D1291063

Duchess

THE STORY OF WALLIS WARFIELD WINDSOR

STEPHEN BIRMINGHAM

BERKLEY BOOKS, NEW YORK

Acknowledgments

Excerpts from *The Honeycomb* by Adela Rogers St. Johns copyright ©1969 by Adela Rogers St. Johns, reprinted by permission of Doubleday & Company, Inc. Excerpts from *Edward VIII* by Frances Donaldson, reprinted by permission of Harper & Row Publishers, Inc., and Weidenfeld (Publishers) Limited. Excerpts from *Chips: The Diaries of Sir Henry Channon*, reprinted by permission of Weidenfeld (Publishers) Limited.

This Berkley book contains the complete
text of the original hardcover edition.
It has been completely reset in a type face
designed for easy reading, and was printed
from new film.

DUCHESS

A Berkley Book / published by arrangement with
Little, Brown and Company

PRINTING HISTORY
Little, Brown edition published 1981
Berkley edition / October 1982

ISBN: 0-425-05651-1

A BERKLEY BOOK ® TM 757,375
Berkley Books are published by Berkley Publishing Corporation,
200 Madison Avenue, New York, New York 10016.
PRINTED IN THE UNITED STATES OF AMERICA

Acknowledgments

There follows a list of individuals who, in ways both great and small, were helpful in the preparation of this book. I am particularly grateful to my late friend and editor Harry Sions, who first conceived the project, and to Genevieve Young, who smoothly assumed editorial guidance following Harry Sions's death. As always, I am also indebted to my friend and literary agent, Carol Brandt, for her encouragement, wisdom and support.

Additionally, I should like especially to thank the late Dowager Lady Christabel Aberconway and her private secretary, Mrs. Bowman-Vaughan, London; the late Mme. Hervé Alphand, Paris; Mrs. Cappy Badrutt, Paris; Sir Cecil Beaton, London; Maître Suzanne Blum, Paris; Lady Diana Cooper, London; Mr. George Cukor, Los Angeles; Mrs. Harriet Culley and Mr. Perry Culley, Paris; Mr. Jeremy Deeds, *Evening Standard*, London; M. Jean-Luc Dubois, Paris; Mr. and Mrs. Robert Fischbach, Richmond, Virginia; Mrs. Edward Gatchell, Andover, Connecticut; the late Mrs. Samuel Goldwyn, Los Angeles; Mr. Douglas Gordon, Baltimore; the late Mr. Michael Greer, New York.

Miss Nancy Holmes, London; Baroness Nancy Hoyingen-Heune, Mexico City; Mr. Thomas Kernan, Paris; Dr. Edward Lahniers, Cincinnati; M. and Mme. Pablo Lozada de Echinique, Paris; the late Miss Julia McCarthy, New York; Lady Alexandra Metcalfe, London; Miss Bernadine Morris, New York; Mr. Eric Mortensen, Paris; Mr. Patrick O'Higgins, New York; Mr. Michael O'Shea, Buckingham Palace; Mr. David Pryce-Jones, London; Baron Alexis de Redé, Paris; Mr. Alasdair Riley, London; Baroness Guy de Rothschild, Paris; M. and Mme. Jacques Ruillier, Paris; Mrs. Adela Rogers St. Johns, Malibu, California; Mr. Martin Shallenberger, New York; Mrs. Ann Kerr Slater, New York; the late Mrs. Lyon Slater, Locust Valley, New York.

Mrs. Benjamin Thaw, Madrid; Mr. Raleigh Trevelyan, London; Mr. John Utter, Paris; Mrs. Jean Stein vanden Heuvel, New York; Miss Gloria Vanderbilt, New York; Mrs. Etta Wanger, Washington, D.C.; Mr. Sam White, Paris; Mr. Jerome Zerbe, New York.

The manuscript was checked for accuracy by the thorough Miss Terry Drucker of New York.

—STEPHEN BIRMINGHAM

For Gene Young

Contents

1

A Girl of
Slender Means

To BEGIN with, she was never pretty. This was a fact that she knew early, and that shadowed most of her early life. In appearance she took after her father's Warfield side and, indeed, she would have made a good-looking boy. The nose was too long and bumpy—in photographs it invariably caught the light and appeared almost bulbous—and the jawline was hard and square. A mole on her chin, on the right, just below her lower lip, was too large to be called a beauty mark. In those days, if a girl was not physically beautiful, much less not even really pretty, she had to develop other attributes to make herself attractive, to boys especially. Or so a southern girl was brought up to believe.

We are, after all, talking about Baltimore in the first decade of the twentieth century, when Wallis was an adolescent. Baltimore was then a rather strange city—neither southern (in the sense that Maryland did not secede from the Union during the Civil War) nor northern, but with strong southern ties and sympathies. It was a proud old city, settled in 1729, which by the outbreak of the Revolution was a booming seaport and shipbuilding center. During the War of 1812, the successful defense of Fort McHenry was Francis Scott Key's inspiration for "The Star Spangled Banner." In 1827, the nation's first railroad, the Baltimore & Ohio, was chartered in Baltimore. In 1904, most of downtown Baltimore was destroyed by fire, but the city quickly and enthusiastically built itself up again, and as World War I approached, the city stretched its muscles with the construction of steel mills and oil refineries. It was a rich city, and in the process of becoming rich, it became an extraordinarily class-conscious city, even more so than Philadelphia or Boston, in which everyone knew, and cared about, who counted socially and who did not. It was a city where Good Family and the Correct Thing mattered a great deal. In this sense, it was an old-fashioned city, jealous of its history, its traditions, its success. Later, such essayists as H. L. Mencken, and his circle of journalists with the Baltimore *Sun,* would give the place an intellectual air. Visitors would also be directed to the home and gravesite of Edgar Allan Poe and, still later, with curiously Baltimorean misgivings, to the home of Wallis Warfield, who became the Duchess of Windsor.

Not being pretty, for Wallis Warfield, was more difficult because her mother was beautiful, a belle. As a girl, and an only child, Wallis was always being reminded of her mother's famous good looks. Alice Montague Warfield had the full figure and tiny waist that were fashionable in the late nineteenth century. Her nose was small and beautifully formed, her hair golden and curly, her eyes wide-set. In an early photograph, she had the delicate loveliness of a Gibson girl. Her family, the Montagues, though very much southern "Old Family" aristocracy, were, by the 1890's, genteelly poor; whatever money the family had had was lost during the Civil War, before which the Montagues had been prominent in Virginia. Montague women had long been noted for their looks and a certain mischievousness and impetuosity, as well as for a certain daring and a wit that, for its day, was considered titillating and even a trifle naughty. There were some who even thought that the Montague outspokenness was a bit vulgar. The Montagues loved plays on words and double-entendres, particularly when it came to social scandal or bedroom matters. Montague bons mots, widely quoted at the time, seem today a little antique and strained. Alice Montague's cousin Lelia, for example, once "scandalized" Baltimore by commenting—about a relative whose baby had arrived somewhat later than had been expected—"It was considerate of the baby to wait that extra week." Its mother had been married barely nine months earlier.

Despite her good looks, Alice Montague—perhaps because her parents were not people of means—appears to have had difficulty attracting serious suitors. It was an era, after all, in which a woman who passed the age of twenty in an unmarried state was considered in danger of becoming a tragic spinster. Alice Montague was twenty-six when she announced her intention to marry, and her choice—a young man named Teackle Wallis Warfield—caused consternation among both the Montague and Warfield families.

There were several reasons for this consternation. It was an era when girls of "good" family were expected to make "good" marriages, and as far as the Montagues were concerned the Warfields were not quite good enough. The Montagues were Old Line. The Warfields were not. At the same time, the Warfields were not entirely without distinction. One relative of Teackle Warfield's, Edwin Warfield, was prominent in Maryland politics, and would later become governor of the state. And some Warfields were rich, particularly Teackle's brother, Solomon Davies Warfield, a self-made millionaire who had become president of the Seaboard Air Line Railroad and president of the Continental Trust Company. Teackle Wallis Warfield's uncommon name had been given to him because his father's best friend had been Severn Teackle Wallis, lawyer, author, and a provost of the University of Maryland, whose statue still stands on Mount Vernon Street in Baltimore.

Though there was money "around" the Warfield family, it was, to the Montagues' way of thinking, "new" money. It was post-Civil War money, made in banking, insurance, railroads, and other forms of trade. Also, the Warfields, as a family, were regarded as stiff, toplofty, puritanical, straitlaced and taciturn. Dour and Teutonic, they were not popular in Baltimore society. A persistent rumor went around the city that the Warfields were, or had been, Jewish—why else name a son Solomon?—and that the name had been changed to Warfield from something else. But the Montagues objected to Teackle Warfield most of all because, of all the Warfields, he was the least prepossessing. He had an unpromising and poor-paying job as a county auctioneer. He was also sickly and known to be suffering from tuberculosis. The Warfields, for their part, suspected Alice Montague of trying to ally herself with a moneyed family, using the ailing Teackle as the avenue. Most suspicious of all, naturally, was the richest Warfield, Teackle's brother Sol.

But Alice, in her stubborn Montague way, was not to be put off. When her parents refused to give her money for a trousseau, she succeeded in borrowing fifty dollars from a Baltimore lawyer named Isaac Straus, and the couple went to a pawnshop to buy the ring—a stolen ring, according to family legend. In the pawnshop, while looking at the large array of clocks on the wall, Alice Montague commented, "What a lot of *time* has been passed here!"—another example of the fey Montague wit. Alice and Teackle Warfield were married in June 1895, and a year later—on June 19, 1896—in Blue Ridge Summit, Pennsylvania, a slightly run-down health resort where Teackle Warfield had taken his expectant wife in hopes of effecting a cure for his tuberculosis, their first and only child was born. The eight-pound baby girl was christened Bessiewallis Warfield, after her mother's older sister, Mrs. Bessie Merryman, and her father. The hope for a cure was vain. Five months later, Teackle Warfield was dead.

Baltimoreans who remember Bessiewallis Warfield as a child tend to be uncharitable, and the reason why this is so may not be too hard to fathom. After all, many years later she became an American success symbol of a certain sort, and her story became translated into a Cinderella fable: the poor little girl who for some reason fitted the glass slipper and was carried off by the handsome prince. She had started as a girl without much to offer and had steadily, through marriages, succeeded in bettering herself. She was transformed, in the minds of her contemporaries, into a heroine of the sort that appeared in so much of the popular fiction of the day. She was like the mousy little salesgirl at the five-and-ten who, when she took off her glasses, was discovered to possess a strange allure, and was swept away by a millionaire from Park Avenue. She was like Eliza Doolittle in *Pygmalion*, one of the most popular plays of the era. With a bit of training in speech and manners, Eliza could dazzle the highest society at Ascot. In short, she embodied every shopgirl's and every debutante's dream. But the trouble was that, to Baltimoreans, Bessiewallis Warfield was not an imaginary creatûre from a play or a novel. She was a very real young woman, and so it didn't seem fair. She was life imitating art, and for Baltimore this was all too much. That the reality was quite different Baltimore could never accept or understand. At the time of her greatest triumph—when she captured the heart of a king—Baltimoreans (all Baltimorean *women*, at least) could only ask: Of all people, why *her?*

Even today, there are those in Baltimore who remind one of Cinderella's jealous stepsisters. In *Who Killed Society?*, for example, Cleveland Amory quotes an "elderly Baltimorean who knew her well" as saying that Bessiewallis's first word was not "Ma-Ma," but "Me-Me." The same source told Amory that, as an indication of her early social aspirations, Bessiewallis's first dolls were named Mrs. Astor and Mrs. Vanderbilt. The first anecdote has the decided ring of a bon mot thought up many years later. So does the second, though extenuating circumstances should be borne in mind. In the year 1900, there were no movie stars. Instead, the newspapers and women's magazines were filled with the doings of "high society" both in America and abroad. By then, Mrs. Astor was in decline, though still a potent memory, and Mrs. Vanderbilt had replaced her as the country's most written-about social figure. If Bessiewallis Warfield did indeed have dolls named Mrs. Astor and Mrs. Vanderbilt—and there is no hard evidence that she really did—there were probably hundreds of other little girls her age who did also.

Looking back, Baltimoreans tend to depict young Bessiewallis as both a liar and a gold digger. Amory also quotes Miss Charlotte Noland, the celebrated headmistress of the Foxcroft School and Bessiewallis's first camp mistress, as saying of her, "I have never known anyone who could so consistently for so many years so successfully evade the truth."

In fact, Bessiewallis was quite a different sort of girl. Like many not-really-pretty girls, she decided to make the most of what she had. Her clothes, for instance, though often home-made, were always immaculate. She was, even as a young girl, weight-conscious, and in an era, the dawning of the Flapper Age, when it was fashionable to be thin and when girls wore brassieres designed to flatten the bosom. She was not tall, an advantage in adolescence when girls often shoot up taller than boys, and when boys won't dance with girls taller than they, or even walk home from school with them. She was popular

with her schoolmates, both boys and girls; at school, she made
at least two close girlfriends who remained her friends for
years. Her contemporaries have spoken of a certain "reserve"
about her. She never seemed to open up completely, and as
a result they tended to treat her, in turn, with reserve, and with
respect. Behind the reserve, there seemed to be a certain shyness, or at least self-consciousness. Years later, she would tell
the story of how, as a girl, she wanted to adorn a white party
dress with a bright-red sash. When asked why, her rather wistful
reply was, "So the boys will notice me." Without some eye-
catching embellishment, she was sure she would go unnoticed.
Behind the reserve, there was also undoubtedly ambition. But
it cannot have been of a pushy, ruthless kind, for teenagers of
both sexes are quick to recognize that sort of thing and will
not put up with it in a contemporary. She was popular with
boys, and liked going out with the "best" boys, but there are
no known examples of her actually setting out to steal another
girl's beau. Had she done that, she would have been ostracized
by her contemporaries of both sexes.

   With boys, she had a reputation of being "fast," but in the
idiom of the era this did not mean promiscuous. Again, according to the code of that day and age, a promiscuous girl
would have been ostracized by her peers. Fast simply meant
that she was coquettish, playful, teasing with boys—in other
words, doing her best to be fun to be with. She knew intuitively
that one key to social success is to develop some sort of trade-
mark, to play up some distinctive attribute. In addition to her
sense of fun, she concentrated on her large blue eyes, her best
feature, which were a surprising contrast to her dark hair. For
a while, as a teenager, she affected a monocle—an amusing,
offbeat thing, rather daring—and fast. The monocle, like the
red sash, drew attention to her in a not unlikable way. Then
there was the fact that, as a young girl, she decided to shorten
her name. Bessiewallis was indeed a mouthful and, as she put
it later, "Cows are named Bessie." Wallis was much more
distinctive and sophisticated. It was "different" from her
friends' names—Mary, Dorothy, Maude, and Helen. And,
again, though the name amounted to a bit of an affectation,
the affectation was of a sort that would not have won her the
disapproval of her peers. Wallis was a "fun" name, with even
a kind of family tradition behind it. Her mother, Alice, often
signed her letters with the more exotic "Alys."

Behind the reserve of this girl who needed so desperately to be noticed lurked fears that, throughout her life, she was never able to shake. She was preternaturally afraid of the dark. She also suffered from claustrophobia, and became panicky in crowds and in small, enclosed places. In addition, she was terrified of heights. Through it all, the fatherless only child was doubtless spoiled by a doting, frivolous mother.

After Teackle Warfield's death, it was clear that mother and child would have to be "taken in" by some charitable relative. This unwelcome burden was assumed by Teackle's sternly religious ("Episcopalian—High Church," Alice used to remind her friends) widowed mother, Mrs. Henry Mactier Warfield, who did so grudgingly. Mrs. Warfield had a substantial and well-staffed four-story town house on Preston Street in Baltimore. This house was also shared by Teackle's bachelor brother, wealthy Uncle Sol, who paid for its upkeep. And so Bessiewallis Warfield's earliest childhood recollections were of a household of affluence and ease, where there was a black valet who padded about on slippered feet, an Irish nurse, a cook and a parlormaid, and a victoria for Sunday outings to church. The elder Mrs. Warfield was a starched and strict observer of the etiquette of the day, and spent many of her waking hours attending to the elaborate ritual of passing out calling cards to her friends and acquaintances, and receiving theirs. Though actual visits were rarely entailed, this was known as "visiting."

At the same time, Alice and her daughter were treated by the Warfields as charity cases, which must have grated on them both. Rich Uncle Sol gave his sister-in-law a regular monthly check, but the check was never in the same amount. And Granny Warfield was always quick to point out that Alice and her child "would be starving in the streets," were it not for the Warfield magnanimity. They led a life, therefore, that was both comfortable and distinctly unpleasant—secure, and yet insecure. "Security" would become a persistent theme in Wallis Warfield's life. After several years, a problem slowly arose. It began to seem as though some sort of liaison were developing between Alice and Uncle Sol. Whether or not there actually was one is uncertain, but in Baltimore there was "talk." The talk was probably inevitable, with an eligible bachelor and his pretty, widowed sister-in-law living under the same roof. Any suggestion of impropriety, much less scandal, appalled Granny Warfield's sense of correctness and what was *comme il faut*. The talk got worse. It was said that Alice Warfield had taken a lover—not Uncle Sol, but another man. To put an end to it, Granny Warfield ordered Alice and her daughter out of the house, which of course only had the effect of escalating the amount of talk. The neighbors said there had to be something to it.

For a while, mother and daughter lived at the seedy old Brexton Hotel, and from there they were taken in by Alice Warfield's older sister, also a widow, Mrs. Bessie Montague Merryman. The next move, sometime in the early 1900's, was to an apartment, again on Preston Street. To make ends meet and help pay the rent, Alice Warfield began taking in paying dinner guests. She was an excellent cook—in fact, perhaps too good a cook because, in the beginning, the costs of preparing her elegant meals outdistanced the returns she received from serving them; not only did ends not meet, they spread further apart. But from her mother Wallis acquired a knowledge of fine food, and an interest in it, that would one day spark her fame as a hostess and menu planner.

After a few years on Preston Street, the little family moved again, to a rented house at 212 East Biddle Street where, according to at least one contemporary account, Alice rented out rooms. There has always been some confusion about this aspect of Alice Warfield's life. Years later, both the British and American press would make much of the story that Wallis's mother "ran a boardinghouse," but Wallis always vociferously denied that her mother did any such thing. Her denials were so heated, in fact, that one began to suspect the lady of protesting too much, and of being deeply ashamed of this part of her mother's hit-or-miss career. A more self-confident woman, if there was even a shred of truth to the boardinghouse story, would have laughed it off, and a truly self-confident woman would have been proud of a mother with enough enterprise to do whatever she could to hold her husbandless household together. But self-confidence was never, nor would it ever become, one of Wallis's strong suits. To her, the social difference between taking in paying guests for dinner and taking in lodgers was always vast, and probably the Baltimore of that time had the same view. Serving meals to strangers was one thing; having strangers sleeping in the house was quite another.

Today, the proud Montagues are quick to point out that their relative's "boardinghouse" was not one in the customary sense. The house at 212 East Biddle Street was in an aging, but still respectable, neighborhood, and it was a *nice* boardinghouse. Alice Warfield carefully screened her guests to make sure that they were only of the highest type, and the establishment quickly gained a reputation for excellence and middle-class decorum. It was tidy and well run, and Alice Warfield was said to serve some of the finest food in Maryland. Also, the Montagues remind us, taking in "paying guests"—one didn't call them boarders—was something that genteel southern ladies often did in those days when they found themselves in straitened circumstances. And it might be added that gentlewomen of slender means frequently did this in England, too.

In any case, from her modest income, Alice was able to send her daughter to a "nice" (though not the most fashionable) private school, Arundel, which no longer exists. And, in 1908, when she was thirty-nine, the real reason for the larger house on East Biddle Street emerged. It seemed that all had *not* been middle-class decorum. The man who had been Alice's lover, about whom all Baltimore had been talking, had decided to take her as his bride. He was John Freeman Raisin, the son of a rather disreputable but well-to-do Baltimore politician. At first, Wallis resented having to share her mother's attentions with Mr. Raisin, but she rapidly grew to like him, though she always addressed him formally and never called him father. For his part, Mr. Raisin had no apparent livelihood, and spent his days sitting around the house, reading, smoking, and, according to at least one account, drinking heavily. But his family's money caused the circumstances of the household to improve markedly. The teenaged Wallis, who had trotted to school in homemade dresses and darned stockings, was now able to appear in store-bought clothes and with spending money in her purse. From Arundel she went on to the equally "nice" Oldfields School, a finishing school just outside the city, where she earned good grades and made the baseball team. Now, at sixteen, she anxiously awaited the only stamp of social approval that Baltimore offered to a young woman—an invitation to be presented as a debutante at the all-important Bachelors Cotillon (always grandly spelled without the second *i*). She also began to dream about an additional possibility—a coming-out ball of her very own.

At this point, we begin to see Wallis Warfield as a young woman perhaps overly concerned with matters of class, status and social acceptance. But it is important to remember that much of Baltimore was also preoccupied with these matters. Though Baltimore was an old city, it was still, in a "society" sense, quite new. Wallis came of age in an era when the delineations and distinctions between the social and economic layers of American society were being drawn more sharply than ever before. The post-Civil War fortunes (most of the great American fortunes were made after the war) had moved into the second generation, and the offspring of the robber barons were cloaking themselves in all the elaborate trappings of gentility and formal good manners. A fixed, moneyed "aristocracy" had emerged, and never before had the wide gap between the rich and the poor been more apparent. Social climbing was the order of the day, and it was even encouraged by the press and by such rags-to-riches writers as Horatio Alger.

If Wallis's ambition to improve her lot—by being invited to better parties, by getting to know the right people—seems to have been stronger than most, there were special reasons behind her drive. Here she was, after all, a girl of good family—with no shortage of distinguished ancestors—in a class-conscious city, who was deprived, by what seemed a trick of fate, of the money that was expected to go with a proud name. With her father dead and her mother forced to work, dependent upon the sporadic charity of wealthier relatives, with social and economic betters on all sides, she must have felt particularly cheated. She was *of* the upper social class and yet, without the financial equipment, out of it, a poor relation. And she had special reasons, too, to be apprehensive about receiving Baltimore society's ultimate nod—an invitation to the Cotillon. Her mother's relationship and marriage to Raisin had been the subject of much local gossip. Alice Montague had become *declassée*. Already, there had been snubs.

"The thing to remember about Wallis," said one of her Baltimore cousins, Douglas Gordon, "and the thing that the British, who called her 'that American woman,' never understood, is that Wallis wasn't an American woman. She was a *southern* woman. Southern women, you know, grow up expecting to get what they want. They expect to be pampered by menfolk. Wallis was a little girl from Baltimore who started out without too much for her, but who wanted to marry a king, and did."

But even this appraisal overlooks the frightened, uncertain, self-conscious side of her nature, her longing for admiration and approval. It also overlooks the romantic, sentimental side. In one of her school yearbooks she wrote, next to her photograph, "Love is all!" Love, of course, is never all, but the same innocent belief that it is would be echoed, many years later, in the title she gave to her autobiography, *The Heart Has Its Reasons,* which could have just as well been the title of a love ballad of the early 1900's. Looking back at her from the distance of decades—a girl approaching her eighteenth birthday, the traditional debutante year, worriedly wondering whether she would be considered good enough to be asked to the ball—one wants to take her by the shoulders and say, "Foolish girl, the heart has no reasons. Love isn't all. Neither is an invitation to a party."

But then one wonders how sincerely Wallis believed in these homilies about love. Love had done little for her mother, and there was little love in the Warfield household. What Wallis needed more than love at that point was luck, and a man to protect her, as southern girls felt they should be protected, and to assuage her insecurities. Love, however, would always provide her with a convenient excuse for her mistakes.

2

Husband
Number One

The report that I will give a large ball for my debutante niece, Miss Wallis Warfield, is without foundation in that I do not consider the present a proper time for such festivities, when thousands of men are being slaughtered in Europe.

This was the frostily worded announcement in the society pages of the Baltimore *Sun* issued in the winter of 1914 by Solomon Davies Warfield. Just where the "report" originated, and why Mr. Warfield felt it necessary to deliver such a rebuttal, is unclear. But it is likely that young Wallis had been hinting to her friends at Oldfields that her rich Uncle Sol might be going to give her a lavish coming-out party, and that the word got around Baltimore and reached the ears of Uncle Sol, who was not pleased. Uncle Sol liked his niece, but in a rather reserved, forbidding way, and he was not a man who could be blackmailed by gossip into spending a large sum of money on anything. Still, humiliating though Uncle Sol's dictum must have seemed to her at the time, Wallis wrote in her memoirs that she accepted it, and understood his reasons for it. Later, she would say that she was always a "little afraid" of her uncle, though whenever she wanted anything he was the man to whom she had to turn. Indeed, Wallis may well have supposed that she would one day inherit some of her uncle's fortune, since he had no direct heirs. In 1910, two years after marrying Alice Warfield, John Freeman Raisin had died, leaving very little money, and the brief financial support he had provided had disappeared. For Alice, this meant returning to the paying guests and, for Wallis, it meant that Uncle Sol still held the major purse strings, and the purse itself remained fat.

That Uncle Sol would not give Wallis a ball of her own was a major disappointment, but she did receive her coveted invitation to the Cotillon. There she made her debut on December 7, 1914, with forty-six other girls, thirty-four of whom, including Wallis, had signed an agreement that they would "refrain from elegance and extravagance of dress" in view of the outbreak of war in Europe.

The stated purpose of the Cotillon was to present young ladies to the older members of Baltimore society, but its real meaning involved the ancient ritual of presenting eligible virgins to the eligible males of the tribe. The list of young men invited to the ball was even more carefully screened than the list of debutantes. It was a premarriage rite, and the girls were dressed as brides-to-be in long white gowns. At this point in their lives, the girls of Baltimore society had little else on their minds but boys and marriage—higher education for women was almost unheard of—and Wallis was no exception. She had already collected a tidy share of "scalps," as the variously smitten males were called, and during her teens did not lack for beaux. She had been delighted when fourteen-year-old Thomas Shryock, the son of General Thomas Shryock, slipped her love notes and passionately worded valentines over the fence of the Arundel School, and delighted when her mother's friends began commenting on little Wallis's "charm," a quality much esteemed in southern women, and one that can often compensate for lack of beauty. Wallis's charm was a Scarlett O'Hara-ish mixture of insouciance and flirtatiousness.

At the age of twelve, she had worn long, carefully constructed curls tied up with flowing ribbons. Later, she adopted a shorter hair style à la Cléo de Mérode, noticeably offbeat for the period, and wore very little makeup. She often appeared in tight-fitting shirtwaists with Eton collars, mannish bow ties at her throat, and wide, tight patent-leather belts that showed off her small waist. At Oldfields, the task young Wallis hated the most was having to make her own bed, but a solution to this problem was to spend as much time as possible away from school, as the house guest of other people. She unquestionably preferred households that were more stable and serene than any of her previous addresses had ever been. After Tom Shryock her most serious beau was a seventeen-year-old named Lloyd Tabbs. The Tabbs family had a large estate called Glen Ora, outside Middleburg, Virginia,* and Wallis was a frequent guest there for Sunday dinners and weekends of tennis and riding. For two summers she had gone to a fashionable girls' camp called Burrlands, outside Middleburg, run by Charlotte Noland, and at Burrlands, when not being diverted by Lloyd Tabbs and his family, she developed a girlish crush on Philip Noland, Miss Charlotte's handsome and wealthy unmarried brother. This caused eyebrows to rise in certain quarters. Philip Noland was then thirty-five years old. For a while, too, she was romantically drawn to her cousin Henry Warfield, who worked for Uncle Sol's bank. Other young men were Tony Biddle and Reginald Hutchinson, both of prominent, well-to-do families. There was also one Carter Osburn, who would recall, years later, that he had been "badly smitten by the Baltimore heartbreaker."

In the spring of 1916, when Wallis was almost twenty, she abandoned the Cléo de Mérode hairdo in favor of the more fashionable Mrs. Vernon Castle look, and took off on a trip to Florida to visit one of her Montague cousins, Corinne Mustin, who was married to a naval officer stationed at the Pensacola naval air station. One day at lunch Corinne announced that her husband was bringing by three fellow officers, all of whom she was eager for Wallis to meet. Wallis could never remember the names of the other two men, but one—Lieutenant (junior grade) Earl Winfield Spencer, Jr.—made an immediate impression on her. It was love at first sight, as she later recalled. "Whenever I turned away to listen to one of the others or to exchange comments with Corinne, the gold stripes on his shoul-

---

*Glen Ora would later become the weekend home of President and Mrs. John F. Kennedy.

der boards, glimpsed out of the corner of my eye, acted like a magnet and drew me back to him," she wrote. Undoubtedly, one of the things that attracted her most to Spencer was the fact that he was an aviator, a new, glamorous, and promising field for a man in those days, even though the thought of flying in a plane terrified Wallis. Also, he was handsome in a rugged, swashbuckling way, and he was equally attracted to her. After lunch, he asked her what her plans were for the following day. She replied, a trifle coyly, "I don't know what the Mustins have planned for me." His answer, full of suave self-assurance was, "Oh, don't worry about that. I really don't care what the Mustins have planned for you, so long as the plans include me."

The Spencers of Chicago were not rich, and so Wallis cannot have set her cap for him in a gold-digging frame of mind. But young Win Spencer must have seemed to her a man of considerable promise and potential. He was one of the first twenty men in the entire United States Navy to win his pilot's wings and, despite his low rank, he was a senior training officer at Pensacola. Also, the future of a navy wife offered a commodity Wallis regarded highly—security—and it promised travel to exotic places. Wallis stayed on and on at the Mustins, developing an art she would practice most of her life, that of being a long-term and apparently attractive house guest. Win Spencer proposed to Wallis on the moonlit veranda of the Pensacola Country Club, and though she later confessed to "some hesitation," she accepted him promptly. Their engagement was announced in September of 1916.

Back home in Baltimore, Wallis discovered that she had scored a personal triumph of sorts. Years later, a former acquaintance would say of her, sneeringly "Wallis always wanted to be first," and, asked to explain, said that Wallis was the first of her debutante "class" to become engaged. Actually, she was not the first, but she was certainly one of the first, and she proudly flashed the big diamond—for which Win had gone heavily into debt—on her left hand wherever she went. Wallis and Win Spencer were married on November 8, 1916, at Christ Episcopal Church in Baltimore, with the bride in a long, flowing white velvet dress with a heavy train and a lace-edged veil, and the groom and his ushers all in trim blue dress uniforms. Uncle Sol, who had approved of the match, gave her away.

Sometime later, when Win and Wallis Spencer's marriage

had begun to go sour, Wallis's cousin Lelia Montague Barnett would remind her, "Well, you know perfectly well—and everybody knew it at the wedding—that you only married Win out of curiosity." Another friend surmised that Wallis married Win "to get out of it"—"it" being Baltimore.

For what happened to Wallis during the next few years, before she became a public figure, we must rely almost entirely on what she tells us in her autobiography, *The Heart Has Its Reasons*. Of course, she exercises the privilege of any memoirist, and tells us only what she chooses, which is far from all. She glides over certain matters, fudges others, and concerning still other events about which we might like to know, she displays a transparent and quite disarming lack of memory. Still, Charles J. V. Murphy, who served as her ghostwriter for the book, was impressed by her general candor. In all that has been written about her, there are, to be sure, annoying discrepancies—the matter of Corinne Mustin's husband's naval rank, for example. In Wallis's memoirs, Henry Mustin was a captain. In *Gone with the Windsors* by Iles Brody he was a mere lieutenant. In J. Bryan III and Charles Murphy's later book, *The Windsor Story,* he was a lieutenant commander, in full command of the Pensacola naval air station. Still, there is no reason to believe that when Wallis wrote her book she resorted to outright lying. This seems clear in her account of her marriage to Spencer, in which she emerges as a young woman of almost shocking naiveté.

In the seven months of their courtship she appears never to have noticed Win Spencer's fondness for drink. That he might be a chronic alcoholic did not occur to her until the first day of their honeymoon, when the couple checked in at the Greenbrier Hotel in White Sulphur Springs. There was an immediate alcohol crisis when Win Spencer discovered that West Virginia was a dry state, and that no liquor could be served on the premises. Faced with this situation, he at first wanted to move to another hotel, in another state. He had, however, foresightedly packed a bottle of gin in his suitcase, enough to carry him over until he could find a source of supply. From that moment on, according to her account, Win Spencer was seldom without a glass in his hand, and in the course of a few memoir pages, the transformation of Spencer from charming and attentive young suitor to raging drunk was dramatic. She had, she insisted, never tasted alcohol before then, except for a sip of champagne at Christmastime. At all the Pensacola parties she had attended, she had wondered a little about the curious consommé ritual in which the officers indulged. Navy fliers were forbidden by regulations to drink within twenty-four hours before flying a plane, but most of the men had devised ways of getting around this restriction. Before dinner, they would gather in the kitchen where—amid explosions of laughter—they announced they were "preparing the consommé." The consommé—actually martinis—was then served in bouillon cups and saucers, and drunk at the table. Everyone exclaimed over the excellence of the recipe, and there were often calls for second and third helpings. While all this was going on, Wallis innocently believed that "naval consommé" was really consommé. It was not until the Greenbrier that she recognized her husband's problem.

For a while, she said, she tried to remonstrate with Win about his drinking, but he only laughed at her and told her not to be a prude. She, meanwhile, always fun-loving and flirtatious, relished the dancing and parties. While she whirled around the dance floor with other young men, and flirted in her southern way—all in fun, of course—Win would settle in a corner with a bottle and become either morose and sullen or insulting and abusive. Later, with hindsight, Wallis's detractors would say that her flirtatiousness "drove" Win Spencer to drink, and he himself would later claim that his wife's refusal to stop paying attention to other men had aggravated his drinking and led to the eventual deterioration of the marriage, and certainly jealousy and alcohol are explosive ingredients in any union. Win also introduced his wife to martinis, to help her overcome a case of hostess jitters before one of her first parties. Thereafter, she always had a double martini before tackling one of the recipes in her Fannie Farmer cookbook, and found that it helped her through an evening. She insisted, however, that one drink was her limit. Win's drinking was something else again.

He would disappear, sometimes for days, without an explanation. Often he would lock her in a bedroom of their cottage before he left, and she dared not call out for help because, after all, what would the neighbors think? Once he locked her in the bathroom for hours, and even when she heard him turn the key in the lock to release her, she stayed in the bathroom, too frightened to come out. Meanwhile, Win Spencer's hopes for exotic travel did not immediately materialize. For a time the Spencers remained in Pensacola. Next, Win was transferred to Boston, and from there he was removed to San Diego, where the Spencers found a place to live at nearby Coronado Beach. In Coronado, Mrs. Spencer was among several hundred officer and civilian wives who attended a reception for, and curtsied to, the young Prince of Wales when he visited California in 1920. Win's next assignment was back east in Washington, and there, of all the places they had been, his wife was happiest. She was immediately at home in the partying world of high government officials, high-ranking military officers, diplomats and titled foreigners. The advent of Prohibition lent a special gaiety to Washington parties, where one could experience the naughty excitement of breaking the new federal law right in the nation's capital. It also did not abate Win Spencer's drinking, and when he was suddenly ordered to new duty in Hong Kong, Wallis announced that she intended to remain in Washington.

It was here, after Win's departure, that she started seeing Felipe Espil, the First Secretary of the Argentine Embassy (he eventually became Ambassador). He was a dashing, handsome Latin, nearly ten years older than Wallis, and all at once she was head over heels in love again. She had already toyed with the idea of divorce, and though Espil was a Roman Catholic, the idea of marrying a divorced woman did not really trouble him. But, as a career diplomat with both great ambitions and expectations, Espil needed a wife with money. This qualification Wallis could not meet. The up-and-down affair with Wallis lasted nearly two years, and ended bitterly late in 1923. (When Espil eventually married, it was to an American who had been divorced twice and was very rich.)

Now, in early 1924, Wallis's cousin Corinne Mustin came to her rescue again. Corinne, recently widowed, proposed that she and Wallis assuage their respective broken hearts with a trip to Europe. Uncle Sol was forthcoming with a five-hundred-dollar gift for this journey—eager, no doubt, to get Wallis's mind off her South American—and so, armed with letters of introduction, gathered in Washington, to leaders of society in the European capitals, the two set sail. Wistfully, and mistakenly, Wallis somehow hoped that Espil would join them abroad to say that all was forgiven but, though this did not happen, the two had a carefree tour.

When Wallis returned to Washington, however, she found the situation much changed. Many of her old friends had departed for other stations and assignments. All at once, Wallis Spencer, without a husband and without an escort, found herself in that awkward social role of extra woman. Win Spencer, meanwhile, had been writing to her, urging her to join him in China. He had, he insisted, reformed, and he begged her to come back as his wife. So, deciding that some attempt at a reconciliation should at least be made, she made plans to join her husband in the Far East.

When Alice Warfield Raisin heard of her daughter's intention to go to China, she had her misgivings, but she did not oppose the trip. "Shanghai is such a long way and such a strange place," she confided to a friend. "But I would not dream of interfering with Wallis. I have always let her make her own decisions." (Alice was a little confused; Wallis's destination was Hong Kong, not Shanghai.) Alice's life had also undergone some changes. In 1921, she had taken a job as social hostess at the Chevy Chase Club, outside Washington, and in 1925, with Wallis on the other side of the world, she would marry for a third time—a man named Gordon Allen, who was Assistant U.S. Attorney General under President Coolidge. ("I'm here with my third for the Fourth," the new Mrs. Allen scrawled, in her witty Montague way, in the guestbook at Wakefield Manor when she and her new husband arrived for the Fourth of July weekend at Cousin Lelia's.)

Wallis set sail on the USS *Chaumont* from Norfolk on July 17, 1924, and arrived in Hong Kong some six weeks later after an uncomfortable trip. Because she was traveling at government expense and was the wife of a junior officer, she was assigned to second-class accommodations and was required to share a cabin with two other women. When she was met by her husband and escorted to the small apartment he had taken, the first thing she spotted was a pair of gin bottles in the bathroom. There was a terrible scene, but eventually Spencer and his Chinese houseboy managed to reassure her that the bottles contained nothing more potent than purified water for drinking.

One of the Oriental delights, it seemed, that Lieutenant Spencer had discovered in his wife's absence was to be found in the Chinese "singsong houses" and local houses of prostitution, where all sorts of unusual sexual specialties were practiced, including group activities that involved members of the same, as well as the opposite, sex. Though Wallis would later claim that she found the idea of going to these establishments repellent, she may well have found them as titillating as her husband did. Even though it was most unusual for a woman to enter such places, she accompanied Win to the singsong houses night after night, perhaps simply because she was trying to be a dutiful wife. Or at least she did so for about two weeks. Then Win Spencer came home drunk, and the attempt at a reconciliation was over.

But Wallis did not turn on her heel and come home. Though she moved out of Win's apartment and would never live with him as his wife again, she stayed on in China—stayed on, in fact, for nearly two years. In her memoirs, the details of her visit are spotty and imprecise, as sketchy as the design of a Blue Willow plate, full of the romantic tinkle of temple bells and vistas of pagodas shrouded in mist and moonlight. She traveled. We see her during this period, a woman fast approaching thirty, leading a restless, rootless, nomadic existence, moving from city to city, from hotel to hotel, in an aimless search for she knew not what, living out of suitcases. Wherever she went her high spirits and love of a good time seem to have stood her in good stead, and she made friends, or at least acquaintances, who would take this migratory creature under their wings for a day or so. And there was never a shortage of male escorts to take her to parties, restaurants, nightclubs and dances. Yet we still see her as a stranger lost in a strange culture, always the gay and laughing outsider, always on the fringe of things. To support her in these wanderings—which, in her vague description of them, have a certain dazed quality—she had only her navy wife's allotment check of $225 a month. But she had become a clever card player and could often win that much in an evening's poker game.

In Paris, with Cousin Corinne, she had made a halfhearted attempt to get a French divorce, but had found it too difficult and expensive. Now she heard that the U.S. Court for China was a good place to get a quick divorce, and so she departed for Shanghai, where she established herself in the Palace Hotel. The Shanghai divorce idea also proved too complicated and costly, but she did manage to meet more friends. At the suggestion of another navy wife, she decided to move on to Peking. In the 1920's Peking was considered a mecca for unattached women. Mothers, in fact, often sent their unmarried daughters to Peking in search of husbands. The white male population—marine and naval officers, embassy officials and attachés—outnumbered the female population by something like ten to one, and many of these eligible young men had not seen a white woman in months. Once more she had no trouble finding escorts. Shortly after her arrival, furthermore, Wallis had the great good fortune to run into an old friend from Coronado days, the former Katherine Moore Bigelow. Since widowed, Mrs. Bigelow had married a wealthy American named Herman Rogers, who had turned his back on his family's banking interests in New York and had decided to become a writer. Rich and indolent, yet charming and cultivated, Katherine and Herman Rogers became, in Peking, what Gerald and Sara Murphy had come to be on the French Rivera: the rich, beautiful and bountiful people whom everybody loved. They had settled in Peking simply because it seemed the most attractive setting they could find in which to lead their pleasant lives.

Later, the Rogerses would play an important role in Wallis's life. But for the moment they were immediately helpful. She must, they said, move out of her hotel and into their luxurious villa. Wallis was delighted to accept. The Rogerses had also beautifully restored a ruined temple outside of town, which they used as a weekend place. Life in Peking was all idleness and ease. Herman Rogers's progress toward becoming a writer was slow, and it was clear that he was no more than a mildly talented amateur. More important to him were the picnics with hampers of wine in the countryside, the glittering parties in the city, the lazy afternoons by the swimming pool. Wallis had expected to spend no more than a few weeks with the Rogerses, but she remained as their happy house guest for a full year. To her astonishing credit, Wallis seemed a woman incapable of wearing out her welcome. She stayed on and on.

Later, to be sure, Wallis would pay a heavy toll for those long, languorous months in China because the "China period" of her life would become the most difficult to explain. When she moved in with Herman and Katherine Rogers, after all, what had she become? To the Rogerses' friends, it seemed that Wallis had become a part of a *ménage à trois*—not, it was assumed, in a sexual sense, but she offered them a lift and a fresh American face. She paid for her board and keep with her charm, which had become her principal profession. It was all, of course, an extension of her transient childhood, much of which had been spent in other people's houses. But now she was an adult, a fading debutante, unattached and yet also vaguely married, an attractive ne'er-do-well, a beguiling vagabond. There were women like her—expatriated, footloose, living by their wits—in the fiction of the era. She was Brett Ashley in *The Sun Also Rises*. In her impromptu China existence, she had become, without realizing it, a *type*. What it earned her was a label that would stick to her for the rest of her life: the scarlet A of Adventuress.

By 1926, however, Wallis was ready to come home. Arriving in Washington again, at her mother's house, she announced her intention of seriously pursuing the matter of her divorce. Both the Montague and Warfield families were scandalized. There had never been a divorce in either family before. To still-puritanical Baltimore society, a divorce was the mark of a fallen woman. But Wallis's mind was made up. She was advised that the cheapest, most convenient place to get a divorce was in Warrenton, Virginia, where a year's residence was required. She set herself up in a small room—without a bath—in the Warren Green Hotel to wait out her year in a rural setting. But there was plenty to amuse her in Warrenton. She was quickly taken up by the town's wealthy horsey set, and her days were filled with riding, lunches, dinners and cocktail parties on wide green lawns. There were also the other guests at the hotel, with whom she rapidly became acquainted. One man in particular, Jack Mason, who was a permanent resident at the Warren Green, became her regular companion and let her use his bathroom. Her life continued to be peripatetic. In midsummer of 1927, to break the routine at Warrenton, Wallis and Aunt Bessie Merryman sailed off for Europe, but that trip was interrupted by a cable announcing that Uncle Sol had died. Wallis returned to learn more bad news.

Her dream of inheriting much of her uncle's fortune turned out to have been wishful thinking, though she was not cut out of his will entirely. Instead, he set up a small trust fund of $15,000 for her, out of which she could be expected to earn an income of about $60 a month. The bulk of his estate, worth about five million dollars, was to go to the establishment of a home for "aged and indigent gentlewomen," in his mother's memory. He also directed that his mother's room in the Preston Street house be preserved, intact, exactly as it had been when she lived in it. (Later, when the room was opened, it was discovered that the house had been burglarized and everything in the room had been stolen.) He evidently also underestimated his niece's future possibilities, for in his will he stipulated that a room in the aged and indigent gentlewomen's home should always be kept reserved for Wallis Warfield Spencer.

Socially, however, there were consolations. She made frequent trips to Washington, to parties there, and to New York. On one of these trips to New York she had dinner with her friends Jacques and Mary Kirk Raffray, at whose Washington Square apartment she often stayed. Among the Raffrays' dinner guests were a Mr. and Mrs. Ernest Simpson.

On another visit, Wallis consulted an astrologer who told her some interesting things. Wallis, would, the woman said, be married three times. She would have a normal life-span, but would die suddenly and "in an unusual place." She would also, between the ages of forty and fifty, wield "considerable power of some kind." Wallis asked, since she was thinking of getting a job after her divorce, if that power would be "connected in any way with a job." No, she was assured. "The power that is to come to you will be related to a man." The astrologer also said, "You will become a famous woman."

3

Husband Number Two

WALLIS was granted her Virginia divorce from Win Spencer on December 10, 1927, some six months after her thirty-first birthday. In the months preceding, on her trips to New York, she had seen Ernest Simpson several more times, but about the nature of these meetings there is some dispute. Wallis, in her memoirs, says that when she met the Simpsons she was given to understand that their marriage was in difficulties. In *The Windsor Story*, Bryan and Murphy claim that Ernest and Dorothea Simpson had separated a year earlier, that Mrs. Simpson had already sued her husband for divorce, and that "the suit was pending when Ernest met Wallis Spencer"; if true, Dorothea Simpson would not even have been present when Wallis met Ernest. Iles Brody says that after Wallis met the Simpsons, "the three adults became close friends." In her biography of Edward VIII, Lady Frances Donaldson tends to go along with Wallis's version—that, though Wallis met the Simpsons as a married couple, the Simpson marriage was "already in difficulties." Not so, according to Dorothea Simpson, who, of course, was to become the woman scorned and replaced by Wallis. She told Cleveland Amory that her whole life had been "ruined" by Wallis. Amory quotes the first Mrs. Simpson as saying, "From the moment I met her, I never liked her at all. I've never been around anyone like that. I've never seen anything like the cold, decayed Society around her. She moved in and helped herself to my house and my clothes and, finally, everything."

In any case, the romance between Wallis and Ernest Simpson developed rapidly, and within months of Wallis's divorce, the Simpsons were also divorced. Wallis had, to be sure, continued briefly to toy with the idea of a career in New York. She entered a magazine fashion-writing contest with an essay on spring hats. A few weeks later, her manuscript came back with a printed rejection slip, and that was the end of that. Then she applied for a job selling, of all things, tubular steel scaffolding of the sort used in the construction of tall buildings. Again, this came to nothing. A proposal of marriage and the security it offered were obviously more alluring. In May 1928 she set off for Europe again, this time alone, for another visit with the Rogerses, who had now moved their base of operations from China to a villa in Cannes, in the south of France. From Cannes, she gravitated to London, where Ernest Simpson awaited her, and there, in a dingy little registry office in Chelsea, Wallis and Ernest Simpson were married on July 21, 1928. She had been single for only a little more than seven months.

Ernest Simpson was an even-natured, round-faced man— like Win Spencer he wore a small mustache—who had a good job. His father had been born in England, had emigrated to America at an early age, and had started a ship-brokerage business in which he had prospered. His son, after graduating from Harvard, had gone into the family business in New York and had also prospered. The family—and the business—maintained close ties with England. During the last year of the war, Simpson had returned to England, enlisted in the Coldstream Guards, and became, in the process, a British subject. His business and social lives were divided between London and New York. In New York, his Harvard connections gave him entrée to the kind of Café Society that was flourishing gaily in the Speakeasy Era. In London, his Guards connection gave him entrée to much the same kind of society there—not the true aristocracy of Great Britain, but the bright young things who would soon animate the pages of the early novels of Evelyn Waugh. It was not the kind of high life that had amused his first wife, who was from a quiet New England family. But it was a life that Wallis, who enjoyed quips and banter and gossip, had come to find decidedly to her liking.

Still, at first, Wallis did not care for London. She found it cold and inhospitable. But as Mrs. Ernest Simpson she had her first real taste of personal financial comfort. Ernest took her on a wedding trip to France and Spain, where they stayed at all the best hotels. He bought her a big car, a yellow Lagonda, hired a chauffeur named Hughes to drive it, and rented her a furnished house in Upper Berkeley Street near Portman Square in the fashionable West End of London. But even so, in the beginning, Wallis had difficulty meeting people in London, particularly the sort of society people she wanted to meet.

Fortunately, her new sister-in-law, Maud Simpson Kerr-Smiley, took Wallis under her wing and was able to give her some social pointers. A friend of Mrs. Kerr-Smiley's explained to Wallis the particular respect and reverence the English have for their aristocracy, and told Wallis that she would have much less trouble dealing with her servants—in addition to the chauffeur, Wallis now had a cook, a butler, and a housemaid—if she could manage to drop a few titled names within earshot of the help. Maud Kerr-Smiley also recommended that Wallis read and memorize the Court Circular, which reported the daily doings of the Royal Family and was printed daily in *The Times*. The Court Circular was a good gauge of who mattered in society at the moment. In addition to the cachet of her hyphenated name and her big house in Belgrave Square, Maud Kerr-Smiley could claim to have once entertained the young Prince of Wales, and—by the wildest of coincidences—to have introduced him to the woman who, for the past ten years, had been considered the major love interest in his life.

That woman was Mrs. Freda Dudley Ward, who was married, with two children, but separated from her husband. One evening, it seemed, in July 1917, Freda Dudley Ward and a gentleman friend named Buster Dominguez had been out for dinner and were strolling home across Belgrave Square. Suddenly, an air-raid alarm had sounded, and Mrs. Ward and Dominguez had sought shelter in the nearest house, which happened to be Maud Kerr-Smiley's. A party was going on, and the Prince, then a soldier on leave, happened to be a guest.

Freda and her escort were taken in, and the entire party hurried to the basement. There, in semidarkness, Freda found herself in conversation with a pleasant young man, and when the all clear sounded, he urged her to stay on at the party. Only then did she realize that he was the Prince of Wales. They danced the night away, and at the evening's end, the Prince escorted Freda home. Mr. Dominguez had conveniently disappeared. Ever since, the Prince and Mrs. Dudley Ward had been inseparable. She was said to account for the fact that the Prince was still a bachelor at thirty-four.

Characteristically, the Prince never thanked Maud Kerr-Smiley for having introduced him, albeit inadvertently, to Freda Dudley Ward, who had become so important to him. He had not even repaid his hostess's hospitality with an invitation of his own. Maud had not been taken into the "Prince of Wales Set," nor had she ever seen or heard from him again. Royalty, of course, never wrote personal thank-you notes, nor did Royalty feel obliged to repay an invitation with another.

Maud Kerr-Smiley now offered Wallis helpful hints in the art of social climbing, which, in London, was a game almost everybody played. It was a game, furthermore, that was more easily played in England than in America because the rules were simpler. All one had to be was pleasant, witty and attractive. Money mattered less than in America. It was easy to meet and mingle with the English aristocracy because members of the aristocracy knew who they were and also knew that outsiders were no threat; outsiders could not join the aristocracy except through marriage, and that did not often happen. And Wallis, an eager pupil, was still clearly the sort of woman whom others tended to feel protective toward. Perhaps some of her early insecurities about herself still showed. In any case, women like Maud Kerr-Smiley became her kindly social guardians and guides.

That first winter, when not studying the Court Circular, Wallis had an opportunity to glimpse the Prince himself—her second since the formal presentation in Coronado eight years earlier. She was driving past St. James's Palace on the way to the City to pick up her husband when she suddenly saw the red-coated guards outside the gate come to attention and present arms. A black limousine turned into St. James's Street and passed the Lagonda, and Wallis was briefly able to see its passenger. What she later described as his "delicate, boyish face" looked, she thought, grave and worried. Her chauffeur in hushed tones announced, "Madam, that was the Prince of Wales."

In the autumn of 1929, Wallis's mother, who had been ill for many months, was dying, and Wallis hurried home to Washington. Her mother died on November 2, three days after Wallis's arrival. Back in London, the Simpsons' lease on the house in Upper Berkeley Street had run out, and the couple began looking for a new one. For a while, they lived in a furnished flat in Hertford Street, off Park Lane, and presently they found the sort of place they wanted, a three-bedroom flat at 5 Bryanston Court, on George Street, near Marble Arch. For Wallis, Bryanston Court became her first real home. Because it was new and unfurnished (the Upper Berkeley Street place had been filled with its owner's furniture), it gave her her first real opportunity to try her hand at decorating. She spent most of the winter of 1929–1930 prowling about London antique shops and fabric houses. Socially, the Simpsons' lives remained somewhat limited to friends of Maud Kerr-Smiley's, who were for the most part members of the American colony in London and had little to do with the world of the Court Circular—of fox hunting, grouse shooting, great balls in London mansions, the ritual of British Court life, or long weekends at stately English country houses.

Some of Maud Kerr-Smiley's friends were promising. There were American diplomats, military attachés, embassy officers. One friend was Major—later General—Martin "Mike" Scanlon, the Assistant U.S. Air Attaché, a handsome bachelor who gave lively cocktail parties and little dinners. Others were the Benjamin Thaws. Thaw was then First Secretary of the U.S. Embassy, and was married to the former Consuelo Morgan, one of the famed trio of Morgan sisters, Consuelo, Thelma, and Gloria.

All three Morgan sisters would feature prominently in Wallis's life, and all three were considered American success stories of their day because they had all made what were considered "brilliant" society marriages and were examples of how a young woman could better herself through marriage. The Morgan sisters were no relation to J. P. Morgan, though they didn't mind too much if someone mistakenly thought they were. The "Miraculous Morgans" were the daughters of Harry Hays Morgan, a minor U.S. Foreign Service officer, and they were essentially the creation of Maury Paul, who as "Cholly Knick-erbocker" was New York society's principal chronicler. Consuelo Thaw's younger sisters, the twins Thelma and Gloria, were once described by Cecil Beaton as "alike as two magnolias, with raven tresses, flowing dresses, slight lisps and foreign accents [who] diffuse an atmosphere of hothouse elegance and lacy femininity." Thelma Morgan had married Marmaduke Viscount Furness and moved to England; Gloria had married Reginald Vanderbilt, a son of Cornelius Vanderbilt II.

To be sure, only one of the marriages, Consuelo's to "Benny" Thaw, had turned out even remotely happily. "Duke" Furness was a foul-tempered man nearly twice his wife's age, and though they would not divorce until several years later, they hardly ever lived together. Reggie Vanderbilt's life con-sisted of drinking, gambling, and driving fast cars, and when, two years after the marriage, he was ordered by his doctor to stop drinking, Gloria wrote: "That was like a sentence of almost complete annihilation. It is difficult to break the habit of a lifetime." Indeed, he did not break it, and died not long after-ward in Newport. There would follow a long court battle over the custody of Reggie and Gloria's ten-year-old daughter, also named Gloria, in which the child's mother would argue that while she, as a widow, had been left with next to nothing to live on, little Gloria was supplied with an income of about $50,000 a year. The mother lost her case, and custody of little Gloria was given to her paternal aunt, Gertrude Vanderbilt Whitney. At the time, the mother was adjudged "in every way unfit, destructive of health and neglectful of her [daughter's] moral, spiritual and mental education."

As her circle of friends widened, Wallis began to entertain at small dinner parties in her new flat, where she had been training her cook to prepare dishes other than traditionally sim-ple English fare. Quickly, the Simpsons got a reputation for serving very good food. A perfectionist, Wallis would do things with her meals that had been unheard of in London, such as insisting on six partridge of identical size and shape to arrange around the serving platter. The English were usually more offhand about such matters, and grocers and fishmongers grum-bled when they saw Mrs. Simpson coming into their shops because her orders were so exceptionally demanding. Wallis also introduced London to the hot hors d'oeuvre, which she had become adept at whipping up during her China days. To

Londoners, hot hors d'oeuvres were a delightful novelty. It was said that Mrs. Simpson had "invented" them, and Wallis cheerfully took credit for the invention.

Her major accomplishment, however, she did not bring off until the early autumn of 1930, after she had been in London more than two years. Following a dinner at Mike Scanlon's, Wallis found herself in conversation with a brown-haired, blue-eyed woman whose name she had not caught. They were talking about the geography and history of England, when suddenly the woman interrupted her and asked, "Do you play bridge?" Wallis answered that she did, a little. "Do you play golf?" Wallis said yes, a little. "Good—then you must come down to Knole this weekend," the woman said. Wallis realized that she had been talking to Anne, Lady Sackville, one of the most brilliant hostesses in London, and the chatelaine of one of the most beautiful and historic country homes in all of England. An invitation to Lord and Lady Sackville's was like a command performance from a king. Social mayhem had been performed in attempts to get on Lady Sackville's guest list. Wallis Simpson regarded this invitation as a passport to a whole new, different, and glittering world. And indeed it was.

It should be pointed out that Ernest Simpson was every bit as socially ambitious as his wife, perhaps more so. It was at his insistence that his older sister Maud had coached Wallis on the ways of the British upper classes, and taught her the strategy of the upward climb. Simpson, a product of Harvard in its most snobbish and class-conscious era, still subscribed to a notion popular in the 1920's—that having rich and influential friends was good for business. It would take another generation of Americans to discover the fallacy of this idea, along with the fact that the rich give the social aspirant very little and, whatever they give, it is almost never money.

For Wallis, high society represented a birthright she had been cheated of all her life. She had been on the fringes of wealth and substance, but never part of them, convinced that she was born to be first rate but forced to accept the second rate. She felt she deserved to share what lay behind the pillared gates and rhododendron hedges of the rich.

Maud Kerr-Smiley had taught Wallis the climber's primary rule: it should never be apparent that you care. If society suspects the climber's motives, the gates quickly close and the walls become impenetrable. The successful social aerialist af-

fects indifference, and this piques society's curiosity; they
wonder why, and ask you to their houses to find out. The fact
that Wallis had been unimpressed by—and had not even
caught—Lady Sackville's name certainly helped elicit the invitation. When Wallis excitedly brought the news of it to her
husband, he was overjoyed. For the next few days the two did
their homework on the Sackville and Sackville-West families,
discussed who else might have been invited, and planned their
respective weekend wardrobes.

The weekend at Knole, a 365-room Tudor mansion, was
not particularly exciting, no different in its ritual and order
from weekends at other great English country houses. Breakfast, brought to the guest bedrooms on trays, was followed by
golf, followed by lunch, followed by bridge, followed by a
walk in the garden or, if the house guest wished, a nap. Then
there were cocktails and—in the somewhat annoying British
tradition—after the cocktail hour guests were expected to repair
to their rooms to dress for dinner. By the time dinner was
announced, any edge of levity from the cocktail hour had worn
off, and one was left to hope that the wine would be potable.
After dinner, there was dancing to the gramophone. Three
changes of clothing were required each day: for morning, for
lunch, and for dinner. The Saturday routine was the same as
Sunday's, with one exception. With Saturday dinner, the Sackvilles always served champagne; on Sunday, burgundy. Still,
for what it represented, that first weekend at the Sackvilles'
was something Wallis always remembered with the profoundest
pleasure. And, with her sly and impish Montague ways, and
her skill at gossipy anecdote (Maud Kerr-Smiley had told her
that the British upper classes liked nothing better than to gossip
about the love affairs of their friends), she was a success. She
was willing to be outspoken and self-mocking, and her practiced attitude of insouciance was perfect. She was, as the British
say, jolly. She was good company. That weekend invitation
was to be the first of many others.

Much has been said and written, over the years, about Wallis
Simpson's celebrated wit. And yet, when pressed to remember,
few of her friends can recall anything truly funny she ever said.
She had, apparently, what the British call a "parrot wit." She
was quick on the uptake, always ready with the pointed response. English humor is based on rapid give-and-take, and
conversation is designed to go lightly over matters, with each

participant adding his or her view. It is chatter, nearly always gossipy, often bitchy. Anything to do with sex is interesting, and amusing. Long, drawn-out anecdotes are considered boring, and are discouraged. At light banter, however, Wallis was very good indeed. For instance, a party guest once commented, apropos of a rumored liaison between two titled people, "I can't imagine what she sees in him." Wallis countered, "Well, darling, I've heard that he is marvelously—*endowed.*"

"*Really?* How do you know that?"

"A little *bird* told me."

Laughter.

Then there is this remembered exchange:

WALLIS   "I wonder what percentage of this season's crop of debutantes are virgins."

GUEST   "Oh, I should imagine about fifty percent."

WALLIS   "Darling, I think that figure is very *high*. It's because of the swimming baths, you see."

GUEST   "*Really?* The swimming baths?"

WALLIS   "Yes. You see, when the mums come to London for the presentation parties, they all stay at their clubs, and the clubs all have swimming baths. After the parties the mums go to bed, but the debs go downstairs, take off their dresses and swim in the swimming baths. The swimming baths all have back entrances, and the boys come in that way. That's when it happens."

And this bit of repartee:

WALLIS   "I hear there's an ancient fertility statue, a Celtic thing, somewhere in Devon. It shows a gentleman in a state of violent erection. The townspeople were so embarrassed that they planted a hedge around it."

GUEST   "Privet, I presume."

WALLIS   (*Pause*) "No, I think it's honeysuckle."

In those days in English society, anyone who talked too loudly or for too long or on too weighty a subject in mixed company was considered a bore, and was not asked back. Heavy topics, like politics, business, or world affairs, were limited to the gentlemen when they had withdrawn from the ladies after dinner for brandy and cigars. Wallis, early on, had managed to master these little conversational techniques and, in some cases, even outdid the British. In the process, to be sure, her personality had acquired a certain brittleness—a very British brittleness—and her faintly scathing comments, delivered in an offbeat southern drawl, went down well with her hosts and hostesses. Again, she was finding it possible to fit in by being a bit different. But of course not everybody found Wallis attractive. Ronald Tree, in recalling his first meeting with her, spoke of her "metallic elegance," which he found distinctly unappealing. In any case, from her successes at the Sackvilles' weekends, it was only a short step to invitations to other houses of the English party-going and party-giving aristocracy—Lady Emerald Cunard, Lady Sybil Colefax, Sir Charles and Lady Mendl, Sir Godfrey Thomas, Sir Philip Sassoon, and the Ormond Lawson-Johnsons. From here, it was only another short step to meeting Royalty.

4

"Strangers When We Meet"

CURIOUSLY enough, considering it would later be labeled "the Romance of the Century"—leading up to an event which H. L. Mencken described as "the greatest story since the Resurrection"—there are at least five different versions, all of them from reliable sources, of how Mrs. Simpson actually met the Prince of Wales. And this does not count the sixth, perfectly true, story of the actual first meeting at the mass presentation at Coronado years earlier, when clearly she had made no impression on him whatever. Even the two parties to the great romance themselves could never agree on when, where, and under what circumstances they first became acquainted. According to one version, reported in the London *Evening Standard* in 1936, they first met in Paris in the summer of 1930, in a railroad station, where both happened to be changing trains for Biarritz. Mrs. Simpson was having some difficulty with her luggage, and the Prince, noticing her predicament, gallantly stepped forward and offered to help her with the French customs agent. He ended up helping her carry her bags, and when they got to Biarritz, his party joined hers, and they all ended up having a jolly time together. It is true that Wallis was traveling in France that summer, with Ernest and Aunt Bessie Merryman. But both Wallis and the future King always denied that such a meeting ever took place—possibly because if, as the story went, they were both staying at the same seaside resort hotel, an adulterous relationship might have been inferred.

A second version is that Consuelo and Ben Thaw were being entertained at the Prince's country retreat, Fort Belvedere, near Windsor, and had to leave a day early. (A subversion of this has it that it was not Connie Thaw, but her sister Thelma Furness who had to leave.) The Prince was devastated that his guests were going, complained that he would be left all alone for the weekend, and so the Thaws (or Lady Furness) suggested that their friends, the Ernest Simpsons, might be persuaded to come up to Fort Belvedere and fill in. The Prince agreed, and the Simpsons were sent for. It seems a little unlikely that the Prince of Wales would accept total strangers as substitute house guests—or, for that matter, that any other host would—simply to ward off loneliness; his circle of acquaintance was large enough to have provided many other choices. But if the story is true, it was probably the Thaws, and not Thelma Furness, who made the suggestion. Wallis has written that at the time she "scarcely knew" Lady Furness, and had met her only once or twice before at large parties. The Thaws, on the other hand, were her good friends. Furthermore, Thelma Furness was then known all over London as one of the current lady friends of the Prince, and was a frequent house guest and traveling companion of His Royal Highness. She had not replaced Freda Dudley Ward exactly, but she and Freda shared him, along with the reputation of being the Prince's "mistress."

As was the case with Freda Dudley Ward, there was a husband in the picture—the money came from his family's Furness Steamship Line—but, for several years, though they shared the same London address, they had seldom appeared together, and were known to have reached an amicable agreement that each was to go his separate way. There is support for the unexpected-guest theory, meanwhile, though it is only rumor. That same fall of 1930, the Prince was playing golf at Sunningdale and is supposed to have remarked dryly to one of his equerries, "I seem to be having some people for dinner whom I've never met—an American couple named Simpson, or something like that."

The third version has it that the Prince and Mrs. Simpson did not meet in 1930 at all, but the following year—on June 10, 1931—the date when she was presented at Court at Buckingham Palace. This is the story provided by Edwina H. Wilson, in *Her Name Was Wallis Warfield,* published in 1936. According to that version, the Prince of Wales was overheard conversing in "muffled tones" at the ceremony with his great-uncle, the Duke of Connaught, and the Duke said to the Prince, "Are there any good numbers tonight?" The Prince is said to have replied, "I hear that Mrs. Simpson is a very attractive American and I hope to meet her afterward." Just who overheard this muffled interchange has never been clear, and for the old Duke to have used an Americanism such as "good numbers" seems more than a little strange. The Wilson story continues that, following the presentation, the Prince and the lady did indeed meet, and went on to a large formal ball given by Lady Furness. (Again, a variant tale has it that the ball was given by her sister Connie Thaw.) It is also said that the Prince offered the Simpsons a lift to the ball in his own car and that they accepted. At the ball, the story goes, the Prince spent most of the evening talking and dancing with Mrs. Simpson.

The fourth version of the meeting is the Duke of Windsor's own and so, in theory at least, it should be given some weight. The year of the meeting, he stated firmly in his memoirs, *A King's Story,* published in 1950, was 1931, and the place was Burrough Court, at Melton Mowbray in Leicestershire, in the heart of the English hunting country. Burrough Court was the country estate of Lord and Lady Furness. It was winter "after my return from South America," and among the Furnesses' guests were the Simpsons. "Mrs. Simpson did not ride," the Duke wrote, "and obviously had no interest in horses, hounds, or hunting in general." As a result, she stayed behind while the others were off to the chase, and she and the Prince fell into conversation.

Immediately, however, comparing sources, one wonders: *Did not ride?* In *his* book, Iles Brody claims that Wallis was "extremely fond of horses and riding and, in fact, possessed a pluck in the saddle which was the envy of accomplished male riders." But let us concede that Brody was probably wrong about this. Wallis was terrified of high places, and on picnics in the country she would frequently sit down in order to descend a slight slope out of fear of slipping and falling. And for the rest of her life she would display no interest in horses or horsemanship.

The Duke of Windsor continued with this now-famous account of their first conversation at Melton Mowbray when, as he wrote somewhat vaguely, the two were "strangers." Aware of the convention that one must not begin a conversation with Royalty until Royalty has spoken first, the Prince took the lead. The subject was the chilly weather. As an American, he asked her, did she not miss the comfort of central heating?

"I am sorry, Sir," she replied, "but you have disappointed me."

"In what way?" he asked.

"Every American woman who comes to your country is always asked that same question. I had hoped for something more original from the Prince of Wales."

"I moved away," the Duke wrote, "to talk to the other guests, but the echoes of the passage lingered."

If Wallis did indeed speak in this rather saucy way to the future King of England, it would have been very like her. It would have fitted with what Maud Kerr-Smiley had taught her about the way to approach British aristocracy: Don't let them think you care, don't let on that you're impressed. It was also shrewdly feminine. One way to get a man to notice you, and right away, is to *almost* insult him. The more *nil admirari* you appear, the easier it is to bowl him over. If a simple smile or a banal answer won't work, try rudeness. He may not like you for it, but at least he won't forget you for a while. The more unexpected your response, the deeper and more lasting will be the impression you make. The Prince of Wales, furthermore, was a man who had long since grown used to women fawning over him. When a woman, for once, didn't fawn, there had to be something extraordinary about her. Wallis was clever enough to know all these facts, and to use them. And from the Duke's own account, her pert responses to his questions did not at all displease him. On the contrary, they "lingered."

From the varying accounts of the historic encounter, now, a common thread appears to be emerging: Lady Furness had something to do with it. She was a plumpish, affable woman who had the unusual distinction of being someone nearly every-

body liked. In 1958, Thelma Furness and her sister Gloria
Vanderbilt published their own volume of reminiscences called
Double Exposure, and in it Thelma refuted both Wallis's and
the Duke of Windsor's previously published stories of the meeting and, in effect, called her former Sovereign a liar. The tale
about the central-heating conversation was, she said, a "fiction." She added that, "Had this been true, it would have been
not only bad taste but bad manners. At that moment Wallis
Simpson was as nervous and as impressed as any woman would
have been on first meeting the Prince of Wales." Wallis's
introduction to the Prince, Thelma Furness claimed, had been
perfectly simple, and she herself had performed it: "I went over
to Wallis, took her to the Prince, and introduced her." Lady
Furness was a little hazy about the date, placing it in either
late 1930 or early 1931—winter, in other words—but was
positive about the place. It happened not in the country but at
her town house in London, at a cocktail party. Also, though
Wallis had claimed that she "scarcely knew" Thelma when she
met the Prince, Thelma added, "Wallis and I became great
friends; actually I came to regard her as one of my best friends
in England, and the Prince and I often would include Wallis
and her husband in our parties. The Prince, consequently, saw
her at least once a week for the next three and a half years."

There are other discrepancies between the Duke's account
and Thelma's. In the *Life* magazine serialization, for which the
Duke supplied the picture captions, he wrote next to the photograph of Wallis's 1931 Court presentation: "Wallis Simpson
was presented to my parents at a Court in the early thirties and
this photograph of her in her Presentation gown was taken at
the time. We were then *almost* [italics added] strangers." (In
the book, the caption was changed to read, "Wallis was presented at a Court at Buckingham Palace on June 10, 1931.")
Obviously, if he and Wallis had been seeing each other "at
least once a week" for the previous six or seven months, they
could hardly have been almost strangers. And at the same time
there could not possibly have been that many meetings during
this period. The Duke had written that he and Wallis had met
during the winter *after* his return from South America in 1931.
The Prince of Wales left on his South American trip on the
morning of January 16, 1931. He did not return from it until
April 29 of the same year, by which date even the bitterest
English winter is well over and the country is enjoying its

loveliest season. Of course, winter is a season that spans two calendar years, and he may have met her in November or December of 1931. But that would have been at least seven months after his return from South America, and it seems strange, after so much time had elapsed, that he would draw a connection between the return from South America and meeting Wallis. More to the point, how could the two have been "almost strangers" in June of 1931, and have "first met" in November or December of that same year, months after Wallis's Court presentation? The Duke of Windsor's chronology simply will not hang together.

Before the Duke's 1950 memoirs were published, Wallis announced that she had gone scrupulously over his manuscript with him, line by line, checking for accuracy. But when her own memoirs were published six years later, she contradicted his story of how and when they met, and added a new version of her own. They did not meet in 1931 at all, but in November of 1930, *before* the Prince's South American trip. She was certain that it was 1930 because of some memorable events that had preceded it. A month or so earlier she had gone to Europe with her husband, and a fire had driven them from their hotel rooms in The Hague. Later, they had gone on to Paris and, for the first time, she had dipped into the small capital from her Uncle Sol's estate and had bought herself several expensive dresses.

Again, Wallis placed the meeting at Thelma Furness's country house at Melton Mowbray but, in her own account, the substitute-guest story was somewhat different. Early in November her friend Consuelo Thaw had telephoned Wallis in some agitation. Connie's sister Thelma, it seemed, had invited the Prince of Wales to Melton Mowbray for the weekend, and had asked the Thaws to come along as chaperones (though why the pair needed chaperones at their age, or at this stage of their affair, is not clear.) Now, at the last minute, a family emergency made it impossible for one of the Thaws—Connie—to go. Would Wallis and Ernest Simpson fill in as chaperones? Though Wallis wrote that she was "scared" by the idea, she was also "dying to meet the Prince of Wales," and so she accepted the assignment. At the time, she was grateful that she had her new Paris dresses to wear for the occasion. All the way up on the train to Melton Mowbray, and to the amusement of their fellow passengers, Benny Thaw stood wobbling in the aisle, trying to demonstrate to Wallis the art of the deep curtsy.

The reason, according to Wallis, why she did not go hunting with the others on the first morning of her visit was that she had a bad cold. Her first conversation with the Prince occurred when she was seated next to him at the luncheon table, following the hunt, and she claimed not to recall whether or not they had talked about central heating. In fact, she said she could not remember what they talked about at all. And certainly if she had made her opening "Sir, you disappoint me" comment at a luncheon table and if, as he said, he then "walked away," it would have meant getting up and leaving the table, which would have created a major crisis for his hostess. Wallis and the Prince did not meet or speak again, she said, until some six months later, when they met at an afternoon reception at Thelma Furness's house in Grosvenor Square. At that meeting, he said to her, "How nice to see you again." That was in May 1931, after his return from South America. The following month, as she tells it, they encountered each other a third time, when she was presented at Court. When the Royal Family was leaving the presentation ceremony, she overheard the Prince mutter to the Duke of Connaught, "Uncle Arthur, something ought to be done about the lights. They make all the women look ghastly." After the ceremony, there was a small gathering at Thelma Furness's house. The Prince appeared—Wallis never claimed that she had been driven to the party in his car—and he complimented Wallis on her dress. "But, Sir," she said a trifle naughtily, "I understood that you thought we all looked ghastly." He looked startled, then smiled and said, "I had no idea my voice carried so far."

Wallis's version of their meeting and budding friendship has, at least, the virtue of a certain logic. And its chronology fits with the Prince's schedule of travel and activities at the time. Nor is there any apparent reason why, when describing the time and circumstances of their meeting, she would have felt any need to dissemble.* The only unanswered question is why, when Wallis read the Duke of Windsor's manuscript for

*Unless, of course, there was something disreputable or embarrassing about those circumstances—if they had actually met, say, at one of the "wild" parties that were so much a part of English high life at the time, and that were gleefully described in the early novels of Evelyn Waugh and Aldous Huxley.

accuracy, she let the central-heating story, which would never jibe with her own, stand and, from the Duke's pages, move on into history. As for the Duke, though it is certainly unusual for a man to forget how and where he first met the love of his life, his lapse of memory is explainable. He was, after all, a great public figure who, in the course of an average day, met many people—some of them notable, some not. He could not, and did not, remember the names of all of them. Because of who he was, on the other hand, those who met him for the first time remembered the occasion clearly. And so the haunting woman of the central-heating comeback may have been an altogether different person.

One thing is certain: by the time of Wallis's Court presentation in the summer of 1931, the "almost stranger" had begun to make a deep impression on the Prince of Wales. As he wrote in his autobiography: "When her turn came to curtsy, first to my father then to my mother, I was struck by the grace of her carriage and the natural dignity of her movements."

Of course the very fact of Wallis's presentation at Court that summer would cause skeptics to wonder, later, whether Wallis and the Duke were telling the truth about how they met, and to insist that the two must have been more than casual acquaintances at that point. The skepticism is based on the assumption that the Prince of Wales was already eager to establish Wallis socially, that the presentation of a divorced American woman could not have been arranged without some high-level help, and that the Prince of Wales would not have offered to help a woman he hardly knew. It is true that, until as recently as the reign of the Prince's grandfather, Edward VII, it would have been impossible for a divorced woman to be presented at Court. But under George V, the rule had been relaxed considerably, and Court presentations had been occasionally offered to divorcées, provided they had been judged the "innocent party" in the divorce. Thelma Furness, for example, herself a divorcée, had been presented at Court four years earlier, in 1927, as an "innocent." Wallis was also "innocent."

Both Wallis and the Duke always denied that her Court presentation had been accomplished with royal help, and there is no real reason not to believe them. For one thing, it was not, at this point, the Prince of Wales who was most interested in advancing Wallis socially. That person was Ernest Simpson.

As Wallis wrote, his sister, Maud Kerr-Smiley, acting on her brother's behalf, had first proposed the presentation and handled the arrangements. Wallis agreed to go along with it because it didn't cost anything. She did not even bother to buy a new dress for the occasion. She borrowed one from Connie Thaw, and borrowed the train, fan, and traditional three white feathers for her hair from Thelma Furness, a veteran of the ritual.

For another thing, following the presentation Wallis and Ernest Simpson did not see or hear a word from the Prince for more than seven months. During this entire period, the woman at the Prince's side and on his arm—at nightclubs, restaurants, private parties—and who acted as his hostess and unofficial chatelaine at Fort Belvedere was inevitably Thelma Furness. When an invitation to the Fort finally came—for the weekend of January 30, 1932—it was Thelma who issued it.

No one could have been more thrilled than Ernest Simpson. Or, of course, Wallis, who was enjoying the heady climb as much as he. It had taken them just three and a half years to get to the very top. It was an American Dream Come True.

5

At the
Summit

IN MANY ways, London was just like Baltimore. The moment it was noticed that a new couple, the Simpsons, had entered the Prince of Wales's charmed circle, there was talk. Who were they? Where had they come from? What does the Prince possibly see in them? It must be *her*. There was jealousy, too. After all, the Prince's circle would only hold so many people, and the Prince had long shown a marked tendency to take up new friends who amused him and to cast aside others with whom he had grown bored. Whom would the Simpsons be replacing? The Prince was already phasing out Freda Dudley Ward—while she was bravely pretending not to care—and concentrating on her replacement, Thelma Furness. Soon he would banish Freda altogether, as he also, in time, would banish Thelma. With the arrival of the Simpsons on the scene, it seemed at though a new pecking order was about to be established.

Wallis was carefully scrutinized, and most of the initial verdicts were unfavorable. One critic commented, "Her jaws show on either side of her face when you sit beside her in the theatre." Another, remarking on her hands, which were large but with rather stubby fingers, referred to "Mrs. Simpson's peasant paws." Even Thelma Furness, who would later describe Wallis as one of her "best friends in England," had a fairly negative first impression: "She was not beautiful; in fact, she was not even pretty. But she had a distinct charm and a sharp sense of humor. Her dark hair was parted in the middle. Her eyes, alert and eloquent, were her best feature. . . . Her hands were large; they did not move gracefully, and I thought she used them too much when she attempted to emphasize a point." Cecil Beaton, who was vaguely related to Ernest Simpson by marriage, had an even less charitable view. As he told Bryan and Murphy, "She looked coarse. Her back was coarse, and her arms were heavy. Her voice had a high nasal twang. She was loud and brash, terribly so—and rowdy and raucous. Her squawks were like a parrot's."

Another who, in the beginning at least, took a dim view of her was "Chips" Channon. Channon had been born Henry Channon III, in Chicago, the son of wealthy parents, and had been considered by his family a spendthrift and ne'er-do-well. He had been virtually banished to England where, to everyone's surprise, he had become a huge success. He had married Lady Honor Guinness of the brewing family and had become a Member of Parliament and a leading London social figure. In the course of time, he would be knighted. Of his first meeting with Wallis, at a luncheon tossed by Emerald Cunard, he noted in his later-published diaries, *Chips*, "She is a nice, quiet, well-bred mouse of a woman, with large startled eyes and a huge mole." After visiting the Simpsons' apartment in Bryanston Court, Channon pronounced it a "dreadful, banal flat." Cecil Beaton's comments on the flat were a little kindlier, but not much. "Like a thousand other apartments, this one displayed impeccable taste and no originality," he said.

But, though the critics might gleefully be carving up the Simpsons with their knives behind their backs, there was no question but that they had been hurled into the limelight by the Prince's sudden attention to them. Ernest and Wallis Simpson, socially, could now no longer be ignored by anyone. In the early days of her friendship with the Prince of Wales, Wallis is said to have been apprehensive about what it all might be leading up to. "No good will come of this, wait and see," she is supposed to have remarked to a friend. "People will turn against me, I will lose all my friends, and I shall end up in the poor house of Baltimore." If, however, she actually made this comment, her gloomy predictions did not immediately come true. On the contrary, Mr. and Mrs. Ernest Simpson were now on every invitation list that mattered. Suddenly, they had more friends than they had ever dreamed of having, and certainly more than they needed. They were catapulted instantly into the highest reaches of British society. Doors that had been tentatively opened for them through the Sackvilles were now flung wide, and society scrambled for invitations to Wallis's little tea and cocktail parties at Bryanston Court. She already had the habit, which would last her lifetime, of worrying about her health, and had become convinced that she had an ulcer. For a while her London doctor put her on a diet that excluded alcohol, and her favorite cocktail-time drink was a half-and-half mixture of milk and club soda. All at once this unappetizing concoction was the rage of fashionable London.

The Simpsons' first weekend visit to Fort Belvedere—an invitation that, as Wallis later described it, had come "out of the blue"—had included some of the Prince's oldest and best friends. Thelma Furness was there, of course, acting as his hostess, along with Benny Thaw and Brigadier General Gerald F. Trotter, known by the nickname "G," the Prince's favorite equerry, who always referred to the Prince as "my master." For Wallis, the weekend was chiefly remarkable in her discovery of the Prince's "secret vice"—doing needlepoint—which his mother, Queen Mary, had taught him (though Thelma Furness also claimed to have been his teacher). He was making a cover for a backgammon table. He had also become an enthusiastic gardener, and during the day he, Ernest, Benny Thaw and "G" Trotter worked in Fort Belvedere's extensive gardens.

Fort Belvedere, a rambling, turreted affair built in no particular style, was what the Prince of Wales considered his true home. It was one of the so-called "Grace and Favour" houses on Crown property bordering Windsor Great Park. These houses were not the personal property of the Monarch, but belonged to the Crown, and were at the disposal of the Sovereign to be given out to favored courtiers or members of the Royal Family. Fort Belvedere was not particularly old as English country houses went, and had been built in the early eighteenth century by William, Duke of Cumberland, the third son of George II. For a long time the Fort was known as Cumberland's Folly because, at some point during the building of the place, the Duke seemed to have forgotten what he had in mind—whether it was to be a pretentious palace or an architectural eccentricity. The Prince of Wales had completely remodeled the house, adding central heating, a modern kitchen, and a steam bath.

For Wallis and Ernest Simpson, their weekend at Fort Belvedere was to be the first of many. There were also invitations to York House, the Prince's official London residence, and there were luncheons and dinners—often as a threesome—at restaurants.

In March 1933—after the friendship had flourished for more than a year—Wallis and Ernest sailed on the *Mauretania* for New York, where Ernest had ship-brokerage business to attend to. They were scarcely out of Southampton harbor when a bon voyage message signed "Edward P." was delivered to their stateroom, and when word spread to the other passengers that Mr. and Mrs. Simpson had received a farewell greeting from the Prince of Wales, the Simpsons were the talk of the ship.

After their return from England, on July 4 of that year, Wallis and Ernest Simpson gave their first formal dinner party for the Prince of Wales at Bryanston Court. There were ten guests, including Thelma Furness and the Thaws. Despite a certain nervousness in the kitchen all went well, and the Prince exclaimed over the food. Wallis had settled on an American menu—black bean soup, grilled lobster, fried chicken Maryland, and raspberry soufflé for dessert—and a red, white and blue color scheme for the American Independence Day. It was a Tuesday night, and the Prince insisted that the Simpsons spend the coming weekend at Fort Belvedere. For the rest of that year, in fact, Ernest and Wallis became almost permanent weekend fixtures at the Fort, with Thelma Furness continuing to act as the Prince's unofficial hostess.

Early in 1934, Thelma Furness departed for America to assist her sister in the custody battle for little Gloria Vanderbilt, a tug-of-war of which much was being made in the press, and which was helping keep Americans' minds off the deepening Depression. Before leaving, Thelma and Wallis lunched, and Thelma said casually, "I'm afraid the Prince is going to be lonely. Wallis, won't you look after him?" Wallis assured her that she would. (In Thelma Furness's recollection of the exchange, it was Wallis who first brought up the Prince's loneliness. "She . . . said suddenly, 'Oh, Thelma, the little man [their pet expression for him behind his back] is going to be so lonely.' 'Well, dear,' I answered, 'you look after him for me while I'm away. See that he does not get into any mischief.'") A few days after Thelma's departure, the Prince telephoned Wallis—the first time, according to her, that he had ever telephoned her personally. He was having a small dinner at the Dorchester Hotel, and would Wallis and Ernest join him? They would. That dinner became memorable to Wallis and her friends because of an unusual occurrence. It had always been a firm, unwritten rule that when in a royal presence one never talked of politics, affairs of state, or other royal matters. But suddenly, at the Dorchester dinner table, the Prince turned to Wallis and began talking to her about what he was trying to do in his job as Prince of Wales, and what he further intended to do when he became King. Eyebrows went up when the others caught the startling drift of the conversation. They went up even further when Wallis not only listened to what he had to say, but encouraged him to say more, and even offered opinions of her own. "But I am boring you," he said nervously. "On the contrary," she replied, "I couldn't be more interested. Please, please go on." He paused, looked at her questioningly, and then said, "Wallis, you're the only woman who's ever been interested in my job."

Soon after this interchange, he developed the habit of dropping by, unannounced, at the flat in Bryanston Court—for a drink in the late afternoon or on his way to and from appointments. Sometimes his visits were only for a few minutes, sometimes he stayed longer. Sometimes Ernest Simpson was there, and sometimes he was not. Now the visits from the Prince to the Simpson flat became an almost daily occurrence. On one memorable occasion he arrived for a small cocktail party and stayed on and on. Even though English etiquette demands that no one leave a gathering where Royalty is present until Royalty itself has left, one by one the other guests did leave, to go on to other dinner appointments. Finally, only Wallis, Ernest, and the Prince remained, and the Prince seemed oblivious to how late the hour had grown. That was when Wallis made her soon-to-be-famous comment to him: "Sir, would you care to take potluck with us?" He jumped up, apologized for keeping them from their dinner, but Wallis assured him that, though they would be dining on modest fare—beef stew—there was plenty for him too. And so he stayed—and stayed.

The more the Prince was seen with the Simpsons in public, the more the speculation about them billowed. If, as some of the gossips insisted, the Prince had taken, in Wallis, a new "mistress," then certainly Ernest Simpson was a most complacent cuckold. He seemed to enjoy the Prince's company as much as Wallis did, and the Prince was equally cordial and solicitous to him. It was also suggested in London that the Prince and the Simpsons might have become a *ménage à trois*. Such arrangements were not at all uncommon in English society, and many were known to have lasted happily for years.

Soon after the potluck dinner, when the Prince appeared for these evening visits, Ernest Simpson—"tactfully," as Wallis put it later—managed to make some excuse, such as work to attend to, to withdraw to another room in the apartment, leaving his wife and the Prince alone with their conversations. The reasons for Ernest's tact were understandable. The constant presence of this particular visitor had caused Ernest's initial enthusiasm about the arrangement to fade considerably. It had become quite clear to him that the Prince was not interested in him, but in his wife.

At Fort Belvedere, and also at York House in Thelma's absence, Wallis had begun advising the Prince on matters of menu planning and decorating. She suggested new furniture arrangements, helped him select new pieces, advised him on color schemes. Presently she was planning all the menus at both the Prince's houses. Needless to say, the Prince's servants did not take kindly to the American woman who had come with new and foreign notions, and had put herself virtually in the position of mistress of the household. With Thelma Furness, it had been quite different—Thelma's approach had been casual and laissez-faire. Wallis was crisp, efficient, a perfectionist who liked things *just so*. But when the servants complained to their master about her interventions and innovations, he told them that they were to take their orders from Mrs. Simpson, as well as from him. No other woman in the Prince's life—not Freda, not Thelma—had ever been given such sweeping authority.

Thelma Furness returned from America in late March, and on the evening of her return the Prince of Wales presented himself at her house. His manner was distant and aloof.

Abruptly he asked her about reports, which were quite true, that she had met Prince Aly Khan a few days before sailing home to England and that he had been so taken with her charm that he had impulsively booked passage on her ship in order to wine and dine her throughout the voyage. The Prince of Wales clearly found this "swarthy" Prince of the Ismailis a member of inferior royalty, and felt insulted that Thelma should have given him the time of day. Thelma did her best to make light of the episode which, she insisted, did not amount to an "affair," but she was clearly worried. She immediately went to her best friend, Wallis, and asked if Wallis could account for the Prince's sudden chilliness. According to Thelma, Wallis merely said, "Darling, you know the little man loves you very much. The little man was just lost without you." Wallis, however, remembers the confrontation somewhat differently. Thelma, Wallis wrote, asked her if the Prince was "keen" on her, and Wallis replied, "I think he likes me. He may be fond of me. But, if you mean by keen that he is in love with me, the answer is definitely no." In a comparison of the two memoirs, Wallis's would appear to be the more staged.

Meanwhile, another weekend at Fort Belvedere was coming up, and Thelma had been invited, along with the inevitable Simpsons. The weekend had not progressed for long before Thelma became aware that the Fort had acquired a new hostess, that she had been replaced. She doubtless noticed the new furniture arrangements, noticed Wallis issuing instructions to the servants, noticed a new intimacy between Wallis and the Prince. The situation became clearest at the dinner table. The Prince had casually reached into his plate to pick up a piece of salad with his fingers, and Wallis, seated next to him, had playfully slapped his hand, as though admonishing a small child. Shocked at such temerity, Thelma had thrown Wallis a sharp look of disapproval. In return, as Thelma put it, "Wallis looked straight at me. . . . I knew then she had looked after him exceedingly well. That one cold, defiant glance had told me the entire story." The next morning, early, Thelma packed and left the Fort, never to return. The woman who had introduced the Prince to his new love would never hear from him again.

That was in April. A month later, Freda Dudley Ward was also cast aside, and in a heartless, offhand way, a particularly stunning act of cowardice that would become typical of the Prince's treatment of people who had outlived their usefulness to him. Freda had for years been in the habit of telephoning the Prince at York House, and the switchboard operator knew her voice. This time, she was told by the regretful operator that the Prince had issued new instructions: no more calls were to be accepted from Mrs. Dudley Ward. That was that, and Freda joined what would eventually become a long list of discarded friends. Now Wallis—and, of course Ernest, who still shared the Prince's attentions—had the field to themselves.

As the relationship developed, furthermore, Wallis's charm began to win over the early critics. A few months after his initial disparaging appraisal of her, Chips Channon's opinion had improved somewhat, and he wrote in his diary, "She is a jolly, plain, intelligent, quiet, unpretentious and unprepossessing little woman"—a few more praising adjectives than damning ones—and a month after that entry he warmed to her even more, saying, "Mrs. Simpson has enormously improved the Prince. In fact I find the duel over the Prince of Wales between Mrs. Simpson, supported by Diana Cooper and, strangely enough, Emerald, and the [Furness] camp is most diverting. In fact, the romance surpasses all else in interest. He is obviously madly infatuated, and she, a jolly, unprepossessing American, witty, a mimic, an excellent cook, has completely subjugated him. Never has he been so in love. She is madly anxious to storm society, while she is still his favourite, so that when he leaves her (as he leaves everyone in time) she will be secure." A few days later, at the opera, "we . . . were joined in Emerald's box by the Prince of Wales and the Ménage Simpson. I was interested to see what an extraordinary hold Mrs. Simpson has over the Prince. In the interval she told him to hurry away as he would be late in joining the Queen at the LCC Ball—and she made him take a cigar from out of his breast pocket. 'It doesn't look very pretty,' she said. He went, but was back in half an hour."

It was true that women had a way of not lasting very long with the Prince of Wales. It was said that he was a less than satisfactory bedmate, and there were even whispers that he was all but impotent. There had been other women briefly in and out of his life. Most of those who accepted his attentions had done so for the glamor and excitement that went with knowing a royal heir, and for the cachet and attention that went with being seen and photographed with him at parties. After a while, the glamor and excitement—if there was no promise of anything more behind them—wore thin. With few of the women he escorted was there any hope or possibility of marriage. In fact, he seemed deliberately to choose women with whom marriage would have been out of the question—like Freda Dudley Ward and Thelma Furness. Also, where women were concerned, he showed a distinct fondness for ladies of the lower rank—women who could not possibly expect to marry the future King of England. And so the women came and went, were taken up enthusiastically by the Prince, and then abruptly dropped. Mrs. Simpson, as Chips Channon assumed, seemed merely another figure in this lengthening parade.

But, to people more observant than Channon, there was something a little different about Wallis and the Prince's interest in her—a certain authority, and power, that she seemed to wield over him and that he, so accustomed to being fawned over by others, almost fawningly accepted. Wallis flabber-gasted London, for example, when she dropped her handker-chief and then waited for the Prince of Wales to bend over and pick it up—which he did. Though she was usually careful, in company, to address him correctly as "Sir," she sometimes forgot herself and absent-mindedly—or was it intentionally?—called him "David," the name reserved for members of his family. The Prince seemed not only to forgive her these lapses of standard etiquette but actually to enjoy them. Instead of waiting, as protocol directed, for the Prince to pass through a doorway ahead of her, she exercised her southern belle's right to precede him. She let him light her cigarettes for her. Then there were those unheard-of little intimacies. Wallis had always been a toucher—a patter of hands and toucher of elbows when she talked to people. Though no one would have dreamed of lay-ing a finger on the physical person of the Prince of Wales, Wallis, at the dinner table, would reach out and tap his wrist reprovingly if she disagreed with something he had said. She would interrupt him—something no one in London society would ever have dared to do. Once, at a party where one of the guests had recently returned from China, she said, "Now David, I don't want to hear any more of your war stories tonight. I want to hear about China." She would reach out and straighten his necktie, or tuck down a protruding collar tab. London was bewildered and, of course, intrigued.

"Let me be candid: the attention was flattering. I enjoyed every minute of it," Wallis wrote. What she did not write—

what she may not have even realized—was that the attention she was now receiving, and her frank enjoyment of it, had effected a change in her personality, manner and bearing. The unpretentious, unprepossessing little mouse with the nervous "startled" eyes whom Chips Channon had observed a year earlier had been replaced by a poised, relaxed and elegant, coolly detached woman. At last she seemed sure of herself, and of everything else. If Wallis had improved the Prince, the Prince had also improved Wallis in terms of her own self-esteem. Chips Channon noticed it. "She has already the air of a personage who walks into a room as though she almost expected to be curtsied to. At least, she wouldn't be too surprised. She has complete power over the Prince of Wales." Even the hard-to-please Cecil Beaton, who had originally found her "coarse," had reversed his harsh appraisal and now found her "immaculate, soignée, as fresh as a young girl. Her skin was as bright and smooth as the inside of a shell, her hair so sleek she might have been Chinese." It was a difference, one might say, as between night and day.

In August 1934, the Prince was planning to leave for a holiday in Biarritz, where he had taken a house, and he asked the Simpsons to join him. Alas, it seemed as though they could not. Ernest had to go to the United States on business, and Wallis's Aunt Bessie Merryman was coming to visit her in England. The Prince immediately expanded his invitation to include Aunt Bessie, who must have been somewhat awed when she learned of her new destination.

The Prince's rented house in Biarritz, a large villa called Morotmont, overlooked the sea. In addition to Wallis and Aunt Bessie, there were other house guests, including the Prince's assistant private secretary, Hugh Lloyd Thomas, his equerries John Aird and "G" Trotter, and Commander and Mrs. Colin Buist. Still, Wallis and the Prince frequently managed to slip away from the others, and were seen having dinner together in small restaurants and bistros around the city. The attention, meanwhile, that the Prince was showering on Aunt Bessie, a plump and lively lady in her seventies, was most surprising. She was Wallis's closest living relative, and he treated her with exceptional deference. He behaved as a suitor would who is trying to impress the parents of his intended with his qualifications as a mate. Aunt Bessie became understandably alarmed, and spoke to Wallis about it, to which Wallis replied, "You don't have to worry about me—I know what I'm doing."

Later that month, the Prince's party was joined by Mrs. Kenelm Guinness, who had an idea. "Posy" Guinness was a cousin by marriage of Lord Moyne, then a leader of the Conservative party, whose yacht, the *Rosaura*, was cruising nearby. Posy was sure her relative would enjoy asking the little group aboard his yacht for a short cruise. As it turned out, she was right; Lord Moyne was delighted. And so the royal party boarded the yacht—all, that is, except Aunt Bessie who, Wallis explained, had been counting on a motor trip to Italy. (In fact, Aunt Bessie may have been so distressed by what she sensed was going on that she wanted no further part of it.)

The *Rosaura* sailed from Biarritz along and down the Spanish and Portuguese coasts, through Gibraltar, into the Mediterranean to Cannes for eleven days and nights. It was during those lazy and unhindered evenings aboard Lord Moyne's yacht, Wallis wrote, when she and the Prince would quietly sequester themselves from the others, that they passed "the indefinable boundary between friendship and love." The Prince had never before presented her with anything more valuable than an orchid plant and a cairn terrier named Slipper. (Was either of them aware of the Cinderella symbolism?) At the end of the cruise, however, he handed her a velvet-covered box that contained a diamond and emerald charm for her bracelet.

Back in England, when Wallis and Ernest were reunited, he asked her how the trip had gone. "I can't describe it. All I can say is that it was like being Wallis in Wonderland," she gushed. She did not mention the Prince's gift of jewelry. Her husband commented dryly that it sounded to him more like "a trip behind the 'Looking Glass.' Or, better yet, an excursion into the realm of Peter Pan's Never-Never Land." And thereafter, Ernest Simpson always referred to the small-boned, delicately featured Prince as "Peter Pan," the little boy who refused to grow up.

That autumn, the engagement of the Prince of Wales's youngest living brother, Prince George, the Duke of Kent, to Princess Marina of Greece was announced, and all London was flung into the whirlwind of social activity that is always precipitated by an upcoming royal marriage. Ernest and Wallis were invited to every gala ball and dinner given for the royal pair, and were invited to the wedding itself, where the Prince saw to it that Wallis and her husband got specially reserved

aisle-side seats in Westminster Abbey. It was that same autumn
of 1934 that Wallis met for the first—and, as it would turn
out, last—time the Prince of Wales's parents, King George
V and Queen Mary. The Prince took her by the arm and led
her across the floor of the reception room at Buckingham Palace, and introduced her to his mother and father. Wallis and
the elderly Queen chatted for a few moments about banalities—
the weather, and the women's dresses. There were some at the
reception who thought that Queen Mary's attitude was reserved,
even chilly, toward the American newcomer.

At that party, Wallis circulated among the glittering and
titled guests and, at the same time, explored and scrutinized
the public rooms of the palace. According to a persistent but
unsubstantiated piece of gossip that has circulated in London
for years, she paused at a window that looked out over the
palace gardens and Queen Mary's famous beds of prize petu-
nias. The flowers were the Queen's personal pride, and the
pride of all of England. As Wallis surveyed the manicured
flowerbeds, she was said to have been heard—by a palace
servant—to comment, "Of course when I live here, this will
all be tennis courts." The remark is said to have traveled up
and down the back stairs of the Palace, and then to have made
its way out into London society. Thus it is claimed that the
servants of the royal household became the first of what would
become many enemies of Wallis Simpson at Buckingham Palace.

6

"What Could It Be He Sees in Her?"

ACCORDING to *Burke's Peerage*, the British Royal Family is simply "the Most Ancient and Splendid Royal House in the World." This grand and sweeping concept has supported and sustained the British Monarchy for centuries and has left its imprint on every occupant of the British throne. True, some English kings have been less splendid than others. The early Saxon conquerors, according to some chroniclers, practiced cannibalism, and this was heartily encouraged at the court of Æthelfrith, King of Northumbria. One of Æthelfrith's courtiers, a doughty Welshman named Gwrgi, is said to have become so enamored of the practice that he slaughtered and devoured one male and one female Briton every day of the week except Saturday. On Saturdays, he killed two of each sex, in order to be spared the sin of breaking the Sabbath and, at the same time, to be assured of having plenty to eat on Sunday.

Still, it is easy to understand the infatuation of a middle-aging American woman like Wallis Simpson—of *any* woman, for that matter—with the Prince of Wales. With the ancient and splendid title, he was easily the world's most eligible bachelor. Then there was the seemingly limitless power that accompanied the title. Wallis wrote, "His slightest wish seemed always to be translated instantly into the most impressive kind of reality. Trains were held; yachts materialized; the best suites in the finest hotels were flung open; airplanes stood waiting." For her, "he was the open sesame to a new and glittering world that excited me as nothing in my life had ever done before."

Who can blame her, or discredit her excitement? To be sure, her infatuation with the Prince was with the symbol, the metaphor. The man behind the lofty metaphor was a person she had not yet fully comprehended. To her, he was still all trappings, all fanfare, all heels clicking to attention, salutes, bows and curtsies, but to her the trappings and the fanfare in themselves were thrill enough.

But while Wallis' bedazzlement with the Prince of Wales was clear and understandable to anyone who saw them, the real puzzle that remained was trying to figure out what in the world he saw in her. In her high-heeled shoes, she stood slightly taller than he. Cecil Beaton continued to try to describe her appearance: "None of her features is classically correct—her nose, for instance; and her mouth is downright ugly—but they all fit together. She's attractively ugly, *une belle laide*. She has an *amusing* face." In terms of her clothes, according to Thelma Furness, "she did not have the chic she has since cultivated." Freda Dudley Ward had been a classic beauty, all soft edges and gentle curves. Thelma Furness had been handsome and bosomy with a strong aura of sex appeal. Wallis's figure was angular, boxy and boyish, broad-shouldered and flat-chested, not the least sexy. What *did* he see in her?

Lord Castlerosse, who knew the Prince well, insisted that the attraction between the two was not primarily sexual. But, at the time, his was the only voice in England that expressed this opinion and, in the ever-prurient eyes of London society, he had to be wrong. It had to be something Wallis was able to do in bed, something no other woman had been able to do, or tried to do, which made him feel more vital, more satisfied, more manly. What it was, of course, could only be a matter of speculation, since, as in all well-conducted romances, there were no eyewitnesses to Wallis and the Prince performing a sexual act. What remained were unproved and unprovable theories. Some said, for example, that during Wallis's mysterious two-year "China period," she learned to perform exotic Oriental bits of sexual business—from the "sing-song houses," perhaps, where her first husband had taken her during the two weeks of their attempt at a reconciliation. From America, a fanciful piece of gossip had it that Wallis possessed an extra vertebra at the base of her spine—supposedly a Montague family trait. This may be why some claimed that she could give an extra twist to the Fish Tail Wiggle, a dance *à la mode* at the time, as well as to other matters.

In the 1920's and '30's, meanwhile, talk of "mistresses" was commonplace, and now that both Freda and Thelma had been dropped from the list of the Prince's women friends, it was assumed that Wallis had become the Prince's "new mistress." Whether she actually was or not would become, as we shall see, a matter of some controversy years later. In fact, throughout what can be described as the Prince and Wallis's "courtship" period, no one saw them so much as kiss. The closest thing to an intimacy ever observed between them was when, occasionally, they were seen rather dreamily holding hands. And yet it was obvious to everyone that he was absolutely smitten with her. He hovered over her, attended to her every wish, and seemed anxious and distracted in her absence. His attitude toward her, while astonishing, was not the least bit attractive. Chips Channon, for one, found it almost sickening. If whatever power she exerted over the Prince made him feel more masculine, he did not show it. His behavior toward her was more like that of a lady-in-waiting.

Wallis herself dismissed sex as the main source of the attraction. She once, years later, told a startled Adela Rogers St. Johns that all the sons of George V—including, Mrs. St. Johns inferred, the man who was by then her husband—"have small-penis complexes." To another interviewer, who asked the Duchess of Windsor why she and the Duke had never had children, she said that the Duke was not "heir-conditioned." (It was a curious echo of a comment Wallis's mother had made when asked the same question after her marriage to Mr. Raisin: "[Mine is] a seedless Raisin.") And, in his memoirs, the Duke of Windsor himself agreed with her. Of that dinner at the Dorchester, when he and Wallis first discussed his work, he said, "Right then I made an important discovery: that a man's relationship with a woman could also be an *intellectual partnership* [italics added]. That was the start of my falling in love with her. She promised to bring into my life something that wasn't there. I was convinced that with her, I'd be a more creative and more useful person."

The partnership he envisioned at the Dorchester may or may not have been passionless, but it was hardly intellectual. He simply did not have the necessary intelligence for an intellectual relationship—which was not his fault. He was descended from dim-witted people on both sides. As Prince of Wales, of course, his own mental dimness could be camouflaged. He was surrounded by aides and equerries and advisers brighter than he who could provide appropriate answers to questions which, without their help, would have been beyond him. The trappings and perquisites that went with the title had kept him propped up and from making a fool of himself.

Noël Coward once said of him, "He had the charm of the world, with nothing whatever to back it up." Once, as a young and unknown talent, Coward had sat up half the night with the Prince of Wales playing accompaniment piano to the Prince's ukulele. The next day, at Hawes & Curtis, a fashionable haberdashery shop, Coward had encountered the Prince again, and the Prince had cut him dead. Years later, when he was famous, Coward would receive many invitations from the Duke of Windsor. Realizing that the Duke was only interested in people who were rich or celebrated, Coward always felt a little guilty about accepting them and becoming a part of the blatant hypocrisy.

If, by the autumn of 1934, Queen Mary was not aware of her son's curiously strong attraction to Mrs. Ernest Simpson, she was the only woman in Court circles who was not. It was the primary subject of London society gossip. But there is no evidence that this stubborn lady, whose iron will was a match for her husband's irascibility, ever mentioned the subject to her son, or that he, more interestingly, ever brought up the matter to either of his parents. That they would have disapproved of the relationship there was no question: they disapproved of most of his friends. He had been careful to present Wallis to his mother only once—at a large, formal occasion, when there was no possibility of any sort of confrontation. Otherwise, he had avoided a scene the easy way, by saying or doing nothing.

And if Ernest Simpson was not aware of the rapidly developing state of affairs, he was doing his best to act that way.

He must have sensed the little silences, followed by the buzz of whispering, whenever he entered a room, and must have guessed that, behind his back, people were beginning to laugh at him. Still, he and Wallis continued to bow and curtsy to the Prince of Wales, and to dress up for every royal occasion to which they were invited. Perhaps Ernest—along with others, including the King and Queen, who knew the Prince and had observed him over the years—believed that the affair could not possibly be taken seriously. After all, the Prince of Wales, now forty, had had a long series of passionate crushes. None of them had ever lasted long. Why should this one vary from what seemed to have become a fixed pattern? But what no one may have also realized was that his youngest brother's marriage had had a profound effect upon the Prince. It fixed, in his head, the idea that he was now middle-aged, and that he too should marry—and marry soon.

Chips Channon, who had grown rather to like and admire Wallis, had never bothered to conceal his low opinion of the Prince. He considered him childish, headstrong, spoiled, and more than a little fickle. Also, by now, Channon had become aware of the Prince's strong pro-German leanings and of his admiration of the growing National Socialist Party. He was also astonished at the absolute power that Wallis seemed to wield over the Prince, the way she seemed literally able to lead him about by the nose. The Prince, Channon wrote in his diary, "is Mrs. Simpson's absolute slave, and will go nowhere where she is not invited, and she, clever woman, with her high pitched voice, chic clothes, moles and sense of humor is behaving well. She encourages [him] to meet people of importance and to be polite; above all she makes him happy. The Empire ought to be grateful."

The Prince, Channon noted, was not always polite. At times, when the Prince encountered old friends, he greeted them warmly. At other times, he ignored them. The Prince could be cheerful and charming. He could also be rude and autocratic and overbearing. All of London was beginning to notice the new jewelry with which Wallis was now being showered, and the source of the jewels was disturbing. At her death in 1925, the Prince's grandmother, Queen Alexandra, had given most of her extensive collection of jewels to him, with the idea that they would one day be worn by his Queen and then passed on to future queens of England. Thus, though not technically part of the Crown jewels, the collection was informally regarded as the property of the Crown. Morally, at least, they were not his to give away. Though the stones that Wallis was wearing had all been given smart new Cartier settings, there were some in London who professed to recognize certain stones as having come from Queen Alexandra's collection.

For the Prince's occasional bad behavior, Channon blamed the influence of Thelma Furness, "who first 'modernised' and Americanised him, making him over-democratic, casual, and a little common." He also blamed the Prince's parents, King George and Queen Mary. "For the 26 years of their reign," he wrote, "they practically saw no one except their old Courtiers, and they made no social background whatever for any of their children. Naturally, their children had to find outlet and their fun elsewhere, and the two most high-spirited ones, the [Prince of Wales] and the fascinating Duke of Kent, drank deeply from life."

The Prince had a habit of embracing—and then dropping—new enthusiasms as quickly as he took up and dropped new friends. He had taken up, in rapid succession, golf, hunting, flying, drinking, and gardening. For two years, with manic intensity, he had played the bagpipes, having abandoned the ukulele. Sometimes he would sit, in his kilt, and play the bagpipes all night long. He had also taken up German and, at times at parties, he would refuse to speak in any other language. At the same time, Channon wrote, "he has the easy gift of smiling, and popular he always was and always will be. He is fanatically loyal whilst his friendships last."

Under Wallis's influence, the Prince had given up the heavy drinking that had characterized his earlier years. At parties now, Channon noted, "he drank next to nothing and then only whisky with plain water, claret or Vichy water, because Wallis drinks these things." Instead of drinking, the Prince had taken up Café Society.

As for Wallis, Channon had warmed to her even more, and wrote, "She has always shown me friendship, understanding, and even affection, and I have known her to do a hundred kindnesses and never a mean act. There is nothing sordid or vulgar in her make-up, but she is modern certainly. She has a terrific personality and her presence grew as her importance increased: we are far from being done with her yet. . . . She would prefer to be grand, dignified and respectable, but if thwarted she will make the best of whatever position life gives her." Channon had honestly begun to hope that one day Wallis would become Queen of England. "No man has ever been so in love," he wrote; ". . . but . . . if he drops her she will fall— fall—into the nothingness from whence she came, but I hope he will not, for she is a good, kindly woman, who has had an excellent influence on him."

Channon's feelings about what London society had begun to call "L'Affaire Simpson" were complicated by his close friendship with the Duke and Duchess of Kent, and his warm feelings for the Duke and Duchess of York, two of the Prince's brothers and their wives. York he described as "good, dull, dutiful and good-natured," and his wife as "well-bred, kind, gentle and slack . . . always charming, always gay, pleasant and smiling . . . mildly flirtatious in a very proper romantic old-fashioned Valentine sort of way. . . . She makes every man feel chivalrous and gallant towards her." The Yorks, of course, stood next in line, after the Prince, for the British throne. They were quiet people. They were not fashionable, not popular in society, and led unpublicized lives. The Duke of York was not as handsome as the Prince, had suffered all his life from a crippling stammer, and his round-faced little wife was downright plain. She was nonetheless strong-willed, a dominating force, and her disapproval of the kind of life the Prince was leading, and her antipathy to Wallis Simpson, were becoming well known.

Thelma Furness, meanwhile, could talk of little else but the collapse of her relationship with the Prince—the snubs and his failure to communicate with her. (Freda Dudley Ward had been more philosophical; she had been hurt, but she was able to shrug it off.) Now London society was being divided into two armed camps, with the defenders of Thelma on one side and the defenders of Wallis on the other. Thelma blamed Wallis for having "stolen" her beau, and tried to gather as many friends as she could muster to her cause—which was to discredit Wallis and to undermine her position. Thelma did manage to gain one ally in the Virginia-born Nancy, Lady Astor. But otherwise, with society's traditional inconstancy, Thelma was having little success. Society heeded only which way the royal wind was blowing at the moment, and had swung immediately to Wallis's side. After all, this was the only way to be sure of receiving royal invitations. Bitterly, Thelma complained that what had once been known as the Furness Set had all but evaporated, and now everybody wanted to be in the Wallis Set. The collapse of the Furness Set, according to Chips Channon at least, was a good thing. Her milieu, as he described it, "while amusing and witty, . . . is small—small and suffocating, with their high-pitched voices and pettiness and criticism and anti-everything. It is destructive. Mrs. Simpson, who wants to get on, is a much bigger better woman than all of them put together."

While L'Affaire Simpson had begun to be the talk of social London, with Wallis's name on everybody's lips, the talk was almost exclusively limited to Mayfair and other fashionable reaches of the West End. What was common knowledge in the perfumed drawing rooms of Eaton Square had not reached the ears of the pub-goers in Ealing. To them, the Prince of Wales was still their handsome, glamorous, golden "Prince of Promise." They knew that he went out a lot, to nightclubs and fashionable restaurants, and that he was often seen with attractive women—they approved of that (though still a bachelor, he couldn't possibly be a "queer")—and they admired what seemed to be his independent spirit and sense of fun. He was a refreshingly modern change from his dour and stiffly formal parents. By 1934, he was easily the most popular public figure in the British Empire, but the general public had only the vaguest knowledge of His Royal Highness's private life.

The British press, meanwhile, was well aware of what the society gossips were saying and of what was going on. But the press published nothing about it. What the press did not know, and what even the London society gossips did not yet know, was that there was also a living ex-husband in the picture. Wallis had discreetly refrained from telling her new London friends about the existence of Lieutenant Earl Winfield Spencer, Jr. The Prince knew about Wallis's first husband, to be sure, but he too had mentioned it to no one.

The names "Mr. and Mrs. Ernest Simpson" had appeared in the Court Circular on lists of guests at the Prince's official dinners—and, because they were commoners, usually at the end of these lists. But the pub-going public did not read *The Times* and, if it had, would have made nothing of a couple with such an ordinary sounding name.

Even in the United States, Wallis Simpson's name was still virtually unknown. At the time of the *Rosaura* cruise, for example, when, as Wallis wrote, that important "indefinable barrier" between friendship and love was crossed, there was only a brief item in the American newspapers:

> The Prince of Wales is evidently enjoying his sojourn in Cannes. To the delight of hundreds of onlookers, last night the Prince danced the rumba with an American woman identified as a Mrs. Simpson. Although it had been announced that the Prince would stay aboard the yacht *Rosaura*, he came ashore yesterday afternoon and shortly before midnight he appeared at the Palm Beach Casino with Mrs. Simpson.

Wallis and Ernest continued to live at Bryanston Court as man and wife, and to appear together as a married couple. But as time went on, Wallis and the Prince would spend more and more evenings alone together, while Ernest Simpson would either retire to his room with "work to do," or would fail to come home altogether, offering the press of business as his excuse. On nights like these, after a visit and a cocktail or two, Wallis and the Prince would continue on to dinner—at Sartori's or the Dorchester or Claridge's—and then, perhaps, on to somewhere else for dancing. Still, Wallis said, "I had taken for granted that Ernest's interest in the Prince was keeping pace with mine." She did, however, notice that Ernest's business seemed to be taking up his evenings with increasing frequency. And when she came home to Bryanston Court after a late night out with the Prince, and popped into Ernest's room—they had long used separate bedrooms—she detected a certain lack of interest, on Ernest's part, in her enthusiastic accounts of where she and the Prince of Wales had been, whom they had seen, and what the other women had been wearing. A certain change in Ernest's "attitude," as she put it, seemed to be taking place.

By late 1934, the Prince of Wales was telephoning Wallis every day, and sometimes several times a day. They were together nearly every night. In January 1935, the Prince telephoned Wallis to say that he was taking a house in Kitzbühel for the month of February, for winter skiing—skiing was just beginning to be a popular sport and the Prince had taken it up with his usual vehemence—and he wanted to know whether Wallis and Ernest would join him there. Excitedly, and without consulting her husband, Wallis accepted for the two of them. That evening, when Ernest came home, Wallis told him happily about the trip to Austria. To her surprise, he did not seem pleased. Instead, he muttered that business would take him to New York for the month of February.

During dinner, Ernest Simpson was strangely silent. At one point he asked Wallis if she was determined to go to Kitzbühel. She replied, "Of course. Why not? I wouldn't dream of missing it."

"I rather thought that we might have gone to New York together," he said. "I see now that I was wrong." He went to his room and Wallis "heard his door bang."

Writing of this episode in her autobiography, Wallis's tone becomes a bit constrained. There was, one feels certain, a bit more to it than that. Sitting there, alone at her dinner table, what did she do next? Surely at that moment Wallis Simpson was one of the most frightened women in London. In going against her husband's wishes in favor of the Prince's, she was taking a giant step—one that would lead her precipitously into unknown and uncharted territory. Here she was, after all, a woman nearing forty, in a country where she was a foreigner. All her friends, no more than party-going pals really, were expatriate Americans like herself, though they were all much more experienced in the ways of the British upper classes than she. There was really no one she could turn to for advice or help. She was about to turn her back upon a man who had been generous, supportive and remarkably tolerant, who might well turn out to be the best husband she could ever have. She had always been a shrewd and spunky gambler, willing to risk her fortunes on the lie of a poker hand. But now all her chips were riding on the Prince, a man she had gotten to know quite well and yet, at the same time, whom she hardly knew at all, whose record for stability, reliability and even loyalty had hardly been impressive. She knew nothing of the immense weight of tradition, of British history, of the inexorability of the British Royal Family that surrounded him. She had not even become acquainted with the Prince's parents or the other members of his family, and he had been noticeably reluctant—or fearful—to arrange for this to happen. Sitting there at her dinner table, about to take the giant step, she must have envisioned the possibility of failure—that the leap would end in a fall, that "fall to nothingness" that Chips Channon had feared for her.

We do not know how Wallis spent the balance of that evening. But it is safe to guess that she spent it thinking hard.

7

Prince to King

As a child, the person who was to become the Prince of Wales had always seemed sad, introverted. The earliest photographs of him show a small, mournful face, the unhappy expression heightened by the deep-set, hollowed eyes that he had inherited from his great-grandmother Queen Victoria. When she first saw him, the Queen commented on what a "pretty" baby he was. That prettiness—a certain fragility and delicacy of neatly arranged features—would last him well into middle age. Victoria had already announced two other heirs to her throne. The first was her son, later to become Edward VII; the second was Edward's son, who would reign as George V; and now there was George's son, destined to become Edward VIII. Arrayed in Victoria's future were three generations of monarchs, almost enough to carry the Monarchy into the twenty-first century. The baby who had been born on June 23, 1894, at White Lodge, Richmond Park, was christened Edward Albert Christian George Andrew Patrick David, and the family had decided to call him David.

At the age of four he still wore ruffled dresses and long golden ringlets, which made him look like an earlier, more solemn Shirley Temple. Because he seemed so delicate and woundable—and remained small for his years—he early showed an ability to bring out strong motherly instincts in women. One was a nurse who, though she served the Royal Family for over three years, was so emotionally unstable that she eventually suffered a complete mental collapse. She virtually ignored little David's younger brother Albert, and fed him so erratically that he developed chronic stomach trouble that plagued him for life. But she lavished so much attention and affection on David that she may have traumatized him even more severely. Few adults retain clear memories of events that occurred before the age of five, but David never forgot how his nurse, when he was summoned to see his parents, would stop him outside his parents' door and "pinch and twist [his] arm." This was so the parents, faced with a sobbing child, would quickly dismiss him and return him to his nurse's care, and she would have him to herself again, to cuddle and kiss and comfort. Eventually, the Prince's parents—then the Duke and Duchess of York—realized that something was wrong, and the nurse was dismissed. But the Duke had long since concluded that his son was a crybaby and a weakling, scolded the boy for his tears, and had begun referring to him as "poor David."

No man could have had a less parental set of parents. Though intelligence tests had not yet been invented and, if they had been, would not have been administered to English Kings and Queens, it is unlikely that, if tested, either of the Prince's parents would have received high scores. Indeed, both actively distrusted intellectual pursuits, which they considered "bad for the mind." Both also detested travel—being proudly English, they saw no reason for venturing off their little island—and they had no use for foreigners, with the exception of certain European rulers who happened to be their relatives. "England is good enough for me," the Duke used to say. "I like my own country best, climate or not, and I'm staying in it." In their nonchalant English way, they were openly anti-Semitic. The Duke of York had been an officer in the Royal Navy, and believed in running his family as a strict commander rules a well-run ship. Discipline was substituted for affection. The Prince wrote later of his father, "It was once said of him that his naval training had caused him to look upon his own children much as he regarded noisy midshipmen when he was captain of a British cruiser—as young nuisances constantly in need of correction." Though his father, he admitted, had an "undoubted affection" for his children, he really "preferred children in the abstract, and . . . his notion of a small boy's place in a grown-up world was summed up in the phrase, 'Children should be seen, not heard.'"

The Duke of York was notoriously averse to criticism of any kind, but once, when a friend remarked that he might be too strict and unbending with his children, he reportedly replied, "My father was frightened of his mother; I was frightened of my father; and I am damned well going to see to it that my children are frightened of me." To his oldest son, the Duke remained a stern, implacable, terrifying and punishing figure. Indeed, the Prince remained frightened of both his parents as long as they lived—too frightened ever to attempt any true human communication with them.

The Duke believed in order and tradition, and resisted anything that smacked even slightly of change. Centuries' worth of royal tradition were trotted out whenever his household, or his routine, was faced with the threat of any sort of innovation. If a chair or a reading lamp had been placed just so in his grandmother's time, there that chair and that lamp were to be placed for all time to come. As a result, the ducal surroundings, while opulent, were at the same time shabby and dated. "It has always been that way" was his answer to every argument. He resisted all forms of progress vociferously, including the telephone, which he refused to use. He was an archconservative, royalist, reactionary. Brought up to believe in the Divine Right of Kings, he had no trouble viewing himself as a godlike figure, the supreme authority in every situation. Believing also that punctuality was the courtesy of kings—and, indeed, he believed in nearly every other time-worn royal slogan—he lived his life by the clock. Appointments were always kept on time, and meals were served at precisely the same hour every day. Bedtime was ten minutes past eleven, not a second sooner or later. His meals were plain, simple, English—and unvarying: kippers for breakfast, roast mutton for dinner with boiled potatoes and brussels sprouts. Once, when his oldest son tried to present him with an innovative dish, his father looked at the unfamiliar object on his plate and shouted, "What the bloody hell is this?" It was, David explained, an alligator pear, from Italy. "Take it away!" his father ordered. Later, the Prince of Wales would sometimes confide to his closest friends, "My father doesn't like me." Then, sorrowfully, he would sometimes add—after a second slug of brandy—"I'm not at all sure I particularly like him." Certainly, if nothing else, his father was an easily dislikable man.

His mother was not much better. Born Princess Victoria Mary of Teck, the Duchess of York was also a firm believer in the Divine Right. When she became Queen of England, she used to say of her children, "I have always to remember that their father is also their King." Reserved and undemonstrative, more concerned with the appearance and seemliness of things than with matters of the mind or heart, she was as incapable as her husband of communicating with her children or of conveying affection for them. She was frightened of sex, and pregnancy disgusted and embarrassed her. She regarded childbearing as a painful but necessary cross that a woman has to endure and, in her own case, as an ultimate duty to the British Monarchy. She considered her children not as children at all, but as successors to the throne. She turned motherhood over to nurses—again, that was the way it had "always" been done—and summoned her children to her side only for brief, fixed periods every day, when she lectured to them on manners and cleanliness and neatness. Her four sons did not enter her chambers for visits with their mother. They were paraded before her and made to stand inspection. Stockings had to be pulled up tight over the knees. The Eton collars had to be starched and white and clean. Neckties must not be awry. Little boys had to carry two fresh white handkerchiefs, and she would ask to see these. She would inspect their shoes for traces of mud or for scuffmarks. Their trouser pockets were sewn shut so that hands could not be thrust in them. Fingernails were checked. When the boys sat in her presence—which they could do when bidden to sit—they were permitted to cross their legs, but only to cross them knee-on-knee, never ankle-on-knee. Little girls, of course, only crossed their ankles. If their mother detected any shortcoming or detail of dress out of place, she would instruct a footman to tell the delinquent son, "His Royal Highness wishes to see you in the Library." Years later, the Prince of Wales would recall the intensity of his terror as he waited for those sessions in the library with his father. In fact, the only moments of closeness her sons may have experienced with their mother may have been when she instructed them in the art of needlepoint.

And so David grew into young manhood plagued by anxiety and painful feelings of inconsequence. Though handsome, with a face so delicately drawn that it verged on beauty, and though he had a radiant smile, he smiled rarely, and was photographed most often wearing a worried frown. He developed certain nervous mannerisms—twisting and tugging at his necktie, constantly clutching at his right wrist with his left hand (perhaps a result of being conditioned never to put his hands in his pockets)—which stayed with him for years afterward. (His next-younger brother, Bertie, acquired a crippling stammer.) David was a slow developer. At the age of sixteen, when he put on the investiture robes as Prince of Wales, he still looked like a pink-cheeked beardless boy of eleven or twelve. He remained small in stature.

At barely thirteen, when his contemporaries and such friends as he had been permitted to have had been heading for Eton and Harrow, David had been shipped off as a naval cadet to Osborne. His father had decided that a more rigorous, disciplined military training was what his oldest son needed, rather than any education in arts and letters (although his third son, Henry, was sent to Eton). "The Navy," his father announced, "will teach David all that he needs to know." At Osborne, the boy Prince was hazed unmercifully, and the Royal Naval College there, as he confessed later, "nearly overpowered" him. If anything, Osborne held more horrors than the traditional public schools of 1907. There was no privacy, and he was placed in a drafty dormitory with thirty other males of all ages. The food was atrocious. His being a royal prince did him no good whatever and, in fact, had an opposite effect. Because of his size he was nicknamed "Sardine." A bullying upperclassman seized him by the collar one day and said, "So you're the Prince, are you? Well, learn to respect your seniors!" Then a bottle of red ink was poured over his head. On another occasion, he was forcibly held down with his head across a windowsill while the sash was brought down across his neck, to remind him of the block and ax that had ended the life of one of his forebears.

From Osborne, he was assigned to Dartmouth for a two-year period of naval training, but his grandfather's death cut his time at Dartmouth short and he was unable to take the final training cruise required for completion of the course. Nonetheless, a few months later, after his father's Coronation, he was sent off on a three-month tour of sea duty, as a junior midshipman aboard the battleship *Hindustan*. This tour was not an unqualified success. The trouble was that *Hindustan*'s captain, an old-school officer and a friend of his father's, expected the fledgling sailor to have all the expertise of a seasoned seaman, which David did not have. The captain reported the Prince's failings to the King, saying, "I would never recommend anyone sailing a ship under his command." This assessment did not please the King, who was more firmly than ever convinced of his son's inadequacy, and must certainly have been a blow to the young Prince's ego.

At eighteen, and against his will, the Prince was sent up to Oxford, where he was enrolled in Magdalen College. He still looked ridiculously young for his years and, for this reason if for no other, he at first had trouble making friends. He was a slight, solitary youth who roamed the streets of Oxford by day, accompanied by his tutor, his valet, or an equerry, or a combination of the three, and who annoyed his fellow students by loudly playing the banjo and the bagpipes in his rooms at night. He was only a so-so student. "Bookish he will never be," commented the president of Magdalen. His father, meanwhile, supervised his spending, and personally went over his accounts. Finding an item of a few pennies recurring every day, he demanded an explanation. It was, he was advised, for His Royal Highness's morning apple.

In the Easter and summer holidays of 1913, he made two visits to Germany, where he stayed with his uncle and aunt, the King and Queen of Württemberg, at Stuttgart, and with the Grand Duke of Mecklenburg-Strelitz at Neustrelitz. He went to Friedrichshafen and met Count Zeppelin, and had dinner with the Emperor in Berlin. It was his second taste of real travel—he had earlier been sent to France to improve his French—and of independence, and clearly he enjoyed it. He had spoken fluent German from childhood. It was, after all, his mother's first language. He snapped photographs wherever he went, and he developed a love for Germany and things German that was to stay with him through the First World War and after.

In June 1914, after two years at Oxford, he announced plans

to travel for the rest of the year, and to return and join the Grenadier Guards the following January. But the outbreak of the war prevented the travel plans, and he was commissioned into the Grenadier Guards in August.

His record during the war became famous. He had already developed a thirst for heroism and bravery that bordered on bravado. He threw himself fearlessly, and often recklessly, into athletic pursuits at which he was never really very good. He had taken up polo, tennis, golf, beagling, and soccer. His disregard for his own safety was the despair of everyone who watched him as he attacked these often-dangerous sports. He was a poor rider, and was frequently thrown from his horse—at one point receiving such a severe concussion that he was bedridden for nearly a month. As he put it, he wanted "to show that, at least in matters where physical boldness and endurance counted," he could hold his own "against others on equal terms." He wanted, in other words, to be considered manly, and to do something for which someone might admire him.

The war he saw as his great opportunity to achieve these goals. At first, however, it was difficult. When his battalion of guards was sent to France, the Prince was kept behind in England because the authorities were afraid he might be taken prisoner. He went to Kitchener to protest this special treatment, and when Kitchener refused his request for European duty, he said, "What does it matter if I'm killed? I have four brothers." He persisted, and in November 1914 he was finally sent to France on the staff of the Commander-in-Chief of the British Expeditionary Forces. Once there, he insisted on volunteering for duty on the front lines, and when this was denied him, he defied his officers and sneaked across to the front lines anyway. He disobeyed orders so often that he should have been placed in the stockade but, of course, being the Prince of Wales, he was not. For his reckless insistence on seeing, and being, where the real fighting and dying was, he was the emotional undoing of his commanding officers. "Thank Heavens he's going," said one general, Sir Frederick Maude, when the Prince was transferred to another command. "This job will turn my hair grey.... He insists on tramping in the front lines." He was transferred several times, and his behavior was equally irresponsible—though the soldiers he visited in the lines were always happy to see him. In Italy, though told not to, he went to the Italian front, and his actions dismayed his host, King

Victor Emmanuel III. A British liaison officer reported: "The King was afraid of the Prince's daily habit of going too near to the Austrian lines. When the Prince went back to Italy in 1918 to stay with the King, he broke away from all warnings and control and flew over the Austrian trenches. . . . The King was perturbed and almost angry at the bravado of his guest."

When the Prince visited military hospitals, he discovered that he was being prevented from seeing the most severely wounded soldiers. He insisted that he see them too. When he heard that he had not been shown the most horribly mutilated soldier of all—a man who had lost, among other things, his hearing, speech and sight—he demanded to be taken to him. The Prince, when he saw the man, knelt beside his bed and kissed him on the cheek.

Needless to say, the news of these daring exploits and acts of self-sacrifice and charity quickly made their way back to England, and he returned from the war to find that he had become the darling of the British public. He was more than a hero, more than a matinee idol; he was the "Prince of Golden Promise," the most popular man in the land. Clearly, this sudden popularity and celebrity pleased him. He rejoiced and reveled in it. The withdrawn and bullied youth was now a man who was wildly cheered wherever he went. The entire British populace, it seemed, wanted to hail him, to kiss him, just to reach out and touch his sleeve. The effect was tonic. Reading the newspaper accounts of his wartime deeds, he saw himself described as "handsome," "dashing," "gallant," and "splendid-looking." He appears not to have given much thought to his looks until then, and when he studied his face in the mirror he clearly agreed that he was indeed handsome, and became particularly fond of his left profile. He also became vain, figure-conscious and clothes-conscious, and soon he would read of himself described as a fashion plate as well. Then he discovered that he was apparently irresistibly attractive to the opposite sex. Understandably, this was all very exciting, heady stuff.

The one person, however, in whose eyes he doubtless most longed to be a darling and a hero was his father. The latter, whose praise came grudgingly if it came at all, still seemed to regard him as a foolish child.

He had always, meanwhile, felt more of an affinity to and affection for his jolly old grandfather, whose namesake he was, Edward VII. Because of Victoria's long life, Edward did not come to the throne until her death in 1901, when he was sixty. In the meantime, he had led a roguish, high-living, hard-drinking life as Prince of Wales—with no real job and, it seemed, hardly a care in the world. He had died in 1910, after a short nine-year reign, when his grandson was only sixteen. But David had always treasured his memories of the easygoing old chap, who was so unlike his chilly, straitlaced father. He enjoyed hearing tales of his grandfather's famous philanderings—of which his wife, the former Princess Alexandra of Denmark, had been famously tolerant. When the old King embarked upon what was to be a seven-year love affair with Lillie Langtry, Alexandra obligingly saw to it that the Jersey Lily was invited to all official functions. And when it was clear that the King was close to death, Alexandra had gone to the rooms of his then-current mistress, Mrs. Keppel, and led her to the bedside of the dying King. The two women rode side by side in the carriage to the King's funeral.

The war seemed to have cured David of his agonizing shyness; or, more likely, the cure was brought about by his immense post-war popularity. Back in London after the war, as the town's best-loved personage, he was enormously in demand and hurled himself into social life with the same frantic enthusiasm that he had formerly devoted to dangerous sport. He was seen—and photographed—dancing all night long in various London night spots: Ciro's, the Café de Paris, and the Embassy Club, usually with some pretty "bit of fluff" on his arm. He was photographed wherever he went, and now he was traveling all over the world, dutifully fulfilling his job as his father's representative. In the process, he was learning how to deal with photographers—when to flash the radiant smile, when to look serious and concerned, which facial expressions allowed the cameras to catch him at his good-looking best. He was also succumbing to a dangerous affliction that plagues many celebrities: he was beginning to believe his own publicity.

The newspapers said he was charming and witty and suave, and he was happy to believe he was all these things. In fact, he was developing characteristics that were somewhat less than charming. He was rude and overbearing and demanding, particularly with people he considered his inferiors, and with servants. He thought nothing of rousing a valet from sleep at midnight to perform some minor function that suited his whim. He kept secretaries standing for hours taking his dictation, while he paced the floor trying to put his thoughts into words (unless Royalty sits down, no one in Royalty's presence can be seated). He was often late for appointments or canceled them at the last minute, and he was discovering that, because he was who he was, he could "get away with" this sort of behavior.

As far as the press was concerned he could get away with anything. Because he seemed to have a taste for low company, or at least for members of the London demimonde, the press labeled him "democratic." Because he had kissed the cheek of a wounded soldier, he was called "deeply compassionate." He was called "generous to a fault," even though he never tipped a waiter or a weekend hostess's maids. Learning from the press that he was a fashion plate, he began to dress the part, favoring large, floppy neckties, suits with bold checks, bright shirts, loud sweaters, and extra-baggy plus fours—all to the distress of his father. The Prince was delighted to see men's clothing advertisements that hawked, in fractured French, "Knickers à la The Prince of Wales." That he was a modern Romeo was celebrated in a popular song of the period called "I Danced with a Man Who Danced with a Girl Who Danced with the Prince of Wales." He was becoming a creation of the media.

The media and the public, of course, did not see the unpleasant side of the celebrity coin—the sulks and rages when he did not instantly get his own way, the arrogance, the stubbornness, the impatient dismissal of advice, the abusive treatment of servants. To the press, he was a paragon of all human virtues. And, reading what the press had to say about him, he appears to have come to another interesting conclusion: that the press was in his pocket, that he controlled it, that it, like everyone else, would meekly do his bidding.

The love affair between the international press and the Prince of Wales continued throughout the gay twenties and into the Depression thirties. The press danced to his tune. The British public was delighted to discover that their Prince had a fun-loving side—he was such a refreshing change from dour old George V—and, in the middle of economic hard times throughout the world, it was pleasant to read that one man, at least, knew how to enjoy himself. In addition, he also seemed to be doing his duty, comporting himself with dignity and aplomb on the various official tours and visits that were a part of the princely job.

Actually, of course, he was not given that much to do, and the one man who would not take his orders was his father. Their relations remained strained. On his return from his world tour in 1925—which the press had hailed as "triumphant"—he was thirty-one, but still he was not allowed to assume duties more responsible than those expected of others in the family. Though he was not actually forbidden to discuss affairs of state with his father's ministers, it was made clear to him that his father disapproved of his doing so. His official position was anomalous. When government papers made their way to his desk, he was aware that they had been given to him to peruse "only with the greatest misgivings and after considerable resistance." He wrote years later, "At the same time, in a manner never defined, I was expected to remain conversant with all that was going on in the world and to give the impression of being knowledgeable and well informed."

By 1935, when it was obvious to everyone that the Prince was madly in love with Wallis Simpson, he could not seem to bring himself to broach the topic with his parents. On this subject, the courageous war hero seemed to revert to the frightened child. Nor, for that matter, could the King and Queen seem to find a way to open up a discussion of the affair with their son, though the King had already expressed his concern to the Archbishop of Canterbury. The King seems to have adopted an ostrich attitude, or to have hoped that, if ignored, the "problem" of Mrs. Simpson would go away. The Prince seems simply not to have been brave enough, knowing that at least their initial reaction would be very disapproving, to have asked his parents for a meeting with Wallis—a meeting at which at least some of the ramifications of the ticklish matter might have been openly aired and discussed. Wallis, too, seems to have been fearful of such a confrontation, preferring to let things glide along as they were, though at such a meeting she would certainly have been on her best, well-bred behavior. It is certainly possible that Wallis might have been able to charm the King and Queen, and to reverse their low opinion of her, as she had managed to do with a number of other people. Had that happened, things might have turned out differently. But, instead, nothing happened, and the four players of the drama—the King, the Queen, the Prince and Wallis—remained frozen and stalemated in Hamletlike indecision and inaction.

The trip to Kitzbühel—originally a two-week holiday—was

extended. The Prince and Wallis and the others in his party moved on to Vienna and, from there, to a sojourn in Budapest. In the process, several of the Prince's appointments had to be canceled, further infuriating his father. Returning at last to Bryanston Court, Wallis noticed a new and perhaps understandable coolness on the part of her husband. Once more, reality loomed, but Wallis tried to dispel it with airy veils of fantasy:

> I was troubled, but my concern was no more than a tiny cloud in the glowing radiance that the Prince's favor cast over my life. I became aware of a rising curiosity concerning me, of new doors opening, and a heightened interest even in my casual remarks. I was stimulated; I was excited; I felt as if I were borne upon a rising wave that seemed to be carrying me ever more rapidly and even higher. Now I began to savor the true brilliance and sophistication of the life of London.

Curiously, for the woman who the Duke of Windsor later declared was the first woman to be interested in his "work," as well as for the man whose work it was, work seems now to have utterly disappeared from their consideration. Their lives had become a kind of extended party.

When Wallis Simpson had first glimpsed the Prince of Wales in the back seat of his car in the 1920's, he had been on his way to Buckingham Palace to see his father, who had been fighting for his life against a streptococcus infection. The King had recovered from that illness, but he had remained an aging and failing man. On January 16, 1936, the Prince was out shooting with friends in Windsor Great Park, when an urgent message from his mother was delivered to him in the field. "I think you ought to know that Papa is not very well," the note began. It continued to say that Lord Dawson, the King's physician, was "not too pleased with Papa's state at the present moment." In her typically constrained way, she suggested that David "propose" himself for the coming weekend at Sandringham. That afternoon, the Prince showed the note to Wallis, who was visiting at Fort Belvedere. The next morning, he flew off to Sandringham.

The following Monday, Wallis was attending a movie with

friends. The showing of the film was interrupted by the reading of Lord Dawson's famous bulletin to the audience: "The King's life is moving peacefully to its close." Five minutes before midnight, January 21, the King died. David telephoned Wallis the news, saying, "It's all over." All she could think of to say was, "I am so very sorry." He said, "I can't tell you what my own plans are, everything here is so upset. But I shall fly to London in the morning and will telephone you when I can."

In the meantime, Queen Mary had stepped away from the dead King's bedside, kissed her eldest son's hand, and uttered the traditional words: "The King is dead, long live the King."

By tradition, successive British rulers face in opposite directions when they are depicted on the coins and stamps of the realm. Accordingly, Queen Victoria faced left; Edward VII, right, and George V, left. But when, as one of his first official duties as England's new King, Edward VIII was asked to select a right-facing pose for the new coins and stamps, he balked. He parted his hair on the left, he explained, and preferred his left profile. Therefore, he wanted to face left. When it was carefully explained to His Royal Majesty that he was breaking tradition, he said, "Why shouldn't I?"

And it was done. On the new stamps, for some reason, though the profile was switched from right- to left-facing, the background colors could not be changed. The left side of the background was shaded, and the right was not. When the direction of the profile was reversed, the effect was of the King looking into the darkness, away from the light. To some people, it was a symbol of ill omen.

8

Rumblings

THE new King, Edward VIII, was six months shy of his forty-second birthday. Like most stages of his development, his period of adolescent rebellion had come late—in his mid-twenties—and had lasted an unusually long time. Fed and encouraged by the press and his adoring public, he had continued to rebel against convention, tradition, parental authority and the Establishment. His rebelliousness had included refusal to consider, as marriage partners, various eligible princesses who were scattered about Europe, and he took up with, instead, various "unsuitable" women, at least two of whom—Freda Dudley Ward and Thelma Furness—were already married. In the press, he read that he was "modern." This sort of thing, he seemed to have rationalized, was what modern princes did. He had often said in private that, when he became King, he would modernize the throne.

According to many reports, his first act as Monarch was one of sheer rebelliousness. Ever since the days of his grandfather, Edward VII, all the clocks at Sandringham had been set one half an hour ahead of the true time. This quaint custom had supposedly been established to ensure the punctuality of the old King's guests at the meeting for the morning shoot. It was also devised as a method of keeping Queen Alexandra, who had a habit of tardiness, on time for her appointments, and it served as a form of daylight saving, adding a half an hour of daylight to each day. Immediately following King George V's death, as most accounts have it, the new King cried, "I'll fix those bloody clocks!" and ordered the clockman to come to Sandringham and return all the clocks to Greenwich time. Lady Frances Donaldson, however, produces evidence that the order was actually issued an hour or so before the King's death.* The reason for this irrational order has never been clear, but perhaps, in the emotional strain of the Royal Family's death vigil, there had been some confusion about time. In any case, the clockman was summoned at midnight and he and most of the Sandringham staff were kept up till dawn changing the many clocks on the estate, much to the annoyance of the household. It was an indication that the reign of the new King would be characterized by thoughtlessness, impulsiveness and sudden whim.

At a state ball in Buckingham Palace in May 1935, one of the many functions celebrating the Silver Jubilee of George V's accession to the throne, Wallis had danced in the arms of the Prince, past his father. Though she had been introduced to him the previous fall, the King did not speak to her, merely looked at her "searchingly." It was, she sensed, only "the glittering tip of an iceberg" of disapproval that was looming about her in the persons of all but one of the Royal Family. Now, eight months later—since there is never a moment in history when Great Britain is without a monarch—David was King, and disapproval from the throne no longer seemed to present a problem.

Though George V and Queen Mary had led lives of singular

*Curiously, in the 1980 television series *Edward and Mrs. Simpson*, for which Lady Donaldson served as historical adviser and production consultant, the clock-changing episode was again placed *after* the King's death, probably because it better suited the needs of drama. In the play, the reason for the new King's order was that his brother Bertie had failed to hear Lord Dawson's announcement because he hadn't known what time it was. This is fiction.

rectitude and moral probity, the Royal Family was no stranger to scandals involving married women. In the late eighteenth century, the Prince of Wales, who later became King George IV, fell in love with a Mrs. Maria Fitzherbert, described as beautiful and "the store of refined good humor and good nature." He proposed a marriage to her that would have been, in light of the Royal Marriages Act of 1772, illegal. She at first refused. But he begged, wept hysterically in front of her, created scenes, and threatened to commit suicide. Finally she consented to an engagement. Mrs. Fitzherbert appears to have been a sensible lady and, after their secret engagement, she went to Europe for a year. But while she was there, the Prince bombarded her with passionate letters, and she eventually returned to England and to him. They were secretly married in 1785. Later, under pressure from his parents, the Prince also married the plump, plain Princess Caroline of Brunswick. And so, when George III finally died, George IV came to the throne a bigamist.

In addition to the new King's own grandfather, Edward VII, there had been numerous other occasions in history when male members of the Royal Family had kept mistresses. The Duke of Clarence, who later became William IV, lived with an actress. Edward, Duke of Kent, set up housekeeping with a Canadian lady. All these liaisons were well known, and accepted.

At the time of George V's death, and during the days of pomp and circumstance surrounding the royal funeral that followed, Ernest Simpson was off on another of his trips to the United States. To watch the ceremony of the Proclamation of Accession at St. James's Palace, Wallis and a small group of the new King's friends had been assigned a private palace apartment across the courtyard. As the group stood at the window, out on the palace balcony came the Garter King of Arms, attended by heralds, pursuivants, and trumpeters in medieval costumes flashing with crimson, silver and gold. Suddenly—and to everyone's astonishment—the new King stepped into the apartment. After the customary bowing and curtsying, the King said airily, "The thought came to me that I'd like to see myself proclaimed King." The party regrouped at the window. Thus it was that Edward VIII was seen being proclaimed King of England with the American Mrs. Ernest Simpson standing at his side. Again, the press made no mention of this. To the general public she was still unknown.

For several days afterward, Wallis saw little of the King, though he was in daily touch with her by telephone. During this period, according to her memoirs—while Ernest Simpson was still out of town—she discovered that her husband was being unfaithful to her. Her discovery, in her account, occurred in a manner that is one of the classic clichés of pulp fiction. And at this point in Wallis's memoir—indeed in her entire loose and inexact description of her second divorce—one is forced to question her truthfulness. A passionate love letter, it seemed, from the "other woman" was misaddressed to "Mrs. Ernest Simpson," though it should have been marked for "Mr. Ernest Simpson," and arrived one day at Bryanston Court. Wallis opened the letter in all innocence, and there, in black and white, was the evidence of the infidelity. Of course it seems hard to believe that any woman would be so foolish as to write a letter to her lover at his own home, and on top of that mistakenly address it to his wife. Ernest belonged to several London clubs, and Englishmen conventionally used the addresses of their clubs in such matters. He also had an office, where confidential letters could have been received.

Bryan and Murphy have added a beguiling element to the incriminating-letter story. The author of the letter, they claim, was none other than Mary Kirk Raffray, Wallis's old friend who had first introduced her to Ernest Simpson. On one of his trips to New York, Bryan and Murphy say, Ernest visited Mary, and a love affair began. Later, Mary came to London and stayed with the Simpsons and even joined them for a weekend at Fort Belvedere. Then Mary moved on to Cannes, where she wrote two letters—one to Wallis, a mere thank-you note, and a second, passionate one to Ernest. She then slipped the letters into the wrong envelopes, posted them, and "almost at once she realized her mistake." She dispatched a hasty wire to Wallis, which said, "DO NOT OPEN LETTER ADDRESSED TO YOU AS IT IS NOT FOR YOU." Wallis, understandably, was more than eager to open the letter.

But this tale does not really hang together either. It is a common enough mistake to place a letter in the wrong envelope. But to have realized the mistake after committing the letter to the post is certainly not common. One suspects that Mary Kirk Raffray, who told the authors this story shortly before her death in 1941, was merely trying to obtain a romantic share of her own in the "Greatest Romance of the Century."

Indeed, she did go on to become the third Mrs. Ernest Simpson.

What is certain is that Wallis, now that the Prince of Wales was King, was laying the groundwork to rid herself legally of her second husband, and that the King was backing her in every possible way. He first offered her the services of his own solicitor, George Allen. When—according to her—she visited Allen in his Finch Lane offices, he asked her, "'Are you quite sure, Mrs. Simpson, that you want a divorce?' I assured him that my mind was made up." At the time, however, she was still insisting to all her London friends, including Chips Channon, that the divorce was entirely Ernest's idea, that she had begged him not to pursue it, and had offered to do anything in her power to save the marriage and make it work. For her apparently noble stance in this situation, the London friends admired and sympathized with her.

George Allen didn't take divorce cases, but with the help of the King's old friend and chief legal adviser, Walter Monckton, an excellent divorce lawyer was engaged in the person of one Theodore Goddard. At the time, Walter Monckton, who had heard all the rumors about the King's affair with Wallis, asked her if she was divorcing Ernest in order to marry the King. This was an important question because, if it could be demonstrated that the divorce was being obtained with Wallis and the King in collusion, it would most certainly be denied. Wallis replied that the idea of her marrying the King was "ridiculous." Monckton, who shared this view, agreed with her.

Perhaps Wallis was learning her deceptiveness from the King. He had a marked tendency toward secret schemes and plots. By confusing and obfuscating his intentions, saying one thing when he meant another, offering one explanation to a friend and a contrary one to a foe, he seemed to gain a feeling that he, and only he, knew the full import of whatever it was, and that only he was in control. With the exception of Wallis, there was almost no one he really trusted, and she was beginning to trust in him alone, the master planner who, it surely seemed, could get away with anything. In any case, with the divorce proceedings comfortably in the hands of royal solicitors, and with Ernest Simpson steadily disappearing from the picture—there was never any sort of confrontation scene, according to her memoir—the King renewed his daily visits to Bryanston Court.

At last he began to try to endear Wallis to other members of his family. It was a task he probably should have undertaken earlier, before they took to referring to her scathingly as "that woman." In the spring of 1936, the King had bought a new car—an American station wagon equipped with gadgetry that had never before been seen in the British Isles. One afternoon, when Wallis was visiting the King at Fort Belvedere, he suggested that they drive over to Royal Lodge to show the car to his brother Bertie, the Duke of York. The Duke and Duchess met the King and Wallis at the door, and while the King took his brother for a spin in the car, Wallis and the plump little Duchess talked about the gardens at the Fort and the Lodge. Wallis got the distinct impression that, while the Duke was impressed with the American automobile, the Duchess was less impressed with the King's other American acquisition. Later, the King gave a dinner party at Balmoral Castle, with Wallis as the guest of honor, and invited the Yorks, and another brother, the Duke of Kent, and his Duchess, as well as several royal cousins. Despite Wallis's efforts at animation and gaiety, the atmosphere remained heavy and sullen, and the Yorks' treatment of Wallis—the Duchess's treatment in particular— was frostily polite to the point of condescension. At still another dinner when the Yorks were present, Winston Churchill made a sly reference to George IV and his illicit marriage to Mrs. Fitzherbert when he had been Prince of Wales. "That was a very long time ago!" the Duchess of York said sharply.

The feelings of strain between Wallis and the Duchess of York blossomed rather quickly into active dislike, and it is not hard to imagine why. No two women could have been more different. Wallis was pert and slender and quick on the uptake: the Duchess was prim, round, domestic and plain. Wallis was interested in society and its latest gossip: the Duchess was not, and preferred to talk about the exploits of her two pretty little daughters. In fact, London society and its leaders, among them Emerald Cunard and Sybil Colefax, had long ago issued a negative verdict on the Yorks: they were dull.* Wallis flashed

*Later on, when the Duchess of York became Queen of England, she is reported to have commented that she and her husband would probably never be invited to Emerald Cunard's parties because "Emerald has never considered Bertie and me social."

and glittered. The Duchess merely glowed gently with moth-
erliness and good manners.

But there were still other reasons for the Duchess of York's
antipathy. As Elizabeth Bowes-Lyon, she had been the only
woman with a rank lower than princess whom George V and
Queen Mary had permitted any of their sons to marry. That
she had found special favor in the eyes of her husband's family
had given her feelings of special importance in the royal scheme
of things. At the same time, her Bertie was not the Prince of
Wales and he was not the King. He was merely next in line
and, as such, was treated as second best. He was not glamorous,
he was not handsome, he was not a daring war hero, he was
not a giant celebrity. The newspapers did not avidly report his
every move, no flash bulbs popped when he appeared, no
woman yearned to dance with him; and no cheering crowds
gathered whenever he hove into view. Indeed, he usually went
about unrecognized. Fewer aides, equerries, secretaries, detectives and servants were assigned to do Bertie's bidding. He
continued to be used by his older brother to fill in, to substitute,
at events and on occasions that the King did not consider important enough to require the Monarch's presence. As King,
his older brother had full authority to order Bertie here and
there to attend to this or that minor matter. This vast difference
in status between the two men, her husband and her brother-
in-law, grated on the Duchess. She had disapproved of all of
David's lady friends, and she would have had a hard time liking
any woman whom David might choose for a wife because that
wife would share the King's superior status. In a word, she
was jealous.

Then, too, with all this frantic party-giving of the King's
to introduce Wallis to his family, there was a sense of haste,
of urgency, of going too fast for comfort. It was as though
Wallis were being pushed on everyone, forced down their
throats—a feeling that the King was *commanding* his brothers
and their wives to take Wallis to their bosoms. To this sort of
thing there was natural resistance. If he could have been a little
more relaxed, or subtle, in his campaign to sell Wallis to his
relatives, the results might have been different. But the King's
mood was far from relaxed. It was harried, aggressive—almost
desperate. His relatives were put off by this.

There was one relative, meanwhile, whose counsel and sympathy he did not seek, and that was his mother. The old Queen

was by no means as rigidly disapproving and despotic as her late husband. Though it was often difficult to penetrate her stern, implacable, and essentially shy nature, she was a sensible lady. She was also well versed and experienced in the ways of British politics, was quite sensitive to the feelings of the British people, and wielded no small amount of influence— not only within her family, but in the government and with the public. Widowed and idle, still not quite able to bring herself to move out of Buckingham Palace to Marlborough House to make way for the new King, she would seem to have been psychologically receptive to an appeal from her son, to at least a discussion of his plans, to a request for her guidance or support. There was no shortage of opportunities for such a discussion, but there was none. In his various meetings with his mother, the King could not seem to bring himself to raise the subject that was most on both of their minds: Wallis Simpson. Nor could the Queen Mother, in turn, seem able to mention the matter to him. Increasingly frustrated, ignored, isolated, and left out of things, she was forced to rely on secondhand reports of what was going on which she received from the King's private secretary, Alexander Hardinge, as well as reports of the love affair that were beginning to float in from America. She seems to have become increasingly angry and even more strongly determined in her resolve *never* to receive Wallis. And who can blame her? It was she who was the woman scorned. The fact that she might regard her son's behavior as insulting seems not to have occurred to him. Nor does the fact that she might well have been willing to meet with Wallis— even grudgingly—if he had had the common courtesy to ask her to. But, by his own admission, he did not. He did not even try. And so the Queen's resistance to the whole idea of Wallis stiffened and hardened as each unproductive day went by. The King, instead of attempting to gain a valuable ally, was acquiring a formidable enemy.

Why was he so shortsighted? Was he so certain of his mother's negative response that to acquaint her with his problem seemed to him futile and a waste of time? Was it egotism— a feeling that, as the new King, he had no need to ask the advice of members of the old regime? Was it his love of secrecy and of cabal-like plots that involved keeping certain people in the dark? Or, though a man approaching middle age, was he still as terrified of his mother as he had been as a child? Doubtless the answer was a combination of all these things. Wallis had brought the matter of the Queen Mother up to him, but he had answered with a worried frown, saying, "That may be difficult." And so what would become a series of staggering public-relations failures began with a failure of family relations.

In May, the King announced to Wallis that he intended to give a dinner party at York House for his Prime Minister, Mr. Stanley Baldwin, and that he wished her to be present. When she demurred, he said, "It's got to be done. Sooner or later my Prime Minister must meet my future wife." It was, she always insisted, the first time the King had mentioned marriage to her. Though to Walter Monckton she had dismissed the idea of marrying the King as "ridiculous" a few weeks earlier, it was now a matter she took quite seriously. She agreed to come and, as usual, to help him plan the menu, the table decorations and the seating.

For the King to have referred to Stanley Baldwin as "my" Prime Minister may sound high-handed, but the usage is correct. Baldwin *was* the King's Prime Minister, even though the designation—which Wallis may have failed to understand at the time—does not mean that the King can tell his Prime Minister what to do. The rest of the King's remark, however, was nonsense. There was no "must" about Baldwin's meeting the King's future wife, and the fact that the King seemed to think there was is an indication of the King's own poor grasp of the situation. Indeed, whereas the King's efforts to have Wallis be accepted by others in his family had been merely fruitless, his decision that she must be accepted by Stanley Baldwin would be the first of a number of major errors of judgment.

Under the British Constitution, there was no provision to prevent the King of England from marrying whomever he wanted to marry. Nothing in the Constitution forbade him to marry a divorced woman, or to marry a commoner, or an American, or any other foreigner. Constitutionally, the only woman he could not marry was a Roman Catholic. To marry, the King of England did not have to have the approval—or the advice—of his Prime Minister, or of his Cabinet, or of either House of Parliament. To be sure, the marriage of the King of England to a divorced American woman with two living ex-husbands would, in 1936, have shocked the country profoundly. The pub-going British public might have been horrified. The Establishment might also have been appalled. The popularity of the new Monarch might have been destroyed, and the prestige and influence of the British Monarchy seriously damaged throughout the world. All this, too, might have been construed as happening at a particularly unfortunate time in history—with Fascism on the rise in Italy and National Socialism in Germany—when the prestige of Britain, as a world power, mattered mightily. The prime ministers in Britain's overseas dominions might have been aghast. Parliament might have thundered its disapproval. The Archbishop of Canterbury would surely have been outraged, the Cabinet might have been staggered, and the Prime Minister sufficiently stunned to submit his resignation. The rest of the Royal Family might have gnashed their teeth and wrung their hands and beat their breasts in rage, and the press might have had a field day. But the King was still the King, and was legally free to marry whomever he chose and let the devil take the hindmost.

This course, however, was not the one Edward VIII had chosen to take. In his apparent belief that Wallis "must" meet Stanley Baldwin, the King was in effect turning the problem over to a politician—and the most powerful figure in Britain. And at the time, there was no legal, constitutional, or other need for Baldwin to have been involved at all. It was the King's first step toward disaster.

The King, like his father before him, had never made any secret of the fact that he had little use for politicans, and certainly his own skill at and knowledge of politics was slight. He had not, furthermore, troubled to conceal his own opinion of Stanley Baldwin, whom he found pompous, boring and excessively verbose. This toplofty attitude had probably not exactly endeared the King to Stanley Baldwin, though Baldwin had always treated him with courtesy, respect and kindness. In any case, Baldwin was a poor choice to turn to for help.

And the cast of characters the King chose to populate the dinner party at which Baldwin was to meet Mrs. Simpson was peculiar in that, in addition to the Baldwins and Wallis, Lord and Lady Mountbatten, the Duff Coopers, Emerald Cunard, Fleet Admiral Sir Ernle Chatfield and Lady Chatfield, and the Charles Lindberghs, the guest list included Ernest Simpson. Though the Simpsons' divorce proceedings were already under way, and the King himself had helped arrange them, Ernest Simpson was at the party. The purpose of the gathering therefore became somewhat confused. Perhaps the King had invited Ernest as an act of defiance to Baldwin, as a way of informing him, at the outset, of the troubling and complicated nature of the situation that lay ahead. Perhaps it was just the opposite, and he had invited both Simpsons to bolster the illusion that, despite the rumors, there was *no* situation, just as the King and Wallis had deceived her solicitors in telling them that no marriage was contemplated. Perhaps the double invitation simply appealed to the King's sense of the outrageous, the unconventional, or to his fondness for creating complexities and ambiguities through which actual motives would be obscured. Even more puzzling was Ernest Simpson's acceptance of the King's invitation. If the evening was a tense one for Wallis, it must have been even more uncomfortable for him.

One person not invited, of course, was Queen Mary. Had she been asked, she might, traditionalist that she was, have felt compelled by the rules of royal protocol to accept. After all, Edward VIII was now no longer just her son; he was her King. Only serious illness or absence from the country would have served the Queen Mother as proper excuses for turning down an invitation from him. But she had not been asked.

In any case, it was a stiff and awkward evening, not made any pleasanter when Charles Lindbergh, just back from Germany, talked lengthily to Baldwin about the superiority of Germany's air power over Britain's. Later, Baldwin commented merely that he had been "intrigued" to meet Mrs. Simpson. Mrs. Baldwin, a more gushy and romantic type, remarked, "Mrs. Simpson has stolen the Fairy Prince."

On July 9, there was another dinner at York House—this time for the King's newly appointed First Lord of the Admiralty, Sir Samuel Hoare, and the Right Honorable David Margesson, the government chief whip in the House of Commons. Hoare was one of Stanley Baldwin's principal lieutenants. The other guests included the Duke and Duchess of York, the Winston Churchills, Diana Cooper, Sybil Colefax, and others of the King's social circle. Upon those she was meeting for the first time, Wallis made a mixed impression. Sir Samuel Hoare, who later became Viscount Templewood, recalled her many years afterward, saying, "In the notes that I made at the time I described her as very attractive and intelligent, very American with little or no knowledge of English life." This time, in reporting the dinner, the Court Circular did not list

Mr. Ernest Simpson among the guests, and to those watching the progress of the affair, including the Queen Mother, the omission of his name did not go unnoticed.

A great deal has been written about the events of 1936 leading up to the Abdication of King Edward VIII. Nearly all the principals, along with many outside observers, have written their respective accounts of the mounting crisis and, in the process, nearly everything that could be said about it has been said. True, Stanley Baldwin ordered his papers on the period locked and sealed for a hundred years, but most historians expect that nothing new or surprising will emerge when this cache is opened in the year 2037. The only thing that will remain a riddle and a mystery is what was on the King's and Wallis's minds at the time. Here, their own memoirs cannot be trusted since both their memories are charged with years of bitterness over the treatment accorded them when the crisis was over. To both the Duke and Duchess of Windsor, looking back, they were simply a pair of innocents, caught up in love, who put their faith in the wrong people, and were betrayed.

Popular psychologists have advanced several theories to explain the King's inexplicable behavior during these first— and last—months of his reign, behavior which was to consist of one monumental blunder upon another. According to one theory, the King subconsciously never wanted to be King at all, and chose Wallis as his unwitting instrument and ally to give him an honorable excuse for stepping down. By choosing an attractive but totally inappropriate woman to be his Queen, he would be seen by his public as modern and courageous. By insisting on making her his wife rather than his mistress, he would be seen as honorable and manly. With her, he could quit the throne and still shine in the public's eye as a noble and sympathetic man, and not—as might have happened if he had quit with a lesser excuse than true love—as a lazy man who would rather let his younger brother do his job.

This theory has gained support in certain quarters. As early as 1927, Elsa Maxwell wrote that the Prince of Wales said to her, "I don't want to be King. I wouldn't be a very good one." A year or so later, Lady Diana Cooper recalls, he said something of the same sort to her: "I think I make a pretty good Prince of Wales. But I don't think I'd make a good King." And one of his brothers, the Duke of Kent, once remarked that

Wales had told him he didn't think he could "take" the pomp and ritual and stuffy conventions of Court life. Finally, Lady Hardinge, the wife of the King's private secretary, wrote that, following George V's death, the new King's behavior became "frantic and unreasonable," and that his display of grief "far exceeded that of his mother and three brothers." It seemed totally out of proportion, particularly coming from a man whose relationship with his father had never really developed. It suggested the grief of a man who realized that the dreaded and hateful task had now fallen on his shoulders.

Wallis, however, always vehemently denied this theory. He wanted, she insisted, very much to be King, had looked forward to replacing his father on the throne, and had spent hours with her excitedly discussing ways and means by which he might enhance the Monarchy, and be an even better ruler than his father. He looked forward to carrying out what he saw as a noble assignment, a God-given mission.

Still another theory, proposed by Bryan and Murphy, has it that the King was a man who needed to be dominated, who needed to be controlled by someone forceful. He was essentially a masochist; he needed a despot. It is certainly true that, in the days immediately following his father's death, the King's passion for Wallis seemed to intensify, and to marry her became his almost hysterical objective—as though, having lost one despot in his life, he needed an immediate replacement. In Wallis—a strong, tough-minded woman who had experienced the rough side of life as well as the polished—he had found the perfect Svengali to whom he could be the perfect Trilby. Other women had ultimately disappointed him by being soft and willing and obedient. Wallis, instead of doing his bidding, let him do hers. It was in the tradition of the southern belle. If a lady dropped her glove, she waited for the gentleman with her to stoop and pick it up. The exhilaration—almost a sexual exhilaration—that the King received from this sort of gentle bullying was at the heart of his profound, almost abject adoration of her, and explained his need to have her constantly at his side. If this theory is true, there is no question but that he wanted to be King. Because to be King was what Wallis wanted him to be.

Perhaps a combination of the two theories makes the most sense. The new King was not bright, but he was at least bright enough to know that he was not bright. He wanted to be King, but not without someone like Wallis—efficient, always organized, impeccably coiffed and dressed, a perfectionist, a bright conversationalist, an attentive and innovative hostess—to help him do the job. Without her it seemed beyond him. She filled in his gaps, glossed over his hollowness with amusing chatter. She made him shine. He found in her literally his other half, the half that he had always sensed was missing. Together, they made one fully operating human being. Without her beside him on the throne to fill him out, he could not see himself as King. Soon he would say as much. To be King, the two of them would have to work in tandem.

His father had long felt that there was something lacking in his son's character or makeup, a certain fiber. Not long before his death, the old King had said to Stanley Baldwin, "After I'm dead, the boy will ruin himself in twelve months." (Though past forty, the Prince was still "the boy" to his father.) And George V had said to Lady Gordon-Lennox, "I pray to God that my eldest son will never marry and have children, and that nothing will come between Bertie and Lilibet and the Throne."

One of the qualities the old King felt his son lacked was self-control, a quality Wallis possessed in full measure. It was ironic that the woman of whom the King most disapproved should have been perfectly equipped to supply that missing factor.

9

Cruising

IN THE series of entertainments the King was providing to introduce Wallis to Britain's leading statesmen and parliamentarians, there were at least two disturbing elements which those close to him noted. For one, the period of official mourning for George V was not over, and all the energetic partying seemed a bit unseemly and out of place. For another, it was all being conducted in a curious atmosphere. The feeling that the new King was in a great hurry, and anxious to get something over with quickly, lent an air of suspense—and foreboding—to the proceedings. But those close to him, who knew of Wallis's plans to divorce Ernest, had merely to count on their fingers to get a good idea of what was in the wind. The Coronation had been scheduled for May 12, 1937. Though, by mid-1936, the divorce hearing had not been scheduled, it was entirely possible that she would be free to remarry sometime before that date. The gossips had started saying that the King intended to marry Wallis as soon as he was able and to go to the Coronation with her at his side as Consort. Indeed, this was exactly what he planned.

A number of experts on British law, meanwhile, have pointed out that the King could certainly have married Wallis without creating a national crisis, and without having to abdicate, if he had been willing to embark on a less precipitous course. He and Wallis, for one thing, would have had to be more discreet about their relationship. She might have removed herself a certain distance from him instead of becoming an almost permanent fixture at Fort Belvedere. The two could have continued to see each other privately, and at small unofficial gatherings, rather than at large official functions(from the articles in the Court Circular, it was becoming obvious that the King regarded Wallis as his official hostess, even at Balmoral, which is considered an "official" royal residence). To his family and to the Establishment he appeared to be publicly flaunting the relationship, which did not win him friends in either group.

His plan should have been something like this: He should have gone ahead with his Coronation in May of 1937 as scheduled, while outwardly keeping up the appearance of attending to his royal duties. He should then have let the excitement from that great national event die down. After a suitable interval, he could have given Wallis, who by then would have been quietly divorced—perhaps in some other country—a title, that of Countess of Cornwall, for example. Again, after another suitable interval, he could have sent the Countess of Cornwall, alone, on an American tour, as a sort of goodwill ambassador. Here, as an American-born woman who had become a titled English lady, she would certainly be received in every important home including, in all likelihood, the White House. At her ladylike best, bringing the good wishes of the King to the people of the United States, we can assume that she would have been a great success. The Countess of Cornwall would then return to England, where the British press, backed by the American press, would proclaim her American visit a huge social and diplomatic triumph for Great Britain. In the meantime, the King might have tried to soften his mother's attitude toward Wallis before it had hardened to steellike refusal to have Wallis under the same roof.

Now, after another interval, the King could have approached his Prime Minister, whoever that might have been, and informed him of his intention to marry the Countess of Cornwall, who by then would be a popular public figure. The Prime

Minister might have replied, "But, Sir, you cannot!" To which the King might have answered, "What do you *mean* I cannot? I can, and I shall, and if you object I can take her down to the nearest registry office tomorrow morning, and marry her in a civil ceremony. *That* would certainly prove an embarrassment to you and your government."

The Prime Minister would probably concede that this might indeed be an awkward possibility. But, he would remind the King, "The lady, Sir, has been twice divorced. She has two living ex-husbands. And in the case of the second divorce, there could be questions raised that there was some sort of collusion, that Your Majesty was influential in arranging certain of the details."

The King would then be in a position to make his final and most telling point, saying something like, "Mr. Prime Minister, I'm surprised at you. Do you not know of the ancient and sacred principle in British law, which is that a British court of justice *can do no wrong?* The Countess of Cornwall was legally declared divorced by a British court of law, which also declared her the innocent and injured party. In granting her a divorce, the same British court of law established that her marriage to Mr. Simpson was legal and proper. By establishing that her marriage to Mr. Simpson was legal and proper, the court simultaneously established the fact that her divorce from her first husband was also legal and proper, and that she, again, was the innocent party. If her first divorce was proper, then, retroactively, so was her first marriage. The Countess of Cornwall, in other words, has been cleared of any wrongdoing by a British court. If you deny my right to marry the Countess, you will be flying in the face of one of the oldest, most important tenets of British law. You will be making a mockery of British justice."

If this dialogue had taken place, the Prime Minister would doubtless have had to concede that the King was correct. From a marriage that would threaten to topple the Monarchy, the King would have deflected the situation to one in which a refusal to let him marry would threaten to shake the foundations of British law. And British law, the Prime Minister would have had to agree, was a matter even more fundamental than the Monarchy. And so a great royal wedding would have been planned, and Wallis Simpson could have become the first American Queen Consort of England.

There was one important ingredient without which the foregoing script could never have been followed successfully, and that was time. To enact it might have taken several years. The King's old friend and chief solicitor, Walter Monckton, who understood British law as well as anyone, might easily have supplied this script, had he been asked for it. Instead, of course, both the King and Wallis had misled Monckton by insisting that marriage was not on either of their minds. And so the King and Wallis pressed impetuously forward toward disaster.

What was the reason for this great haste? It would not be long before the King would begin saying—with very much the ring of an ultimatum—"No marriage, no Coronation." Why did one event have to precede the other? Wallis would not be legally free to marry until the scheduled date of the Coronation was barely two weeks off. The King's explanation would be that he could not go through the sacred ceremony of the Coronation "with a lie on my lips." This sentiment has an honorable and pious sound, but what did he mean? Nothing in the Coronation ritual involved declaring marriage plans.

Though Wallis does not say so in her memoir, the only conclusion one can draw is that she was the person pressing for an early marriage. After all, who could blame her? As she often said, the King never actually made a formal proposal of marriage to her. Instead, he had simply begun acting on the *assumption* that they would be married. Without a formal commitment, either verbally or in writing, she might well have been a little nervous lest her mercurial intended suddenly change his mind. She had seen how fickle he could be, how quickly, and how cruelly, he had cast aside former loves. If she was merely patient and took her time—what might happen? Someone else, younger and prettier than she, might come along. Or the King might gradually be drawn into the routine of his royal duties and travels and ceremonies, and little by little the walls of royalty would close around him, leaving her outside. Also, she was now in the process of shedding Ernest, her support and provider. She had only the King to support her now. She was not young, time was running out, the King was the bird in the hand. If she lost him, where would she be? Poor again. From her book we see how fortunate she felt to have got as far as she had with him in so little time. The slow and patient course that would have saved the day had to be unacceptable to Wallis. She had to secure him now with marriage.

It was now or never. Of course she had no idea of the thicket of problems involved. As an American, how could she?

For fifteen years, King Edward VIII had been listening to a press that had told him he could do no wrong and that he was the most popular fellow in England if not the world. In 1936, however, he began making errors of judgment, one after the other, that would cause people to wonder whether their confidence in him had not been misplaced. The first was his tardiness about—and apparent lack of interest in—moving into Buckingham Palace, where he had told his mother she could remain as long as she wished. It was true that he had never cared for the palace, and that Buck House, as it is known to Londoners, is a large, drafty, and generally uncomfortable collection of cheerless rooms. Still, it is the official residence of the British Monarch and, as such, it has a symbolic significance to the British people, particularly to the residents of the city of London. Seeing the royal standard flying over Buckingham Palace, the Britisher feels reassured that "the King's at home," that all is well and the Empire is in good hands. It is much the same as in Washington. When the presidential flag is not flying over the White House, there is the feeling that somehow the chief is not on the job. For this reason, if for no other, generations of British monarchs before Edward had dutifully endured the discomforts of Buck House and made it their home for set periods of each year. The fact that the royal standard had not yet flown over the palace for the new King was vaguely disquieting.

Meanwhile, various of the new King's friends had come up with suggestions for brightening up Buck House. Lady Elsie Mendl wanted to paint all the rooms and furniture white. White rooms were one of Lady Mendl's trademarks as a pioneer interior decorator. Sybil Colefax, on the other hand, who also possessed important credentials in matters of taste, proposed doing the whole place in beige. But so far nothing had been started, and the King was spending most of his time at York House or Fort Belvedere. By the spring of 1936, Wallis was living there with him practically full time.

There were other setbacks for the King. In March of that year, he sent a memorandum to Parliament, the subject of which was royal finances. He asked, among other things, that a provision be made for a fixed income for his future Queen.

He suggested that an annual sum of £50,000—about $200,-000—would be adequate and reasonable. Such a request would have to be approved by both Houses, and it could not have been more ill-timed. For one thing, the Great Depression had deepened, and the country was undergoing great social and economic unrest. For another, nearly everyone in Parliament knew about the King's relationship with Wallis, and though her name was not mentioned in the memo, it seemed quite clear who the King had in mind as his "future Queen." The proposal was summarily turned down by both the House of Commons and the House of Lords.

At the same time, social London could not help noticing how rapidly Wallis's wardrobe was expanding, along with her collection of ermine, mink and sable wraps. Now, when she ventured forth on a shopping outing, she was accompanied by a detective from Scotland Yard—paid for, presumably, with the taxpayers' money. Then there was the matter of her jewelry, of which she suddenly seemed to have a great deal. In his diaries, Chips Channon described her at a party as "smothered in rubies"; later, he added that "her collection of jewels is the talk of London," and "the King must give her new ones every day." To some, this was interpreted as a rather tasteless example of conspicuous spending during hard times, but among others there was the growing suspicion that the King was cannibalizing his grandmother's famous collection and bestowing it all on Wallis. He had always had a fondness for jewels, and frequently dropped in at Cartier to look at pieces. The trouble was, he usually just looked and didn't buy. Where were the diamonds, rubies, emeralds, sapphires and pearls coming from? To counter this criticism, the King proudly pointed out to his friends that, under Wallis's shrewd stewardship, the royal household was operating far more economically than it ever had before. At Wallis's suggestion, he had fired several servants, thereby further swelling the ranks of the English unemployed.

In 1936, public relations was not the science—or craft— that it has since become, but certainly during the first few months of his reign the King exhibited no public-relations sense whatever. He assumed, for example, that the pub-going public would be pleased to see a photograph in the press of the new Monarch trudging down a street on a rainy day carrying an umbrella. In fact, the public's feelings were mixed. It was fine for the Prince of Wales to walk, but the British looked for far more pomp and grandeur from their King. So did the Establishment, but the King seems not to have grasped this. In his memoir, he belittlingly tells of a Member of Parliament who criticized his stroll in the rain as too informal, and said, "We can't have the King doing this sort of thing. He has the Daimler." A small matter, perhaps, but it stood out in the minds of the British public, who expected their King to uphold certain standards and demanded that he subscribe to a certain amount of formality.

Kings did not walk; they rode in great closed cars. And an undue amount of fuss seems to have been stirred up concerning the King's chosen methods of locomotion. He had taken to calling the royal limousine "the Crystal Palace." In the days before air conditioning, a closed car could be hot and stuffy, and he preferred his American automobile, with the windows rolled down. In some quarters, this was interpreted as a snub to the venerable British automobile companies of Rolls-Royce and Daimler. One evening, a peer jokingly complained to the King that earlier that day a speeding royal car had very nearly run him down. The King reportedly replied, "Couldn't have been me. It must have been Lascelles [his brother-in-law, Lord Lascelles]. He's the one who drives around in state. You know—he's getting royaler and royaler, while I'm getting commoner and commoner." This sort of attitude raised eyebrows, and H. G. Wells commented sniffily, "Nowadays princes come plain—like chicken without stuffing." The British admire stuffing.

Perhaps even more disturbing was the King's apparent attitude toward the Church. Though he was Defender of the Faith of the Church of England, it was noted that he rarely attended church services of any sort—a fact that further gave his statement about not wanting to go through the sacred rite of Coronation with a lie on his lips a hollow ring. The Archbishop of Canterbury paid him a visit and brought up this subject as tactfully as possible. Speaking of the King's late father, Dr. Cosmo Lang said, "I want you to know that whenever the King questioned your conduct I tried in your interest to present it in the most favorable light." The prelate's comment mystified the new King. "My conduct, I wondered. What was Dr. Lang driving at?" he wrote in his memoirs.

In August of 1936, the King embarked on what was to be

his greatest public-relations misadventure yet. His father had been dead barely seven months, and the nation was still in its traditional year-long period of mourning. The news from the Continent was daily growing more alarming, with both Hitler and Mussolini by now firmly in power. The worldwide Depression showed no signs of ending, and it was surely a time when the King should have been showing the public that he was settling seriously into the job of running the Empire. Yet at this moment it was announced that he was chartering Lady Yule's palatial yacht, the *Nahlin,* and was taking a group of close friends on a European cruise for an extended holiday. It was as though, having sensed that his behavior was coming under criticism in his own country, the simplest solution was to go away and leave it for a while.

It was revealed that the King was having the *Nahlin*'s library removed—there was obviously to be little time for reading on the cruise—to make space for an extra bedroom, as well as for the enormous cargo of liquor that was to be taken on board. There had already been rumors that the King was drinking heavily again, and the size of the *Nahlin*'s liquor supply did little to dispel them. The King was also taking along three thousand new golf balls. When asked about these, he explained that he intended to keep in golf practice on the voyage, and would be driving the balls from the deck into the sea. "I love a splash!" he said.

The guests on the boat would be a familiar group, among them Lady Diana Duff Cooper and her husband, Lady Emerald Cunard, Lord and Lady Brownlow, Herman and Katherine Rogers, and of course Wallis. The King's old friend and aide "G" Trotter, who for years had been called his "wet nurse," had meanwhile been banished from the royal circle. He had been seen dining at the Savoy with Thelma Furness, and Wallis had accused him of disloyalty; those who had seen the King's best friend in public with the former object of his affections might assume that the King's connection with Thelma was not completely severed. The King had called Trotter on the carpet and asked if the story about the Savoy dinner was true. Trotter admitted that it was. "You are no longer in my service," said the King, and another friend tumbled into oblivion.

When it was asked whether Mr. Ernest Simpson would also be on the cruise, the naive answer was that of course he would not. That, someone speculated, would bring the number of guests to an unlucky thirteen. But this was untrue. Additionally invited were Lord Dudley, Lord and Lady Louis Mountbatten, Mrs. Evelyn Fitzgerald, Archie Compston (a golfer), Major Sir John Aird (the King's equerry), Major Humphrey Butler (an equerry of the Duke of Kent's) and Mrs. Butler, Sir Godfrey Thomas (a private secretary of the King's), Commander Colin Buist (another of the King's equerries) and Mrs. Buist—bringing the guest list to a total of nineteen.

Originally, the *Nahlin* cruise was to have begun in Venice. But at the last moment a harried Mr. Anthony Eden, who was then Foreign Secretary, succeeded in persuading the King not to visit Fascist Italy. Reluctantly, the King agreed to change his itinerary and to sail along the Dalmatian coast to Greece and the Aegean Islands and the Bosporus. It was a rollicking voyage, as boisterous as it was ill-timed. In Yugoslavia, Prince Paul, the Regent, insisted on a visit from the King of England and his party, and organized a noisy motorcade that tore across the countryside, scattering Balkan peasants in its wake—a display that horrified the British Foreign Office when they heard about it. As the *Nahlin* called at various Adriatic ports, the yacht was inevitably met by a huge and cheering crowd, armed with cameras, singing serenades and shouting "Long live love!"—for by now everyone in the world seemed to know about the King's interest in Wallis Simpson. The King responded to these worshipful throngs with obvious relish, moving through the crowds with smiles and handshakes, posing for photographs, signing autographs—apparently unaware of the international uproar he was causing or that the publicity might be getting out of hand.

Everywhere he went he displayed what he liked to think of as his informality, but which others considered his lack of dignity. On shore as well as on deck he went about in baggy walking shorts and short-sleeved pullovers. Sometimes he was shirtless. He posed, topless, in bathing trunks, and, with Wallis, puttering about in a rented paddle boat. Topless again, he posed standing on his head on the deck of the yacht, his shorts dropping down about the royal thighs, exposing the knobby royal knees and the almost-hairless royal armpits. During one shoreside procession, he had trouble with a shoelace and bent over to retie it while the others waited. Diana Cooper wrote, "We were all left staring at his behind." At one point, while swimming off the yacht at dusk, the *Nahlin*'s captain, Jessel, ran afoul of his own motor launch and got badly cut up by its propeller. The King took command of the ship, saying, "I've told them not to worry about us if we're delayed. It doesn't matter a bit."

In Istanbul, the party was greeted by the dictator Kemal Atatürk, who treated Wallis as though she were already married to the King, and in Bulgaria they were met by King Boris III, a locomotive enthusiast who let the King ride in the cab of his private train and pull the whistle and throttle the engine up to full speed. At times, even the King's guests became concerned about his abandonment of decorum, and Diana Cooper spoke to Wallis about the public appearances in the shirtless state. Couldn't Wallis speak to him? Wallis replied that it was a man's world, and when the man happened to be the King of England it was even more so. He had already succeeded in making her believe in the principle of *le roi le veut;* if the King wished it, he could do it.

In Budapest, Wallis, with a large diamond in her hair, tried her hand at gypsy dances until the wee hours, and the King, in an expansive mood, took over the bartending behind the bar of the Ritz Hotel. The King and his party were entertained in Hungary by the semidictator Admiral Horthy, and the King developed a liking for the Hungarian peach brandy called barack. After one particularly long and bibulous evening at the Ritz, the King appeared on the balcony of his hotel suite and, to demonstrate his marksmanship, shot out a row of street lights along the Danube embankment.

In Germany, Hitler had already been declared Führer, and the infamous "Night of Long Knives" had disposed of a number of his political adversaries. Workers' homes had been bombed in Vienna, where the merry royal party also stopped for a festive visit. Back home in London, the British Foreign Office watched with a kind of abject horror as the reports drifted in of the King's larking visits to one after another Nazi-sympathizing chief of state. Early in September, the royal party left the yacht, and the King and Wallis parted company in Zurich. She left for Paris and a few days' shopping; he flew to London, where he was met and driven to Fort Belvedere in a new car, a 1936 Buick, which he had registered in Wallis's name. Once more the Establishment bristled.

The British press, meanwhile, led by the two "press lords," Lord Beaverbrook and Lord Rothermere, had, at the urging of

Walter Monckton and the King, entered into its famous gentlemen's agreement to publish nothing about the King's and Wallis's affair, and to print only the barest details about her impending divorce. Geoffrey Dawson, editor of Britain's "official" newspaper, *The Times,* had also agreed to print nothing, though Dawson's reason was that he was "embarrassed" to publish the story. The press in other parts of the world, however—particularly in the United States—had been having a field day with the *Nahlin* cruise. Puzzled Britons, purchasing American newspapers and magazines at the stalls, were finding these publications mutilated by the censor's shears. Britons who subscribed to American publications by mail, or who received clippings from relatives or friends in America, were of course aware of what was going on, and the news was spreading by word of mouth. Just how long the British press could manage to keep the lid on these stories was becoming a matter of serious question.

It was in Paris, apparently, where mail was waiting for her at the Hôtel Meurice, that Wallis learned of the storm of publicity that the *Nahlin* cruise had generated throughout the world. Letters from American friends were stuffed with clippings, and her Aunt Bessie had shipped her a particularly large packet. Not all the stories were accurate, and not all were flattering. Few failed to note that Wallis's mother had "run a boarding house." For the first time, Wallis said, she was "troubled." She telephoned the King about it, and he told her not to worry. The press lords had kept their word. There had been nothing whatever in the British press. To him, the British press was all that counted. Still, it was at this point that Wallis allegedly wrote home to Aunt Bessie, "Please send my family papers. People are saying that I'm a plumber's daughter." The Montague-Warfield family tree, she apparently felt, would establish her as a member of the American aristocracy. Aunt Bessie is said to have written back. "Your family papers are on their way. They are very fine. Just don't behave like a plumber's daughter."

The foreign press continued to be unfavorable. In Germany, for example, the *Deutsche Allgemeine Zeitung,* which had not yet been brought into line by Hitler, commented tartly: "King Edward VIII does as he wishes. It would have been unthinkable, during the reign of George V, that a divorced woman should be received at Court. It is well known that the views of the

Church of England are very strong about divorced women. The King is only a few months on the throne, but one has no doubts that it will be an extraordinary reign."

In the United States, understandably, the reaction of the press was less critical. On October 26, 1936, William Randolph Hearst's New York *Journal* appeared with a banner headline that announced, "KING WILL WED WALLY," and went on to say: "In all human probability, in June 1937, one month after the ceremonies of the coronation, will follow the festivities of the marriage [of King Edward VIII] to the very charming and intelligent Mrs. Ernest Simpson, of Baltimore, Maryland, U.S.A."

The story achieved more weight and significance from the fact that Hearst himself had just returned from England, and it was rumored that he had visited the King at Fort Belvedere. In fact, the story was one that could have been put together by anyone who had been paying attention to high-level London gossip. Hearst was enchanted by the whole idea. He had already begun to gear up the machinery of his giant press empire to publicize—and promote to the world at large—the idea of Wallis Simpson's being the first American woman to become Queen of England.

The Hearst story, furthermore, made it increasingly difficult for the British press to keep their promise and suppress what was beginning to look like one of the biggest news stories in history. Hearst's bold speculations would be only the first glimmerings of what would become a huge media event. During the course of it, the media barons—the Hearsts, Beaverbrooks and Rothermeres—would completely take charge of the proceedings, leaving Wallis and the King to a fate that not they but the media would decide, and during which the King would discover that he did not control "his" press at all. In the process of helping the media sell millions of copies of newspapers and magazines, the King and Wallis would become the media's playthings.

Still, the two continued to fuel their joint delusion: *le roi le veut.*

10

Divorce Number Two

THE willingness of the British newspapers to suppress news stories that might be embarrassing to the Royal Family is not based entirely on a policy of genteel good taste and respect for the institution of the Monarchy. Royal scandals are kept out of the papers for other, more practical reasons. One is Britain's tricky libel laws. Had the press reported that the King of England was apparently having an affair with a still-married woman, both Ernest and Wallis Simpson could have sued and might very well have collected. There was also the touchy matter of advertisers with royal warrants. An advertiser might risk losing his prestigious "By Appointment" designation if he bought space in an offending newspaper that printed matter unflattering to Royalty. Purely economic factors such as these dictate a policy of extreme caution when it comes to royal carryings-on, and the Prince of Wales's earlier dalliances with married ladies—Freda Dudley Ward and Thelma Furness— had also gone unreported.

On the other hand, when an American publication breaks

a story of a royal scandal, the British press no longer feels under any restraints. It can simply print what the American publication said and place all the blame, as it were, for the shocking story on the Americans. The British feeling toward Americans has long been somewhat ambivalent—a mixture of envy and disdain—and the habit of letting Americans break the nasty news first has become something of a tradition. As recently as 1975, for example, while all of London buzzed with rumors that Princess Margaret and Lord Snowdon had all but officially separated, that Snowdon was seeing other women, and that the next step would probably be a royal divorce, no word of the untidy business was published in Great Britain. It took an American magazine, *McCall's,* to print the story of the disintegration of the Snowdon marriage. With that, the news became banner headlines all over Britain. By sitting quietly on a billowing royal scandal until it erupted in print across the sea, the British press could treat it as a sensation. It was a technique that sold newspapers.

The situation in the autumn of 1936, however, was unusual on two counts. First, the press had agreed to extend its policy toward Royalty to include an American commoner, and to print no more than minimal details of Wallis's upcoming divorce, to treat it merely as a legal notice. Second, even after William Randolph Hearst gave British newspapers all the green light they needed, the British press continued, despite increasing pressures, to remain silent. That it remained so for as long as it did can perhaps be partially explained by the press lords' hunch that when their story finally broke it would be a bomb-shell bigger than anything in the history of the Fourth Estate. A bombshell and a gold mine.

While the *Nahlin* had been gaily cruising, with three thousand golf balls plopping into the azure waters until it was necessary to send out for more, Wallis's solicitors in London had been soberly at work on their client's marital problem. It had been decided that, in order to create as little public attention as possible, the divorce proceedings should take place some-where outside London. The sleepy little city of Ipswich, about an hour's drive from the capital, was selected. Here, in the birthplace of Cardinal Wolsey, amid gentle Tudor surround-ings, Wallis's divorce, it was hoped, would be quiet, unher-alded, tasteful. In order to be properly divorced in Ipswich, of course, Wallis had to be a resident of the county of Suffolk. With the guidance of the King's solicitors, this also had been arranged, and a small cottage called Beech House in nearby Felixstowe had been rented in her name. At the time, her actual address was aboard the peripatetic *Nahlin*, a technicality.

On October 27, 1936, the Circuit Court of Assizes in Ipswich was presented with a file labeled "Simpson W. vs. Simpson E. A." It was the first case to be heard in the afternoon session, and presiding was Justice Sir John Hawke, an elderly jurist whose features were emphasized by his traditional full, below-the-shoulder, pale-yellow wig. Mr. Norman Birkett, representing Wallis's counselors, rose and addressed His Honor, promising to be brief. He ushered Wallis, who had dressed for the occasion in almost mouselike simplicity, into the witness box. She looked, according to some reports, more than a little nervous, as well she might. William Randolph Hearst's story, published just a day earlier, had alerted London-based reporters, not bound by the Beaverbrook–Rothermere pact, who were waiting in large numbers, with their cameras, just outside the courthouse door.

She repeated the oath, "I swear by Almighty God that the evidence I give to this court shall be the truth, the whole truth, and nothing but the truth," with her hand on a Bible. The oath done with, Birkett reminded the judge: "My Lord, this is an undefended case"—that is, Mr. Simpson was not contesting it.

Later, when the details of the divorce proceedings became public knowledge, and when Wallis's lawyer and the judge who was deciding the case were accused of being in collusion, it was pointed out that both Mr. Birkett and Justice Hawke had quite a bit in common. Both were King's Counsel—members of a select and prestigious legal fraternity in England, of which there are only a few hundred members. Both judge and lawyer were Fellows of the Inner Temple, an even more august and selective legal club, and the two men were also close friends. But if there was collusion, the judge asked one off-putting question of Wallis's lawyer at the outset. "Why has the case been brought *here?*" he wanted to know. There was no answer, and Birkett merely riffled through some papers. Finally, the judge said, "Proceed, Mr. Birkett."

Mr. Birkett asked Wallis her name, and then asked, "Do you reside at Beech House, Felixstowe?"

"Yes, I do."

This, of course, was not quite true. For the past year or so, her residence had been principally Fort Belvedere in Windsor Great Park, and after the *Nahlin* cruise the King had moved Wallis out of her Bryanston Court apartment into more sumptuous quarters in Cumberland Terrace, Regent's Park. But the judge accepted Felixstowe as her residence. There were a few more perfunctory questions about previous addresses, and the date—July 21, 1928—of her marriage to Ernest. These points established for the record, Mr. Birkett turned to Wallis and asked, "Were you happy with Mr. Simpson until the autumn of 1934?"

"Yes."

"But then came a change. Please tell us what that change was."

"He was indifferent. Very often he went away for weekends. Alone."

"Did you complain to him about this matter?"

"I did complain."

"And yet he continued to do what you complained of? Going away alone, and staying for whole weekends?"

"Yes, he did."

"Now, on Christmas Day, 1934, did you find a note lying on your dressing table?"

"Yes."

Mr. Birkett withdrew a letter on pale-blue stationery, handed it to the clerk, who passed it to the judge, who read it silently.

"Has there been another letter?"

"Yes. A letter came to our house. . . . It *seemed* to have been addressed to *me*, but when I opened it I found that the contents could have been meant *only for my husband.*"

In her memoirs, of course, Wallis mentioned only one letter. For the court record, she mentioned two. The judge did not ask the plaintiff to produce the second, and her attorney proceeded to have her narrate what she had done next: consult her solicitors, who on her instructions hired detectives to follow and observe her husband's comings and goings.

"What was the result of that observation?" Birkett asked.

"Certain information which made me bring this divorce action," Wallis replied.

Birkett reached in his briefcase and produced another letter. "On the twenty-third of July, nineteen thirty-six, did you write to your husband the letter I now hold in my hand?"

"Yes."

The lawyer handed the letter to his client and asked her to read it.

In a calm, steady, self-assured voice, Wallis read: "Dear Ernest: I have just learned that while you have been away, instead of being on business as you led me to believe, you have been staying at the Hotel Bray with a lady. I am sure you realize this is conduct which I cannot possibly overlook and must insist you do not continue to live here with me. This only confirms the suspicions I have had for a long time. I am therefore instructing my solicitors to take proceedings for a divorce."

The letter was so carefully constructed and punctuated that it had the distinct sound of having been composed especially for the occasion. It did not sound like a letter written by a wronged and angry wife, but like a document put together by a committee of lawyers. It said just enough, and no more. It contained no adjectives and only one terse adverb. It did, however, contain one mistake. The hotel, it turned out, was not the Hotel Bray but the Hotel de Paris in the town of Bray-on-Thames, but that could have been some law clerk's small oversight.

Wallis was then asked to identify the signature on the hotel's registration form as her husband's, which she did, and she was then told to step down.

Three more witnesses were called, all of them employees of the Hotel de Paris. Two were waiters, Archibald Travers and Dante Buscalia, and both—who seemed thoroughly rehearsed and ready for their questions—swore that on the nights of July 21 (which, though no one noticed it, would have been Ernest's and Wallis's eighth wedding anniversary) and July 23, 1936, they had seen, and waited on, Mr. Ernest Simpson in Room 4 of the hotel, and that the lady with him in the room was definitely not the Mrs. Simpson who sat before them in the courtroom. One of them had served Mr. Simpson and the unidentified lady their breakfast in bed. Both were asked to identify Mr. Simpson from a group photograph, and both did so without hesitation. The third witness was Christian Haesler, the hall porter. He had witnessed Mr. Simpson register at the hotel with the lady. He too could readily identify Simpson from the same photograph, and he attested to the signature in the hotel register.

"Upon that evidence," Wallis's attorney said, "I ask your Lordship for a decree nisi with costs."

For a moment, Justice Hawke seemed indecisive. "Well," he said finally, "I suppose I must come to the conclusion that there was adultery in this case." The judge hesitated again, and then made this puzzling comment: "But there is one question, I should have liked to ask you. I suppose, Mr. Birkett, you know that question."

"That the name of the lady who stayed with the petitioner's husband has not been mentioned here?" Mr. Birkett replied quickly. "But, my Lord, the name of the lady is plainly disclosed in the petition and the lady has been served with a copy of the petition."

"That was what was in my mind, Mr. Birkett," replied the judge, somewhat ambiguously. He scribbled something with his quill pen. Then he muttered, almost crossly, "Very well, decree nisi"—that is, not final—"with costs, I am afraid." And he added, "Unusual circumstances."

What Justice Hawke meant by unusual circumstances will, of course, never be known; whether he suspected that the petitioner was divorcing her husband to marry the King of England must be left to conjecture. Otherwise, there was nothing particularly unusual about the circumstances. Ernest Simpson had done what countless other unhappy British husbands, as well as American husbands, did in those days. To spare his wife's name, he had agreed to appear in a compromising situation with another woman, hired for the occasion, in an understanding hotel, also hired, where the necessary employee-witnesses would do their jobs in return for appropriate compensation. The hired lady's name, which was politely kept out of the transcript, was Mrs. E. H. Kennedy, whose nickname was Buttercup. After the hearing, Buttercup Kennedy dropped conveniently from sight, never to surface again. The proceedings, meanwhile, had lasted exactly nineteen minutes. Now, unless the action was contested, which seemed unlikely, Wallis was free to marry again in six months. And Ernest Simpson, for his compliance and cooperation, had been ordered to pay the court costs as well.

Under English law, any man who takes a trip with a woman other than his wife, and stops with her at the same hotel, has given his wife the opportunity to sue him for divorce on the grounds of adultery. A husband, too, can sue his wife for staying in the same hotel with another man. Wallis Simpson and the King of England had stayed in the same hotels several times—in Vienna and at the Budapest Ritz, to mention just two. But if Ernest Simpson had thought of bringing the divorce action himself, he would have been out of luck. In England, no one can sue the King.

The moment Justice Hawke announced his decision, the reporters from the foreign press who had been waiting outside came flooding in amid cries of "Silence! Silence!" from the bailiff. A hasty attempt was made to spirit Wallis out through the back door of the courthouse, but reporters and photographers also awaited her there beside her chauffeur-driven car. The police had been alerted too, and tried barricading doors, and suddenly there was a dreadful scuffle between the press and the police, with the police swinging riot sticks and seizing and smashing cameras. Needless to say, this sort of treatment did little to initially endear Wallis to the press. Eventually, she made it to her car, and was driven to Beech House, where she hastily gathered the few personal effects she had needed at her temporary residence, and was sped back to London. That night, she and the King dined alone.

Wallis's divorce was headlined all over the world, and, as a result of the camera-smashing rout outside the courthouse, many of the verbal depictions of Wallis were unflattering. In the process of the ensuing publicity, anyone who had the remotest connection with the King or Wallis was interviewed and quoted. In Kansas City, a housewife named Mrs. Earl E. Bryson, the daughter of an Olathe undertaker, came forward and claimed to be the second cousin of the King's sister-in-law. She was quoted as "feeling sorry" for the King and Mrs. Simpson. The fact that Mrs. Simpson had not one, but two, living ex-husbands was unearthed, and Earl Winfield Spencer was reached for comment. He was gallant. His former wife was, he said, "a wonderful woman." The chief reason for their divorce, he went on, was that he had not felt cut out for the "society" life which she so obviously preferred. He wished her well. Both Wallis's former husbands had bland, round, rather forgettable faces with small mustaches, and looked suddenly so much alike that the newspapers had trouble telling which was which and, in their captions, usually mixed them up. In the absence of hard news, the newspapers made things up. One report had it that fun-loving Wallis was fond of practical jokes, and that a favorite one was pulling chairs out from under dinner guests who were about to sit down at table.

The first Mrs. Simpson, when reached for comment, was not charitable. She and her daughter Audrey were living in New York at 1331 Madison Avenue, an address which today brushes the fringes of Harlem. They were, she claimed, in straitened circumstances. "If what the newspapers say of my former husband's financial standing is true, Audrey and I wish he could find it possible to provide adequately for her education and maintenance. The present Mrs. Simpson has enough of 'what it takes' to steal a man. Mr. Simpson walked out on me while I was ill in a hospital in Paris."

Ernest Simpson maintained a dignified silence, despite having become the butt of all the jokes ("The Unimportance of Being Ernest," was one). He did, however, write Wallis an extraordinary letter, the contents of which were somehow leaked to the press. He wrote, "And would your life ever have been the same if you had broken it off? I mean could you possibly have settled down in the old life, and forgotten the fairyland through which you had passed? My child, I do not think so." He apparently regarded both Wallis and the King as children, an appraisal which, in retrospect, seems one of the more perceptive."

In New York, where the news of the Simpson divorce had followed immediately on the heels of Hearst's announcement that the King and Wallis would marry, the royal romance was the primary topic of every fashionable cocktail party, as well as among passengers on the city's subways. The press, furthermore, had already succeeded in vulgarizing it. A typical tabloid headline, in language hardly suitable to "The Most Ancient and Splendid Royal House in the World," had blared:

KING'S MOLL RENO'D IN WOLSEY'S HOME TOWN

It was not a situation designed to enhance Britain's prestige abroad. The American press followed with ancillary stories— one, for example, listed the various European princesses whom the King, at one time or another, *might* have married. He might have married the Italian Princess Yolanda of Savoy—a Roman Catholic, to be sure, but she might have converted for him. He might have married Princess Maartha of Sweden, the niece of the Swedish King, and in the 1920's it had been unofficially reported that he was engaged to her. Maartha also had two lovely sisters, Margarita and Astrid; he might have married either of them, or their cousin, King Gustav's daughter Ingrid. In Denmark, there had been another trio of royal sisters— Alexandrïna Louise, Theodora, and Caroline Matilda, nieces of King Christian. In Germany, there had been Princess Cecile Victoria, daughter of ex-Crown Prince Wilhelm and a granddaughter of the Kaiser. Or the Prince could have ventured farther afield—to Rumania, where there were two royal princesses, or to Austria-Hungary, where there were several more. All these possibilities had been passed over in favor of a twice-married American woman who was not even pretty. The effect of all these stories was to stress the striking "unsuitability" of Wallis as the future wife of the King of England.

In England, meanwhile, both the King and Wallis were continuing to deny to their friends and advisers that marriage was in the wind or even stirring in the breeze. "Ridiculous!" and "Impossible!" had become Wallis's stock responses to friends who brought it up. It didn't matter. No one believed them now. The arrangements for the marriage had already been taken over by the media.

11

Villains

In a number of the many books about the Abdication of King Edward VIII, the role of villain in the drama has been assigned to Prime Minister Stanley Baldwin. Cold, stubborn, hidebound, convention-bound, unmoved by evidence of true love, Baldwin has been portrayed as the chief plotter of the King's downfall, abetted by the Archbishop of Canterbury, Cosmo Lang. In both the Duke of Windsor's and the Duchess's memoirs, Baldwin is cast as the heavy, and in his personal account of the Abdication, Lord Beaverbrook also accuses Baldwin of having precipitated the crisis. Actually, Baldwin was ill-suited for the villain role. Though the King may have found Baldwin pompous and windy—he indeed seemed to have had little use for politicians in general—Baldwin was extremely fond of the King, as he had been of his father, and considered the King his friend. During at least the first few months of Edward's reign, he had spoken proudly of how well the King was doing his job. Also, as we shall see, Baldwin entered the crisis only in its lattermost stages, and then with great personal sadness, with downright reluctance, and after delaying as long as he felt he possibly could.

Another candidate, though an unlikely one, for the role of villain was Winston Leonard Spencer Churchill, then approaching his sixty-second birthday but, with his round pink baby face, looking a good fifteen years younger. Like Stanley Baldwin, Churchill was a loyal Tory. There the similarity ended. Unlike Baldwin, who was merely rich—a fortune amassed by his father in steel mills and collieries—and a product of the Industrial Revolution, Churchill was a member in full standing of the British aristocracy. Born at Blenheim Palace, he was a lineal descendant of the first Duke of Marlborough and a product of Harrow. Baldwin's ancestors were small Worcester landowners and farmers. The difference in social class was vast, and important.

Churchill, of course, did not conceive of himself as cut out for villainy. In 1936, his was one of the few voices from the Establishment raised in the King's behalf. His reasons for backing the King were somewhat complex. For one thing, as an aristocrat, Churchill supported the Royal Family and its whims and desires as a matter of course and as a matter of tradition. For another, he was then temporarily out of power, and may have seen the King's cause, which he assumed to be a popular one, as a way of getting back in again. Like the King, Churchill had also been trying to warn the British government and the British people about the superior strength of German air power, and he refused to be sanguine about the possibility of avoiding a German confrontation. These views and grim warnings had thus far gone unheeded, and by being a gloomy Cassandra he had only succeeded in making himself disliked. (It would be several years before he would be proved right in his predictions and hailed as a hero.) Most of all, however, Churchill backed the King because, like a true English gentleman, he would always be a champion of the underdog—which was what he saw the King to be at the time. Like others, Churchill counseled patience—hoping secretly, perhaps, that, given time, the King's lovesickness would cure itself.

Ironically, by supporting the King, Churchill would only further complicate the situation by making others in the Establishment, including Baldwin, more steadfast in their determination to take an opposing position. Churchill's well-meaning interference marked him as a gadfly and a mischief-maker.

Besides Baldwin and Churchill, there were several other good candidates for Chief Villain, not counting the romantic pair themselves. One was Queen Mary. "If only," Walter Monckton said later, "Queen Mary had received [Wallis], the crisis might have been avoided. Queen Mary alone of all women had the power and the love to make her understand what was involved. Instead, the royal family had all but expelled her." If only . . . If only the King had shown his mother the respect she wanted and had taken her into his counsel before it was too late, before her distaste for Wallis had congealed into obstinacy and cold fury. The old Queen knew the power she wielded. She was the most admired and respected woman in the realm. That which displeased her displeased England.

Then, long before Wallis's divorce, another villain had emerged in the United States in the person of William Randolph Hearst. Though the American press described her in unflattering terms—"moll" was one—and spoke openly of "adultery," in general it was sympathetic to Wallis, and so was the American public—particularly the female segment of the public. The story had that Cinderella quality—the poor little girl from the middle-sized city who had captured the heart of the world's wealthiest, most titled lord. It was the radio soap-opera plot of *Our Gal Sunday,* or a Joan Crawford movie. That the King of England should have chosen an American woman was flattering in itself. That the woman was not a title-hunting heiress named Astor or Vanderbilt or Gould, but bore a plain, American-sounding name like Simpson, made it all the more romantic. To the American mind, divorces did not carry any particular stigma.* On the contrary, the soap operas and films of the era were filled with divorces. All this William Randolph Hearst—at the time the most powerful single figure in the American press—knew well.

Hearst himself was not a man who felt bound by the conventions of middle-class morality. Indeed, he felt himself to be well above them. He had long ago abandoned his legal wife and had been living openly with the movie star Marion Davies. To Hearst, the King–Mrs. Simpson story had all the elements of a sensation, one that might produce good copy for months,

---

*It was different in England, particularly among the lower classes. As an anonymous patron of a London pub is supposed to have said in 1936, "It just won't do. We can't have two other blokes going around saying they've slept with the Queen of England, can we?"

even years. It had the glamor of royalty: the handsome King, one of the most popular men in the world. It had money, and it had sex. It had international political significance. With Europe heading in the direction it was, Hearst reckoned correctly, England might soon need the United States as its ally. Hearst could see why it might be important for England to have an American woman on the throne. Best of all, the story would sell newspapers. Early in March 1936, from his castle, San Simeon, in California, Hearst telephoned one of his top reporters in New York, Adela Rogers St. Johns, with an assignment. She was to leave for England immediately, and bring back the story of the *real* Mrs. Simpson. "Let us see," said Hearst, "if we can make her Queen of England."

In her autobiography, *The Honeycomb*, published in 1969, Mrs. St. Johns gives an account of that visit. To begin with, though she was able to interview a number of people in the King's circle, she found nobody at that point—Wallis's divorce from Ernest was still six months off—who seriously believed that the King would ever marry Wallis. Most people assumed that she was the King's mistress, and some people were scandalized about that. But everyone assured Mrs. St. Johns that marriage was out of the question. One of the people interviewed was Thelma Furness who, Mrs. St. Johns accurately deduced, no longer cared for Wallis and who told her much the same thing. Wallis was just another of the King's famous crushes; he could not and would not marry her. Viscountess Astor was interviewed and was even more vociferous in her agreement with the others. She had been born Nancy Langhorne of Virginia and had been divorced before marrying Viscount Astor. But lately she had become very English, very religious, and very moral. She now disapproved of Americans, of divorce, and of adultery. She regarded Wallis Simpson as a conniving, ambitious, social-climbing and tuft-hunting American adventuress who had come to England to bag a title, and who was now trying to make off with the biggest title of them all. As for marriage, that was "patently impossible." The British would never stand for Mrs. Simpson as Queen.

As for discovering what "the real Mrs. Simpson" was like, Mrs. St. Johns found herself in similar difficulties. Though everyone she spoke to had met Wallis, few people could say what she was like. Even Fred Bate, the head of the National Broadcasting Company in Europe, who had been one of the guests at the Dorchester dinner, couldn't say much about her. In fact, as Mrs. St. Johns talked to more and more of Wallis's London acquaintances, she discovered that they were as curious as she was, and asked *her* what Wallis Simpson was really like. Perhaps, as a fellow American, Mrs. St. Johns could explain her. Mrs. St. Johns approached the visiting Alexander Woollcott, whose devastating wit had brought down the Algonquin Round Table at luncheon after luncheon, and he provided her with a string of familiar but not very helpful adjectives: Wallis was bright, amusing, charming, witty. *Witty?* That sounded promising for a lively anecdote or two to spark up the story, but for the life of him Woollcott could not think of anything clever that Wallis had actually said—no Wildean epigram, no Churchillian bon mot, not even a Dorothy Parkerish wisecrack. Her wit "will not travel," Woollcott said finally.

Mrs. St. Johns was unable to interview Wallis herself—the King had forbade interviews—but she did manage to meet the lady briefly at a large gathering. She was impressed with Wallis's large blue eyes, her best feature, and her carefully plucked wing-like eyebrows, her thin fashion-model figure, her sense of style, and the huge sapphire earrings that almost exactly matched her eyes. Mrs. St. Johns also noted that, though Wallis's feet were beautiful, she had large, bony, "ugly" hands.

At an after-theater supper at Quaglino's, Mrs. St. Johns ran into a man named Marcel Hellman, an Oxford-educated foreigner and dandy, and out of desperation for some clue to Wallis Simpson's elusive reality, she interviewed him. Hellman did not know anything about Mrs. Simpson, but was something of an expert on both the written laws of England and the subtle but powerful unwritten laws that really ruled the realm. The King, he pointed out, was technically free to marry anyone he wanted to except a Catholic, but at the same time "there would be a number of other things involved." The most important of these was the ancient principle that the Sovereign cannot— *must not*—bring the Crown into controversy. The only reason the Monarchy had survived as long as it had, Hellman explained, was that the Crown had steadfastly refused to become the center of conflicting factions or the focal point of contention about any matter whatsoever. What most disturbed Hellman was that the King seemed to be gathering about him a group of supporters who were *for* Mrs. Simpson—what amounted to a King's political party. On the other side, an equally vocal group was forming that was *against* Mrs. Simpson. Hellman saw these factions becoming polarized and heading toward each other on a collision course. If they collided, the unwritten law that insisted on the Crown's absolutely complete political neutrality would be threatened. The King was a human being, but the Crown was an institution, and the Crown would have been brought into controversy. If that happened, he would have to go, Hellman said. "He *can* marry anyone. But he *may not,* as lesser persons do, make his own choice, for upon it depends the future and welfare of the State."

While all this was an interesting lesson in the delicacies and intricacies of British constitutional law, it did not exactly add up to the story Mrs. St. Johns had been sent to England to obtain. Discouraged, she returned to New York to tell her boss that the story was not there. The King was not going to marry Mrs. Simpson, and if he did he would no longer be King, nor would she be Queen. The real Mrs. Simpson was not to be found in England; she was either merely "charming," as her defenders claimed, or a ruthless headhunter, if one listened to her detractors, and neither fact added up to a news story. Perhaps the secret of Mrs. Simpson's historic allure was that she was a riddle, but whatever the allure was, it lay locked somewhere in the King's imagination. He had called her "the perfect woman" and "the most wonderful woman in the world," but these encomiums were not exactly hot copy. Some said her attraction to the King had to be connected with something she did in bed. Others claimed just the opposite, that the key to her allure was that she was the first woman the King had known who had refused to sleep with him, that his ardor was thwarted sexual desire, even though this made Wallis seem something of a monster. Both points of view, of course, were entirely speculative, and neither would be suitable for reporting in a family newspaper. So, Mrs. St. Johns said, there was just no story.

But W. R. Hearst was not a man who lost confidence easily, particularly in a story that was his own idea. He was not the least bit fazed by Mrs. St. Johns's misgivings. Nor was he interested in a character analysis of the real Mrs. Simpson. What he wanted was Wallis portrayed in the most favorable possible light, presented as a woman with every conceivable queenly virtue—warmth, intelligence, gentleness, charm, cultivation, taste, and an impeccable family background. Alice Warfield's quasi-boardinghouse background would not be emphasized, nor would the fact that she had later worked as a hostess at the Chevy Chase Club—and had been fired for incompetence. Hearst wanted Wallis depicted in such a way that American readers would open their hearts to the girl from Baltimore. So that the American public would apply pressure on Washington. So that American diplomats there would apply pressure on the Court of St. James's. And so that, in the end, any official disapproval of the King's marrying an American commoner would evaporate. The series of articles Hearst envisioned would stress the fact that, should there be a war in Europe, England would need America and that therefore England needed an American woman as Queen. The articles should also point out that, should there be a war and should the King be forced to renounce Wallis, how well could the King rule his people through a war if he were doing so with a broken heart? His aim was to force the British Establishment to do an about-face, to make Britain *crave* Wallis as Queen, to convince the world that no one but Wallis would possibly do. As he put it, "I must emphasize that you are never to write about Mrs. Simpson except as an American woman who may become Queen of England, and one worthy of that high position."

Mrs. St. Johns warned him: "A lot of this may have to be fiction."

That was quite all right with Hearst. In fact, he said, if Adela St. Johns, in researching Wallis's family background in the South, could trace her ancestry back to either George or Martha Washington, the point could be made that, if Washington had chosen to take the title King instead of President, Wallis today would be a royal princess.

It was a large order, and Mrs. St. Johns reminded Hearst that it would take time. He agreed, and also that the timing of the articles was most important.

A few days later, St. Johns had a telephone call from Marion Davies. "W. R. wants me to tell you he has decided to go to England to see the King," Miss Davies said.

Adela St. Johns was flabbergasted. "Can he do that?" she wanted to know.

"He can do anything," Miss Davies replied. "He says to tell you he will do his best to get us more time."

He could and did. Hearst never revealed the exact content of his conversation with the King at Fort Belvedere, but Mrs. St. Johns later deduced that he had wanted the King's assurance on two matters. First, were the King's intentions toward Mrs. Simpson honorable? And, second, would the King agree to proceed slowly, cautiously, not rush headlong into things and provoke a crisis, and let the St. Johns articles sink in and do their intended work? The King answered both these questions in the affirmative. Thus reassured, Hearst returned to the United States and advised St. Johns that she could commence publishing her series of articles, a sixteen-installment exercise in the blending of fact, fiction, speculation, sentimentality and high romance. The first began:

THE REAL STORY OF THE KING AND WALLIS

Once upon a time—so all good fairy stories begin—a prince looked down from his place beside the Throne and saw bowing before The King his father and The Queen his mother, a slim dark woman with eyebrows like the wings of a swallow.

Wallis Warfield Simpson. The woman of destiny, the woman who was to be the one great love of the Prince Charming, of the King of England—the woman for whom today he battles those graybeards of his empire who may demand that he sacrifice either her or his throne. What manner of woman is she?

And so it went. Though Adela St. Johns had been unable to establish a George Washington connection, she portrayed an American background that was thoroughly aristocratic, and a woman whose personality could perhaps best be described as both regal and elfin.

When the St. Johns articles reached them, both the King and Wallis were delighted. It was clear that, in William Randolph Hearst, they had an important American champion. Still, though the Hearst newspapers were not distributed in England, the stories created a small but significant backlash. Those in high government circles, and in the Royal Family—including Queen Mary—who were paying close attention to what the American papers were saying, were rather put off by them. Hearst, it seemed, was taking matters into his own hands and promoting Wallis as a candidate for Queen with more than a little hard sell. Also, the soft, gauzy, fairy-princess creation which Adela St. Johns had devised seemed difficult to reconcile with the chic, stylized, hard-edged and worldly woman that the "new" Wallis—the royal Wallis—actually appeared to be.

With perfectly terrible timing, after three or four of the St. Johns articles, all glowingly extolling Wallis, had appeared, the news from Ipswich arrived: she was divorced. Hearst was bitterly disappointed. The King had kept only one of his two promises. The more important one, that he and Wallis would not move hastily, had been broken. The importunate schedule of events the King was planning was now quite clear. Wallis's divorce decree would become absolute in six months' time, on April 27, 1937. She would then be free to remarry, with the Coronation only fifteen days away. Hearst realized then that his patriotic hopes to have an American Queen of England had been a pipedream. But the story was still sensational news. The headline in his New York *Journal* read: KING WILL WED WALLY. Meanwhile, the St. Johns articles of the lovers' struggle with the wicked "graybeards"—Baldwin, the Archbishop— continued.

That the King should have begun to court the press, and to believe that he could manipulate it to suit his ends, was in itself unusual. It had become almost a tradition in the British Royal Family to distrust the press and to cooperate with it as little as possible—and for good reason. The Royal Family was constantly in the eye and consciousness of the public, and to maintain even a minimum of privacy the press had to be kept politely at bay. Buckingham Palace employed press officers whose main duty was to answer daily questions from reporters in a way that would obfuscate matters as much as possible. According to long-standing policy, members of the Royal Family never granted interviews. And yet, beginning with his meeting with Hearst, the King made the press lords his confidants and chief advisers. It was a tactic that would only lead to confusion and disarray because the King was demonstrating a habit of saying one thing and then doing another. At the same time, the lovers themselves were sending out differing signals to the world around them. By November 1936, the King had told close associates, among them Walter Monckton, that he planned to marry Wallis. And yet Wallis, a few days later, when asked outright by Sybil Colefax whether the King had suggested marriage, "looked surprised" and replied, "Of course not."

In England, the counterpart to William Randolph Hearst was the legendary Maxwell Aiken, first Lord Beaverbrook, owner of the *Evening Standard*, the *Daily Express,* and founder of the *Sunday Express.* Physically, Lord Beaverbrook and Hearst could not have been more unlike. Hearst was tall and magisterial; Beaverbrook resembled a tiny, paunching elf with an oversized, balding, beetle-browed head. Most photographs showed Beaverbrook wearing a crooked, toothy grin. His nickname was "the Beaver," and he looked a bit like a beaver. There was a definite raffish side to the Beaver's nature, and he often said he enjoyed the company of rogues and scamps and scoundrels more than that of kings and queens. Still, he had become one of the most powerful newspapermen in the world, and was widely conceded to be a genius.

On October 12, 1936, Percy Cudlipp, the editor of Beaverbrook's *Evening Standard,* learned of Wallis's impending divorce hearing. The fact that its venue would be Ipswich, and not London, where Wallis lived, made Cudlipp immediately suspicious that something of great importance was being covered up. He went straight to his boss, who agreed that there was a major story here. In it, the King's name would not need to be mentioned, but the implications would be clear and the *Standard's* readers would draw the obvious inferences. Beaverbrook, furthermore, was an old friend of Wallis's solicitor, Theodore Goddard, whom he promptly telephoned to ascertain whatever additional facts he could. Goddard, taken aback that his Ipswich plans were about to backfire and that the *Evening Standard* was about to break with a story of the divorce and its out-of-the-way location, asked for an immediate conference with Beaverbrook. In the evening, the two men met at Cherkley, Beaverbrook's country place.

Goddard begged Beaverbrook to give the story no more space than would be routinely allotted to a standard legal notice. Any pretrial publicity, he argued, might seriously jeopardize his client's case. Wallis's action, he insisted, was a purely private matter, based on her husband's alleged infidelity. There was nothing more to it than that. Yes, Goddard had heard the rumors, but they were quite untrue. The King had no plan and no desire to marry Wallis Simpson, nor had she any plan or desire to marry him. The meeting ended inconclusively, with Beaverbrook making no promises.

The next morning, a Tuesday, a very worried Mr. Goddard met with Walter Monckton and George Allen, the King's solicitor. The Ipswich idea, it seemed, had not been a good one after all; it was making the whole circumstances of the divorce look fishier, and Max Beaverbrook was threatening to spread its whole fishiness across his newspapers. It was too late, however, to stop what had already been put in motion unless, of course, Wallis could be persuaded to call the divorce off. The three men agreed that the problem should be immediately taken up with the King.

The King, at that point, must have wished it could have been possible to remain happily cruising aboard the *Nahlin* forever. The newest development was another in a series of misfortunes which had been besetting him since he had first put foot again on English soil, and which would continue to beset him for the next seven weeks as problems mounted with the inexorability of a rising toilet bowl. To ward off the present one, Goddard suggested that the King personally telephone Beaverbrook and enter a plea of his own. Monckton and Allen also suggested—as others had done before and would continue to do through the next weeks—that if the King could persuade Mrs. Simpson to withdraw her divorce action, or at least postpone it for a while, much unpleasant publicity could be avoided. That, the King said, was out of the question. As her friend, he had no right to interfere in her personal business. He would, though, telephone Beaverbrook, which he proceeded to do, suggesting a meeting and adding, airily, "Name your own time!"

The wily publisher was in no hurry for the royal audience. He apparently had a little more journalistic digging to do. He explained to the King that he was suffering from a particularly irksome toothache and that the next few days would be consumed with dental appointments. He would not be able to see the King until Friday, the sixteenth. (In her book, Frances Donaldson notes that in Beaverbrook's calender for that week, there were no entries for dental appointments, but at 5:30 P.M. on Thursday, the fifteenth, was a notation reading "Mr. Ernest Simpson." Whether Beaverbrook interviewed Simpson that afternoon is not known, but if he did, it is likely that Ernest was properly discreet and noncommittal.)

The King and Lord Beaverbrook still knew each other only slightly, having met, at most, on two previous occasions. But that Friday meeting would sweep Beaverbrook into a prominent place in the history of events leading up to the Abdication, and it was a prominence that, for the next weeks, Beaverbrook would clearly relish. Never was he happier than when he felt himself to be at the helm of great power, when he could demonstrate his ability to wield it, and when the rich and powerful stood before him, hat in hand, requesting large favors.

What the King was asking him for, at their meeting, turned out to be much more than Mr. Goddard had suggested. He asked not only that Beaverbrook's papers minimize all news of Wallis's upcoming divorce to the point of suppression, but that Beaverbrook do what he could about "limiting publicity after the event." Finally, he wanted Beaverbrook to use his influence to see to it that other publishers would do the same. In his book *The Abdication of Edward VIII*, Beaverbrook wrote that he found the King's reason for this large order sound and convincing: "The reasons he gave for this wish were that Mrs. Simpson was ill, unhappy, and distressed by the thought of notoriety. Notoriety would attach to her only because she had been his guest on the *Nahlin* and at Balmoral. As the publicity would be due to her association with himself, he felt it his duty to protect her."

And so Beaverbrook agreed to do whatever he could. Later, he would say that he would have agreed regardless of whether or not he had known that the King planned to marry Wallis. Simple chivalry toward the distressed lady would have dictated that he do so. But one wonders. Beaverbrook was not a man who ever had a simple reason for doing what he did, and it was not chivalry—but peddling stories about the peccadilloes of the mighty—that had made him a rich man.

Beaverbrook, it turned out, could do quite a lot. He first visited his Fleet Street rival, Esmond Harmsworth, whose father, Viscount Rothermere, owned the *Daily Mail* and *Evening News* group of papers and was chairman of the Newspaper Proprietors' Association. Harmsworth was a friend of the King's, and readily agreed to the news-boycott proposal. Provincial newspapers were telephoned, along with papers in Ireland and Scotland, and all fell into line. Beaverbrook's influence extended even beyond the English Channel. *Le Figaro* had been grandly paying the affair no heed, but *Paris-Soir* had been having a field day with it. At Beaverbrook's urging, however, its editor agreed to publish nothing more on the matter. It was a coup of considerable proportions. As for the United States, Beaverbrook was less sure of himself. As he put it, "Negotiations with the Americans promised to be both difficult and tedious, and quite likely to end in failure." Still, he was planning a mid-November trip, part business, part holiday, to his native Canada, and he proposed to stop in New York to see what he could do.

On November 5, at the King's suggestion, his lord-in-waiting Perry Brownlow invited Lord Beaverbrook to dinner. The purpose of the dinner was to thank his lordship for his good services, as well as to allow him to meet and get to know the lady for whom he had done so much, and who now had her decree nisi. Beaverbrook had met Wallis only once before, and then very fleetingly, but now he was able to size her up. Perhaps Wallis had deliberately dressed down for the occasion because Beaverbrook's description of her that evening makes her sound almost drab:

> She appeared to me to be a simple woman. She was plainly dressed, and I was not attracted to her style of hair-dressing.
> Her smile was kindly and pleasing, and her conversation was interspersed with protestations of innocence of politics and with declarations of simplicity of character and outlook, with a claim to inexperience in world affairs. Throughout the evening she only once engaged in political conversation, and then she showed a liberal outlook, well maintained in discussion, and based on a conception which was sound.
> I was greatly interested by the way the other women greeted her. There were about six women who were present at the dinner or who came in afterwards. All but one of them greeted Mrs. Simpson with a kiss. She received it with appropriate dignity, but in no case did she return it.

Beaverbrook had already begun to suspect that the "no marriage" assurances were untrue, and all through the evening he waited for the King to take him aside and confide his true plans. The King did make a few critical remarks about Stanley Baldwin and his Cabinet, but otherwise he seemed unready to make a full disclosure. Toward the end of the evening, however, the King did tell Beaverbrook that he had "something

further" to discuss with him. When several days had passed
with no further word from the King, Beaverbrook suggested
to Perry Brownlow that it might be helpful to those who were
trying to assist the King if the King would try to be candid and
truthful. It was a sensible hint. Whether it was passed on to
the King is unknown. Certainly it was not heeded.

From the beginning, to those close to the King the choice
of Lord Beaverbrook to be one of the champions of the King's
cause seemed an odd—even ominous—one. On the one hand,
it seemed a bold and brilliant public-relations move. And yet,
looked at another way, it may have been suicidally fatal. What
was in it for Beaverbrook? people wondered. He had to have
some ulterior motive. He was no royalist, for one thing, and
had often, both publicly and privately, been mocking and dis-
dainful of the Monarchy and the Royal Family. At the same
time, he was no friend of Stanley Baldwin's, and the two were
old political enemies who had been trying to do each other
in for years. (Later, when asked why he had joined the King's
team, Beaverbrook is alleged to have impishly replied, "To
bugger Baldwin!") But as all who remember him attest, the
Beaver loved mischief, and here was opportunity for mischief
at its best. The Beaver enjoyed seeing Royalty in a pickle, and
if Baldwin were part of the pickle so much the better. According
to at least one longtime Beaverbrook staffer, Sam White, if
Beaverbrook could have succeeded in ousting both the King
and Baldwin in the crisis, he would have liked it best of all.
Max Beaverbrook seemed to enjoy making enemies more
than he enjoyed making friends. An ardent Republican, he
despised the Monarchy in general and the House of Windsor
in particular. King George V had opposed his peerage. Beaverbrook also hated Stanley Baldwin, who had publicly attacked
the "press lords"—Beaverbrook and Rothermere—for wield-
ing power without responsibility. To round off matters, Beaverbrook also hated Winston Churchill, and usually came out in
favor of anything Churchill opposed. Churchill's son, Randolph, also wrote for the rival *Daily Mail,* and had launched
journalistic attacks on the Beaverbrook papers for being a law
unto themselves. On more than one occasion, using his father's
high-level connections, Randolph Churchill had succeeded in
scooping the Beaverbrook newspapers on important stories.

The fight to save King Edward marked a rare Winston Church-ill-Beaverbrook alliance.

As for Beaverbrook restraining his own and other news-papers from reporting what was going on, he had absolutely nothing to lose. The story was still there, it was not going away, it would come out sooner or later. When it did, it would sell hundreds of thousands of newspapers, and Beaverbrook papers would have the inside track. The only ones with anything to lose were Wallis and the King. If, as some said, the King was a Hamlet-like figure of inaction and indecision during the crisis, Beaverbrook was his Iago, come in through the wings from another play.

The entrance of Beaverbrook into the fray caused other, more immediate, disruptions. For one thing, it further enraged Queen Mary, whose late husband had had no use for Beav-erbrook. Stanley Baldwin, upon learning that Beaverbrook was one of the King's new defenders, was puzzled and hurt. Bald-win was already under heavy pressure and criticism for having made no decisive move in the Mrs. Simpson situation, and had been abjectly waiting for the King to come to him and make clear his intentions. Instead, the King was defecting to the enemy camp. The pressure on Baldwin to act was now even greater.

Not long before leaving for Canada, Beaverbrook made an appointment with Walter Monckton to discuss means by which the American press could be persuaded to stop printing stories that the King of England was about to marry an American divorcée. At the last minute, however, Monckton had to cancel this meeting, explaining that he had been detained "by Royal command." And so Lord Beaverbrook set sail for Canada aboard the *Bremen*, disappointed, perhaps, that he was not at the moment needed.

Major Alexander Hardinge, the King's chief private sec-retary, had a thankless job. It was his duty to act as liaison, a kind of ambassador, between the King and Number 10 Down-ing Street. He was also assigned the chore of keeping the King abreast of the opinions of Parliament and the Cabinet, and of public opinion, and he was the collector of the King's press cuttings. As he later wanly wrote, "The King's Private Sec-retary is a solitary figure, and ploughs a lonely furrow." Still, he did his job conscientiously and well. The only trouble was that the news of Cabinet, Parliamentary and public opinion Hardinge was now required to deliver to the King was for the most part bad. So were the press cuttings from the foreign press.

By early November, many figures in the government were becoming alarmed at what seemed to be the do-nothing policy and ostrich attitude of Prime Minister Baldwin. At least one sternly worded message (". . . there is but one course . . . namely to put an end to Your Majesty's association with Mrs. Simpson") had been drafted for Baldwin's signature. When this was shown to Hardinge, he protested that it was much too severe, and begged for softer language. Neville Chamberlain then had a hand at emending it, but the tone of the letter remained harsh (". . . your association with Mrs. Simpson should be terminated forthwith.") Baldwin, still wavering, refused to sign either version.

By November 13, Major Hardinge felt that the time had come for the King to face certain unpleasant facts, and that it was his duty to present them to him. That evening, when he returned to Fort Belvedere, the King found a letter marked "Urgent and Confidential" on top of the customary pile of red leather boxes. He started to chuck it aside in favor of joining Wallis for a cocktail, but his very nervous butler informed His Majesty that Major Hardinge had asked that he read it immediately.

Sir,

With my humble duty.

As Your Majesty's Private Secretary, I feel it my duty to bring to your notice the following facts which have come to my knowledge, and which I *know* to be accurate:

(1) The silence of the British Press on the subject of Your Majesty's friendship with Mrs. Simpson is *not* going to be maintained. It is probably only a matter of days before the outburst begins. Judging by the letters from British subjects living in foreign countries where the Press has been outspoken, the effect will be calamitous.

(2) The Prime Minister and senior members of the Government are meeting to-day to discuss what action should be taken to deal with the serious situation which is developing. As Your Majesty no doubt knows, the resignation of the Government—an eventuality which can by no means

be excluded—would result in Your Majesty having to find someone else capable of forming a government which would receive the support of the present House of Commons. I have reason to know that, in view of the feeling prevalent among members of the House of Commons of all parties, this is hardly within the bounds of possibility. The only alternative is a dissolution and a General Election, in which Your Majesty's personal affairs would be the chief issue—and I cannot help feeling that even those who would sympathize with Your Majesty as an individual would deeply resent the damage which would inevitably be done to the Crown, the corner-stone on which the whole Empire rests.

If Your Majesty will permit me to say so, there is only one step which holds out any prospect of avoiding this dangerous situation, and that is for Mrs. Simpson to go abroad *without further delay,* and I would *beg* Your Majesty to give this proposal your earnest consideration before the position has become irretrievable. Owing to the changing attitude of the Press, the matter has become one of great urgency.

I have the honour, etc., etc.

Alexander Hardinge

P.S. I am by way of going after dinner to-night to High Wycombe to shoot there tomorrow, but the Post Office will have my telephone number, and I am of course entirely at Your Majesty's disposal if there is anything at all that you want.

It was a letter that was extraordinarily polite, considerate and humane in tone, but the King's immediate reaction to it was shock and outrage. As he wrote angrily in his memoirs, "They had struck at the very roots of my pride. Only the most fainthearted would have remained unaroused by such a challenge." He had reached a point, obviously, where anyone who was not in complete agreement with him was an enemy. It is also interesting to note the plural "they" in the lines just quoted, because he immediately assumed that Hardinge's letter was part of a plot, and that Stanley Baldwin was behind it.

In fact, Hardinge had been to see Baldwin, but only to ascertain whether the Prime Minister's Cabinet would indeed meet that day, and to ask whether the meeting might be postponed. Baldwin had replied that he was under too much pressure from his ministers, and that it could not be. Furthermore,

Hardinge had just finished a draft of his letter when he received a visit from Geoffrey Dawson, the editor of *The Times*, who showed him a strongly worded editorial on the situation which *The Times* planned to publish imminently. Hardinge had then shown Dawson a copy of his letter to the King, urging Dawson to wait for the King's reply before publishing his editorial. The same day, Hardinge had had lunch with Stanley Bruce, the High Commissioner of Australia, which had resulted in Bruce's sending a message to Baldwin in which he said, "If there was any question of marriage with Mrs. Simpson the King would have to go, as far as Australia was concerned."

Though Hardinge, in his letter, had been merely doing what his job required of him—keeping the King informed of government and public opinion—the King soon added the names of Dawson, Bruce and the Archbishop of Canterbury to the list of alleged plotters. Because Hardinge had also carried messages between Queen Mary and her son, since she seemed incapable of speaking to him as his mother, the Queen was also assumed to be a member of the cabal.

When the King showed Hardinge's letter to Walter Monckton, Monckton somewhat guardedly agreed that the letter was "impertinent." But he urged the King not to fire Hardinge summarily, as the King proposed doing. Instead, Monckton advised him to do what a great many people were now urging him to do, to wait and be patient.

Next, the King showed Hardinge's letter to Wallis. She read it, she tells us, and was "stunned" by its contents. Immediately, according to her account, she offered to do what Hardinge suggested and leave the country. But the King, she says, would not hear of it. He needed her by his side now more than ever. Tearfully, she agreed to stay.

Hardinge's letter was never answered.

Instead, the King asked to speak to Lord Beaverbrook, and was somewhat surprised to learn that Beaverbrook was already two days out to sea aboard the *Bremen*. A radio telephone call was put through, followed by radiograms and more telephone calls—all with the same message: Beaverbrook must come home at once. It was even suggested that the *Bremen* and its passengers be turned around in mid-Atlantic, and if the *Bremen* had been a British and not a German vessel, it might have been done. Beaverbrook, while no doubt delighted at being brought back into the eye of the storm, was more than a little worried about all the wires and telephone calls, which could easily be intercepted and monitored. Beaverbrook also wondered why the King had been unaware of his Canadian visit. It had been in all the papers. But he agreed to cancel his Canadian trip and to book passage on the *Bremen's* return voyage.

During his brief New York stay, while the *Bremen* restocked and refueled, Beaverbrook called on Joseph Patterson of the *Daily News*. While he was in Patterson's office making a plea for American press restraint, a call came through from the King, who had traced him there. Once more, he was appalled at the King's indiscretion to call him about what was supposed to be a secret matter in a newspaper office. Beaverbrook tried to keep his end of the conversation noncommittal, but the King, at his end, could not seem to get the point. He finally told Beaverbrook that he intended to marry Wallis, and now he wanted Beaverbrook to come home to help him do it. Beaverbrook was certain that the call was being monitored, as indeed it was—by the entire *Daily News* switchboard and half the newspaper staff.

And as soon as the *Bremen* was ready to embark again, Beaverbrook was aboard. Of course, what the Beaver was intended to accomplish on this return mission to London was something no one—certainly not the King—could possibly imagine.

12

Needs and Wants,
Ways and Means

WHAT was it, one must ask at this point, that they wanted—
these two middle-aged people who seemed about to confront,
and rearrange, British history? Did they both want the same
thing? Probably not. Was it simply the implacable power of
"true love"? It would not seem so, looking back at the pair in
the delicate balance of the late autumn of 1936. Though those
who observed them in those days were convinced that the King
was truly smitten by Wallis, and madly—quite literally
madly—in love with her, the same friends were equally certain
that Wallis was not really in love with him. She was flattered
by the attention he paid to her, yes, and she enjoyed the power
that her friendship with the King gave her over others. She
enjoyed, as any woman would, the gifts of jewels, furs, and
dresses that he showered upon her, and she liked moving about
in the topmost echelon of London society. But Wallis, after
two marriages and two divorces, was too wise in the ways of
men and women, too experienced in the vagaries of love, to
believe in it any longer. Love seldom lasted. Other things—

emeralds, palaces, power, to name a few—were longer-lived. Though she would give her memoirs an almost maudlinly sentimental title, *The Heart Has Its Reasons,* the woman who emerges from its pages is not the sentimentalist of her girlhood. Nor is the book in any way a love story, nor does she make much use of the word *love* in connection with any of the men in her life, nor does she talk of her heart, or really tell us what its "reasons" were.

Wallis Simpson—or, as she had begun calling herself after her second divorce, Wallis Warfield—was, despite her sophisticated poise, naive in many ways, but she was no child. The King, on the other hand, was still a child, and a rather neurotic one at that. From his stiff, rejecting, self-conscious and defensive parents, he may well have acquired a deep fear of responsibility, a fear which may secretly have humiliated him and which he tried to hide with public statements about "duty" and "responsibility." From watching the antics of his roguish old grandfather, whose namesake he was and whom he thoroughly admired, he had also developed a penchant for rebellion against anything that smacked of authority. Authority, in fact, seemed to anger him almost to the point of irrationality. He had grown up, by his own admission, anxious, fear-ridden, and uncertain of what it was to be King, and of what was expected of him as a man.

Then, as a young man, learning that he was handsome and universally adored, he had doubtless acquired a deep need for praise, for publicity, and loyalty. He needed loyalty and yet, when it seemed he had it, he was almost always suspicious of it. When loyal friends appeared—from his own social circle, at least—he was always inwardly convinced that their loyalty was based on his rank, what he was rather than who he was. Such friendships as he had were usually fleeting, broken off at his instigation. He had countered this by cultivating a series of friendships with women who were inaccessible or otherwise inappropriate. (Did squiring married women make him feel more like a man? the amateur psychologist might ask.) Because Americans were considered socially inferior to the English, he cultivated Americans, looked for American values, tried to speak in the American idiom, preferred American cars. This defiance of tradition, which his friends regarded as a kind of madcap manliness or stubbornness, or even as an indication that the King was very modern and part of a younger generation that was healthily questioning worn-out values, may have been—if he had been able to analyze it—just another expression of his inability to accept the responsibilities of the throne.

Most of all, he craved attention. It was a child's craving. He loved sweeping into rooms to the rustle of bows and curtsies. In many ways he used Wallis as an attention-getting device, flaunting her around the town aglitter with gems and wearing gowns that could have only come from him. She was also a device by which he could publicly even the score with his parents. And surely he must have derived a childish delight in discovering that, at age forty-two, he was still attractive enough to break up what had previously seemed a perfectly happy marriage.

It is possible, too, that the King was using Wallis for still another reason—to provide him with an acceptable and honorable excuse for abdicating: love. If he resigned his kingdom for love, the world would love and sympathize with him for it. The world might even love him all the more. "Look what he has given up for love!" the world would exclaim, and he would remain a hero. He would no longer be the King by title, but he would forever be the King by adoration. He could retain all the trappings of a monarch, and the publicity he so adored, and yet he would have none of a monarch's tiresome duties. Though both he and Wallis would spend the rest of their lives hotly denying the charge that finding his way out of the job had been his primary, if unconscious, aim, there is no doubt that his feelings about the kingship were ambivalent.

As for Wallis, did she really believe she *would* be Queen? Probably not, in her secret soul, though we shall never know since she was always too shrewd ever to answer that question. The wanter never really believes he will get what he wants until he has it. And yet there was that naive side to Wallis's nature, her understanding of British constitutional law was limited, and her grasp of the power of the British Establishment and the huge invisible force of British tradition was even more tenuous. She may have half believed the King's vague reassurances that "we'll work it out, don't worry," and "I can get away with it." She may have half believed that the King of England was more powerful than the Almighty, and that he could move mountains as easily as he could commandeer yachts, summon great cars and servants, and make trains stop at unscheduled stations to suit his whim. She was, after all, an American woman from a small southern city, with a schoolgirl education that had stressed manners more than history and literature. Even in middle age, she may still have believed in the myths of kings. She may also have believed, now that Lord Beaverbrook was on his way home, that he was about to perform some sort of miracle.

One of the King's greatest problems, meanwhile, was himself. Instead of sticking to one principal adviser—as the absent Beaverbrook still assumed himself to be—he had begun seeking the counsel of others. Inevitably, the pieces of advice he received in return were often conflicting, and even when the advice was sensible, the King had the unfortunate habit of not heeding it. Now, with Beaverbrook still on the high seas aboard the *Bremen*—transatlantic flights had not yet been inaugurated—the King decided to take matters into his own hands. The upsetting letter from Private Secretary Hardinge had reached him on the evening of November 13, a Friday. At his old friend Walter Monckton's urging, he had agreed not to follow his first impulse and fire Hardinge on the spot for his "impertinence." But he had immediately asked Monckton to take over all Hardinge's former duties, which Monckton had agreed to do—even though this would amount to a considerable personal sacrifice (he would receive no additional compensation). The King then announced that he intended to summon Stanley Baldwin and tell him that, unless he could marry Wallis as he wished, he would abdicate.

This, of course, was in direct defiance to the plan Lord Beaverbrook had laid out to him before he left. At all costs, Beaverbrook had urged him, he should not place the marriage question in the hands of the politicians. Monckton also urged him not to take this course, saying that Baldwin would not like to hear such an ultimatum. Nonetheless, the King went right on to deliver one. The following Monday, the sixteenth, Baldwin was called to the palace, and the King delivered his impetuous and stunning statement: "I want you to be the first to know that I have made up my mind and nothing will alter it— I have looked at it from all sides—and I mean to abdicate to marry Mrs. Simpson."

Of course the King may have thought of this as a tactical

ploy, and hoped that, faced with such a drastic alternative as Abdication, Baldwin would immediately capitulate and let the King have his way. This may have been why the King stretched the truth in telling Baldwin that he was "the first to know" that he was considering Abdication (the first to know had been Monckton). But Baldwin was a literal man, and he took the King at his word. His shocked reply was, "Sir, this is a very grave decision and I am deeply grieved."

Later, in his book *The Abdication of King Edward VIII,* Lord Beaverbrook would have many harsh words for his old enemy Baldwin, calling him "cunning...a relentless foe," claiming that Baldwin was already "discredited in his public career," and accusing him of deceptive and misleading tactics. But up to this point Baldwin had been merely a politician trying to play his hunches, hoping that the problem would somehow go away or solve itself without his intervention. Now, with the King's ultimatum presented to him, there was nothing for him to do but seek the counsel of his government and ministers. Thus far, Baldwin had tried to treat the King's romance as a private matter. Abdication, however, was a public one.

That same day, the King went to his mother and made the same pronouncement. To the Queen, of course, it did not come as a great surprise; it was what she had been dreading all along. Her biographer, James Pope Hennessy, reports her reaction: "It can be simply stated that Queen Mary greeted her son's decision to give up the throne with consternation, with anger and with pain.... No single event in the whole of her life— which, we may recall, had not been an invariably happy one— had caused her so much real distress or left her with so deep a feeling of 'humiliation.'"

Two days later, on November 18, the King departed on a long-scheduled royal tour of Wales, where special attention was to be paid to unemployed miners and steelworkers who were undergoing one of the bleakest periods in their history. As he addressed the haggard and hungry faces of the miners and their ragged wives and children, he said, "These works brought all these people here. Something must be done to find them work." The next day, at another stop on the tour, he made a similiar assertion: "You may be sure that all I can do for you I will; we certainly want better times brought to your valley." At yet another stop, he told the chairman of the Unemployed

Men's Committee, "Something will be done about unemployment."

Later, it would be speculated that these royal remarks might have further distressed Stanley Baldwin. The King, after all, seemed to be overstepping his authority—since he had no power to "do" anything about poverty and unemployment. Once more, he seemed to be involving the Crown in politics. But what is more interesting about the King's comments in Wales is what they reveal about his character. While delivering lofty sentiments and promises to his subjects, who were certainly overjoyed to hear them, he had just three days earlier announced his intention to abandon his throne and country for the sake of an American woman.

The King, obviously, was having a busy week. And how was Wallis passing her time? She was doing, it would seem, very little. Nor had the King yet taken her into his confidence with his thoughts on Abdication. A number of the King's advisers, and several of her friends, had suggested to her that she might ease the growing tension around the throne if she would just slip out of the country for a while—to Europe, perhaps, or home to America—until the situation simmered down. She and the King could continue to communicate by letter and by telephone: absence, after all, was alleged to make the doting heart grow fonder. But clearly Wallis was unwilling to make such a move and gave, as her argument, this: If she left, he would simply follow her—he would follow her to the ends of the earth. He had told her so. If the King began chasing Wallis across the globe, there would be an even greater scandal. Her rationale made a certain amount of sense. The King did seem sufficiently love-crazed to behave in such an irresponsible manner. But one wonders. She may have been afraid that just the opposite might happen and that, if she left England, he might *not* pursue her.

Wallis's general policy of inaction seems to have been one of her own devising, and at this point it might be well to pause and consider what she *might* have done. In retrospect, she could have done, or tried to do, a great deal. She had never, for example, made any attempt to approach the woman whom she now, under any circumstances, expected to be her future mother-in-law. The old Queen presented a proud and imperious façade, but she was not rude. She was also human, and a woman. Another trait that those closest to her recognized was her overwhelming *shyness*. Her shyness served as a principal barrier between her and her family, including her children, and yet, once penetrated, the shyness revealed a sensitive and often uncertain person. The properly worded note from her son's intended bride, requesting an interview and a chance to talk, might not have gone unanswered. Inexplicably, this simple notion seems never to have occurred to Wallis. And so it is possible that the Queen, never having had a single word from Wallis, thought that Wallis was the one who was behaving insensitively and rudely.

Why hadn't she ingratiated herself with some of the Old Guard? Ingratiating herself was something she was good at. Didn't she realize that these people would be some of her future husband's most important subjects? And what about Baldwin? At the Baldwin dinner—in advance of which the King had said to her, "Sooner or later, my Prime Minister will have to meet my future wife"—why hadn't she tried harder to exercise some of her famous charm on him? It might have helped. They might even have become friends. But Wallis seems to have made no such overture or effort. After the dinner, Wallis noted that the Baldwins were "pleasant but distant." For all her celebrated gifts as a hostess, Wallis apparently did absolutely nothing to reduce this distance or to defrost the chilly atmosphere. In retrospect, it is no wonder that Mr. Baldwin thought little of Wallis as the King's future helpmeet. She helped him not at all.

Was she simply awed and frightened of such powerful people? It seems unlikely. She was already a nimble and successful social climber, and had developed the social climber's muscles, including the most important one—a skin of rhinoceros toughness. Was she simply naive? During those agonizing days, a number of people tried to size her up and plumb the mystery of her character. According to Lord Rothermere, Wallis was just "a nice woman who has suddenly found herself catapulted into this absurd position." Beaverbrook may have been closer to the answer when, after his first evening with her, he described her as "simple."

But what Beaverbrook failed to understand was that, for a southern woman of Wallis's background, simplicity was a carefully cultivated and practiced art. Demureness was a southern tradition, and helplessness a pretty southern pose. Her generation had been taught that to be a lady meant knowing how to cook and sew and manage servants, to sip cocktails and play bridge, to look her nicest for her man at parties and, by acting innocent and a little silly, to make the menfolk feel important. In particular, the man of the house had to be given the illusion that he was in charge of things. It was all a little game, a show. And it meant that when the King could have used her help and guidance most, she was busily trying to make him feel that he was guiding her.

Nor should we underestimate the size of Wallis's ego. It had never been small and now, fed by the King of England's attentions and expensive gifts, it had enlarged to generous proportions. As the fiancée of what she believed to be the most important man in the world—the master of the greatest plantation she had ever known*—she now believed that she was the most important woman. She had become a woman who received kisses but did not need to kiss back. She had gone beyond ingratiating herself to anyone but the King himself. Instead of all the things she might have done, she did nothing. In so doing, it became clear that if the King was unconsciously conspiring to have himself removed from the throne, he had picked the perfect co-conspirator.

But what she may not have realized was that she had become perilously isolated. With the exception of the King, she had no advisers who had her interests at heart. Those who understood the issues and were thumping for the King—Beaverbrook, Harmsworth, Winston Churchill—had the King's and the country's interests in mind, not hers. Such friends and supporters as she had in the world of high society were more concerned with their own social fortunes than with hers. In the end, she had only the King for guidance, and he would prove to be an untrustworthy guide.

Wallis had figured in one important event that week, albeit somewhat passively, when another newspaper publisher entered the arena with an offer to help the plighted pair. With Beaverbrook out of the country, Esmond Harmsworth of the *Daily Mail* and *Evening News* group may have felt himself

---

*On June 30 of that year, Margaret Mitchell's *Gone with the Wind* had been published. Britons might have looked to that novel for clues to Wallis's character.

entitled to act as Beaverbrook's stand-in; after all, the two rival newspaper chains had agreed to ally themselves behind the King's cause. On November 19,* Harmsworth took Wallis to lunch at Claridge's, and asked her if she had given any thought to a morganatic marriage. There is evidence that Harmsworth did not give great weight to the notion. Someone in Lord Rothermere's office had mentioned it to His Lordship, who had found it an interesting suggestion, and Rothermere had passed it along to his son. In a morganatic marriage, Harmsworth explained, the King's wife would accept a rank and title lower than Queen. Also, if there were children of the union, they would not stand in line to inherit the throne. The idea of morganatic marriage was not popular in England for reasons that were mostly snobbish. They were fairly commonplace among the minor royal houses of Europe, the families whom the British Royal Family sneeringly called "bicycle royalty." In Britain, which did not consider itself in the same league with such countries as Portugal, Rumania or Yugoslavia, a morganatic marriage was considered *déclassé*. At first, according to her account, Wallis found the idea "astonishing," and the Duke recalls that she called the notion "strange and almost inhuman." But she seems quickly to have warmed to it as a workable compromise. When she relayed Harmsworth's suggestion to him, so did the King.

When Max Beaverbrook set foot on English soil again the following week, and immediately presented himself to the King, he was aghast to learn of what had transpired in his absence. The King had threatened to abdicate, and had made his threat to none other than the Prime Minister. Harmsworth had not only planted the idea of morganatic marriage in Wallis's head, but now the King was enthusiastically committed to the notion. And Harmsworth had gone one step farther, and had already presented *that* suggestion to Baldwin. Clearly, Beaverbrook resented Harmsworth's interference and the split it

*There is some question about this date. Wallis had said it was the nineteenth, while the King, in his memoirs, says it was the twenty-first. Wallis is probably correct. If it was the nineteenth, the King was away on his tour of Wales. If it was the twenty-first, a Saturday, he had returned and would probably have joined the luncheon group. Also, most weekends Wallis spent with the King at Fort Belvedere.

represented in what Beaverbrook had wanted to be a united front among the press lords. Also, he pointed out to the King, morganatic marriages were not only unpopular, they were illegal—or, at least, there was no provision for them under British law. To accomplish a morganatic marriage, special legislation would have to be enacted, and Beaverbrook was certain that Parliament in its present mood would not cooperate with such a law.

The King, he insisted, must revise his thinking. And, fortunately, Beaverbrook had come up with an alternate plan, one he had been devising while pondering the question during his days on shipboard. The first piece of business to get out of the way, he said, was to withdraw the morganatic proposal from the Cabinet immediately. Then, though the King kept muttering, "No marriage, no Coronation," Beaverbrook stressed again that the Coronation must take precedence, should proceed on schedule, with Wallis remaining quietly in the background. Then, after a suitable period during which the dust would be allowed to settle, the marriage question might be broached again. Beaverbrook had uncovered an interesting technicality. When the King is in Scotland—at, say, his castle at Balmoral—he is a member of the Church of Scotland. The Church of Scotland regarded marriage as a contract, not a sacrament, and had no strictures against the marriage of divorced persons. Suppose the King were to marry Wallis at Balmoral? This, of course, might have repercussions in Parliament, splitting the House along religious lines, the English Anglicans versus the Scottish Presbyterians. But there were many Anglicans in Parliament who did not accept their Church's narrow restrictions on marriage, who subscribed to a more liberal view, and who would side with the King. In the end, Beaverbrook felt, any objections the Church might have could be successfully dealt with.

It was also possible that Baldwin and the Cabinet might then propose a morganatic marriage, which would be easier for them to accept. The King could then consider this, and accept, thereby putting him in a position of granting a favor, rather than asking for one. Instead of playing into the Cabinet's hands as he was now doing—and putting his head, as Beaverbrook put it, "on the executioner's block"—the Cabinet would be playing into his. Meanwhile, both the Beaverbrook and Rothermere newspapers would continue to thump steadily in support of the King. The King closed the meeting saying that he agreed with Beaverbrook's recommendations. Still, when Beaverbrook left the Fort that afternoon he was uneasy.

He went next to Walter Monckton, and told him what had transpired. Monckton enthusiastically endorsed the Beaverbrook plan. Then, though it was growing late, Beaverbrook called on Sir Samuel Hoare, the First Lord of the Admiralty. He asked Hoare to be the King's advocate within the cabinet— not necessarily to endorse the King's marital plans, but merely to be a man who could fairly and calmly put across the King's point of view. The meeting with Hoare was less satisfactory. Hoare not only opposed morganatic marriage; he opposed any marriage at all and preferred Abdication. Still, he did agree to talk to his friends in the Cabinet and to let Beaverbrook know the outcome of his discussions in the morning.

What Beaverbrook had not yet realized was that, in his absence, Baldwin's Cabinet ministers had been becoming increasingly alarmed about the King's ability to carry out his royal duties. He was becoming a security risk. Reports had floated back to the Cabinet of sensitive and highly secret documents lying about the King's desk at the Fort, while an international array of party guests flocked to the house. There were even dark mutterings that Wallis might be some sort of German spy.

It was nearly midnight when Lord Beaverbrook got home to his Stornoway House in London, and it had been a long and tiring day. At two o'clock in the morning, Beaverbrook was awakened by the ringing of the telephone beside his bed. It was the King. Mrs. Simpson, the King said, wanted a morganatic marriage; that was all there was to it. Once more, Beaverbrook was appalled at the King's indiscretion in using the telephone for such urgent and confidential matters. Though he tried to hedge his answers and to suggest that both the King's and Beaverbrook's lines might well be tapped—there was already evidence of this—the King talked on and on. It was as though he had heard nothing that Beaverbrook had told him earlier in the day. In the end, the King agreed—again—to go along with Beaverbrook, but added that a morganatic marriage was what Wallis definitely "preferred."

Beaverbrook hung up the receiver quite certain that, whatever the King said to the contrary, he would not withdraw the morganatic marriage proposal from the Cabinet, and that the fat would remain in the fire. He was right; the King did not. True to form, Wallis was letting her man do all the heavy work. But her preference had become his command.

Admirers of the late Max Beaverbrook, who died in 1964, have often commented that he was a perfect "foul-weather friend." This is an apt description of him. Foul weather was the climate that he most enjoyed. To be sure, his advice to the King was sound. And it is ironic that the fatal counterproposal—morganatic marriage—should have come from a rival newspaperman. It permanently tipped the scales. Up to that point, those in the government who opposed the marriage had been merely in the position of begging the King, as a favor to the country, not to proceed with it. Now he was asking the government the favor—to propose a distasteful piece of legislation that would never pass. The balance of power had shifted, and the game was all but over. The King no longer had the choice of renouncing either Wallis or the throne. Even if he renounced Wallis at that point, as Beaverbrook wrote, "it would become publicly known that the King had been refused permission by the British Cabinet to marry the woman of his choice and it would be morally impossible for him to remain on the throne, a discredited man who had abandoned his intended wife."

But Beaverbrook remained in the fight, knowing that the weather would get fouler before it cleared again.

13

Storm . . . and Flight

ON Wednesday, November 25, there was disastrous news. Malcolm MacDonald, Secretary of State for the Dominions, had advised Mr. Baldwin that any legislation providing for a morganatic marriage would require corresponding measures in certain of the Dominions. Whether Mr. MacDonald was correct in this opinion is unclear; after all, there was no real precedent for anything that was going on, but MacDonald felt that the Dominions must be consulted on the subject and their opinions weighed. The Dominions had long exerted a strong, subtle, almost mysterious influence on the thought of official England. What would they think, how would they react, those little-understood people off in the far-flung reaches of the Empire? The Dominions represented nothing but question marks, but Baldwin was not optimistic. There had already been strongly negative reports from Canada, where readers had had full access to American newspapers and magazines. Nonetheless, Baldwin quickly informed the King of Mr. MacDonald's opinion, and asked him whether the views of the Dominions' prime ministers should be sought. The King replied "Yes," and thereby helped further to seal his fate.

Once more, Max Beaverbrook was horrified. The King, he pointed out, "was under no compulsion to let Baldwin put the question [to the Dominions] for him," and also had the right, under the statute of Westminster, "of sending out his own question, framed in his own terms, in the manner most favourable to himself," which might gain more sympathetic responses. Beaverbrook hurried to the palace to explain all this, but it was too late. Telegrams to some seventy-five of the Dominions' prime ministers had already gone out.

Beaverbrook would always claim that Baldwin's telegrams had been "cunningly framed," and with "loaded dice" against the King—that the question asked had been a blunt, "Do you recommend the King's marriage to a woman with two husbands living, or do you recommend Abdication?" Thus expressed, the overwhelming response would surely favor Abdication. But there is no evidence that Baldwin's queries were not entirely fair. In each of his wires, which went out on November 27, Baldwin outlined his unsuccessful interviews with the King, the King's proposal for a law that would enable him to marry morganatically, the King's threat to refuse Coronation if he could not marry, and finally that Abdication had been considered in favor of the King's younger brother, the Duke of York. Of course the King would have been within his rights to ask to see the text of the telegrams before they were sent out. But he did not.

A few days later, the King asked Baldwin what the responses from the Dominions had been. Baldwin answered that they were not all in yet, but that they were running heavily negative to the marriage proposal, Baldwin mentioned a particularly hostile letter from Mr. Lyons, the Prime Minister of Australia, and he showed Mr. Lyons's reply to the King. It was the only one that Baldwin showed him, but then it was the only one the King had asked to see. The King did not see, among others, the reply from Mr. Savage, the New Zealand Prime Minister who, though a Roman Catholic, had expressed no opposition to a morganatic marriage. Nor did the King see any other of the favorable, or merely noncommittal, replies that eventually came in. The Dominions were far from unanimously opposed. But the King, believing Beaverbrook's "loaded dice" theory, seems to have felt that he had fallen victim to yet another round of bad luck. With despair, now, Beaverbrook watched the King enter upon "a policy of total drift which carried him inevitably to disaster."

Events were now moving very fast. On Sunday, November 29, Beaverbrook and Sir Samuel Hoare had dinner at Stornoway House, and it was a far from cheerful gathering. Hoare warned Beaverbrook that the Cabinet had scheduled a meeting for Wednesday morning to decide finally on the King's request for morganatic-marriage legislation. The King's request would almost certainly be denied, and the clash between the King and the government would then be head on. At that point, what Marcel Hellman had warned Adela St. Johns must not happen would have happened. The Crown would have been brought into controversy. The next step would have to be Abdication.

On Monday, the thirtieth, Beaverbrook went to the King again with a last-ditch proposal. He begged the King to send word to Baldwin that he wished to withdraw the whole question of marriage, morganatic or not, for the time being. Let some time go by, Beaverbrook begged, during which his own and the Rothermere papers could launch their public opinion campaigns. After all, Beaverbrook argued, Wallis's decree did not become final for five more months. Why was the King in such an insane hurry? In five months' time, with luck, the Baldwin government might fall anyway, and the enemy would be out of the way. The meeting was long and, throughout, the King kept insisting that he was going to marry Wallis come what may. "Mrs. Simpson will not be abandoned," he kept repeating. But, in the end, he agreed to instruct Walter Monckton to tell Baldwin that he wanted no further advice on marriage at the moment. That evening, Monckton telephoned Beaverbrook to say that he had received the King's instructions, and would be meeting with Baldwin in the morning to withdraw the King's request for advice on his marriage. Beaverbrook heaved a temporary sigh of relief.

The next morning, however—Tuesday, December 1— Monckton telephoned Beaverbrook again and told him of his interview with Baldwin. It had not gone well. In Beaverbrook's words: "When Monckton delivered his message Baldwin asked if this represented any change of attitude by the King—in other words, did it mean that the marriage was to be abandoned?" Monckton could not lie to his Prime Minister but, in his lawyerly way, he did his best to be evasive. He answered that he had been given no instructions on the matter. This was not answer enough for Baldwin, who merely waved him out of the room. Beaverbrook and Monckton agreed that little had been accomplished.

That same day would be the last day the press would keep silent on the subject of the King's romance with Wallis Simpson. In the north of England, the Reverend Dr. Blunt, the Bishop of Bradford, was addressing his diocesan conference and, in the course of his remarks, he asked his audience to pray for the King who, with his great responsibilities, had so much need for God's grace. But, he added, the King at the moment seemed to have a *special* need. Dr. Blunt went on, in an oblique way, to deplore the King's inattention to religious matters, and said, "Some of us wish that he gave more positive signs" of his need for grace. At the time, it was assumed that the Archbishop of Canterbury was behind, or had at least inspired, Dr. Blunt's remarks. Though both Blunt and the Archbishop denied this, it was true that the Archbishop had summoned all the Anglican bishops to London just before Blunt's speech, and that one of the topics under discussion was "the King's matter."

The next morning, Wednesday, December 2, the *Yorkshire Post* and other northern newspapers printed the comments of Dr. Blunt—aptly named, the wits pointed out—and commented editorially on them to a readership which, for the most part, wondered what Blunt was talking about. But the lid on the press was off. Immediately, Beaverbrook telephoned the King and begged him to release the press restrictions he had placed upon him, and to allow his papers to present the situation—and Wallis—in as favorable a light as possible. The king refused. And so, on the following morning, every newspaper in England except Beaverbrook's carried banner headlines that screamed GRAVE CONSTITUTIONAL CRISIS! and page after page of stories about, and pictures of, Mrs. Wallis Simpson.

There were—and still are—roughly four distinct classes of British society. At the top stood the members of the Royal Family, surrounded by members of the Court and the upper aristocracy, proud old landed families such as the Cecils and the Howards. Into this relatively small circle were permitted a few others—the country's great industrialists, bankers, and solicitors, upon whom the aristocracy depended to guard their wealth and position. It was an upper echelon based on inherited titles and ancient wealth, in which lives were conducted with almost Victorian probity, formality and ritual between sprawling country estates and decorous London mansions.

Just below this topmost stratum and yet, socially, completely removed from it, was another small group which in the 1930's was called Café Society. These were the "bright young things" of Evelyn Waugh's early novels, whose counterparts in America were John Held's flappers. It was a gay and rich and party-going group, which dined out in restaurants and danced all night in nightclubs. The women daringly smoked cigarettes and drank gin—the poor man's drink—and indulged in mild profanity. In England, Café Society's only base was London, and it included a certain number of titled folk, but few of higher rank than baron or viscount. Café Society opened its circle also to include visiting moneyed Americans and other foreigners, as well as to celebrities in the theater, one or two popular writers, and the fashionable interior decorators of the moment. Also, because its doings were usually more newsworthy than those of the staid aristocracy—and because it thrived on being reported in the gossip columns—Café Society included certain people from the press. Though the King had not been born to this class, it was the one whose company he—as well as Wallis—clearly preferred.

Below this social level were arrayed the members of Britain's large and working middle class, almost none of whom had had the opportunity to curtsy to a duchess or dine in the same restaurant with a famous stage star. And, below this, were the masses of the British working and nonworking poor.

For months before December 3, 1936, the aristocracy had known of the King's infatuation with Wallis Simpson, and had been appalled by it. To this group, the very phrase "American divorcée" carried a double stigma. And of course the members of Café Society had also known, and had been titillated by it. Neither approving nor disapproving of the King's affair, they were merely curious about what might be the outcome. But as for the rest of England, thanks to the rigidly drawn class barriers, almost no one had heard of Wallis Simpson until that gray December morning.

In retrospect, the collaboration of the King and Beaverbrook to stifle the press on the subject of the King's goings-on was probably the most disastrous of a series of wrong decisions concerning the handling of the media. Bursting, as it did, all at once upon a general public that was grimly going about the business of preparing for a belt-tightening Depression Christmas, the crisis seemed much more dire and drastic than it really was. If, instead, the British public had been permitted to read the gathering details of their King's romance throughout the preceding year, they would doubtless have read of his intention to marry the American woman with a collective shrug, and gone on to the crossword puzzle. As it was, the first public reaction to the headlines was one of shock, confusion, dismay and disbelief. What did this mean for England, for the future, for their golden "Prince of Promise"? In the City, stockbrokers were flooded with orders to sell, and the stock market plummeted. Outside Number 10 Downing Street, pickets appeared with placards that declared SAVE OUR EDWARD VIII and OUT WITH THE MATCH BREAKER! Outside Wallis's house in Cumberland Terrace, pickets gathered with less sympathetic messages: DOWN WITH THE WHORE! WALLY—GIVE US BACK OUR KING! OUT WITH THE AMERICAN GARBAGE! Bricks and stones were hurled through her windows, even though she was not there.

By nightfall, the pros and cons of the King's situation were the only topic of conversation in every pub in England. The public seemed almost violently divided, and the arguments led to insults and fist fights. Suddenly, England was an armed camp. Because Wallis was an American, and the English had been avidly reading reports about such American enterprises as Murder, Incorporated, there were some intemperate Englishmen who suggested that Wallis should be "bumped off" or "taken for a ride." Others, just as intemperate, defended her, and the King's right to marry whomever he chose.

The lady herself, meanwhile, had received that morning's newspapers on her breakfast tray in her bedroom at the King's redoubt at Fort Belvedere. It was her first hint, she later said, of the gravity of the situation. One must believe her. Her view of England and the English was a very narrow one. So, one suspects, was the King's.

When Wallis joined her intended husband that Thursday morning in the drawing room, he too was reading the papers. Hastily, he tried to hide them from her, but she told him not to bother. She had already seen them, thanks to the efficiency of the Fort's servants. It was a habit she would never lose—reading everything that was written about her, the favorable and the damning. Many people who achieve sudden fame quickly learn the wisdom of ignoring their press, but Wallis could not be so cynical. The press obsessed her. Even though her friends warned her not to be, she was just as obsessive about the mail she received—vast bundles of it would arrive throughout the ensuing months—reading every letter, the crank letters, the hate letters, the letters asking for money and other souvenirs, along with the letters of sympathy and support. The letters often frightened her. Frequently they depressed her. Still, she insisted on reading them all.

Now she insisted that Alex Hardinge had been right all along; she should leave England immediately, and stay away until the storm blew over. The newspapers had been full of violent talk, of threats on Wallis's life, of possible bombings, of the brickbats hurled at her house in London. The woman who William Randolph Hearst had dreamed would one day cement a great bond between the United States and Britain was having just the opposite effect: never had anti-American sentiments in England run stronger. The King agreed. She must be taken out of England, not only for her personal safety but to shield her from further "publicity." In fact, he had already begun making the arrangements; it was what he enjoyed doing most, planning Byzantine cloak-and-dagger escape schemes. In retrospect, the decision that Wallis should leave England at once seems an odd one. Where in the world could she be better protected from the press and potential wrongdoers than the King's own Fort, which was heavily guarded around the clock? Still, the decision that she must flee was made.

Wallis placed a hurried telephone call to Cannes, where her friends Katherine and Herman Rogers were living in a spacious villa called Lou Viei. Yes, the Rogerses agreed, she could come to Cannes and stay with them. The King, meanwhile, telephoned his old friend and lord-in-waiting Perry Brownlow, and asked Brownlow to accompany Wallis to France. Because she was terrified of flying, a surface route was planned. Brownlow and Wallis were to depart that night under cover of darkness, driven by Field, Brownlow's chauffeur. In the meantime, the King's chauffeur, George Ladbrook, would drive Wallis's Buick to Newhaven, where the car would be put aboard the night ferry to Dieppe, across the Channel. The reason for the double-chauffeur arrangement was that the Buick might be recognized, but if it was seen without a passenger no suspicions would be aroused. On the ferry, Ladbrook, Brownlow and

Wallis would rendezvous. The King also assigned the group a bodyguard, one Inspector Evans from Scotland Yard, who would continue on with them to Cannes. A maid was dispatched to London to collect a few personal items of Wallis's from the Cumberland Terrace house. Wallis would leave Fort Belvedere heavily veiled. False names would be used. Brownlow and Wallis would travel to France as "Mr. and Mrs. Harris." While Wallis frantically packed, the King marched around the Fort issuing orders. Simultaneously, he was trying to prepare a radio address that he hoped Stanley Baldwin would permit him to deliver to the nation, explaining his situation and asking for support. As soon as Wallis was safely off, the King planned to return to London.

When nightfall came and everything was in readiness, with Brownlow waiting with his car and driver and Inspector Evans, Wallis's bags were carried out and there was a passionate and tearful farewell between the King and the veiled lady in the great arched doorway of Fort Belvedere. Wallis was sure, she said, that she and the King would never meet again. But his words to her, as she remembered them, were, "You must wait for me no matter how long it takes. I shall never give you up." Wallis had, in the meantime, executed a new will, leaving almost everything to Aunt Bessie, and naming the King as an executor. Then she was off, down the dark and winding roads to Newhaven. It would be almost three years before Wallis would set foot in England again.

Wallis and Brownlow rode in silence for a while. Then Brownlow said he had a suggestion for her. He asked the chauffeur to pull over to the side of the road for a moment, and speaking in whispers so that Inspector Evans and the chauffeur could not hear them from the front seat, he outlined a plan of his own. Instead of going to France, why didn't Wallis go to the Brownlow estate, Belton, in Lincolnshire? Here she would be remote from London, and could be guarded and protected much more securely than at a popular winter resort on the Riviera. She would still be in England, and that would be a comfort to the King. Brownlow was certain that, with Wallis out of the country, the King would grow even more distraught and irrational, more apt to make rash and politically suicidal decisions. The last possible chance of keeping the King on the throne might depend on his knowing that he was within proximity of her.

But, Wallis reminded Brownlow, they both knew perfectly well how angry the King became when he was crossed. The King had made and approved these plans. He would be furious if they were changed without his knowing it. Brownlow agreed, but said that he was willing to stake his friendship with the King against this possibility. He was certain that he was right. "We do, don't we, both want the same thing for the King?" he asked her. Confused, Wallis did not seem to know the answer to this. "The King told me this morning," Brownlow said, "that if you leave he will not stay in England. He spoke of going to Switzerland. This means only one thing—abdication."

No, Wallis said finally, she could not disobey the King's orders, no matter what it meant. There could be no change in plan. She must do as she had been told and go to France. Brownlow sighed and, through the speaking tube, ordered the chauffeur to drive on. And so the car continued on its night journey to the coast.

At this point, of course, Wallis probably did not want the same thing that Brownlow wanted—which was for the King to remain on the throne at all costs. She wanted him to remain on the throne, but she also wanted to marry him, and it was now quite clear to her that she could not have both things. Abdication was a huge, irreversible step. Would he really take it, just for her? How could she be sure? She knew his mercurial nature. How can any woman be sure how much a man will sacrifice for her sake until the sacrifice is made? By going away she may have felt she could force the issue.

Or there may have been another reason. In *The Windsor Story,* Bryan and Murphy speculate that Wallis may have been more than a little in love with the tall, handsome—and of course wealthy—Herman Rogers, and that more than friendship may have developed between the two during her long sojourn in China. It was certainly true that Rogers was very fond of her. If she really believed, when she left the Fort that night, that she would never see the King again, did she choose the villa in Cannes because she saw in Rogers not only a sanctuary but also another possibility? Was he the next man on her list? If this sort of thing was on her mind—and there is no evidence that it was—we would have to take a harsher view of her: that she was indeed the schemer, the home wrecker, the "scalp hunter" that certain acquaintances claimed she was. Or the woman who, as she tells us Aunt Bessie said of her, "always had a plan."

All the way to Newhaven, meanwhile, Perry Brownlow was working on quite a different rationale. Something had to be done, he insisted, to make the King give up—or at least postpone indefinitely—the idea of marriage, and stay on the throne. Somehow, he must be persuaded. If Wallis could not, or would not, do it, then someone else must be found. Wallis suggested Lord Derby, an old friend of the King's father and a man whom the King admired. Possibly the King would listen to Derby, and she promised to telephone him from the pier at Newhaven. But, when they arrived at Newhaven, Wallis decided that there was no time to telephone Derby. So, though it is doubtful whether her call would have done any good, another opportunity was lost. Or avoided.

Ladbrook, the chauffeur, was waiting with Wallis's Buick when "Mr. and Mrs. Harris" boarded the Channel steamer. This, however, was the only detail of the King's elaborate plan for Wallis's flight to France that went according to the blueprint. From that point on, nothing went right. When the ferry docked at Dieppe, it was discovered that the registration papers for the car were still in Wallis's name. The King had forgotten about passports, perhaps because the King of England never travels with one, and while she was trying in her limited French to explain to the French customs officials that she was Mrs. Harris, a look at her passport revealed that she was Mrs. Simpson. To clear the car through customs, telephone calls had to be placed to Paris and, around the confused scene, a little crowd quickly gathered. As it pushed and shoved, the word went out, *"Voilà la dame!"*—the woman the French had been reading about in all their newspapers. Within minutes, the news had been flashed to every editorial desk in the republic: Mrs. Simpson was in France. The King's hope of having Wallis leave England "to avoid publicity" was permanently dashed. The journey, in fact, would create more publicity than anything that had happened thus far.

When the big, expensive, and enormously conspicuous American automobile was finally cleared to set off into the streets of Dieppe, it was still night, but the "hounds of the press," as Wallis put it, were now in full pursuit. Fortunately, Perry Brownlow had thought to bring a map. The distance from Dieppe to Cannes is about 650 miles—too long, Perry decided, to be undertaken in a straight run. Normally, in those days, the route to take would have been to Paris, then southward through Lyon. But now that they had been recognized, Brownlow decided upon a more circuitous route, avoiding Paris, to throw the press off the scent. He also suggested breaking the trip for a few hours' rest and continuing the next morning— a plan which, with luck, would bring them to Cannes by midnight of the following day. It was two in the morning by the time they reached Rouen, about thirty-five miles south of Dieppe, and Perry suggested that they stop there for the night, at the Hôtel de la Poste. The sleepy room clerk did not recognize them when they registered, nor did he ask to see their passports, and the lobby seemed deserted. All seemed well. Brownlow said good night to Wallis and promised to awaken her for an early start "before the first light." Wallis lay down on her bed fully clothed, and went immediately to sleep.

It was full daylight, however, when Brownlow banged on Wallis's door in the morning. He had overslept. They must be off at once. There was no time for Wallis to bathe or change, barely time for her to gobble the roll and sip the cup of tea that Brownlow had sent up to her. When Wallis appeared in the lobby, looking rumpled, a large crowd was waiting. Outside, an even bigger crowd had gathered around the American limousine with the British license plates. As Brownlow and Wallis made their way into the car, a blond girl stepped in front of the automobile. When Inspector Evans of Scotland Yard asked the girl to move aside, she said something to him in French and aimed a camera at Wallis. Evans struck the girl, and knocked the camera out of her hands. She screamed, and there were angry shouts from the crowd. The little party of four was not in good spirits when it finally started off. There is evidence, too, that a certain amount of friction had developed between Wallis and Inspector Evans. Several months later, *Time* magazine elected Evans as "the Englishman who most dislikes Mrs. Simpson," saying that throughout the trip, she "kept telling the detective he was a stupid Scotland Yard flatfoot, who had not been smart enough to enable her to give reporters the slip."

Because of their late start and the zigzag route Brownlow had chosen, it was lunchtime when they reached Evreux, some twenty-five miles farther south. Here they decided to stop to eat at the Hôtellerie du Grand Cerf, where Wallis wanted to telephone the King. No one in the restaurant appeared to recognize her, but the only telephone was a public one in the bar. When Wallis finally got through to Buckingham Palace the connection was so bad that neither party could understand the other. Wallis, shouting, tried to explain why they were in Evreux, which had not been on the originally planned route, and the King, shouting back, tried to explain something to Wallis that she could not make out. It was all made more complicated and incomprehensible by the ridiculous code the King had worked out for telephone calls, since he was certain that they would be monitored on both sides of the Channel. According to the code, Beaverbrook was "Tornado"; Baldwin was "Crutch"; Churchill was "W.S.C."; the King was "Mr. James," after St. James's Palace; and Wallis was "W. M. Janet." Wallis had written out the code words on little slips of paper which she spread out in front of her as she telephoned. Wallis and her entourage were some five miles out of Evreux before she realized that she had left the slips of paper at the bar.*

What the King had been trying to tell her on the telephone was that the press had correctly guessed her destination, and that reporters from all over Europe were gathering outside the Villa Lou Viei to be there when she arrived. Also, at some point outside of Evreux, Ladbrook had taken a wrong turn, and the group had driven a number of miles before they realized that they were no longer heading south, but were driving north-westward toward Deauville, or roughly in the direction of Dieppe, from which they had originally started. Now poor Ladbrook had to bear the brunt of everyone's frayed nerves and short tempers.

As a result, it was nearly dusk when Wallis and her party reached Orléans. They had driven for hours, and only managed to land seventy miles south of Paris. In Orléans, a great deal of time was spent searching for a telephone. When one was finally found, Wallis was unable to get through to Buckingham Palace and got only screeching, echoing noises from the other end of the connection. It had started to snow and sleet, and

---

*Where they were discovered by the hotelier who, sensing their importance, kept them to himself. Several years later, Sir Harold Nicolson, passing through Evreux, happened to stop at the same hotel. Knowing that Nicolson knew Wallis, the hotelier insisted on giving the notes to Nicolson, who returned them to her.

had grown bitterly cold. Even the most luxurious Buick of 1936 was inadequately heated. In the back of the car, Brownlow huddled in an astrakhan-collared coat with fur lining and Wallis, in furs, wrapped herself in a heavy fur lap robe. The roads grew icy and treacherous, and Ladbrook had to slow the car to a snail's pace. It was after seven when the beleaguered party arrived in the little town of Blois, not far from Orléans, and decided to stop and spend the night. They checked in at the Hôtel de France et de Guise. Here, as a special courtesy, the *patron* gave Wallis the room in which the Duc de Guise, a sixteenth-century nobleman and a leader of political intrigue, had spent the last night before he was murdered.

Several years later, a novelist named Ann Bridge, who claimed to have psychic powers, spent the night in the same room, number nine, at the same hotel in Blois. In the room, she experienced a "sense of desperation," and had nightmarish dreams involving suicide. She was certain, she said, that Wallis had contemplated suicide that night. Whether or not Wallis did, she slept again in her clothes and, as the *patron* reported, did not even use the towels.

Downstairs in the lobby a crowd of reporters and photographers quickly gathered and, spread out on sofas and table tops and on the floor, were prepared to spend the night in order to catch their quarry leaving in the morning. To elude them, Brownlow told Wallis that they would leave at three in the morning. This time, he did not oversleep, but when the little party gathered in the dark outside the hotel they discovered that one of the reporters had foresightedly parked and locked his car directly in front of the Buick, blocking it from the exit. Finally, however, with some persistent maneuvering, Ladbrook succeeded in getting the reporter's car pushed out of the way, and the group managed their getaway undetected.

On the cold and icy road to Lyon, the car skidded, and Brownlow was jolted to one side of the vehicle. There was a sound of breaking glass, and immediately the back seat filled with the unmistakable smell of Scotch whisky. A supportive flask that Brownlow had kept in the pocket of his fur-lined coat had broken. To get rid of the fumes, Wallis insisted that the car windows be opened. Now the drive was even chillier, and for Brownlow, damper, and without his whisky he grew irritable. At this point, it is hard to believe that anyone in the car was on speaking terms with anyone else.

Outside Lyon, Ladbrook got lost again. More time was spent looking for the right road—for fear of recognition, no one dared stop and ask directions—and more recriminations were heaped on Ladbrook who, by now, must have wondered why he had ever considered entering the service of the King of England. Then, when they finally reached the city of Lyon— no way had been found of avoiding it—the big Buick was instantly recognized. When the car was forced to stop at intersections, crowds pressed against the windows, pushing and shoving for a glimpse of the famous passenger. By the time they left Lyon, they were being followed by a long caravan of automobiles bearing reporters, photographers, and others of the merely curious. At Vienne, the party stopped for lunch at the famous Restaurant de la Pyramide, where the proprietress, Mme. Point, quickly ushered them into a private room. The reporters flocked into the main dining room. Mme. Point had a suggestion for escaping from them. She would offer to prepare for the press some of her most renowned dishes—canny Frenchwoman that she was, Mme. Point was quick to grasp the value of the international publicity which this event would provide for her restaurant. Then, while the press were gorging themselves, Wallis—who would have time to gobble a quick omelet—could exit down a back staircase, through the kitchen, to where there was a table. Wallis could climb up on the table to a small window, through which she could climb and then drop a short distance to an alley below, where the Buick would collect her. Wallis agreed and, using this route and shredding her stockings in the process, she once more managed to leave the press behind her.

By eleven that night, the party was still three hours from Cannes. A journey that should have taken two days at the very most was now well into its third. In a town called Brignoles, Perry Brownlow tried to telephone the Rogerses to assure them that Wallis was still on her way, that they intended to press on now without stopping, and to prepare the Rogerses for a post-midnight arrival. This telephoning took more time, but Brownlow eventually got through to Herman Rogers, who warned him that hordes of reporters were already encamped around the villa, and that a cordon of French police had had to be summoned to keep the press from forcing their way through the gates.

Sure enough, when the Buick finally reached the entrance

to the Villa Lou Viei—it was two-thirty in the morning of December 6—the scene was one of siege, swarming with reporters, with floodlights, cameras, armed and shouting policemen and, it seemed, the entire population of Cannes. It took more time to convince the police that the Buick and its passenger were what the commotion was all about, but finally the car was permitted through the gates with Wallis crouched on the floor of the car, huddled under the fur lap robe. Then the gates clanged shut against the shouting and screaming crowd. The Buick pulled up to the door, stopped, and the disheveled house guest jumped out and ran up the front steps into the arms of her equally distracted hostess, Katherine Rogers, who could only say, "Wallis, *dear!*"

The bizarre journey across the face of France raises all sorts of perhaps unimportant but nonetheless interesting questions. Why, since Wallis refused to fly, hadn't it been arranged for her to travel by train, where she could have remained comfortably in a locked compartment with the shades drawn? Why, if the journey had to be made by automobile, couldn't an anonymous French car have been hired, along with a French driver who knew both the language and the countryside? Why, if it had to be the ostentatious Buick, hadn't hampers of food and drink been provided, so that the party would not have had to stop at public restaurants? One reason for the car, rather than the train, may have been Wallis's wish never to be far from a telephone, her last line of communication with the King. But most of all the unwieldy travel plans seem to have been undertaken because the King wanted them that way. Again, it was a case of *le roi le veut*.

14

The End of
Edward VIII

BACK in England, things were in an equally confused state. On December 2, the day before Wallis's departure, the King had told Beaverbrook that he intended "to retire into private life." But Beaverbrook could not be certain whether he was serious. Though the King now often talked of Abdication with his various advisers, he always coupled these remarks with a repeated insistence that he intended to remain on the throne. He had also mentioned to Beaverbrook his idea of going to Switzerland with his close friend and equerry Piers Legh. But this, he said, was merely for a rest and a holiday, and did not mean an act of Abdication. In fact, it was no longer clear to anyone what the King's intentions were. Meanwhile, he was scribbling on the speech to his subjects which he hoped to make. This was a notion that Wallis favored. It called to mind the enormously successful "fireside chats" that President Franklin Roosevelt was making in America at the time.

On December 3, while Wallis frantically packed for her flight to France, George Allen, the King's solicitor, arrived at

Stornoway House in the afternoon with a draft of the King's proposed speech. Beaverbrook read the draft, and then called Winston Churchill and read it to him over the telephone. Churchill, who was on his way out to deliver an important address at Albert Hall, said that he would come by Stornoway House after his meeting and discuss the speech. In his Albert Hall address, Churchill made a friendly reference to the King, and received a wild and prolonged burst of applause—an indication of strong public feeling in the King's favor. It had become clear to Churchill, Beaverbrook and others that the King had his most loyal supporters among the young. This fact had also become unpleasantly clear to the King's opposition. When the Archbishop of Canterbury had called a meeting of the leaders of the Free Churches Federation, the purpose of which was to present a united front against the King's marriage, a number of the younger clergymen had refused to go along with him.

When Churchill arrived at Stornoway House, he, Beaverbrook and George Allen went over the King's speech in careful detail. They made a few suggestions. The term "Britishers," for example, they felt should be changed to "British men and women." But Churchill was not sanguine about the King's chances of ever being able to deliver his speech. To do so, he would need Baldwin's permission, and Churchill suspected that Baldwin would regard the speech as an attempt to go over the heads of the executive branch of the government. The King's best strategy, Churchill decided, would be politely to telephone Baldwin and read him the speech. Under no circumstances should the King give Baldwin a copy, which would enable Baldwin to study it, consider it, discuss it with the Cabinet, and decide negatively. George Allen promised to convey these suggestions to His Majesty.

In his memoirs, the Duke of Windsor said that he was "uncertain" whether he had given Baldwin a copy of the speech or not. This seems odd, since it was such a crucial point. In any case, the lights burned late in Stornoway House on the night of Wallis's departure. Suddenly Beaverbrook's mansion seemed to be the center of everything. There was a great deal of coming and going, and the subject of all the meetings was how to persuade the King to renounce Wallis. Later, in his memoirs, the King described these gatherings of his friends and well-wishers as "The Conspiracy." But the "renunciation" that his friends wanted was not intended to be permanent. All that was needed was a period of respite, and calm. If only the King would make a statement saying, "I have no plans for marriage in the foreseeable future," or something equally vague, the world, the press, and his government would be able to turn their attention to other matters. "Give Us Time!" the newspaper headlines implored. But, like Napoleon, the King seemed to be saying, "Ask me for anything except time."

The following morning, a Friday, it turned out that Beaverbrook's and Churchill's efforts to edit and emend the King's speech had been time completely wasted. Somehow the speech had already made its way to Stanley Baldwin, and it could only have come from the King himself. Baldwin arrived at his Cabinet meeting with the speech in his briefcase and passed it around. After due deliberation, the Cabinet vetoed the whole idea for the reasons Churchill had anticipated.

Thus, with the King silenced, the day began gloomily for Beaverbrook and Company. But all at once there was a bright burst of hope. The *Catholic Times*, which had always been opposed to divorce, came out editorially in strong support of the King. Whether divorce was an issue or not, the *Times* declared, the King should not be made the pawn of the politicians. Even more encouraging—and shattering to Baldwin—was the editorial attitude of the *News Chronicle*, which came out stirringly in the King's behalf, and enthusiastically endorsed the idea of a morganatic marriage. The *News Chronicle* had been one paper that Baldwin had been certain would back him. Led by the *News Chronicle*, public opinion was now swinging heavily in the King's favor. As the day progressed, there was even more reason for rejoicing among the Beaverbrook faction. As long as Wallis had been closeted with the King at Fort Belvedere, there had been no way of approaching her. But now she had left for France in the company of Perry Brownlow. If anyone could successfully persuade her to announce her willingness to give up the King, even temporarily, it was Brownlow. A way to avert the crisis seemed suddenly at hand.

On Saturday, December 5, a public statement was issued from Wallis. It was not exactly the statement Beaverbrook wanted. It said simply, "I need calm and rest. I have no plans. The King is the only judge. While waiting for his decision, I am going to withdraw into silence and rest." That evening, Winston Churchill issued a more moving statement to the press. "I plead for time and patience," it began, and went on:

> There is no question of any conflict between the King and Parliament. Parliament has not been consulted in any way or allowed to express any opinion . . .
>
> This is not a case where differences have arisen between the Sovereign and his Ministers in any particular measure. These could certainly be resolved by the normal processes of Parliament . . .
>
> No Ministry has the authority to advise abdication of the Sovereign. Only the most serious parliamentary processes could even raise the issue in decisive form. The Cabinet has no right to prejudice such a question without having previously ascertained at the very least the will of Parliament . . .
>
> If an abdication were to be hastily extorted, the outrage so committed would cast its shadow forward across many chapters of the history of the British Empire.

It was one instance, however, when the famous Churchillian rhetoric should have been curbed. Churchill was saying that Parliament should decide the issue and he was wrong. With the best intentions in the world, he was advocating a course that would fly in the face of a great unwritten British tradition, the one Marcel Hellman had correctly explained to Adela St. Johns: the King can remain King only as long as the Crown is not drawn into public controversy. To ask Parliament to decide would be to do just that. The British humor magazine, *Punch,* published a cartoon in which Churchill was parodied as Winnie the Pooh stirring up a hornets' nest. It was worse than that. Without intending to, Churchill was administering the coup de grace. Once the King's problems were turned over to Parliament, the people's elected representatives, the King would have to abdicate. Abdication, furthermore, now seemed to be the course the King himself had chosen.

Though now, technically, it was really all over for Edward VIII, there was still to be a good deal more shouting and agonizing and faint glimmerings of hope. They would not matter. On the same Saturday morning as Churchill's statement, the King had summoned Walter Monckton and said to him, "I want you to go to London and tell the Prime Minister that when he comes to see me this afternoon, I shall formally tell him that I have decided to abdicate." Duly, Walter Monckton performed his sad duty.

Beaverbrook learned the news later that morning. Despondently he said to Churchill, "Our cock won't fight." In effect, it was all over. And at that very moment Wallis and the Buick were zigzagging across the map of France on a purposeless journey to nowhere.

Once in Cannes, Wallis was finding very little of the "calm and rest" she had come to the Rogerses' villa to obtain. Hundreds of reporters and photographers and French policemen milled outside the gates, and the crowd flowed over into the garden of the Michael Arlens' villa next door, trampling roses and flower beds. Photographers literally climbed into trees for better views of Wallis's bedroom windows, and when she made a brief appearance on a balcony, flashbulbs popped from behind every bush. When they tried to leave their house, the Rogerses were pursued by a clamoring horde of newspapermen. Telephone operators were bribed to intercept telephone conversations, and two special operators from the French Foreign Office in Paris were summoned to help handle, and protect, the telephone traffic to and from the villa. The Rogerses' servants were offered huge bribes for "inside" stories—bribes which, with Gallic alacrity, they eagerly accepted—providing the press with such lively copy as what Wallis had eaten for breakfast (a soft-boiled egg, tea, and a *croissant*), and who was sleeping where. (Herman Rogers had taken the bedroom on one side of Wallis's, and Inspector Evans flanked her on the other side; poor Ladbrook had been relegated to the servants' quarters.) On Sunday afternoon, December 6, her first day at Villa Lou Viei, Wallis suddenly fainted, and was ordered to bed.

Perry Brownlow, meanwhile, had been gently but urgently trying to persuade Wallis that an act of renunciation on someone's part now seemed the only way to keep the King on his throne. If he would not renounce her, then she must renounce him. Naturally, she was unwilling to do this, saying that it would "hurt" the King. Hurt feelings aside, Brownlow persisted, it must be done. Then he made a telling point. Renouncing the King, he reminded her, would be the only way she herself could come out of the situation with a shred of self-respect. Self-respect was something Wallis cared a good deal about, and so, reluctantly, on Monday morning, December 7, she agreed and began to prepare her new statement.

By noon she had completed it, but when she read it to Brownlow he was disappointed. He had wanted a firm, une-quivocal statement saying that Wallis had no intention, plan, or even thought of marrying the King. Instead, her statement was somewhat self-serving and unforthright:

> Mrs. Simpson throughout the last few weeks has in-variably wished to avoid any action or proposal which would hurt or damage His Majesty or the Throne.
>
> Today her attitude is unchanged, and she is willing, if such action would solve the problem, to withdraw forthwith from a situation that has been rendered both unhappy and untenable.

Brownlow begged her to change the word "willing" to "determined," and "if" to "because." But Wallis was adamant. This was as far as she would go. She would not commit herself to any action. She would merely offer.

That afternoon, she telephoned the King in London to read the statement to him. Once more, the connection was bad, but when she finally managed to read the statement to him, he sounded, as she had expected, hurt and angry. There was a long silence, during which she thought he might have hung up on her. Then she heard him say, "Go ahead, if you wish; it won't make any difference." At seven o'clock that evening, Brownlow delivered Wallis's statement to the press.

Though the statement was essentially noncommittal, the immediate reaction of the press was not to interpret it that way. The next morning, Tuesday the eighth, the headlines jubilantly announced: "MRS. SIMPSON RENOUNCES KING! CRISIS ENDED!"

But it had not even halfway ended. The next afternoon, the King telephoned Wallis to say that he had learned that Theodore Goddard, who had represented her in her divorce case, was on his way to Cannes to see her. What Goddard's mission could possibly be was a mystery to the King. But, he said, "I know that Baldwin is behind this," and he urged Wallis not to see Goddard when he showed up. Now confusion reigned at the Villa Lou Viei. What in the world did Mr. Goddard want? Was it possible that Wallis's lawyer and Stanley Baldwin were somehow in collusion? Lord Beaverbrook always thought so—there was no end to Baldwin's deviousness and treachery in Beaverbrook's mind—though it would have been downright unethical for Mr. Goddard to scheme against his own client. All day long, Wallis and her hosts waited for word of the alleged arrival of Mr. Goddard. Finally, at two-thirty Wednesday morning, when Wallis and the Rogerses were about to go to bed, a message was delivered to the villa signed by four British newsmen from the group outside. The note said, "Mr. Goddard, the well-known lawyer who acts for Mrs. Simpson, has arrived at Marseilles by special plane. He brought with him Dr. Kirkwood, the well-known gynecologist, and his anesthetist."

Confusion turned to consternation. The presence of a gynecologist would quickly be inferred to mean that Wallis was pregnant. An anesthetist implied that Wallis might be on the verge of giving birth to the King's unborn child. The whole comedy of errors was taking on the aspect of farce.

Angrily, Perry Brownlow marched out and confronted the mob of reporters. He denied that Goddard's visit had anything to do with the state of Mrs. Simpson's health and, to explain it, he resorted to a glib lie. Goddard, he told the press, merely wanted to discuss the disposition of the lease on Mrs. Simpson's London house. In a harried state, everyone went to bed.

In the morning, after breakfast, Mr. Goddard arrived in Cannes and telephoned the villa. Still angry, Perry Brownlow demanded to know what his business was with gynecologists and anesthetists. Goddard explained. The alleged "gynecologist" was his personal physician; Goddard had a heart condition, and his doctor had insisted on accompanying him on the flight—his first experience, in fact, with an airplane. The "anesthetist" was one of his law clerks. Goddard asked to see Mrs. Simpson on an important legal matter.

Though the King had asked her not to, Wallis—perhaps out of curiosity—agreed to see him. Goddard's mission, it turned out, was a delicate one. He had come to Cannes to recommend that Wallis drop her divorce action. There was a possibility that the decree absolute—normally granted six months after the decree nisi—might be challenged on the basis of collusion; this would create an even deeper scandal, and Goddard's stance was vaguely threatening. If she dropped her action, Goddard explained, any question of the King's marriage to her would dissolve into thin air. Furthermore, any reinstatement of the action in the future would be difficult, if not impossible, and "possibly somewhat untidy."

In her memoirs, Wallis wrote that she replied to Mr. Goddard, "I will do anything in my power to keep the King on the Throne." But instead of doing anything—particularly anything as drastic as what Goddard recommended—she stalled. She was suspicious. *Was* Baldwin behind this? Evasively, Mr. Goddard said that Baldwin would be "pleased" with such a development. It was true that Baldwin had summoned Goddard to Downing Street, and had somehow approved this mission. He had dispatched Goddard in a government airplane, and told him he could take along his doctor if he was worried about his health. What were Baldwin's motives in this? Baldwin had known for days of the King's decision to abdicate. Wallis suspected that Mr. Goddard was merely a little man trying to seize this opportunity to play a major role in British history.

In any case, Wallis told Goddard that she could do nothing about her divorce without consulting the King. It took most of the morning to get through to London, while Goddard waited. When she finally reached the King, it was noon, and when she told him what Goddard had proposed he was silent for a moment, and then said he would let her talk to George Allen, who had something important to tell her. Allen came on the telephone and, in his crisp lawyer's way, told her that there was nothing to be gained from withdrawing her suit. The King had decided to abdicate immediately. In fact, he was already in the process of doing so.

In her memoirs, Wallis wrote that this was the first she had known of the King's intention—on noon of Wednesday, December 9. Others had known it for nearly a week. He had managed to keep one of the most important figures in the matter completely in the dark, and then, instead of breaking the news to her himself, had given the task to his solicitor. How does one account for such callousness? Possibly, of course, he was simply frightened of what her reaction might be, certain that she would not approve. Or he may simply have been too ashamed of what he was doing to tell Wallis until it was too late for anything to be done about it. In abdicating, he was taking the weak and easy way. He had been unable to stand up to the bullies. He had refused to fight. In another telephone call later that day, he said to her, "The only conditions upon which I can stay here are if I renounce you for all time. And this of course I will not do." It was a sad attempt at a show of courage and strength of purpose, but it was not even the truth. No one had demanded that he renounce Wallis "for all time."

In *The Heart Has Its Reasons,* Wallis leaves the impression that she took the King's decision calmly, with resignation, without anger or contempt. But surely her emotions that day must have been in a very confused state—a mixture of bitterness and bewilderment that the man she considered the most powerful figure in England should have given up so easily. Where was the power now? It seemed to have fallen into her hands, for all that the King was doing now he was doing on her behalf. Somehow, it was going to be up to her to provide him with some sort of substitute for everything that he was giving up. It was a heavy duty he was handing her, along with the gift of his devotion. The future that day must have looked particularly frightening and uncertain. He was showing that he would do anything in the world to have her at his side. How many men would give up a life's calling just for a woman? If she ever had any doubts about it, she was now sure that she had him in the palm of her hand. But, she must have wondered, had she really wanted that?

Of the many stories printed about Wallis's reactions to the news that the King would indeed abdicate the throne for her, there was this one in the New York *Times:* "When the King telephoned to Cannes to tell the lady for whom he was giving up his throne that his decision had been taken and he would abdicate, she answered with her slightly drawling southern accent, 'But, David, can't you remain Emperor of India even if you are no longer King of England?'"

The *Times* went on to comment that the story seemed hardly credible, but printed it anyway.

Wallis, meanwhile, was also preoccupied with extricating herself from another muddle with the media, whom she and the King still seemed to think they could control. It all started several weeks before the British press finally broke its silence on the subject of the King's romance, and the saga of this extraordinary public-relations blunder is recounted in Bryan and Murphy's *The Windsor Story*. Mr. Newbold Noyes, the associate editor of the Washington *Evening Star*, was married to Lelia Gordon Barnett, who was Wallis's second cousin.

Noyes knew Wallis and liked her, and had become concerned about the many lurid stories that were appearing about her in the United States. It was his notion—rather like Hearst's earlier one with Adela Rogers St. Johns—to use his friendship and family connection to obtain a series of interviews with Wallis, and to write a series of articles about her that would reveal her in a favorable light—as a woman, in other words, fit to be Queen of England. He was certain that he could syndicate these exclusive stories, and that they would sell many newspapers. He cabled his suggestion to Wallis's Aunt Bessie, who relayed it to Wallis, who wired back her approval. Newbold Noyes set off for London.

He arrived on November 30, and the next evening he joined Wallis and the King for dinner at Fort Belvedere. He found the King in a mood that was nothing if not expansive. He chatted candidly about the morganatic marriage proposal, weighing its pros and cons. Later, Noyes would recall with some surprise that the subject of Abdication never came up, but he did not realize that this was a taboo topic in Wallis's presence. The King offered Noyes a special office in Buckingham Palace—a gesture completely without precedent—and the next morning Noyes repaired there, and began working on his articles.

That was December 2 and, of course, the next day Wallis departed on her flight to Cannes. It was clear that there would be no more interviews with either the King or Wallis, and that Abdication was probably no more than a matter of days away, and so Noyes was forced to use his journalistic inventiveness to stretch material from an evening's visit into a ten-article series of some fourteen thousand words. The stories, when they appeared, were almost abject in their flattery, and Wallis and the King were described in the most glowing terms. And yet, no sooner had the first of them hit the newsstands than there was trouble.

For one thing, no British monarch in history had ever given a personal interview to the press of the sort that Noyes was reporting. It infuriated the rest of the Fourth Estate—particularly those in Britain—that the singular honor of this sort of exclusive had been handed to, of all people, an American. The rest of the press responded by increasing the degree of venom aimed at Wallis. Then there was the problem of the European press, who were not only angered but disappointed in the bland-ness and sugar-sweet prettiness of the story Noyes had to tell. In the United States, the syndicates which picked up the articles were faithful to Noyes's copy, but in France, particularly, it was deemed necessary to spice it up a bit. In one French "translation," for example, the venue of the meeting between Wallis, Noyes and the King was shifted from the sitting room and dining room of the Fort to Wallis's bedroom. Though Noyes had written that the King, greeting Wallis, had bowed and kissed her hand, in the French version, the kiss was turned into a wild embrace. It was these hyperventilated versions of Noyes's prose that reached Wallis with her morning breakfast tray. She was furious.

She immediately shot off an angry denial, repudiating the articles "published under the signature of Mr. Newbold Noyes, styling himself as her cousin." Now it was Noyes's turn to be hurt and angry; Wallis's statements questioned both his journalistic credibility and professional honesty, and, needless to say, rival newspapermen were happy to make a point of this. Noyes now issued a statement of his own. He had never claimed to be her "cousin." He could document his visit to Fort Belvedere and prove that the King had supplied him with an office in Buckingham Palace, which he had used. He also cabled Wallis in Cannes, pointing out the wide discrepancies between what he had written and the French "translations." It did no good. As Bryan and Murphy wrote, "The truth could not overtake the lie. . . . Protestations of 'misunderstanding' met with accusations of 'betrayal.'" Wallis and the King had become so accustomed to what they saw as treachery that they found it everywhere they looked, and Newbold Noyes's name was added to the growing list of well-meaning friends who had come forward, offered to help, failed to satisfy, only to be permanently cast aside.

15

"Rat Week"

WALLIS and the King felt particularly betrayed by that great voice of the British Empire, *The Times* of London, which could be traditionally counted upon to be royalist and supportive of the Monarchy. Under the editorship of Geoffrey Dawson, however, *The Times* launched a full-scale psychological offensive against the King. It was as if, even though he was already as good as gone, *The Times* was determined to see him go down in ignominy. First, *The Times* let it be known in Fleet Street and in certain influential London clubs that it was preparing a story on "the real Mrs. Simpson." The story would tell the "truth" about her, would include photographs of her two former husbands, unflattering photographs of Wallis—including an absurd one of her taken as a teenager wearing a monocle—and a picture of her mother's former boardinghouse in Baltimore, which was by then in a run-down area. The King was aghast when he heard of the projected story, and sent Walter Monckton to find out about it. Monckton was merely assured that *The Times* did not plan to publish its story "in the next issue," leaving the distinct implication that it might do so any day after that. The King was thus kept in agonizing daily suspense, waiting for the dreaded story to appear.

On December 8, *The Times* published an attack on Wallis of a different variety. In reference to the morganatic marriage idea, the newspaper declared indignantly: "The Constitution is to be amended in order that she may carry in solitary prominence the brand of unfitness for the Queen's throne," and added that the King's late father had had his last days "clouded by anxiety for the future."'

The Times's voice was, as usual, sonorous and grave, and yet, at the same time, the King that week suddenly saw himself becoming the butt of ridicule and jokes. Christmas was at hand, and schoolchildren had begun to chant, "Hark, the herald angels sing, Mrs. Simpson stole our King!" George Bernard Shaw, at the height of his fame as a humorist, published a rollicking fictitious dialogue between "the King, the Constitution, and the lady," which was widely being chuckled over. A joke circulated that the King, who had been Admiral of the Fleet, had now settled on becoming "the third mate on an American tramp." Worst of all must have been the abrupt change in the attitudes of his old circle of friends, who now seemed to be decidely of the fair-weather variety. With amazing alacrity, the old group which had fawned over him and courted his attention disbanded and formed new alliances. The standbys—Sybil Colefax, Elsie Mendl, Emerald Cunard, Diana Cooper, along with the guests on the *Nahlin* cruise that had first put the throne in jeopardy, and all those who had been weekend regulars at Fort Belvedere—were suddenly no longer available, and were regrouping around the new Monarch-to-be. All at once the shy young Duke of York and his plump little Scottish Duchess found themselves the focus of attention in London society. Wallis, had she been there, might have been dismayed at how rapidly her Simpson Set was evaporating, and how her old chums and playmates were saying that they "never really liked her." It was very much like rats leaving a sinking ship, but this one was a Ship of State. People were saying that the King— already referred to in the past tense—had been "too obstinate," and others said that he was actually "insane." It was said that he was now "drunk all the time," though even Queen Mary had been able to concede one point in Wallis's favor, acknowledging that under Wallis's influence he drank much less.

Osbert Sitwell, disgusted with the sudden hypocrisy, wrote a poem called "Rat Week," in which he bitterly denounced the people who were now turning their backs on the King. He spoke derisively of Lady Colefax and Lady Mendl, and of dandyish John McMullen, the fashion plate, and of all Wallis's old friends who were now confessing that they "never really thought her *nice.*" The poem, which was about to be published, circulated through Mayfair and stirred up such a fuss that Sitwell withdrew it and suppressed it. It was never published.

On December 8, Emerald Cunard gave a great party at her house at 7 Grosvenor Square. It was to have been in the King's honor, and he himself had selected the date. Without him, of course, it went on anyway, as gay as ever. It was a brilliant gathering—the Duke and Duchess of Marlborough, the Duff Coopers, the Londonderrys, the Fitzgeralds, the Ribbentrops and a gaggle of other ambassadors and social potentates. At one point, the Duchess of Marlborough cornered Chips Channon and asked him if he did not think that all the while Wallis had been playing a double game. Channon did not know the answer, and was not even sure what the question meant. The Duchess went on to say, "We had her to stay at Blenheim; I liked her"—again in the past tense.

Later, when the music had started, the butler hurried to Channon and told him that he was wanted urgently on the telephone. It was the Duchess of Kent, who wanted to see Chips and Honor Channon right away at her house in Belgrave Square. The Channons departed through the cold night. At the Duchess's house, she told them that her husband had spent the last two days at Fort Belvedere secluded with his brother, using every argument and every means in his power to try to persuade the King to remain on the throne—but to no avail. The King had told Kent that he could not "'stick' being King, . . . could never tolerate the restrictions, the etiquette, the loneliness." In Channon's opinion, if this particular issue "had not arisen something else would have."

What the point was of summoning the Channons to the Kents' house was never clear to them.

Someone said that, in his infatuation with Wallis, the King was behaving like a man "bewitched."

December 9 was a day of waiting. The King's silence now was costing him supporters by the thousands everywhere. By six o'clock that evening it was learned that the Instrument of

Abdication was being drawn up. That night, two last-ditch friends who had not joined the scramble of the rats, Colin Buist and his wife, arrived at Kitty Brownlow's house, hysterical and weeping. They had a mad idea of rushing out to Fort Belvedere, and in effect storming it, in a final attempt to get the King to change his mind. But when they had telephoned Osbourne, his valet, they had been told that the King refused to see them or even come to the telephone.

On the ninth it was also learned that the previous evening, when the King had failed to show up at Emerald Cunard's party, he had been tossing a dinner party of his own—a stag affair, a sort of pre-Abdication celebration which seemed, to some, not quite in the best of taste. Still, it was a festive evening. The King's brothers, the Dukes of Kent and York, were both there, and Walter Monckton, and the King's friend Tommy Dugdale, and even Stanley Baldwin. Much brandy was consumed, and the two adversaries, Baldwin and the King, toasted each other in eternal friendship. After dinner, the King got out his bagpipes and played, and the men sang "Over the Sea to Skye," and other drinking songs. It was perhaps the only gathering in the empire that night where "Topic A" was not brought up.

After the departure of the weeping Buists, Kitty Brownlow telephoned her husband in Cannes. In despair, he told her that Wallis had spent hours with the King on the telephone—pleading, begging, cajoling, threatening, doing everything in her power to make him stay, to make him wait. But now the King would not even listen to her.

December 10 dawned coldly. At Fort Belvedere, the King quickly read through the Instrument of Abdication that had been drawn up for his signature. It was a simple statement:

> I, Edward the Eighth, of Great Britain, Ireland, and the British Dominions beyond the Seas, King, Emperor of India, do hereby declare My irrevocable determination to renounce the Throne for Myself and for My descendants, and My desire that effect should be given to this Instrument of Abdication immediately.
>
> In token whereof I have hereunto set My hand this tenth day of December, nineteen hundred and thirty six, in the presence of the witnesses whose signatures are subscribed.

Then he picked up a pen and signed it with a flourish, "Edward R.," letting the long tail of the "E" sweep under the other letters. It was witnessed by his three brothers, Albert, Henry, and George.

In Parliament, Stanley Baldwin rose and delivered a half-hour address. He appeared a little muddled, and his notes, which he seemed to have trouble organizing, were scattered about him as he spoke. He reiterated his many conversations with the King, praised the King in tribute after tribute, saying that throughout everything the King had behaved in a noble, upright, constitutional manner. He shifted the blame from himself to his Cabinet, and said that he himself had not really had time to consider the morganatic marriage proposal. (Commenting on Baldwin's speech in his diary, Chips Channon noted that, though the Cabinet and the Dominions had been opposed, Baldwin could have—if he had wanted to, and if he had been given time—surely brought them around to a different way of thinking. Now, of course, it was too late.) To many, Baldwin's speech was a final act of rattishness. Throughout it, Winston Churchill sat doubled up, his head in his hands. And, after it, as the chamber was clearing, the irrepressible Lady Astor called out to Chips Channon, "The people who have been licking Mrs. Simpson's boots ought to be shot!" Channon pretended not to hear her.

Only a few formalities remained. On December 11, at eleven in the morning, Parliament gave its assent to the Bill of Abdication. Lord Halifax made the motion, and then the Royal Commission was sent for, and the Lords Onslow and Denman filed solemnly out of the chamber, and returned in full robes and wigs. The Speaker was summoned and, followed by his Commons, he appeared at the bar. The clerk read the Royal Commission, and the Lords bowed and doffed their hats. The bill was read. It was one fifty-one in the afternoon, and the clerk bowed and uttered the words, *"Le roi le veut."* With these words, Edward, the beautiful boy Prince of Promise, became an ex-King.

That evening, the ex-King went on the radio to deliver his famous address, in which he said, "At long last I am able to say a few words of my own," and continued:

> You must believe me when I tell you that I have found
> it impossible to carry the heavy burden of responsibility and

to discharge my duties as King as *I* [the first-person pronoun was heavily stressed] would wish to do without the help and support of the woman I love.

And I want you to know that the decision I have made has been mine and mine alone. This was a thing I had to judge entirely for myself. The other person most concerned has tried up to the last to persuade me to take a different course. I have made this, the most serious decision of my life, upon a single thought of what would in the end be best for all. . . .

It was an eloquent, moving, and manly speech. At the time, it was assumed that Winston Churchill had written it. In his memoirs, the Duke of Windsor—who remained proud of the speech for the rest of his life—insisted that he himself had written it, and that Churchill had made only a few slight changes in the wording. Actually, the writing of the speech was a collaborative effort between the King, Churchill, and the writer Harold Nicolson.

Also questioned was how forcefully "the other person concerned" had tried to dissuade him from his course. And yet when Perry Brownlow returned to England he was able to produce a letter in his own handwriting, dictated by Wallis, authorizing her lawyers to withdraw the divorce proceedings at Ipswich, signed by Wallis and witnessed by both Brownlow and Mr. Goddard. It was too late, of course, but she had tried.

In Cannes, Wallis listened to the speech over the crackling French radio, lying on a sofa in the Villa Lou Viei, weeping silently—whether in triumph or defeat, or both, it was hard to say.

In London, the Edward Stanleys were having a small dinner party for a few of the King's remaining friends. At ten o'clock, the wireless was turned on, and they heard the words, "His Royal Highness, Prince Edward." They listened to the speech, then sat in silence. Chips Channon bowed his head in prayer and wept—tears of relief, no doubt, that the ordeal was over.

Then they played bridge.

"THE ROMANCE OF THE CENTURY"
THE STORY IN PHOTOS

Wallis in 1920. The eyebrows became a fashion statement.

United Press International

United Press International

TOP: Bessiewallis as an infant with her mother.
BOTTOM: Mrs. Earl Winfield Spencer, Jr., in 1918.

The young Prince of Wales flanked by his parents, Queen Mary and King George V, with his sister Mary, the Princess Royal, in 1922. *Behind stand, from left:* Sir Alan Lascelles, the Duke of Gloucester, the Duke of York.

The Bettmann Archive

Keystone Press

TOP: "The Magnificent Morgans": Gloria Morgan Vanderbilt, *left,* and her twin sister Thelma, Lady Furness.
BOTTOM: Freda Dudley Ward at her wedding.

The National Archives

United Press International

TOP: A skiing holiday at Kitzbühel. When this photograph was published in 1935, the woman was "unidentified."

BOTTOM: Ernest Simpson in the mid-1930's.

The National Archives

The Bettmann Archive

TOP: The Coronation parade of King Edward VIII, 1936.
BOTTOM: Attending the first Armistice Day ceremony of his short reign—Edward VIII and his mother.

The National Archives

The National Archives

TOP: Sympathizers outside Buckingham Palace, December 1936.

BOTTOM: Stanley Baldwin leaving 10 Downing Street during the Abdication crisis.

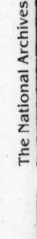
The National Archives

The National Archives

Keystone Press

TOP LEFT: Ever loyal: Walter Monckton.
TOP RIGHT: The King's champion: Lord Beaverbrook.
BOTTOM: Taking sides: Winston Churchill and Sir Samuel Hoare.

TOP: Reading his Abdication speech.

BOTTOM: A wedding photograph. Major Edward Dudley ("Fruity") Metcalfe watches in the background.

TOP: On their visit to Hitler's Germany, 1937.

BOTTOM: The swearing in as Governor of the Bahamas, 1940. The Duke perspired so much he could barely see to sign the register. His Duchess employs a fan.

TOP: At the Duchess of Windsor's Ball, New York, 1953, with Jimmy Donahue and Mrs. Lytle Hull.
BOTTOM: New Year's Eve, 1953, the year of the Coronation of Queen Elizabeth II. The Windsors in paper crowns.

In the garden of the house in the Bois de Boulogne,
with one of the many *petits chiens*.

Pictorial Parade

Pictorial Parade

Paris Match/Pictorial Parade

TOP: The Duke of Windsor's party at the Paris Lido.

MIDDLE: A soulful moment with columnist Suzy Knickerbocker (Aileen Mehle). The year was 1969, the hostess Liza Minnelli, and the evening's theme was "Love."

BOTTOM: The Duchess discovers the Twist at the Club Saint-Hilaire in Paris.

Central Press/Pictorial Parade

United Press International

TOP: "Reconciliation" at last: the Queen receives the
Windsors in 1967.
BOTTOM: The keeper of the flame, Maître Suzanne
Blum, the Duchess's canny lawyer.

Leaving a Paris hospital in 1979: a gallant wave for photographers.

16

Other People's Houses

EVERYONE wondered what old Queen Mary thought. When the King had opened Parliament in November, she had been conspicuously absent—her first such absence in twenty-five years. She stayed away, presumably, because she suspected that Wallis would be there. For the past months, she had kept a discreet and reticent silence and, in fact, had been against her son going before the public with a radio broadcast. The next morning, however, a statement she had issued was published in the English newspapers:

> I need not speak to you of the distress which fills a mother's heart when I think that my dear son has deemed it to be his duty to lay down his charge, and that the reign which had begun with so much hope and promise has so suddenly ended.
>
> I know that you will realize what it has cost him to come to this decision; and that, remembering the years in which he tried so eagerly to serve and help his country and Empire,

you will ever keep a grateful remembrance of him in your hearts.

I commend you to his brother, summoned so unexpectedly and in circumstances so painful, to take his place. . . . With him I commend my dear daughter-in-law, who will be his Queen.

On the surface, it sounded restrained, dignified, Queenly. To others, it sounded cold, cynical—the reference to "cost," the pointed reminder that the new King had a respectable wife—and remarkably like an epitaph.

People had already begun speaking of Edward as "the late King," and the Archbishop of Canterbury, in his "farewell" address to the departing Monarch—which shocked many people with its harsh and blanket condemnation of the King's circle of friends—also spoke of him as a dead person, saying: "He had a craving for private happiness. Strange and sad that for such a selfish motive he should have disappointed hopes so high, abandoned trust so great. We have loved our King. Let the odd circle which got him away from us, stand rebuked by the nation." The "odd circle," meanwhile, was doing its best to disassociate itself from him. The friends who had been his guests on the *Nahlin* became social pariahs. The Brownlows, who had been so loyal to him, found themselves socially in Coventry. In the weeks before the Abdication, Lord Beaverbrook had been suffering intermittently from a toothache. Now, on December 11, the day after the Abdication and the day of the ex-King's broadcast, he had a dental appointment and was sitting in the dentist's chair when a call came through from Buckingham Palace. Beaverbrook's first reaction was, "No, I won't talk to them." The dentist expressed surprise at his patient's unwillingness to talk to the palace and so, somewhat grumpily, Beaverbrook got out of the chair and went to the telephone. It was the ex-King calling to say goodbye. The two men chatted pleasantly for a few minutes. Though Beaverbrook's initial aim may have been to cause mischief, there were apparently no words of thanks for the time and effort he had spent in the ex-King's behalf, for the trip to Canada canceled at the King's bidding, for the dashing back and forth across the countryside on the King's errands, for the late-night telephone consultations, for blockading the press as long as he had—nothing. Beaverbrook tried to make his voice sound cheerful, but inwardly he was disgusted. His only thought was the cliché "Journeys end in lovers' meetings," but he didn't utter it. He returned, with what amounted to relief, to the unpleasant business of the dentist's chair. More or less simultaneously, the rest of Britain returned to the banalities of daily living.

The London stock market, which had plunged sharply during the days previous to the Abdication, staged a brisk rally the day after.

Already, millions of pounds had begun to flow into the government exchequer from private individuals as gestures of gratitude for the way Stanley Baldwin had "saved" the Crown, even though, as we have seen, Baldwin's role had been simply that of the pragmatic politician—that is, he had passively let matters run their course, hoped for the best, and tried to keep his own head above water. Lord Nuffield, the Oxfordshire automobile tycoon of Morris Motors, sent a personal contribution of ten million pounds—the equivalent of fifty million 1937 dollars.

On the night of the ex-King's departure into self-exile, he met briefly with his brother, the new King. As Bertie, who was now George VI, put it in his diary, "When David and I said goodbye, we kissed, parted as Freemasons, and he bowed to me as his King."

Soon after his radio broadcast, the man who had spent 325 days as King of England entered a limousine and was driven with a detective to Portsmouth. There he was to board the destroyer *Fury,* which was to carry him across the wintry, fogbound Channel to Boulogne. Now he was not only a man without a country but, technically, also a man without a title. Though he had been introduced as "Prince Edward" on the broadcast, the title of Duke of Windsor would not be conferred upon him until the following day. At the entrance of the Portsmouth naval harbor, the car was stopped by a guard who cried, "Halt! Who's there?" The detective replied, "The King!" And then, in some confusion, remembering that his passenger was the King no longer, he added, "I mean . . . can't you see who is sitting in the car?" The former King was permitted to pass through the gate. With him was Slipper, the little cairn terrier he had given Wallis, which she had been unable to take with her on her own trip to France.

A few friends joined him on board the *Fury* for farewells.

To one of them he said, "I always thought I could get away with the morganatic marriage." Was he that naive? He had been told often enough, by Beaverbrook and others, that he could have got away with it only if he had been willing to wait for the proper moment. But he would not wait. Though he would forever refuse to see it that way, no one had made the decision to abdicate but himself.

It was only an hour or two before boarding the *Fury* that he had any idea of where he was going to go. He had telephoned Wallis in Cannes and told her that he planned to motor from Boulogne to Switzerland, where he would stay in a hotel. She had been shocked. It struck her as another example of the inhuman cruelty with which the others in the Royal Family were treating their relative—not only to force him out of the country, but also to refuse to provide him with a suitable place to live. Fortunately, however, Perry Brownlow had been able to find him better accommodations.* The Baron and Baroness Eugène de Rothschild had a castle called Schloss Enzesfeld near Vienna, and even though considerable work was involved in order to open up a large estate that had been closed for some time, the Rothschilds agreed to take him in.

He, of course, would have much preferred to go to France, but his lawyers had advised against it. In ordinary divorces, it is perfectly acceptable for a divorced woman to live in the same city as her intended new husband during the decree-nisi period. But this was no ordinary divorce, and the lawyers felt that, in order not to jeopardize the final decree, at least one national frontier should be kept between them. And so the former King headed for a stay at Schloss Enzesfeld while Wallis languished with the Rogerses at Cannes, waiting for the magic day in April, and freedom.

The big story was over for the time being, and the press had departed from the streets around the Villa Lou Viei. Now Wallis was free to wander about Cannes virtually unnoticed and unmolested. The Rogerses did their best to amuse and entertain her. They had friends in for dinner. They played cards. On warm days they took picnics to the beach or drives in the country.

Edward VIII's farewell radio address had won him sympathy

---

*Later, Lady Mendl would claim that it was she who was responsible for making the arrangements.

and love, almost universally, over half the world. Letters of cheer and comfort to the departed King poured in. This, however, was not the case with Wallis. She seemed to have stirred up an equally enthusiastic hotbed of hate. The bags of mail that arrived daily at the Villa Lou Viei contained almost nothing but abuse.

It was curious, but there was something about Wallis's personality, or perhaps it was her *appearance*—the practiced smile, the "metallic elegance"—that made people who did not know her dislike her. To her friends, she was good fun and good company, an excellent conversationalist and a talented hostess. And yet to millions of people who had never met her she was a bitch. It was a problem that would plague her for the rest of her life. Women, in particular, tended to take offense at the very *idea* of Wallis Simpson. She was called a home wrecker, but whose home had she wrecked? Her own? As we have seen, the King of England did that. The truth was that she did not look the part of a glamorous seductress. Women more beautiful, and less beautiful, than she could not imagine how this bony, flat-chested creature with the punishing jawline, the mole, and the schoolmarmish hairstyle had ever been able to bring it off. She seemed to touch deep sore spots of envy and resentment in all of womankind. Quite irrationally, the female response to her was that she *had no right* to what she had got. Added to this would be the galling fact that, for the rest of her life, she would cleverly refuse to reveal what her secret was, or—if she even knew—what it was that he saw in her.

Every insulting epithet that has ever been cast at a woman was hurled at her. Some of the letters were violent and threatening. Many were obscene. One particularly alarming series came from a man who identified himself only as an Australian and who said he was on his way to France to kill her. As a result of these, Herman Rogers kept a loaded pistol beside his bed. For some reason, the worst letters seemed to come from Canadians; next were British people living in the United States, and Americans of British birth or with British connections. But she did receive one letter from a man who must have been extraordinarily warm and gentle, and who was certainly long-suffering. He wrote:

I did not have the heart to write before. I have felt somewhat stunned and slightly sick over recent events. I am not, however, going into that, but I want to believe— I do believe—that you did everything in your power to prevent the final catastrophe.

My thoughts have been with you throughout your ordeal, and you may rest assured that no one has felt more deeply for you than I have.

For a few pence each day I can keep *au courant* with your doings. . . .

The writer was Ernest Simpson, who must have loved her very much.

To her credit, Wallis was an excellent house guest. The old maxim that "house guests, like fish, should not be kept for longer than three days" did not apply to her. After all, she had spent much of her life making a home for herself in other people's houses. She was exceptionally neat and orderly. She had sent for her maid, Mary Burke, from London, to help ease the strain on the Rogerses' household staff. She did not demand to be constantly entertained, was able to amuse herself, and spent much of her time alone in her room, reading. When the Rogerses wished to entertain her, she was good company. She never complained or criticized. For all these things, she was appreciated. Though it might be supposed that her host and hostess would weary of having their home the center of so much storm and controversy, the days, at least, were never exactly boring. There is no indication that the Rogerses did not enjoy all the excitement.

The new Duke of Windsor, on the other hand, perhaps because he had had less practice at visiting, turned out to be just the opposite sort of guest. Enzesfeld was a schloss of properly Rothschildian proportions—a huge baroque hunting lodge decorated with regal splendor, surrounded by a vast park and beautiful gardens, with hothouses, stables, and numerous other outbuildings. But the Rothschilds had been living in Paris, and the castle had been empty for several years, maintained by a skeleton staff. Now, and in a great hurry, Kitty de Rothschild had to open her house, staff it, and prepare it for her Very Important Visitor. All this she was perfectly willing to do; to be entertaining the former King of England carried a certain amount of social cachet—particularly to someone like the Baroness, who had started out in life as Kitty Wolff, the daughter of a Philadelphia doctor. She had struggled her way upward through two other marriages and, in the process, had shown a certain religious flexibility. She had been born Jewish. With her first husband, she was a Protestant, with her second a Catholic, and now, as the Baroness Rothschild, she had again become a Jew.*

Fortunately, there were a great many unemployed Austrian imperial servants in and around Vienna, so assembling a household staff was no problem for Kitty. But there were also paintings and silver and porcelains to be taken out of vaults, rugs to be unrolled, furniture to be uncovered, chandeliers to be taken out of their bags, ballroom floors to be polished, flowers to be arranged in all the rooms. All this had to be done, furthermore, by long distance from Paris. But Kitty was an efficient girl, and by the time the Duke of Windsor arrived in Vienna, all was in readiness down to the last detail—including a string of matching, pure white Lippizaner horses that had been installed in the long-unused stables, just to make the stables look lived in.

The Duke of Windsor arrived in Vienna by train, was met by the British Minister, Sir Walford Selby, posed for photographers, and then started off by motorcade to Enzesfeld, where he comfortably settled in. Kitty de Rothschild arrived two days later. Somewhat to her surprise, he did not greet her with any particular friendliness. He seemed preoccupied with other matters and blandly unaware of the elaborate preparations she had undertaken for his indefinite stay. She had been somewhat unprepared for the size of his retinue—with aides-de-camp, equerries, a financial aide, a butler, valet, chauffeur, and a Scotland Yard detective, there were eleven in all. But most outrageous was the fact that the Duke already seemed to regard Enzesfeld as his own domain, and to consider Kitty, his hostess, as a somewhat unwelcome house guest. He had replaced the Rothschild cellar of wines and liquors with his own private stock. When his dinner was announced, he did not invite his hostess to join him.

Most of his day, his hostess discovered, was spent on the

*She died, however, a Roman Catholic, and had a solemn high requiem mass.

telephone. It was what he called his "work." He telephoned Wallis in Cannes several times a day, and there were lengthy telephone conversations with London as he wrestled with the continuing problem of separating his personal fortune from the monies and properties of the Crown. He often called his Canadian ranch in Calgary (where he had hoped to strike oil, but had not), and there were calls to other, more remote parts of the world. When the first telephone bills floated in, the Baron de Rothschild, though a very rich man, was more than a little annoyed. There were other, minor annoyances. The Duke liked to play cards, and when he felt in the mood for a game a card-playing group was summoned by royal command. He played for high stakes, and when he won he cheerfully collected his winnings. But when he lost he did not pay.

Then there was the matter of his royal moods. At times he would grow incredibly sullen and surly, shouting at servants and issuing commands. He lost his royal temper easily. At other times he would seem to grow deeply depressed and uncommunicative, and at still other times he would merely seem bored. Still, Kitty de Rothschild did her best to amuse and entertain him. Supposing that his Christmas, parted from his beloved, might be a particularly sad and lonely time for him, she quietly planned a surprise Christmas Eve gala. She summoned musicians and entertainers and decorators from Paris, and redid an entire salon for the party, complete with an immense Christmas tree. On the night of the party the Duke sent word that he could not attend. This disappointed Kitty, who had placed a special Christmas gift for him under the tree. Now there was a question of how to get it to him. The next morning she had the gift—a set of sapphire studs from Cartier—placed on his breakfast tray. The gift caught him quite by surprise, and when he thanked her, he said he had had no time to think about Christmas presents, but would try to come up with something. Later in the day, he presented her with an autographed photograph of himself.

When he stopped in Vienna, he did not buy much—which did not endear him to the Viennese merchants—and instructed that the bills should be sent to the British Minister. When these bills had gone unpaid for some time, his equerries paid them out of their own pockets. When the British Minister advised the Viennese merchants that the ministry was not responsible for the ex-King's bills, the bills were forwarded to the Baron de Rothschild who, again, was not pleased. It had been the Rothschilds' understanding that they were loaning the house to the Duke, but that he would pay the household expenses. It soon turned out that the Duke was under quite a different impression. The household bills mounted with alarming speed on the Baron's desk, and Kitty de Rothschild's patience was beginning to wear thin. In talking to a London friend on the telephone, she snapped, "As far as I'm concerned, anyone can have him any time!"

In January, one of the Duke's oldest and dearest friends, Edward Dudley ("Fruity") Metcalfe, was skiing in Kitzbühel, and telephoned the Duke to ask if he would like him to come for a visit. The Duke replied that he would be delighted, and Metcalfe arrived for what would turn out to be a fairly extensive stay. When not on the telephone, the Duke and Fruity Metcalfe skied together, and talked and visited late into the night. During the long telephone conversations with Cannes, though Fruity Metcalfe did not intentionally eavesdrop, it was occasionally impossible for him not to hear some of what was going on since the poor long-distance connections frequently made it necessary for the Duke to shout to be understood. In writing home to his wife, Fruity Metcalfe noted his ominous impression that many of the conversations with Wallis did not seem to go too well—that she appeared to be badgering the Duke, complaining of this or that that he should or should not have done. Sometimes the Duke emerged from these telephone sessions looking nervous and depressed. But then he would soon place another call, and the substance of that one might lift his spirits.

Early in February, when Kitty de Rothschild was starting off for Paris, she was understandably quite hurt to learn that, owing to a telephone call to Cannes, the Duke had not yet dressed for the day and would therefore be unable to come downstairs to thank her or say goodbye. Nor would he be able to thank or tip her servants who were leaving with her. Fruity Metcalfe was shocked by this behavior. At his insistence, the Duke reluctantly wrote a thank-you note to Kitty, which Fruity delivered to her at the railroad station. This mollified her somewhat.

In early March, when he had been in residence at Enzesfeld for nearly three months, his hosts dropped a rather strong hint that he might pay some sort of rent, or at least expenses. He appeared apprehensive, but went right on living on the same grand scale—with the bills for all of it directed to the Roths-childs.

Out of his kingly element, it seemed that he could be re-markably insensitive. Once, at a luncheon—to which he had invited himself—at the Vienna home of Sir Walford and Lady Selby, he seated himself at the table and said, "You know my inquisitive nature. So I must ask you, what are those curious little silver rings around your napkins?" He was told that they were napkin rings, used to hold napkins from meal to meal. He looked astonished. "Do you mean," he said, "that you don't get fresh linen with every meal?"

One reason why the Baron de Rothschild tolerated his rude and ungrateful guest was the Duke's announcement that one of his projects, now that the king business was out of the way, would be to write a book in defense of the Jews. He had been interviewed by the press about it, who had asked him if he thought the time was right. "To know what is the right thing to do and not to do it, is cowardice!" was his reply. Rothschild, of course, was delighted with the idea. He equipped the library at Enzesfeld with reference books, a special desk with pencils and other writing tools. In the library, the would-be author periodically flipped through folios and drew doodles. He spent a great deal of time planning the physical appearance of the book—it was to be bound in royal-blue Morocco, and the cover would bear the coat-of-arms of the Prince of Wales, even though he no longer was that, and the motto Ich Dien (I serve). He found nothing ironic in this, apparently.

By March, though, it was apparent that the proposed book would never go any further than its cover, and Eugène de Rothschild was losing patience. The household bills for the Duke's stay were now causing genuine alarm, and Rothschild took up the matter with legal experts in Vienna. They had a clever idea. The city fathers would stage a little ceremony, and the Duke of Windsor would be proclaimed "Master of Castle Enzesfeld," which would flatter him. Thereafter, all bills would be directed to the Master of Castle Enzesfeld, and that would be that. When the bills, so addressed, arrived, the Duke had a hasty conference with Sir Walford Selby in Vienna. He could not stay at Enzesfeld any longer, he declared; a new, less expensive place must be found. Selby came up with a pleasant little boardinghouse called Pension Appersbach, on the shores of a lake at St. Wolfgang. Guests were in short supply, it was off season, and the proprietress, in consideration of the nice publicity the Duke's presence would give her place, agreed to take him in, with his entire party—and also to install a new bathroom off his bedroom—for a mere ten dollars a day. The Duke and his entourage moved out of Schloss Enzesfeld and into the pension in late March. By then, Fruity Metcalfe had left for England. There was now no one to remind the Duke that a thank-you note to Kitty de Rothschild might be in order, and so she received none.

While the new Duke of Windsor was carefully saving pennies, his future Duchess was merrily spending. Just how her finances were being handled during her months in France has never been clear—whether the ex-King had turned over to her an outright sum or was sending her an allowance or was merely paying her bills—but, for the first time in her life, Wallis was enjoying the sensation of being a rich woman. Lucius Beebe once said that when a person moves from poor to rich, there is a change in physical appearance—"a new set to the jaw." Wallis was acquiring this too, along with an increasingly practiced eye for beautiful and expensive dresses. If her wedding was going to be, as it was already being touted, the Wedding of the Century, an elaborate trousseau seemed to be required, and assembling it was one of her tasks during the early spring of 1937. Four designers had been selected, and Wallis had chosen an international assortment: Mainbocher, an American; Molyneux, an Englishman; Paquin, a Frenchman, and Mme. Schiaparelli, an Italian who worked in Paris. For colors, her new clothes were to feature a patriotic theme of red, white, and blue, in keeping with the flags of both the United States and Britain. And the gem of the collection was to be the wedding dress, which Mainbocher was creating for her in a color he named Wallis blue—which was really just a new name for the ancient shade of blue of the ribbons worn by Knights and Dames of the Garter.

Originally, there were to have been forty-eight dresses in the bridal trousseau, but Wallis soon decided that she needed eighteen more—eleven more for daytime, six for evening, and a particularly glamorous negligée of blue and silver lamé with long tight sleeves, cut high in the front and slashed daringly low in the back. (Because of her prominent collar bones, Wallis never wore anything cut low in the front.) Wildlife was another theme in her new wardrobe. One day dress in black crepe was overlaid with small white turtles. Another evening ensemble, in Wallis blue, was scattered with yellow butterflies. On one flared evening skirt, a large red lobster was appliquéd from the waist to below the knee. All these outfits, of course, had to be accessorized with coats, hats, gloves, shoes, bags, and jewels. Of his share in the preparation of Wallis's trousseau, Mainbocher has said that it was the biggest job his salon had ever undertaken. To style Wallis's hair for the wedding, Antonio Magnagnini was summoned from his establishment in Paris. Magnagnini charged fifty dollars a trip to Cannes, plus expenses, which was considered a great sum in those days, and many trips were required before he had decided on what was to be his "creation." (Wallis always insisted that she had problem hair. Curly and recalcitrant, it would never stay in place through the night. Years later, after discovering the Paris hairdresser Alexandre, she telephoned him in the morning and said, "What have you done to my hair? It stayed in place all night!")

While the Duke of Windsor did not at all mind living like a king, he also liked to spend like a king—which meant that he did not like to spend at all; or rather, that he had always obtained everything he wanted without ever handling money or facing the nuisance of paying a bill. Now, in middle age, he was too set in his ways to change. Wallis was just the opposite—she loved to spend money and never felt confident unless her purse was stuffed with large bills. The Duke's last few days in England had been spent with his family and advisers in heated disputes over money. At one point, he grew so angry at what he felt was their unfair treatment of him that he flew into a rage and hurled account books and ledgers onto the floor.

Actually, separating his personal fortune from the Royal Estate had presented an enormously complicated problem, and his bankers and lawyers were still working on it. He had owned the royal estates at Sandringham and Balmoral outright, and it had been agreed that he would sell these to the new King for about a million pounds, or five million dollars. He had also technically owned other royal residences—Buckingham Palace, St. James's Palace, Windsor Castle, Fort Belvedere, and other choice pieces of real estate in and around London which composed the Crown properties. Crown lands comprised over half a million acres. But these properties were subject to "entail"—that is, they were in a kind of loose trust to be enjoyed, used, and passed on from Monarch to Monarch. They were not the King's to sell, and, as an ex-King, he could no longer use and enjoy them. Technically, again, he had owned the contents of Buckingham Palace—the collection of paintings, the antiques, the royal library, the gold banquet service, George V's superb stamp collection, and the Crown jewels. These items, of course, earned no income and, with his Abdication, were withdrawn from him and placed in the Royal Establishment for future Kings and Queens. There was a particularly bitter haggle over the stamp collection. The Duke had never been interested in it, but he appreciated its great value and wanted it. In the end, it was decided that, because most of the stamps had been given to his father by his subjects around the world, the collection belonged to the nation.

The Duke of Windsor, as King, had always assumed that he was imperially rich. Now, upon Abdication, he learned with dismay that, while hardly poor, his wealth had limitations and that, in giving up the throne, he had also given up considerable tangible assets. His grandmother, Queen Alexandra, had been one of the richest women in the world, and she had left substantial sums to all her children and grandchildren—how much has remained a closely guarded secret since royal wills are never probated or published. George V had left money to all his sons—except Edward. He had reasoned that Edward would be drawing a substantial royal paycheck throughout his life. From his grandmother's estate and other inheritances, it is assumed that, before his Abdication, the King was personally worth in excess of four million dollars in cash, jewelry, real estate and securities. The effects of the Great Depression, which had struck England as well as the United States, had doubtless reduced this sum somewhat. As Prince of Wales, he had invested some of his money and, in the process, had become, to an extent, land poor. His 4,000-acre ranch in Canada, for example, after failing to produce oil, had been next planned for raising prize herds of cattle. But nothing had yet come of this, and so his Canadian property, which included a comfortable ranch house, was standing idle and unproductive—as well as costing him something he had never paid much attention to: taxes. He had assumed that he would receive a lifetime revenue of five hundred thousand dollars a year from the Duchy of Cornwall, and perhaps the greatest blow of all was when he was told by the royal solicitors that he was incorrect in this assumption.

And so, to the man who had always supposed that he was a billionaire and would always be able to live like one, the bitter truth was that, upon leaving the throne—what with the sale of Balmoral and Sandringham, and his personal money— he was only worth somewhere between eight and ten million dollars. The new King had done his best to be generous and fair to his brother, and had agreed to pay him an allowance, which would be tax-free, of $125,000 a year—a gesture he had been under no obligation to make. Still, the Duke was stunned by his sudden "poverty." In a premarital agreement that was being drawn up with Wallis, the Duke had at first grandly offered to settle £300,000 on her—about a million and a half dollars in those days—so that she would have a comfortable lifetime income. Now, when he explained the sorry state of his finances to her, there was a bitter exchange over the telephone between Austria and Cannes. Wallis interpreted the situation as he did—as yet another example of his family's miserliness and vindictiveness. To punish him, they were punishing her. In the end, Wallis tore up the original agreement and signed a new one giving her only a third of the original amount, or about half a million dollars. After all, to her, ten million dollars seemed like a lot of money—more than she had ever known. Why shouldn't she have unlimited spending money? It was a battle they would always have, between her natural extravagance and his anxiety that if he let her have her way they would soon both be in the poorhouse; or a battle between the heedless way he had spoiled her in the past and his new grasp of the bottom line.

In March, Wallis had also moved. From the Villa Lou Viei in Cannes, she had gone, along with the Herman Rogerses, to stay in the Château de Candé, in Monts, near Tours, which was the home of Mr. and Mrs. Charles Bedaux. She had become the house guest of a couple she had never met. Here, it had been decided, Wallis and the Duke of Windsor would be married. The choice of the Château de Candé had been made by the new King, George VI, in preference to various other large places that had been offered for the ceremony, and the King's selection seems to have been based primarily on his wish to shift the venue of the event away from the Riviera, with its reputation as a playground for the rich and frivolous. It was a curious choice and, as it would turn out, a sinister one. Charles Bedaux was a strange man. He had made a huge fortune as the inventor of something called the Bedaux System, which he sold to various manufacturers. The Bedaux System was based on "B-units," which were applied to factory workers, and the system determined how many B-units an average worker, in a given job, could produce in a single hour. Workers who produced more B-units than average were paid bonuses; those who were working under B-unit capacity were paid only the guaranteed basic wage. What it amounted to was a speed-up system, and the Bedaux System had attracted considerable interest in Nazi Germany. In the United States, labor organizations had complained bitterly about the system, claiming that companies subscribing to it set their basic B-rates too high. Of where Charles Bedaux stood politically, there was no question. "I am an out-and-out Fascist!" he had declared, but no one at the time seems to have taken such matters into account. When Mr. Bedaux had offered his château for the wedding, Wallis had briefly wondered whether this total stranger was doing so simply because he wanted the publicity. But she dismissed this unworthy thought. Actually, as it would turn out later, Bedaux had another, much more ambitious plan.

Wallis's divorce from Ernest Simpson became absolute at the end of April, but she did not receive official word of it until May 3. Immediately, the Duke of Windsor made plans to join her, and arrived at the Château de Candé the following day. As usual, being a man who disliked waiting for anything, he wanted to get married right away. But the Coronation of the new King, George VI, had been scheduled for May 12, and so they agreed, for reasons of "taste," that the wedding should be put off until early June. "June is the month for weddings," she reminded him. But more than taste and tradition were involved. If their marriage were to take place while the attention of the world was riveted on the panoply surrounding the Coronation, the Wedding of the Century would become a mere footnote in the news. So the date was set for June 3.

Meanwhile, on the day before the Duke and Wallis were reunited, tragedy struck. The Duke had shipped Slipper, the cairn terrier, to Wallis in France to keep her company, and that afternoon in May, Wallis and some friends were walking across a nearby golf course, followed by Slipper and a pair of Scotties.

The dogs romped and played, and suddenly Slipper disappeared. The group called and searched for him, and finally found him lying limp and quivering in the tall grass. When Wallis picked him up, he twisted in her arms and tried to bite her. The dog was rushed to a veterinarian in Tours, where he died. Though poisonous snakes are rare in France, the verdict was that Slipper had encountered one in the underbrush and had been fatally bitten. Wallis had a deeply superstitious nature. She had already had elaborate astrological charts drawn up for herself and the Duke of Windsor—she a Gemini, he a Cancer—and also for his parents, Queen Mary and King George, by a New York actress-turned-astrologer named Nella Webb. (The thrifty Miss Webb had promptly tried to sell the charts, which also showed an "opposition" in the stars to a May wedding, to the New York *Daily News*. And, though Wallis doubtless did not know it, it was a capital offense in England to cast a horoscope of the Monarch. It is interesting to surmise what turn royal history might have taken if Mrs. Simpson had been apprehended for her crime and hanged.) Wallis also subscribed to the ancient belief that there is magic in the touch of kings. Slipper had been her gift from the King. His death struck her as an ill omen. Others saw even deeper symbolism in Slipper's violent death. Slipper was the glass slipper presented by Prince Charming to the Cinderella from Baltimore. Now the glass slipper was broken.

Certainly things began to go poorly. The Duke, as part of his preparation for the marriage, had urgently requested of his brother the King that the wedding be given public recognition in England, and that his youngest brother, the Duke of Kent, be sent to serve as best man. He also urged that his mother, Queen Mary, attend the wedding. By late May, however, it had been made painfully clear that no member of the Royal Family would attend the wedding, nor would it be given any official recognition whatsoever. Nor, for that matter, would many of the bride and groom's old circle of London friends be present. For a time, too, it seemed as though there would not even be a clergyman to officiate, since most Church of England clerics refused to marry divorced persons. Then, out of the blue, there appeared an English clergyman named R. Anderson Jardine, the vicar of St. Paul's Church in the obscure parish of Darlington, who offered to perform the ceremony and thus confer upon the couple the blessings of the Church. The

Duke was delighted with the Reverend Jardine's offer, and no attention at all was paid to a telegram that was delivered to Jardine the day before the wedding from the Bishop of Durham, who was Jardine's superior. It read: YOU ARE WITHOUT EPIS-COPAL LICENSE OR CONSENT TO UNITE THE DUKE OF WINDSOR AND MRS. SIMPSON. SINCE YOUR LICENSE HAS BEEN REVOKED, UNDER THE CIRCUMSTANCES YOU ARE UNABLE TO LEGALLY SO-LEMNIZE THIS MARRIAGE. Mr. Jardine said that he would so-lemnize it anyway and united the beleaguered couple in the eyes of God.*

As the wedding date approached, the event began to take on a carnival aspect. Outside the gates to the château, hawkers were setting up stalls to sell trinkets and souvenir postcards. Nearby, the American newspaper columnist Cornelius Van-derbilt, Jr., was camped in a rented house trailer to cover the affair for his syndicate. Within hours of the ceremony the Duke received the most crushing blow of all. He had also asked his brother the King that his new wife be recognized as a Royal Duchess, with the title of Royal Highness, and addressed as "Madam" or "Ma'am." Now came a wire from Buckingham Palace informing the Duke that while he himself could be styled His Royal Highness, the Duke of Windsor, his wife would merely be the Duchess of Windsor. She would not be a Royal Highness. The Duke, naturally, took this as yet another "insult" to his wife-to-be. Actually, though the gesture does seem cal-lous, mean-spirited and spiteful, there were reasons for it. The designation Royal Highness in England is reserved for those who, however remotely, stand in line for succession to the throne. Since Wallis could never succeed to the throne, to address her as "Your Royal Highness" would have been both presumptuous and improper. Also, the new King and his family seem to have been bearing in mind the past performances of both the Duke and Wallis. Wallis had already shed two hus-

---

*Self-promotion rather than Christian charity seems to have motivated the Reverend Jardine. Later he would embark on a lecture tour through the United States as the man who married the Windsors and, according to Iles Brody, six years later Jardine and his wife, as proprietors of some-thing called the Windsor Cathedral in Los Angeles, were arrested for having overstayed their visas. The Jardines appealed to the Duke of Wind-sor for help and were told that he could do nothing for them. So much for royal gratitude.

bands. The Duke had cast aside a series of other women. The Royal Family simply did not believe that the marriage could possibly last, and the title Royal Highness, once it is conferred, is irrevocable. If either the Duke or Wallis married again, their respective spouses could also demand the designation, and the Royal Family no doubt could envision Royal Highnesses proliferating across the face of the globe.

Wallis always insisted that the matter of her designation was of little importance to her, that she really didn't care. But she had to care, if only because he cared so much. He regarded it as the snub of his lifetime, and would remain embittered about it until he died. The Duke immediately decided to ignore the verdict from the palace. Wherever they went in life, he insisted, he would see to it that Wallis was always addressed as "Your Royal Highness," whether she was really a Royal Highness or not.

To others, her situation seemed faintly comical, and jokes about the lowness of her would-be Highness began to circulate about London. A reporter named Hannen Swaffer wrote:

> Gone all the glory, all romance.
> "Honi soit," Queen Wally pants.
> No golden crown will grace her hair.
> Her throne is but a Windsor chair.

Instead of the Royal Family, the guests at the wedding would be a mixed bag. They would include Herman and Katherine Rogers, the Walter Moncktons, the Fruity Metcalfes, the Baron and Baroness de Rothschild, Charles and Fern Bedaux, and Wallis's faithful Aunt Bessie. Still, there would be lavish touches. Constance Spry, the fashionable London florist, had been brought in to do the flowers at the château, and Cecil Beaton, the London photographer, would take the pictures, with instructions to shoot from the Duke's left side only. *Vogue* had been given exclusive rights to the photographs. Nuptial music would be provided by Marcel Dupré, the celebrated French organist, who would play Bach's Cantata No. 29, Schumann's Canon in B minor, a prelude, a fugue in G minor of his own, and "O Perfect Love." For an engagement ring, the Duke had given Wallis a large, rectangular emerald set in platinum. The wedding ring would be a plain band of rare Welsh gold, of a sort usually reserved for royal weddings. As a wedding gift, he would give her a complete set of jewels—a diamond necklace, a bracelet, a ring, a brooch, and a diamond-studded coronet to make up for the crown she would never wear.

And yet, for all this, as the date and hour approached, there was a heaviness in the air, a feeling of sadness and incongruity—that this, only this, was what it had been all about, nothing more. The months of ordeal had taken their toll on both the Duke and Wallis. Neither looked their best, and both seemed tired, drawn, pale and anxious. As the house guests at the château assembled for the festivities, they were struck with how out of keeping, physically, Wally appeared for the part in the heady drama she had played. Even Cecil Beaton, who was fond of Wallis, could not resist describing her waspishly: "She twisted and twirled her rugged hands. She laughed a square laugh, protruded her lower lip. Her eyes were excessively bright, slightly froglike, also wistful." On the day before her wedding, he wrote, "Wallis hovered about in yellow, slightly more businesslike than usual; with her face showing the strain: she looked far from her best." It all added to a mood of sorry anticlimax.

Shortly before the wedding, Wallis completed the formalities of having her name legally changed to Wallis Warfield, so that she would be married as such, with no reminders to her new husband of his predecessors, though, at the brief rehearsal for the ceremony, Wallis said, "You don't need to tell me what to do. Don't forget, I've been through this a couple of times before."

At noon on June 3, the little group gathered in the music room of the Château de Candé. Dr. Charles Mercier, the Mayor of Monts (who also doubled as the town's physician) was there in his best shiny-blue suit to perform the brief civil ceremony. Dr. Mercier was understandably nervous and perspiring, and there were several questions which, according to the statutes should have been asked but were not. Had Dr. Mercier taken the legally necessary step of verifying the couple's birth certificates? Had permission for a Royal Prince to marry even been granted, as required by the Royal Marriages Act? The feeling seemed to be that this was an unusual marriage and that, under the circumstances, certain procedural details could be overlooked. Then Dr. Jardine took over, even though his words would be regarded as having no effect by the Church of England. When he came to the words, "Wilt thou love her, comfort her, honor her and keep her?" the Duke of Windsor cried, *"I will!"* in such a shrill, high-pitched voice that those standing nearby were startled. At 12:14 P.M., the Duke and Wallis Warfield became husband and wife.

After the ceremony, there was champagne, and a buffet luncheon of chicken à la king, followed by French pastries and fresh wild strawberries and cream. The Duke then introduced a creation of his own, the Wallis Cocktail, a sticky concoction of Cointreau, peppermint, gin, lemon juice and soda that he had devised for the occasion. Outside, from the sky, a gallant French aviator flew low over the château to scatter hundreds of rosebuds on the scene—or so he claimed. If he did this, the blossoms must have blown in some other direction, because no one at the wedding party was aware of any falling rosebuds.

Shortly past six, after the coffee and the brandy, the Duke and Duchess of Windsor stepped into the famous Buick and started south for their honeymoon. Accompanying them, according to one report, were 226 pieces of luggage, of which 183 were large trunks. According to another report, there were 266 pieces, of which 186 were trunks. Whatever the correct tally, it would mark the beginning of a tradition. Wherever the Duke and Duchess traveled, throughout their lives, there would always be a reporter waiting to count their suitcases.

William Randolph Hearst had asked Adela Rogers St. Johns to cover the Windsor wedding for his newspapers, but she had declined the assignment. To Mrs. St. Johns, the Romance of the Century had already entered the realm of show business. At her suggestion, Mr. Hearst sent Louella Parsons in her place.

17

Unemployed

FOR their wedding trip, the Duke and Duchess motored—driven by the ever-faithful George Ladbrook—as far as the Italian border, where they boarded a luxurious private railroad car said to have been personally loaned to them by Benito Mussolini. After the wedding, Herman Rogers had begged the press not to follow the couple, but the press, needless to say, ignored him. The press were there when the Windsors' car was hooked on to the Simplon Orient Express, and were able to report that the car contained a complete bathroom and a bedroom containing a large double bed fitted out with standard Thomas Cook and Sons *wagons-lits* brown blankets. The Duke wore bright-red pajamas to bed and, in the morning, had early tea followed by an English breakfast of bacon and eggs. How the press obtained such intimate details is unclear, unless it was by bribing railroad officials.

After such a tumultuous courtship, it would be pleasant to envision a wedding night spent in passionate lovemaking. But one wonders, and whether sex had anything at all to do with the Romance of the Century is open to question. Though in many ways a ridiculous woman, Emerald Cunard was a shrewd one. She was certain, she once told Bruce Lockhart, that throughout their long affair, Wallis and the King had never slept together. Though, in his diary, Lockhart wrote, "I doubt this," Emerald Cunard may have guessed correctly. Wallis herself once said to Jack Aird aboard the *Nahlin,* "I have had two husbands, and I never went to bed with either of them." Aird's response to this announcement is unrecorded, but what is one to make of this strange confession? For one thing, it puts the lie to Wallis's repeated claim that one of the greatest disappointments of her life was that she had not had children. In the end, it is possible to conclude that neither Wallis nor the Duke was interested in sex. He had been reared from a Victorian female perspective which held that sex was a nasty business. Her upbringing had been the opposite, with a strong male figure —Uncle Sol—at its center. To her, sex may have been meaningless against the pleasures of money, power, and possessions. In that sense, the "romance" was a charade. The union was pragmatic in that Wallis offered her new husband freedom from sexual responsibility. She demanded nothing of him other than the perquisites that went with his rank and that allowed him to indulge his personal tastes, which were gentle ones and ran to gardening, needlepoint, playing musical instruments, and dressing up in kilts and bright red pajamas. From this perspective, it is possible to see why each considered the other his personal salvation.

In any case, the honeymooners first visited Venice, where they did the traditional things—toured the canals in a gondola, strolled in the gardens of the Hotel Excelsior, visited the Lido. Everywhere they went there were demonstrations of affection from the Fascists, who were eager to do whatever possible to annoy and embarrass the British government. In front of photographers the newlyweds were showered with flowers, and the Duke responded by giving the Fascist salute. From Venice they went to Milan, and then on to several Italian coastal resorts. It was the beginning of a meandering, peripatetic existence that would characterize most of their lives. From Italy, they made their way to Austria, to the beautiful Castle Wasserleonburg, near Arnoldstein, which had been loaned to them by Count Paul Münster, complete with its lady ghost, a "Bluebeard Duchess" who had murdered eight husbands. (A dependence on the kindness and hospitality of others would also characterize their lives.) Reporters were lurking in the shrubbery when the couple arrived, by moonlight, and watched as the Duke carried the Duchess over the threshold of Wasserleonburg, and heard her laugh shrilly. The next morning, the Duchess removed some stag's horns and elephant tusks from the walls, and got down to business with her housekeeper. Castle Wasserleonburg was to be their home for some three months.

In Vienna, the Duke ordered some stationery with his initials encircled by the Garter, and bearing the motto, *"Honi soit qui mal y pense."* Barely three weeks later, the Garter Principal King of Arms, Sir Gerald Woods Wollaston, claimed in a lecture at the Lyceum Club in London that Edward VIII had "speeded up" his father's funeral. The Duke was furious, and for several days he could talk of nothing but "that rotten story." In the end, he wrote a letter to the London *Evening Standard* about it, protesting that his mother had wanted a faster funeral for his father than had been given to his grandfather, who had waited above ground for two weeks. Wollaston apologized for the remark, but that night, invited to sit at dinner opposite the Duke and Duchess of Kent, Wollaston found that his place card had been moved.

Keeping track of these snubs and countersnubs kept the new Duke of Windsor busy, but not very busy. Wallis's first two marriages may have been sexless, but at least her previous husbands had been gainfully employed and had gone off to work every morning. Now she was having to become accustomed to life with a man who was, in a very real sense, out of work. Her days were filled with the duty of keeping him company, keeping him amused and occupied, and warding off boredom. Since his interests were limited, this was obviously no easy task, but to Wallis's credit she would prove herself up to it for the next thirty-five years. Shortly before his marriage the Duke had asked his brother the King that he be quickly given some government post appropriate to his rank. This also had been denied, and it became increasingly clear, as the months went by, that the Duke of Windsor had been given a title that carried with it no responsibilities whatsoever. His mother, of course, was behind it all, supported by the new Queen. The Duke of Windsor's famous popularity, it now seemed, was working against him. Both the Queen Mother and the new Queen Elizabeth were convinced that if the Duke were given any significant position in British life he might outshine the new King, and the matriarchy was determined that this must not happen. There could not be two Kings. To permit the new King to achieve a popularity of his own, the former King must be forced into the shadows. After all, a new King traditionally reached the throne only upon the death of a predecessor. Officially, the Royal Family had decided to treat the ex-King, as much as was possible, as though he were a dead person.

The snubs from the Royal Family were beginning to mount up. It had been announced that the Duke and Duchess of Kent would be the first family members to visit the Duke of Windsor and his new Duchess. In August, two months after the marriage, it was announced that the Kents' visit would be indefinitely postponed, with no reason given. To counter this unfortunate publicity, the Windsors made public their plans for social work, which turned out to be not particularly extensive. The Duke sent the equivalent of five hundred dollars to a Leicestershire agricultural society, and the Duchess sent twenty-five dollars to a church school in Warfield, Berkshire, her "family seat." But the British government conspicuously omitted the Duke's name from the list of those who could confer royal warrants—"By Appointment, etc."—to merchants and manufacturers, though the names of his two younger brothers, Kent and Gloucester, were included. To Wallis and the Duke there seemed to be no end to his family's spitefulness.

In September of 1937, the Windsors left Wasserleonburg for Paris, where they ensconced themselves in a two-bedroom suite at the Hôtel Meurice. Here, in October, Mr. Leslie Hore-Belisha, His Majesty's Secretary of State for War, became the first British Cabinet minister under the new King to have an audience with the Duke of Windsor. The topic under discussion was the Duke's desire to be given some sort of government post; what he wanted most was the governor-generalship of Canada. It was an unrealistic request. Of all the Dominions queried about the ex-King's marriage plans, none had reacted with greater hostility than Canada, and when presented with the Duke's suggestion Mr. Hore-Belisha was noncommittal. The Duchess, it was announced, was "too busy" to attend the audience—another public-relations gaffe. What she had been busy doing, it turned out, was shopping—for Mainbocher dresses, Paquin furs, Georgette shoes, and Suzy hats.

Meanwhile, their new friend, Charles Bedaux, had come up with a lavish plan for the Windsors. He would send them, at his own expense, on an extended grand tour of the United States. It was an invitation that Wallis—understandably eager to return to her native land as an almost-Queen and an international celebrity—was keen to accept. The Duke also approved—he liked anything where the travel and accommodations would be free. But when the news of the projected tour reached the American press, there were loud outcries of indignation. That the former King of England should come to America as the guest of a self-proclaimed Fascist seemed more than a little inappropriate. Several of the Windsors' friends dropped respectful hints. In Washington, the Roosevelts gave no intimation that the ducal pair would be received at the White House. To many observers it seemed clear that Mr. Bedaux merely wished to use the Windsors as traveling advertisements for his controversial Bedaux System. But Bedaux continued to press forward with the arrangements.

Just before the wedding, Bedaux had come up with another idea for the royal couple that was, if anything, even more ill-conceived and ill-timed: a tour of Nazi Germany "to inspect the Third Reich's industry and social institutions," which would be topped off by an audience with Adolf Hitler himself. The Duke had frequently given the Nazi salute—affecting, in fact, Hitler's own somewhat languid version of it. He had also long prided himself on his mastery of the German language and, at times, would insist on conversing only in that tongue. In England, he had often held forth on the superiority of Germany's air power over Britain's, to the consternation of his ministers. Hitler's personal reaction to the Abdication is said to have been mixed. When he first heard the news, the Führer allegedly fell into a deep depression, saying, "I've lost a friend to my cause!" Then he suddenly shifted moods and became exultant, crying, "I told you! The English are decadent!" In any case, Hitler's government had made elaborate arrangements for the Windsors' visit and, in October, they left Paris for Germany.

For the Duke, the German visit was almost a sentimental journey. For Wallis, it was a chance—the first in nearly five months of marriage—to give her husband something to do. For fourteen days, the Windsors toured German factories, greeted everywhere with "Heil Windsor!" to which they responded "Heil Hitler!" Their tour director was the Nazi Labor Front leader, Dr. Robert Ley. At one factory, Dr. Ley stopped and asked a worker, "You *are* happy, aren't you, my worker comrade?" The worker glanced nervously at a huge sign which said, "HUSH! Remember it is your duty to be silent!" and mumbled, *"Ja, ja."* The Duke reminded the Germans that the Windsor family name at the time of his birth had been Saxe-Coburg und Gotha, and had been changed to Windsor as recently as 1917, and as the Duke's well-dressed wife moved smilingly among the German workers, one woman was overheard to whisper, *"Wie schön sie aussient!"* ("How well she looks"). Another worker said, "It would be better for Germany if he had stayed on the throne." At one of the hotels where the Windsors stopped, a large German woman stood outside the front entrance and sang "For He's a Jolly Good Fellow" at the top of her voice. All these reports were read in England with some embarrassment and distaste.

After their drawn-out pilgrimage across the face of Germany—during which the Duke pointed out that his younger brother Kent had had to quit for a rest after three days of this sort of thing, saying, "I'm all in!"—the Windsors came at last to Hitler's retreat at Berchtesgaden, where they were given a somewhat puzzling reception. They arrived a little earlier than had been expected, and were kept waiting at the foot of the Führer's private mountain for almost an hour before an escort appeared to usher them into the dictator's presence. Hitler seemed to be making the point that a King might deserve one sort of courtesy, but an abdicated King deserved quite another. Still, when the Duke and Duchess were finally presented, the Führer greeted them warmly and gave them a full two-hour audience. The Duke and the Führer talked energetically in German, and though an interpreter was provided, Wallis, who spoke no German, had no idea what the men were talking about. All she knew was that the Führer kept squeezing her hands effusively. Apparently, Wallis never did find out what was being discussed during that historic meeting. Though she asked her husband later, all he would say was that their talk had been "very interesting" and that Hitler was "against Bolshevism." In her southern-girl's way, she never pursued the subject further, saying, "In one respect, at least, men are pretty much alike. Statecraft is an art into which they will not readily initiate women, no doubt on the theory that it is over their heads."

What she seems not to have realized was that her husband was no longer in a position to practice "statecraft."

According to the *New York Times*, during his meeting with Hitler, the Duke reportedly was "very critical of British politics as he sees them and . . . [declared] that the British ministers of today and their possible successors"—including, no doubt, his old friend Winston Churchill—"were no match either for the German or the Italian dictators." Afterward, Hitler commented, "If it had been possible for me to talk to King Edward the Eighth for just one hour, the abdictation of His Majesty could have been avoided. He had a responsibility not only to Britain but to Europe of which he did not seem to be aware." And one of Hitler's aides said, "The tour of the Fatherland has shown how right *Der Führer* was in judging that King Edward's abdication would be a serious blow to German interests."

There were other festivities for the Duke and Duchess in Germany. Ribbentrop gave a dinner party in their honor at a fashionable Berlin restaurant, and they clinked glasses and exchanged more Nazi salutes with German dignitaries and Foreign Office officials, including Heinrich Himmler, Dr. Ley, and Herr Herman, Hitler's adjutant. At this dinner, however, the Führer could not be present, and offered pressing state business as his excuse. Only a few weeks earlier, at a Court function at Buckingham Palace, Ribbentrop had approached the throne, clicked his heels, and had given the Nazi salute three times, shouting "Heil Hitler!" with each gesture. The King had looked straight through him and made no response to the salutes whatever—which was understandable, since Britain was already girding itself for the inevitability of war with Germany. In Nuremberg the Duke of Coburg—a cousin—gave the Windsors a grand dinner, and Wallis's place card, which all of German society had been speculating about, read, *Ihre Königliche Hoheit der Herzogin von Windsor*—Her Royal Highness the Duchess of Windsor.

In England, when these German doings were reported, it began to be assumed, particularly in Court and government circles, that the Duchess was responsibile for her husband's political leanings, just as she had been responsible for his abdication. Antipathy to her grew, and now even King George VI was expressing signs of annoyance. After all, here was the Duke of Windsor still behaving as though he were King. Certainly it began to seem out of the question that the Duke should be given any post in the British government. If war came, he—or, more likely she—would perhaps be put in the position to leak military secrets to the Germans! But Wallis was no Mata Hari. Though her husband might appear to stand, politically, somewhere to the right of Louis XVI, she was, if anything, more politically naive than Marie Antoinette.

Actually, both were political innocents, and an aspect of the Duke's character was beginning to emerge that had not been apparent when he was the charming, party-loving, debonair and "democratic" Prince of Wales or King of England: he was a terrible snob. He was, furthermore, a money snob. Though Wallis might appear to some to be the archetypal social climber, her husband was turning out to be every bit as ambitious. There was his preoccupation, for instance, with the tiny nuances of social distinction between a Royal Highness and a Duchess. His fascination with Hitler was based primarily on the fact that Hitler, up to that point, had been extraordinarily successful. Anyone who was successful or rich qualified for the Duke's friendship, and his attraction to men like Charles Bedaux, whose personality was not the least bit attractive, stemmed from the Duke's awareness that Bedaux had obviously made a lot of money.

Plans were continuing for the Windsors' tour of America under Bedaux's aegis. It was, of course, to be very grand. Little attention was being paid by the prospective travelers to reports that Bedaux was being denounced in the United States as a "Fascist bloodsucker," and that his Bedaux System was being described as "nothing more than a method of forcing the last ounce of effort at the smallest cost in wages." American labor leaders were up in arms over the auspices of the visit, and Joseph P. McCurdy, the head of the Baltimore Federation of Labor, reminded Americans that the Windsors had just visited Nazi Germany, that neither the Duke nor Duchess had shown any concern for the poor, and he warned Baltimore trade unionists of a "potential threat" if the Windsors visited that city. The president of the AF of L, William Green, agreed. "Bedaux made his money from the sweat of textile workers," he said and added, somewhat mysteriously, "Mrs. Bedaux likes the lavish use of lavender scent."

Everyone began taking sides about the proposed visit, and, through it all, the Windsors' own sense of public relations continued to be remarkably dim. They approved a hasty trip to Washington by Bedaux to make final arrangements, and they agreed to his hiring the Arthur Kudner advertising agency in New York to handle publicity. At one point, Bedaux offered to bow out of the picture, but the Duke refused to let him. In Paris, the Duke lunched with the American and British press, saying, "I'm a very happily married man. Sportsmanship is absent from some newspaper comment on the activities of the Duchess and myself. We are looking forward to our tour of the United States to study methods of housing and industrial conditions." In the United States, the author Sinclair Lewis commented, "There is no longer any way for the Duke of Windsor to make himself useful to the world." In Britain, the press comment was more restrained. The *Evening Star* merely said, "The Duke is as much in need of wise and experienced councillors as . . . when he was King."

The U.S. State Department was cool to the whole idea of the tour, and was unwilling to confer royal status on the Duchess. Nor was the State Department sure how the Duke and Duchess should be addressed. Bedaux explained that it was merely necessary to call her "Ma'am," and him "Sir." (Bedaux himself, whose English was quite uneven, called the Duke "Sire.") In Paris, meanwhile, the U.S. Ambassador to France, William C. Bullitt, was in favor of the visit. He thought it would be good publicity for the United States. In Canada, where the Duke had asked to be sent as governor-general, Ramsay MacDonald, the former Prime Minister and Labour party leader, announced that he did not want the Windsors in that country. And in Bermuda, a photograph of the Duke and Duchess that had been tacked up by a newsstand counter clerk named Mrs. Evalyn Stovell, with a caption that read, "They're Happy Now," was angrily ripped down by the seventy-three-year-old Bishop of Bermuda, the Right Reverend Arthur Heber Browne. (Miss Stovell chased the Bishop home; she wanted her picture back.)

Back home in Baltimore, the old house in East Biddle Street had become a tourist attraction. It had been fitted out with likenesses of King George V and Queen Mary, and of Wallis herself in the act of curtsying to Their Majesties. A dollar was being charged for admission—a stiff figure in those Depression days—plus twenty-five cents to lie down in the bathtub where Wallis had supposedly bathed (it was claimed that lying in the magic tub would increase one's sexual prowess). The wax museum had been doing a thriving business, and an entrepreneur from New Jersey had begun negotiations with the city of Baltimore to have the Windsor Museum, tub and all, moved closer to New York, where the box office would presumably be greater. But then a curious rumor started. It was said that the only object in the house dating back to Wallis Warfield's time was an ancient kitchen stove, on which she had once made fudge. The number of admissions suddenly dropped. The entrance fee was reduced to fifty cents, but business did not improve. Eventually the museum, which had been billed as "A Shrine to Love," closed its doors, never to reopen.

In London, a few stragglers remained in support of the departed King. Something called the Octavian Society met at irregular intervals in a second-rate restaurant in the Holborn District of London to lament the loss of Edward VIII. A pet speaker was the Reverend Jardine. At one of these gatherings, the novelist Compton Mackenzie spoke stirringly, saying, "We want him back! We don't want to send greetings to France. We want to send them to Fort Belvedere. The country needs him, for he is the greatest influence for the peace of Europe!" The Duke replied with thanks to Mackenzie. Another group, called the Henchmen of Honour, had been founded by a retired barrister named Robert Elton, who also appealed to the Duke to return to England. Elton tried to have the 1936 Abdication Act repealed and declared illegal because, though it had been passed by Parliament, it was not a mandate of the people. But Elton's claim was denied on the grounds that it was not on the regular schedule of cases. For his efforts, Mr. Elton received no thanks at all from the Duke.

Aside from these scattered and ineffectual groups, the Duke and Duchess seemed to have no political friends at all, except in Italy and Germany. One former English friend of the Duke's from pre-Abdication days, Hector Bolitho, wrote of him in 1937 that he was "harassed, unreasonable and vain...he had no friends"; that he "preferred to amuse himself in the way his will and fancy guided him"; that he was "selfish...distraught, unreasonable." At Windsor, the armorial banner of the Duke of Windsor was taken down from its original place, in the first stall on the right, in St. George's Chapel—the lodge room of the Knights of the Garter—and moved three places down the line. In the 1937 edition of *Burke's Peerage,* the Duchess of Windsor was ranked thirty-third lady in the land, though *De-*

brett's Peerage ranked her eighth. Of this, the Royal College of Arms said, "Only the King is able to decide and state the exact position. The less said about this the better."

They were right. The Duke and Duchess of Windsor could return to England whenever they wanted, but the Duke refused to do so unless his wife was granted full status as a Royal Highness and received at Court. This the King, backed by the two women closest to him, his mother and his wife, refused to do.

The main pressure against the Windsors' visit to the United States was coming from the same source—the throne. Still, the Windsors continued with their plans. Then came a stunning blow. The White House, which had thus far had little to say about the plan, announced that Mrs. Roosevelt would be unable to entertain the ducal pair. Unfortunately, she would be "out of town" at the time of the proposed visit, off on an extended lecture tour. It seemed that the best that official Washington could do would be a small reception at the British Embassy. With this, the Duke decided to call off the trip. But then he changed his mind, and started to pack twenty trunks and fifty suitcases. Two days before the Windsors were due to sail for America aboard the *Bremen*, under a German flag, the Duke was invited to the British Embassy in Paris for lunch with the Ambassador, Sir Ronald Campbell. He was informed that under no circumstances were he and his wife to take Mr. Bedaux's proffered trip. Glumly, the Duke returned to the Meurice. That night, "with great reluctance," the cancellation of the Windsor American Housing Tour was announced.

The American press—which had been looking forward to another national circus such as had been provided by Queen Marie of Rumania's tour in 1926—was greatly let down. Though Wallis had been named "Woman of 1936" by *Time* magazine, there suddenly seemed to be nothing more to say about the Windsors.

The press, to give it credit, did its best. It reported that an impostor signing his name as "Edward Windsor" had run up huge hotel bills in Paris. The man was sued for fraud, but got off on the grounds that he had never actually claimed to be the former Edward VIII.

From Hollywood it was reported that Will Hays had offered the Duke of Windsor a salary of $100,000 a year to be an international representative of the Hays film-censorship office.

Hays denied the report as without foundation.

In London, the Duke brought a lawsuit against the publisher William Heinemann and the author Geoffrey Dennis, whose book, *Coronation Commentary*, "repeated the rumor that the lady who is now the plaintiff's wife occupied before his marriage to her the position of his mistress." The Duke won this libel action and, as is customary in English courts, was awarded an unspecified, but insignificant, amount in damages.

Other libel actions would follow at any printed suggestion that the Windsors' union had been consummated before they had taken their marriage vows. Years later, even after the Duke's death, as we shall see, this matter would be given what might seem an inordinate amount of weight.

Perhaps the liveliest Windsor story toward the end of 1937 was a statement by Ernest Aldrich Simpson, who on November 8 arrived in New York on the *Queen Mary*. Asked if he would ever marry again, he replied, "Oh, let's have another drink."

18

Limbo

A REPUTATION for parsimony began developing around the
Duke and Duchess of Windsor soon after their marriage.
Though both enjoyed luxury and all the trappings of wealth,
neither seemed at all to enjoy spending money—not, at least,
when it was their own money. When close friends teased Wallis
about this, she indignantly and self-righteously explained that,
after all, the Windsors were not *that* rich. When her husband
had outlined to her the financial arrangements of the Abdication, he had stressed to her the importance of saving every
penny possible. By pinching pennies wherever she could, she
was merely obeying her man's instructions.

Their honeymoon had been spent almost entirely in borrowed castles and châteaux, in borrowed railroad cars and free
hotel suites. They had done a great deal of dining out at other
people's houses and almost no entertaining of their own. The
American tour had appealed to both of them because it would
be both luxurious and free. In Paris, the Hôtel Meurice had
been happy to give the Windsors a special discounted rate. It

was not merely that the Windsors' presence gave the hotel cachet; the Meurice had long been a favorite royal stopping place and did not really need more cachet. But the French, a breed not noted for either openhandedness or fondness for the British, were turning out to be exceedingly generous when it came to entertaining the Windsors. The French promptly gave the ex-King diplomatic status. He would be permitted to live in France tax-free, and the French would provide the Windsors with round-the-clock police protection. On the surface, it seemed odd that the French would extend such courtesies to an Englishman, even a duke—the English being their traditional enemies.

Actually, there were several good reasons for this. One was an effort to consolidate the *entente cordiale*—a deliberate gesture of friendship to the British and to Buckingham Palace—by offering to shelter Britain's problem child in a place so close to England that exile would not seem like exile. At the same time, it was a sly way to point up British stuffiness and inhospitableness, to subtly demonstrate the pettiness of British attitudes. After all, France had taken in Oscar Wilde after he had been ostracized in England. Paris also enjoyed emphasizing its reputation as "the city of love," and where better to welcome the most famous lovers in the world? Finally, the canny French realized that there would no doubt always be value in the Windsors' presence as a tourist attraction. France no longer had a Royal Family of its own. Now it had one.

When it came to obtaining free merchandise, however, it was another matter. For years after the Windsors' marriage, there would be heated speculation about whether the Duchess of Windsor did, or did not, pay for the clothes that composed her extensive and constantly renewed wardrobe. The answer is that sometimes she did and sometimes she didn't—or, rather, that she paid when she couldn't get what she wanted any other way. Early in 1938, the French designers had named Wallis the Best Dressed Woman in the World, and obviously it behooved some of these ladies and gentlemen—particularly those who felt that the publicity of dressing her would be good for business—to dress her for nothing, or for substantial discounts. One of her favorite designers was Pierre Balmain, and Balmain directors recall that she often requested, but did not always get, a discount. Some couturiers and jewelers were willing to let her borrow dresses and jewels for special occasions. But others, more secure in their position of fashion eminence, felt differently, and insisted that the Duchess of Windsor be charged exactly the same prices that were paid by their other customers. For Wallis, whether she paid or not became a matter of trial and error because, in the ups and downs of the French fashion industry, designers often changed their minds. In one salon, which she had patronized in the past. Wallis admired a dress and asked that it be sent around to her at the Meurice. But the couturier demurred and requested that he be paid first by check. The Duchess stalked angrily out of the salon. Later that afternoon she returned with her checkbook and bought the dress. Shopping, for her, became a curiously will-they-won't-they sort of adventure. It is ironic that now, though on a much grander scale, Wallis was having to indulge in the same sort of scrimping and haggling that she had done as a poor girl growing up in Baltimore.

At home, meanwhile, there was another problem. Though the Duke clearly enjoyed seeing his wife in elegant dresses and jewelry—often accompanying her on shopping trips and seeming to encourage her spending—he became visibly unhappy when the bills for the finery inevitably arrived. He tucked them into a drawer in his desk where they went unpaid for months at a time. It was no wonder that certain designers began insisting that Wallis pay for her purchases in cash, and for Wallis it meant that she was left in a kind of financial limbo, never certain of what sort of figure lay at the bottom line. Though he could not live without a personal valet, though she must also have a personal maid, and though life was intolerable without a chauffeur and a detective following in a second car, Wallis was also required to do what many rich women do who do not like to be seen in the same outfit twice. She supplemented her clothes budget by selling her gowns to thrift shops.

In London, there was noisy muttering about stacks of unpaid bills that both the Duke and Duchess had left behind them. But, by February 1938 it was announced that all the London debts had been settled, including the largest one, a $600,000 bill from Cartier. But in Europe shopkeepers learned not always to expect too much in the way of business from the Windsors. In Vienna, the Duke spent an entire day shopping for jewelry, picking over priceless things for hours, but by day's end he had made only one purchase—a sixty-cent flashlight from a hardware store. In the Balkans, Wallis bought three tiny dolls and paid for them with a twenty-dinar Yugoslavian bill, worth approximately fifteen cents. The dolls cost only fifteen dinars, and Wallis told the clerk grandly, "Keep the change." In the spring of 1938, Wallis sent another small doll to Wales with the instruction that it be given to the child of a Welsh miner. The other stipulation was that the child must name the new doll Wallis. At about the same time, when the Duke was asked whether he could make ends meet on his royal allowance, he replied, "Well, if worse comes to worst I can always pick up a living showing people around Schönbrunn Palace—I know it so well." And, throughout all this, the Duke continued to demonstrate, as his old friend Fruity Metcalfe put it, "slight lapses [of cheerfulness] when a bill has to be paid."

In February 1937, the Duke's only sister, Mary, the Princess Royal, had been the first member of the British Royal Family to visit him during his lonely exile at Castle Enzesfeld. "Well, you do look fit!" she said to him when she met her on the railway station platform in Vienna. He, however, was visibly on the verge of tears. Now, during the cold winter months of 1937–1938, he made more attempts at a reconciliation with his family across the water. But all overtures were rebuffed, and some of the snubs must have been particularly disheartening. The Duchess of Kent, who was the former Princess Marina of Greece—and the only English duchess who was herself a member of a royal family—had appeared to support the King and Wallis during the bitter days before the Abdication, and Wallis had considered Marina one of her closest friends. (Wallis had given Marina a pair of lamps—bought on sale at Fortnum & Mason for ten guineas each—as a wedding present.) It now seemed that Marina's friendship had been strictly of the fair-weather variety and that she had defended Wallis merely to spite her Scottish sister-in-law. Now the Scottish sister-in-law was Queen of England, and Marina let it be known that she would never spend the night under the same roof as "that woman."

The winter of 1937–1938 was cold and dreary, and the darkening war clouds across the face of Europe only added to the weather's bone-chilling gloom. The Duke and Duchess divided the winter between the Meurice and a furnished villa, the Château de la Maye, in Versailles. The Duchess was taking French lessons, but by now it must have already become clear to her that, just as she was an outcast in England, so would she always be, in a sense, an outcast in France. She would never be able to attract to her table the crusty old aristocracy of Paris—the old titles with strung-out names separated by *du* and *de*. (With some justification, she pronounced these inbred people incredibly dull.) Instead, her set would be *le tout Paris,* the party-going set that floated in and out of town with the seasons between the Côte d'Azur, St. Moritz, Palm Beach, New York and Long Island. They were the new and self-made rich, people like Charles and Fern Bedaux; Bettina, the model, and her husband Gaston Bergéry, who later became a Nazi collaborator; Edmund Bory, who owned Fauchon, and Louis Vaudable, who owned Maxim's; and of course the Rothschilds who, for all their money, were always second-rate French simply for being Jewish in a Catholic country. Then there were the visiting Americans and movie stars and members of the elegant Parisian homosexual set, which included some of the most fashionable couturiers and hairdressers. It was an amusing and expensive circle; it flattered and fawned, but neither loyalty nor kindness was high on its list of priorities. For those qualities, it began to seem, the Duke and Duchess of Windsor would only have each other.

The Duke was becoming restless, preoccupied and irascible as he pondered what must have seemed a very empty future. All his overtures to London and requests to "be of service" were ignored. His Paris friends began to notice that he was drinking more than a little, and a large cologne bottle in his dressing room was discovered to contain brandy. During the Paris days, while the Duke brooded, Wallis shopped for apartments. But each time she found one that she thought might be suitable and brought him to see it, he said, "No, no, no—it won't do." What he longed for, it seemed, was the country— not suburban Versailles, but vast acreage such as that which surrounded Fort Belvedere, where he could putter in the garden and clear paths through the underbrush. This was one of the two great differences that they would spend their lives trying to reconcile—her love of the excitement of big-city living and his love of rural pleasures. The other was his tendency to lateness, and her insistence on absolute punctuality.

The French Riviera wasn't the country exactly, but by the spring of 1938 it was at least an escape from the chilly weather in the north, and Wallis and the Duke journeyed there and ensconced themselves in a handsome rented villa called La

Croë at Cap d'Antibes. La Croë, also furnished, was owned by a British newspaper executive named Sir Pomeroy Burton, and had been one of the houses offered to the Windsors for their wedding. At La Croë, Lloyd George and Winston Churchill called to pay their respects to the Duke, and the actress Maxine Elliott—who had lent her villa in Cannes to the Windsors for a holiday before their marriage—gave a large party for them and their guests.

La Croë was a somewhat unusual house. It was large, with seventeen bedrooms and eight baths, one of which was reported to contain a gold bathtub. The Duchess was always careful to point out that the tub wasn't *solid* gold—it was merely painted gold. The roof of the house had been fitted out like the deck of a ship, with fake guns, a telescope, life belts and jackets, and three "cabins." For all its oddities, the Duke liked the house, and his spirits seemed to improve. He and Wallis decided to lease La Croë, and the next few months were spent wandering with their entourage and luggage between Cannes and Paris and Versailles. They were in Cannes to celebrate Wallis's forty-second birthday in June, and cruised on a borrowed yacht, the *Frixos,* which belonged to another of their somewhat déclassé circle of acquaintances, "Nicky" Zographos, the head of the Greek gambling syndicate in Monte Carlo. Four days later, they celebrated the Duke's forty-fourth birthday less spectacularly at home.

And so they wandered, aimlessly, rootlessly, and unemployed about France, stopping in this or that rented or borrowed house or hotel suite, perching here and there to rest like weary birds after a long flight. Piles of conspicuous luggage—large Louis Vuitton trunks, each numbered and emblazoned with tall letters announcing THE DUKE OF WINDSOR followed them and preceded them. He called her "Darling," or "Sweetheart," or "Peaches," and she called him "Darling," or "David," or— which raised eyebrows—"Little Man." He didn't seem to mind this diminutive, nor did he seem to mind when she occasionally chided him with, "Don't forget, darling, you're not King anymore!" One afternoon in Paris, when Wallis was entertaining friends for cocktails at the Meurice, the Duke of Windsor appeared, his arms laden with dress boxes—shopping that he had picked up for her at various dressmakers. He disappeared into a bedroom to deposit his parcels, and his wife leaned forward and confided to her friends, "No one will ever know how hard

I work to try to make the little man feel busy!"

In the fall of 1938, Wallis and the Duke decided at last on a Paris house, a huge mansion at 24 Boulevard Suchet near the Bois de Boulogne, and took it on an extended lease. It was their first dwelling that was not decorated, at least in part, with other people's tastes and furnishings, and Wallis fell to the task of decorating this house with enthusiasm. If anyone still asked what it was he saw in her, and if it was not sex, then one of the answers must have been her extraordinary domesticity and organizational ability. The Duke of Windsor once commented to a friend, "If Wallis were ever stranded on a desert island, the first thing she would do would be to organize the grains of sand on the beach." As for decorating, she not only had a fine eye for beautiful things, but she was also an absolute perfectionist. Every drape must hang *just so*. Every tiny precious object displayed on a table top must be arranged *just so*. Every ashtray—both she and the Duke smoked—must be emptied and polished immediately after it was used. Her perfectionism extended to areas of her house that guests never saw— her closets, with her dresses arranged according to color, length, and season, with a note attached to each to remind her when and where it had last been worn; her drawers, with gloves, blouses and underthings arranged according to color and labeled according to the shoes, bags, belts and hats each item accessorized. For the next few months, her perfectionism in decorating 24 Boulevard Suchet made her the despair of designers, antiques dealers, and craftsmen all over Paris as rooms were painted and repainted until just the shade she wanted had been achieved. Though her tastes ran to the baroque—heavy brocades on walls and window hangings, sculptured mirrors, tall sconces, chandeliers, and large, rather pompous flower arrangements—the results were spectacular. Under her hand, 24 Boulevard Suchet became exactly what she wanted—a showplace, built for entertaining on the most lavish scale—and as her handiwork progressed, her husband clearly admired every last detail of it. If she could not keep her husband busy, she had at least created an environment for him that appeared to make him happy.

While Wallis was absorbed in turning the house on the Boulevard Suchet into a setting for gala balls, the eyes and interests of the world were turning to other, more pressing matters. The Windsors were at La Croë on September 3, 1939, the day that Britain and France declared war on Germany and Italy. That morning, Windsor had tried to telephone London, but the international circuits were jammed, and he finally gave up, saying, "I'm sure that I shall hear from my brother the moment any decision is taken. Let's go for a swim." But he did not hear from his brother. The first official word came in a telephone call from the British Ambassador in Paris. He returned from the telephone, said, "Great Britain has just declared war on Germany," and dove into the pool.

Much later in the day, he finally got through to Walter Monckton, who was still acting as his liaison with the government. He told Monckton, "I want to offer my services in any capacity my brother deems appropriate, and I must return to Britain." Monckton promised to get back to him, but there were no more calls from Monckton that day.

Actually, there was great concern in official London about what was to be done with England's former King. It was not merely a question of his personal safety, though of course this was a factor. More troublesome was the uncertainty about the Duke's political views, which could make him untrustworthy, even dangerous, in France. He had been entertained by Hitler. He had been loaned Mussolini's private railroad car. Many of the Windsors' friends were outspokenly pro-Fascist. But the question was: Where would they go? Over the more than two years since the Abdication and the Windsors' marriage, the Royal Family's icy attitude toward the Duke and his wife had, if anything, grown colder and more unrelenting. Both the Queen and the Queen Mother continued to make it clear that, if the Duke of Windsor returned to London, his wife would never be received by either of them. Within the family, the Duke and Wallis were now treated as nonpersons, as if they simply did not exist. The Duke, just as stubbornly, was still insisting that the only conditions under which he would return to England were if Wallis were recognized by his family and given the title of Royal Highness. Thus things stood at an impasse. In a stubborn family, his mother's and sister-in-law's stubbornness matched his own. Furthermore, they both outnumbered and outranked him.

On the evening war was declared, there was a particularly lurid late-summer orange sunset in London. As Cecil Beaton recalled it, the glow made it look as though all of London were on fire.

On the French Riviera, the Windsors attended another party, and the Duke appeared to be in one of his black moods. When it was over, they returned to La Croë. Wallis had always hated the Duke's habit of playing the organ and bagpipes—interestingly enough, his late father had played them also and always claimed that his son played both instruments very badly. But the skirl of bagpipes symbolized something to the Duke, and he would often sit for hours playing the mournful music, seeming, in the process, to remove himself from the living earth into some more romantic, tragic, lonely time and place. That night after the party he insisted on putting on his kilt and going up to the strange, gun-turreted roof of La Croë to play his pipes. He wanted to play, he said, for Mussolini's troops that were gathering just beyond Cannes, across the Italian frontier. What message he wished to convey to Mussolini's troops is unclear, but after listening to the wild music of the pipes coming from the rooftop for some time, Wallis had had quite enough of it. She rang for her steward, Ernest King, and said, "Please go up on the roof and tell His Royal Highness that it's past midnight." The servant did as he was told, but still his Royal Highness would not come down.

19

On the Road

THE following morning Walter Monckton telephoned. As usual, the connection was poor, but the conversation was made more difficult by the decision, for security reasons, to speak in French, a language in which neither the Duke nor Monckton was fluent. Monckton, however, said that there had been "promising discussions," and promised to come to France shortly with full details. Three days later he arrived by government plane at La Croë. There were two possible wartime positions for the Duke, Monckton explained. One was as a member of the British Military Mission attached to the French General Headquarters at Vincennes. The other was as Deputy Regional Commissioner to Wales, a civil defense job. Both were pitifully unimportant posts, pointedly far removed from sensitive areas and from the capital cities of either Britain or France. But, swallowing his pride, the Duke said that he preferred the one in Wales since that, at least, would bring him back to Britain. In any case, Monckton said, the King wanted to see him, and would send his own airplane to fly the Windsors back to England. The Duke was to announce his decision to his brother upon arrival in London.

But flying back to England presented problems. Wallis had always had a deathly fear of airplanes. One of her many superstitions and dreads—black cats, walking under ladders, thirteen at table, hats on beds—was the certainty that the "unusual circumstances" of her death, which the astrologer had predicted, would involve an airplane crash. The Duke, who had flown his own plane as a young man, now seemed to have contracted this irrational fear of flying from her. He, too, was terrified. They would not fly, even if it meant dodging U-boats in the English Channel, and that was that. And so, on September 8, the Windsor party set off by automobile for the Channel coast, accompanied by their three cairn terriers—Pookie, Preezi, and Detto—and with a station-wagon load of possessions, hastily packed in cardboard boxes, following behind them. Though U-boats were indeed a threat, Wallis's chief worry was that the British would impound and quarantine the dogs when they reached Portsmouth.

At the start, the journey proceeded smoothly. They spent the first night at Avignon, and stopped at Vichy for the second. But when they arrived at Vichy, they were advised that there would be a delay. Plans, it seemed, had not been completed for the rest of their journey, and they were instructed to remain at Vichy until further notice. When, after two days, no word had come, the Duke decided to continue on to Paris to confront the British Ambassador. There, somewhat glumly, the Ambassador told the Duke that his party could continue on to Cherbourg, where a destroyer, the HMS *Kelly*, would carry them overnight to England.

In England, though a red carpet was laid down for them in Portsmouth, the ceremony to welcome the ex-King after nearly three years' absence was minimal. They were to stay at the Sussex house of the Duke's old friend Fruity Metcalfe—far enough from official London so that their presence would go almost unnoticed—while the Duke would meet with the King. No functions had been planned for the Windsors. No invitations were waiting for them. The mood of the visit was one of tension and apprehension. Would the Duke accept either of the lowly offers? Or would he attach the customary string that Wallis must be recognized as a Royal Highness? Writing of her guests' visit, Lady Alexandra Metcalfe, Fruity's wife, said, "They arrived on the 12th & today is the 25th. The visit has gone easily & well. There have been moments when the ice seemed dangerously thin & ominous cracks have been heard but the night has brought a thickening & we have skated on again. . . . we have every evening a quatre."

The Duke's meeting with the King was very disappointing, and also very brief. The royal mind had changed, apparently, since Walter Monckton's visit to La Croë. The Welsh post that the Duke had hoped to get was not even mentioned. The options for wartime service had narrowed down to one—with the mission at Vincennes. It was that or nothing. Furthermore, there were humiliating conditions attached to the offer. Though the Duke still retained the rank of Admiral of the Fleet, Field Marshal in the Army, and Marshal of the Royal Air Force, he would have to waive all this and accept the lowlier rank of Major-General. When saluted by an enlisted man, he was told, he must not return the salute since the salute would be technically intended for the Monarch, and he was Monarch no longer; it was a petty and hair-splitting point that needed not to have been made, since all officers routinely return the salutes of enlisted men.

And yet, with an admirable swallowing of pride, the Duke accepted all these restrictions and conditions. And so, after what must have seemed an almost completely unnecessary trip, the Windsors turned around and headed back to France. They had been in England barely two weeks, and had seen or spoken to almost none of their old friends. Indeed, it seemed that with a few exceptions such as the Metcalfes and the Moncktons, all the old friends from the carefree days had evaporated. The only courtesy extended to Wallis had been the British customs' willingness to waive the quarantine regulations in her case, and let her bring the cairns into the country.

In Europe, the winter of 1939–1940 became the period known as the Phony War. Though a state of war officially existed, no bombs fell and few shots were fired. At Vincennes, the Duke took up his insignificant post while Wallis languished in the house on the Boulevard Suchet, picking up her extensive redecorating chores where they had been left off. She also joined the motor branch of the French Red Cross, and helped to deliver plasma, bandages, and cigarettes behind the Maginot Line. One of her inventions during this period was a design for a pair of woolen gloves for riflemen, with all fingers covered except the trigger finger. Then in early May 1940, when everyone had begun to think that the Phony War might go on forever, it abruptly ended. Also, as far as France was concerned, it seemed all but lost. Frightened, the Windsors conferred with William Bullitt, the U.S. Ambassador, who, agreeing that Paris might soon be under siege, suggested that the Duke and Duchess might be safer somewhere in Central France. Wallis remembered Blois, the little town where she had stopped with Perry Brownlow on her hectic trip across France in 1936, and suggested that this might provide a haven for them. The Duke agreed, and so, in the well-traveled Buick, the beleaguered Windsors were off again, on roads jammed with the traffic of evacuating Parisians.

But Blois was so crowded with refugees—not only French but Dutch and Belgian as well—that the Windsors were forced to spend the night on two narrow cots in a rented sitting room. England, it began to seem, had lost all interest in the welfare of its former King and was leaving him to his own resources. The following morning, the Duke had a new plan. They would drive to Biarritz. From there, if the Nazis overran France, Wallis would be able to make an easy escape across the border into neutral Spain. He would return to what remained of his mission, which by then had moved from Vincennes to Paris. After a hasty breakfast, they headed southwestward again.

Biarritz was also crowded with refugees who had had the same idea, but Wallis was able to find a room at the Hôtel du Palais. Here, however, the Nazis decided to make propaganda use of her. The German radio blared out the news that Wallis was in Biarritz, staying at the Hôtel du Palais, and even broadcast her room number. This did not exactly make her the hotel's most treasured guest. Fortunately, her stay was brief. Barely a week later the Duke telephoned her to say that Italian forces were massing at the French border. It was essential, he said, that they go at once to the south of France and gather whatever remained of their possessions in the house at La Croë. It was a somewhat foolhardy idea, under the circumstances, and Wallis wondered as they drove eastward toward the Côte d'Azur—in the face of traffic that was westward, away from the Italian frontier—if they weren't possibly going the wrong way. But her husband insisted that saving their possessions and his papers was more important than their personal safety.

They arrived at La Croë on May 29, and though the war

was now almost within earshot, they started to pack and make arrangements for closing up the house. They even found time to do a bit of entertaining, and had Maurice Chevalier to lunch. But then, on June 18, the British Consul General at Nice, Major Dodds, sternly warned the Duke of Windsor that instructions had come from London. He and the Duchess must leave France as quickly as possible. Major Dodd's best advice was that the Windsors join him and his staff and head for Spain. The Duke, meanwhile, had been given a leave of absence from his mission in Paris. It would turn out to be permanent. And so—off again—the Windsors and everything they could carry with them got into the Buick and joined the throng of westward-escaping refugees.

The British government had become painfully aware of—and embarrassed by—rumors circulated by the Nazi propaganda office that the Duke and Duchess sympathized with the German cause, had praised Germany's air power as superior to Britain's, and favored (as Hitler then did) a peaceful surrender of Britain to Germany. Obviously London, not knowing how much weight to attach to these stories—but knowing the Duke's pro-German sentiments almost too well—was alarmed. The Windsors must be gotten out of Europe, and preferably as far from Europe as possible. Winston Churchill argued in favor of inviting them back to England. But the King, the Queen Mother, and most of the Court Establishment—still unforgiving—remained stonily opposed. And there, as the Duke and Wallis made their way across the Spanish border to Barcelona, matters rested at a stalemate. In Barcelona, the Windsors rested for a few days. Then they continued to Madrid and the relative calm of a suite at the Ritz.

The sojourn in Madrid turned out to be for about two weeks. Though the news of the war continued to worsen, there were parties, receptions and balls for the Windsors. By coincidence, the British Ambassador to Spain was now Sir Samuel Hoare, to whom the ex-King and Beaverbrook had turned for help during the early days of the Abdication crisis—and from whom very little help had been forthcoming. But Sir Samuel received the Windsors cordially and, scrupulously, no mention was made of unhappy differences in the past. And soon Sir Samuel was able to deliver what he hoped was good news for the Duke. Winston Churchill, who was now Prime Minister, had succeeded in persuading the King to invite the Windsors back to

England for the duration of the war. They were to make their way as speedily as possible to Portugal, where two flying boats of the Coastal Command would meet them and carry them back to London. Also, the Duke of Westminster had offered the Windsors his house, Eaton Hall, near Chester. It began to seem as though the ice might be beginning to thaw.

Wallis, in her memoirs, insisted that she was willing to go along with this plan, and thought it very "sensible." She even said that, to comply with it, she would try to suppress her lifelong fear of flying, and would board one of the flying boats. She claimed that she found the Duke's attitude—which imposed conditions on Churchill's offer—"a little silly." But conditions there were, and they were drearily familiar ones. First, he must be given an important wartime post in England; second, she must be awarded the same status as his brothers' wives, as a Royal Highness.

It could be argued that the Duke showed rather poor taste in continuing to haggle over such petty matters as titles and forms of address while soldiers were dying in the battlefields. And Winston Churchill certainly showed remarkable patience and forbearance in haggling with the ex-King over social minutiae so soon after promising to give England only "blood, toil, tears and sweat." On the other hand, the Duke, very much aware of how desperately the British government wanted him off the European continent, undoubtedly felt that he held very strong cards—the strongest he might ever hold, in fact—and that he had a now-or-never chance to get his brother and the rest of the Royal Family to capitulate and give him what he wanted. And so one can either deplore his insensitivity and stubbornness, or admire his persistence and gallantry. For several days, the coded wires and telegrams went back and forth between Madrid and London as Churchill and the Duke bargained over his conditions. Early in July, the Windsors continued on to Portugal to await the final outcome.

Here, alas, the bad news reached them: the Duke's conditions were unacceptable. Churchill, however, had a compromise offer. If the Duke wished, the King would be happy to appoint him Governor of the Bahamas. It was almost an insulting offer—almost too humiliating to accept. The Bahamas was Britain's least significant West Indian colony, thousands of miles from England, a handful of winter-resort islands with no military importance whatsoever, which would never remotely be touched by the war in Europe. Governorship of the Bahamas was customarily handed to a military officer or civil servant on the verge of retirement. In fact, Churchill's offer was not an offer at all. It was more like an ultimatum. Nor was Churchill able to pretend to his old friend that this would be a post of importance. He did, though, try to soften the blow by saying that, if the Duke did the Governor's job well, more significant duties would surely be given to him in the future. When the Duke broke the news to Wallis, he tried to put a cheerful face on things. He said, "Well, darling, they've finally found a job for me."

What happened during the next few weeks in Portugal has become a matter of great controversy—one that would erupt, periodically, as we shall see, for the next forty years. It involved the alleged German plot to kidnap the Duke and return him to some neutral country—like Spain—or, even better, to make use of his increasing anger and bitterness over his government's treatment of him, and lure him of his own accord to the Nazi cause.

In their respective memoirs, the Duke and Duchess both made light of this plot, treating it as a kind of joke or comic-opera ploy. But when, after the war, certain captured files from the German Foreign Office were opened, indicating that the Duke and Duchess were both aware of the plot and hinting that they themselves may have been part of it, the Windsors' lawyers immediately began rattling their swords—suggesting that the Windsors took these allegations very seriously indeed.

A few facts are clear. Hitler, by the summer of 1940, still believed he could succeed in bringing England to its knees through nonmilitary means, and certainly the Duke of Windsor would have provided Germany with a very valuable hostage and bargaining chip in this endeavor. Even more lucrative, from a propaganda standpoint, was the possibility that the Duke was angry enough to disavow Churchill and the rest of his brother's government. In return, in the event of a German victory, the Germans could offer to send Edward VIII back to England as a puppet King with Wallis as his Queen. It was a plot that was not without a certain logic, considering the Duke's sentiments at the time and the fact that he had often said that he could have dealt with Hitler without going to war.

Portugal, meanwhile, during those early days of the Second World War, was a strange place. Though neutral, the country teemed with Fascists, and the smells of intrigue were every-where. The British Ambassador to Portugal was now Sir Wal-ford Selby, who had entertained the Duke during his waiting-out period in Austria. Though there is no evidence that Selby was pro-Nazi, he certainly selected a curious place for the Windsors to live while they were there. It was the country estate, in Estoril, of a wealthy Portuguese banker, Dr. Ricardo de Espirito Santo e Silva, who was a well-known Nazi sym-pathizer. Here, the Nazi offensive to secure the Windsors seems to have been mounted on two fronts. One was fear. A note was slipped into a bouquet of flowers that was delivered to the Duchess. A mysterious caller arrived in Estoril, saying that he had an "extraordinary offer" of a luxurious house for them if they would return to Spain. The visitor turned out to be an emissary of Joachim von Ribbentrop. And the German Minister wrote to Ribbentrop, "A firing of shots through the bedroom window scheduled for July 30 was omitted, since the psycho-logical effect on the Duchess would only have been to increase her desire to depart [but], through steady undermining of their sense of security, the Duke and Duchess are being strongly influenced." They were being influenced, furthermore, to be-lieve that the offer of the governorship of the Bahamas was a ruse, that the *British* wanted to kidnap them, and that, once aboard their ship to Nassau, the British planned to murder them.

The second front involved diplomatic persuasion, and in this we must rely on what the captured German documents reveal. On July 25, for example, the German Ambassador to Madrid, Stohrer, reported that a Spanish emissary, Miguel Primo de Rivera, the son of the old Spanish dictator, had returned from Lisbon. While there, Rivera

had two long conversations with the Duke of Windsor; at the last one the Duchess was present also. The Duke ex-pressed himself very freely. In Portugal he felt almost like a prisoner. He was surrounded by agents, etc. Politically he was more and more distant from the King and the present English government. The Duke and Duchess have less fear of the King, who was quite foolish ("reichlight toricht"), than of the shrewd Queen who was intriguing skillfully against the Duke and particularly the Duchess.

The Duke was considering making a public statement

and thereby disavowing present English policy and breaking with his brother.

In a second telegram, Stohrer continued:

When he gave the Duke the advice not to go to the Bahamas, but to return to Spain, since the Duke was likely yet to be called upon to play an important role in English policy and possibly to ascend the English throne, both the Duke and Duchess gave evidence of astonishment..... They replied that according to the English constitution this would not be possible after the Abdication. When the confidential emissary then expressed his expectation that the course of the war might bring about changes even in the English constitution, the Duchess especially became very pensive.

On August 1, the Duke and Wallis sailed for the Bahamas aboard an American ship, leaving, presumably, the German plot to use them failed and thwarted, except for an August 2 document which indicated that it might be taken up again at some later date:

The message which was conveyed to the Duke made the deepest impression on him and he felt appreciative of the considerate way in which his personal interests were being taken into account.... The Duke paid tribute to the Führer's desire for peace, which was in complete agreement with his own point of view. He was firmly convinced that if he had been King it would never have come to war. To the appeal made to him to cooperate at a suitable time in the establishment of peace, he agreed gladly. However, he requested that it be understood that at the present time he must follow the official orders of his government. Disobedience would disclose his intentions prematurely, bring about a scandal, and deprive him of his prestige in England. He was also convinced that the present moment was too early for him to come forward, since there was as yet no inclination in England for an approach to Germany. However, as soon as this frame of mind changed he would be ready to return immediately.... He would remain in continuing communication with his previous host and had agreed with him upon a code word, upon receiving which he would immediately come back over. He insisted that this would be possible at any time, since he had foreseen all eventualities and had already initiated the necessary arrangements.

While the evidence above is fairly damning, it is still not sufficient to support the claim that the Duke contemplated treason. To the German approaches he was polite and noncommittal, and it is also important to remember that diplomats, politicians, and bureaucrats of any government are skillful at writing reports to their superiors that say what the superiors want to hear. This latter report has such a ring to it, an attempt to make a failed mission sound like a success of sorts.

The Duke's last days in Portugal, meanwhile, had been consumed with other matters pertaining to his appointment in the Bahamas, some of them astonishingly trivial. For one thing, before taking up his post in Nassau, he wanted to visit the United States, and another series of coded wires went back and forth between Estoril and London on this matter. Though he did not specify what her ailment was, he insisted that the Duchess needed to go to New York for medical reasons. The Colonial Office was firmly opposed to this, pointing out that Roosevelt, facing an election in November, would feel seriously embarrassed by a royal visitor from a warring European country. The Duchess, of course, could make her own arrangements from Nassau for her New York doctor's visit. After much pleading, the Duke's request was flatly denied.

Next, he wanted two young guardsmen named Fletcher and Webster released from military service to accompany him to Nassau as valet-butler and chauffeur. The War Office pointed out the inappropriateness of removing two able-bodied servicemen from the wartime British army to serve as ducal servants, and suggested that he settle on two men past military age. More telegrams flew back and forth on this issue. Finally, as a compromise—and to get the Windsors out of Portugal, where they seemed imminently in danger of causing great trouble, as quickly as possible—the Duke was allowed to have Guardsman Fletcher, but not Webster. It was the only concession he got.

Since most of the Windsors' last days in Portugal were spent bickering over servants for the Nassau post, it seems hard to believe that they were simultaneously considering becoming Nazi collaborators. And the rendezvous with the Germans in 1940 might be dismissed as an interesting footnote to history if it were not for one brief document unearthed in the captured

German files. It was a telegram dated August 15, two weeks after the Windsors' departure from Lisbon, sent by Hoynegan Huene, the German Minister to Portugal, to his superiors in Berlin. The Duke had changed ships in Bermuda, and the Huene wire read as follows:

> THE CONFIDANT HAS JUST RECEIVED A TELEGRAM FROM THE DUKE FROM BERMUDA, ASKING HIM TO SEND A COMMUNICATION AS SOON AS ACTION WAS ADVISABLE. SHOULD ANY ANSWER BE MADE?

It is not clear who the "confidant" was, or what, if any, reply to this wire was sent. Nor was the wire itself discovered. Two possible explanations of this "telegram from the Duke" (if indeed there was one) present themselves. It could have been a forgery—but from whom and, more important, to what purpose? As far as the Germans were concerned, the issue was closed, and it could have been to no one's advantage to try to revive it. Or the Duke could have sent the wire himself. Frances Donaldson, the Duke's biographer, comes to the latter conclusion. Lady Donaldson writes:

> . . . it is . . . likely that on the sea voyage to Bermuda, having completely failed to get recognition for himself or his wife, having received an appointment which he regarded as petty and provincial, holding an entirely false idea of his own capacities and the genuine opinion that British policies were mistaken, the Duke became persuaded that he had too precipitately refused an opportunity to serve his country. If this view is accepted, it must also be accepted that he decided to reopen the door by sending a telegram to a man who, when he had last seen him, had delivered a message direct from Ribbentrop—a message which, even to someone of the Duke's limited understanding, must surely have been seen to have the most sinister implications.

Also, if this view is accepted, he had missed an opportunity to wreak the ultimate revenge upon his brother, his sister-in-law, and his mother.

20

Decorating

DURING the Windsors' first months in the Bahamas, Wallis would amuse herself, when writing to friends, by perversely crossing out "Government House, Nassau," on her letterhead, and substituting "Elba" or "St. Helena." In this exile, she liked to say, she and the Duke had been "put out of harm's way." Still, for all her bitter complaints, life in Nassau did not seem to present too many vicissitudes. Within a few days of her arrival in August 1940, Wayne Forrest, a former assistant of the hairdresser Antoine, was flown down from New York to do Wallis's hair. He brought with him a number seven carton of cosmetic refills for her beauty case, and picked two bottles of rum and five eggs to prepare a special shampoo.

When Wallis first saw Government House, which was to be the Windsors' official residence, it reminded her of a southern plantation house—a huge, rambling structure, circled with wide verandas and set on a grassy knoll surrounded by palms. As a welcoming gesture, the ladies of Nassau society had filled all the rooms with bouquets of bright tropical flowers, and the house had been thoroughly cleaned and was considered ready for occupancy. But, on closer inspection, Wallis decided that there was a great deal more to be done. In fact, as far as she was concerned, what Government House needed was a complete renovation. The Bahamas House of Assembly had already set aside an appropriation for repairs, but now, at the Windsors' insistence, an additional sum was voted to cover the renovation and the addition of an entire new wing. Within a week after their arrival, the Duke and Duchess pronounced Government House uninhabitable and moved out. The Duchess had spotted termites and, on an inspection of the basement rafters, found dry rot. The house was turned over to workmen. At first the Windsors borrowed a house—as they had become accustomed to doing—from Mr. and Mrs. Frederick Sigrist, Nassau worthies. Later, as the work on Government House went on and on, they moved to Westbourne, one of several estates owned by the Canadian mining magnate Sir Harry Oakes, who was then the richest man in Nassau. Westbourne was also loaned to them.

The decision to renovate Government House was one of several diplomatic mistakes the Windsors were to make during their sojourn in the Bahamas. Once again, their timing was terrible. True, the war in Europe was going a little better for England; despite the Duke's dire predictions of the vast strength of the Luftwaffe, the RAF had won the Battle of Britain. But watching the Windsors move into, and then immediately out of, Government House, hurt the feelings of the conservative, tradition-proud Bahamians. They had always loved their old Government House, and felt intensely possessive about it. Other colonial governors had lived in it comfortably for years without complaining. Why was it suddenly unsuitable for the Windsors? Who was *she* to suddenly decide that everything was wrong about the place? The island's Old Guard were even more miffed when they learned—not from the Duchess, which would have been more tactful, but from their daily newspaper—that she was going to gut the entire house, rebuild it and redecorate it from top to bottom—using a decorator imported from New York, of all places. Weren't the local artisans and craftsmen good enough for her? What was more, the islanders liked Government House exactly as it was—the whitewashed walls, the muslin curtains blowing at the open windows, the comfortable late Victorian furniture that the Duchess now planned to discard. "Does she have to do all this so soon?" one Nassau society matron asked. And another said, "Couldn't she have at least consulted *us?* What does she—or any other American—know about decorating for the tropics?" The islanders were even more indignant when they learned that among other things, the Duchess had ordered portraits of two of the Duke's ancestors, Queen Victoria and George IV, removed from the walls, and that one of the public rooms was being painted in a soft pink that had been specially mixed to match the Duchess's face powder (her powder puff, it was reported, had been sent to New York in order to get an exact match). Still, the Duke and Duchess seemed unaware of the distinct antipathy their project was creating, and their work progressed.

How to explain this remarkable lack of sensitivity? There were some observers who felt that, in the four years since the Abdication crisis, Wallis had been hardened and toughened by the treatment she had received from the Royal Family, and had learned to conceal her bitterness beneath a careful façade of brittle superficiality. Behind the mask was an angry woman who no longer cared whether or not what she did was criticized, and who no longer felt she owed anything to anyone except her husband—and he happened to like it when she decorated. Certainly he, too, seemed to have changed. His dependency on her was complete. In her new toughness, she was simply being tough for both of them.

In New York that summer, William Randolph Hearst summoned Adela Rogers St. Johns to his office again. The woman who had written about the real Mrs. Simpson before the Abdication was now being given another exclusive—the follow-up on the married life of the Duke and Duchess of Windsor, who were settled at last in Nassau. The story was to be called "At Long Last, the Windsors' own story," and furthermore, it was to contain "no warts." It was to be all sunshine, serenity and marital bliss—that was the only way Hearst had been able to obtain sole rights from the Windsors. All other newspapers, magazines, and book publishers had been turned away.

At first, as Mrs. St. Johns tells us in her autobiographical volume, *The Honeycomb,* she was less than enthusiastic about the assignment. "To start out with the truth," she said, "I've lost my taste for the Windsors." But, Mr. Hearst suggested shrewdly, wasn't she nonetheless just a bit *curious* about them? After all, she had already written thousands of words about them, without ever having met either party. Wouldn't she really enjoy knowing what the Duke and Duchess were like? She had been given complete freedom of access to them both. They had offered her the hospitality of their borrowed house for as long as she liked. (She decided to turn down this invitation.) She could ask them whatever she wanted—all that had been promised. She would, as well, be regally entertained in Nassau. It would be a lovely, fully paid vacation, in the company of the world's most famous couple.

"Mr. Hearst," Mrs. St. Johns wanted to know, "will I be allowed to write the truth?"

Typically, Hearst replied, "You need not write anything but the truth. Let us cross the bridge of what is the truth in this case when we come to it."

And so, in early November 1940, Adela Rogers St. Johns set off by plane for Nassau. She was met at the airport by Major Gray Phillips, the Governor's aide-de-camp, and was advised that the Duchess would receive her immediately at Government House, where she was supervising the renovation. Mrs. St. Johns was given a briefing on protocol. The Duke was to be addressed as "Your Highness" or "Sir," and he was to be referred to as His Royal Highness. Wallis was to be addressed as "Duchess," and referred to as the Duchess.

At Government House, after making her way across drop cloths, around pails of plaster, cans of paint, and scattered debris from the carpenters and masons, Mrs. St. Johns was ushered into a small, bare-walled office furnished with a modern desk and two chairs. Behind the desk, flanked by telephones, jars of pencils, and long sheets of paper covered with figures, sat the Duchess of Windsor.

Adela St. Johns's strongest impression of Wallis was the blue eyes. She was so transfixed by them that, later on, she could not remember what Wallis was wearing other than sapphire earrings, though she knew she was in the presence of one of the best-dressed women in the world. She also noticed that Wallis looked young for her age, and yet, at the same time, she was *aware* that the Duchess looked young for her age. She also looked cool, despite the tropical heat and lack of air conditioning—crisply efficient and a bit worldly-wise. Later, Adela St. Johns recalled, "While she had a look of breeding—she *moved* right—she did not have what we call *class*." There was an air of mannered artificiality about her that was off-putting, and that made everything she said and did seem artificial and calculated. To Mrs. St. Johns, she seemed a woman who was all veneer, and if there was any depth of feeling underneath the veneer she had learned never to let it show. Adela St. Johns was also immediately aware that she did not like the Duchess of Windsor—disliked her intensely, in fact—and was at the same time confident that the Duchess of Windsor did not like her. She knew right away that it was going to be difficult to write Mr. Hearst's Happy Ending.

The mutual antipathy that the two women instantly felt for one another is understandable. On the surface, they could not have been more unlike. Wallis was a woman who, other than to keep house, had never worked. Adela St. Johns was a California-born woman who had worked all her life, starting at the bottom in newspapers and working her way up in the tough, competitive, male-dominated world of the Fourth Estate to the point where she was one of the top woman reporters in the world. She had tackled unpleasant assignments and, in the process, had become earthy-tongued, humorous, candid, and cynical, with a well-developed ability to cut through pretense, which she would have called by a juicier epithet. At the same time, she and Wallis were also very much alike. Both were ambitious, and both were strong-willed. Adela St. Johns, for example, in the course of her newspaper career had earned a reputation as a two-fisted drinker who could outlast the best of the men at the bar. At the same time, when her son Bill went off to the war, she made a vow with herself never to drink until her son came home. He never came home, and she never drank again. She was a woman who, well into her eighties, would still swim a mile a day in the icy Pacific surf outside her home in Malibu. It was the similarity in their two female natures that was at the root of their dislike and distrust of each other. They were cut from the same American brand of cloth. Both were American success stories, though in different fields.

After the usual courteous preliminaries, the Duchess immediately began talking. "I did everything I could to prevent the abdication of the King, even though it might mean I would live to the end of my life—alone. . . . But I would have chosen to keep him on his throne, where he would serve his people and the world. . . . . Someday you will know, you will understand what was done to him, the sacrifices he made. This man is—you will know—is almost a saint."

She continued at length in this vein. Did she, Adela St. Johns wondered, actually think of her husband as a kind of holy martyr? "Her deep concern [was] that this man, almost a saint, who had been Ambassador Extraordinaire, instead of being used in a world-wide position only he could fill, for which only the former Prince of Wales had been trained, he was wasted on this rock in the ocean. She was bitter. He would, she felt, be even better as once more a roving diplomat, with all his experience, than he would have been as King, for his experience had not been within the narrow confines of constitutional monarchy. That this man should be worrying about the failure of the sponge crop—'We are determined to do our duty like good soldiers and he—he bears it like a saint—but it is the world that suffers his loss.'"

She went on, speaking with emphasis: "You know, when I first met the Prince of Wales, and he fell in love with me, I was not exactly young, and I was not exactly—shall we say inexperienced? Believe me, I would much rather have been the mistress of the King of England than the wife of the Governor of the Bahamas!" Adela St. Johns thought it was interesting that she spoke of "when he fell in love with me." She never once mentioned her falling in love with him, or their falling in love with each other.

Then the Duchess stretched out her arm, pressed a buzzer on her desk, and picked up one of the two telephones. "Darling?" she said. "Have you time to come in a moment?" Apparently he did, for almost immediately the Duke of Windsor appeared at the door, and Adela St. Johns rose and curtsied the way she had been taught to do by the nuns at her convent school. He smiled at the curtsy, and it was a radiant smile. But Adela noticed that when the smile faded, the man—saint and martyr or not—looked haggard and, even under the ruddy tropical tan, weary and old. She also noticed that the Duchess's expression had softened visibly—into something that might have been taken for a look of love, or possibly pity.

Twin conclusions jumped to Mrs. St. Johns's mind. He had reacted to the events following the Abdication with terrible disappointment and sorrow. She had reacted with an almost inarticulate rage. Since her reaction was focused on his family—his mother, his brother, and his brother's Dowdy Duchess—she could not express it to him. Nor could he express his to her, without confessing his loss of manhood. Unlike some marriages, which are held together by an ability to communicate, theirs was cemented by an inability.

That evening at dinner, in the Sigrists' elegant manor house, at a table filled with flowers and candlelight, Adela St. Johns was seated beside the Duke and was stirred when the kilted Governor rose to his feet, lifted his wine glass, and said, "Gentlemen, the King!" After that, the conversation was more mundane. At another dinner party she attended, the Duke wanted to talk about American table manners. He wanted to know why Americans put their forks in the left hand when they cut things, and then transfer them back to the right hand to eat—while the English keep the fork in the left hand and use the knife to build up a small package of food on the back of the fork. The English method, the Duke felt, made more sense, and was more efficient. The conversation reminded Mrs. St. Johns of the alleged exchange about central heating when Wallis Simpson first met the Prince of Wales.

At one point, the Duchess called down from the other end of the long table, "Darling, Mrs. St. Johns knows Mickey Rooney." It turned out that the Duke was a great Mickey Rooney fan, and he was full of questions about what the actor was really like. That evening, Adela St. Johns did notice what the Duchess wore—a long gown of floating blue organdy, her best color, and a crown of diamonds in her hair.

Major Phillips had instructed Mrs. St. Johns on the protocol of conversing with Royalty. There were three rules. She must never open a subject or ask a question until Royalty had given her permission. She must never turn away from Royalty or terminate a conversation. She must answer every question Royalty asked her, even if her answer was that she didn't know the answer to the question. But she was momentarily caught off guard when the Duke turned to her at the dinner table and asked her why the American press had reacted so adversely to the pray-for-peace speech he had delivered at Verdun shortly before the war. The press had criticized the speech on the grounds that it seemed inappropriate for an ex-King to speak out and steal the spotlight while his replacement on the throne, even then en route to the United States for an official visit, was doing his best to rule in his place. After some hesitation, Adela St. Johns replied:

"In my country, sir, we have a tradition of enormous sympathy for a pinch-hitter. A pinch-hitter, in case that sports term isn't familiar to you, sir, is a man who, when a star is injured or out of the lineup or in a slump, is sent in for him. He bats for him in a pinch, when the game may be won or lost. He is a substitute. He is on the spot. All American hearts go out to someone who is, let us say, pinch-hitting for Babe Ruth. We are rooting for him, poor guy, to do well, get a home run, win the ball game."

"I understand this," the Duke said.

"To us, sir, your brother King George VI was, in our eyes, a pinch-hitter. When you left the game he came in as a *substitute*. You were a great and popular star, sir. He, with some handicaps we had heard about, and without your buildup, was suddenly called on to take your place. We felt it wasn't right for *you* to appear in an heroic role and speak from a battlefield in *France* when he was trying so hard to bat in your place, to get a hit—as though Babe Ruth ran up and down the sidelines hitting fungoes when a pinch-hitter was at the plate in his stead."

The Duke was silent for a moment, and of course Adela St. Johns could not turn away from him or terminate the conversation. Then he said, "Do you know that the Duchess was the first woman who ever spoke to me about my *work?*" He mentioned the speech he delivered just after he became King. "I used to discuss my speeches with her even then—that phrase *I am still the same man*—that was hers. The Verdun speech, we thought that any man who had an opportunity to speak for peace should do so. It was meant only as a plea for peace."

Listening to him, Adela St. Johns had another sudden flash of insight. She and many others had been surprised and puzzled by the sentence from his Abdication speech—"I cannot carry my burdens as King as I would wish to do without the help and support of the woman I love." Public declarations of love are very un-English, and they are very un-upper-class. It was a line that echoed from the pages of a *Cosmopolitan* novelette. Now she was certain that that sentence had been Wallis's also.

On other occasions, during what turned out to be a three-month stay in Nassau, Mrs. St. Johns had opportunities to observe what great power Wallis exerted over her husband. At a party at the Emerald Bay Club, for example, she noticed how the Duke had kept moving seat by seat around the table until at last he sat beside her. She manipulated him beautifully, flattering him and feeding his ego, saying things to him like, "David, darling, tell your wonderful story about—" and so on, helping him look and sound his best. One night Mrs. St. Johns watched as the Duke led his wife out onto the dance floor. They were both beautiful dancers. Watching them dance—two diminutive, no-longer-young people moving perfectly to the music in each other's arms, absolutely synchronized and interconnected, it was really possible to conclude that they had been made for each other, if only for moments like these. And yes, Mrs. St. Johns decided, it was possible to believe that theirs was a great love story after all.

During her Bahamas visit, Adela St. Johns learned that the Windsors were again planning a trip to America. "I felt a cloud of dark foreboding concerning this visit," she wrote. Somehow she was certain, all would go wrong, all they did would be held against them by the press, held up to ridicule and scorn: the wartime skylarking of the world's most famous and frivolous couple. With the help of a Windsor aide, Adela drafted a short list of Dos and Don'ts designed to help Wallis and the Duke get the friendliest possible reception in America:

DO

Land somewhere other than New York.
Go to Wakefield Manor, the Duchess' ancestral home, as the first stop.
Wait for the White House to move before making any social engagement.
Keep very strictly to all war-time regulations.
Bring as small a staff as is possible to do with and as little luggage.

DON'T

Go to a big New York hotel.
Bring too much luggage!!!!!!!
Have too many servants.
Wear jewelry.
Attend any parties in either Washington or New York unless guests are carefully checked.
Same about Wakefield Manor.
DO NOT GO to cafes or restaurants.

BE SURE TO

Consult the heads of our Press, this as Press is an international matter in war-time, and they will wish to help
and advise you: William Randolph Hearst, Roy Howard,
Kent Cooper, Sulzberger, Ogden Reid, Roy Roberts,
Colonel McCormick

The purpose of all this sensible advice was to undo, if
possible, some five years of public-relations blundering, to gild
the notoriety with a heavy coating of respectability and responsibility, and to build a new "image" for the Windsors as
serious, sensible, quiet, well-mannered and well-meaning people.

Perhaps one should never offer unsolicited advice to anyone.
It is almost never heeded. Certainly Wallis and the Duke paid
no attention to any of Mrs. St. Johns's cautionary words. Almost perversely, it seemed (were they stupid? was it the nose-
thumbing syndrome again after all the slights and snubs? had
they simply stopped caring what anyone thought, and determined to do only what pleased themselves?), they ignored it
all. They arrived in America that winter—in New York, of
course—like two bulls in a china shop. They ensconced themselves in one of the biggest, flashiest, most publicity-conscious
hotels in town, the Waldorf-Astoria, where they took an entire
floor. They "brought more trunks and suitcases than harassed
customs officials could count." With them came the Duke's
valet—indispensable as always—two maids for the Duchess,
a secretary for each, all four dogs, and all Wallis's jewelry.
Immediately, they were taken up with enthusiasm by what was
then known as Café Society, the playboys and playgirls of the
era, the newly rich and the would-be rich, the second-rate and
lower-than-second-rate pretty and handsome and silly and gay.
Night after night they danced and drank and partied, and stayed
at nightclubs until the wee hours of the morning. They never
bothered to consult the press chiefs, but were contented with
the offerings of Cholly Knickerbocker, Walter Winchell and
Elsa Maxwell, and all the other gossip columnists. They never
bothered to visit Wakefield Manor, which the Duke had often
said he wanted very much to see. They never received an
invitation to the White House. They never set foot inside an
opera house, a concert hall, a symphony auditorium, a lecture
hall, a church.

As for her story, Adela Rogers St. Johns dutifully sat down and wrote what Mr. Hearst wanted—a Happy Ending—tender, romantic, loving. As before, her heart was not in it. The Duchess, she wrote, had told her that the Duke would "always want to improve living conditions." Certainly, from what one read of their doings in the gossip columns, he was interested in improving his own. To describe the Duchess, Mrs. St. Johns found herself resorting to adjectives she hated: *"frail—tiny— delicate—floating—graceful—dainty."*

Her real feelings she saved until 1969, when she wrote in *The Honeycomb,* "I always had the impression that Wallis Warfield Windsor could play tackle for the Green Bay Packers."

But then, no doubt, so could have Adela Rogers St. Johns.

21

✥

Wandering

THOUGH the Duchess of Windsor in her memoirs referred to the Nassau period as "five fruitful years," they were not particularly onerous years, nor, with one exception, were they very exciting ones. The exception was 1943, when Sir Harry Oakes was murdered. Until the refurbishment of Government House was completed, he had been the Windsors' principal host in Nassau. Sir Harry's son-in-law, Count Alfred de Marigny, was arrested and tried for the murder, but he was eventually acquitted and the crime has remained unsolved. Later, the Duke of Windsor would be accused of having bungled the case by calling in, as chief investigators, two Florida policemen, Edward Melchen and James Barker, instead of turning the matter over to Scotland Yard or the FBI. The Oakes murder would be the first of a series of violent ends that would overtake people who had, at one time or another, befriended the Windsors. Within seven months, Charles Bedaux was also dead. He had been arrested in North Africa and charged with trading with the enemy, after he tried to buy up a North African orange crop for the Nazis. The penalty could have been ten years in prison and a $10,000 fine. While awaiting a grand jury hearing to decide whether he should be indicted, Bedaux committed suicide in his Miami prison cell by swallowing a massive dose of sleeping pills.

Once the renovation of Government House was finished, Wallis often complained in private of acute boredom and, indeed, most of the high points of her life in Nassau were unpleasant ones. A writer named Helen Worden wrote a critical appraisal of the Windsors for the *American Mercury* in which she said, among other things, that the Duchess kept a photograph of Herr von Ribbentrop in her bedroom and that, in return for the Bahamian government's care for United States soldiers, Wallis had asked to have dresses sent to her from New York. "Absolutely untrue!" fumed the Duke in a letter to the editor, demanding a retraction. The *Mercury* printed a retraction of sorts.

The Duke had also taken time to point out to reporters that the heavy circles under his eyes were not, as rumor had it, the result of overindulgence in alcohol. The circles, he said, were hereditary, and he pointed to a portrait of his great-grandmother Queen Victoria, saying, "Look—she had bags under her eyes too." Wallis, meanwhile, had found time to go to New York for the first of what would be several face lifts. At the hospital she checked in as "Mrs. Robertson"—a mischievous way, it was suggested, of twitting her friend Cordelia Biddle Robertson, a woman known for her success at remaining young-looking.

Though the Windsors complained of boredom with the islands' slow-paced life, which Wallis tried to alleviate by doing some Red Cross work, they made numerous trips to the United States. In May 1943, they visited Bahamian farm workers in Swedesboro, New Jersey, who were not happy about the northern climate and the food. The Duke explained, "You see, they're used to eating peas and rice covered with pork fat. It's a horrible mess, really, but they like it." He recommended more blankets, raincoats, and a look-see into the workers' menus. Later that month, when Winston Churchill addressed the House and Senate in Washington, the Windsors appeared and were applauded—she looking "taut-faced" according to one reporter in a sly reference to the face lift. Inexplicably, when films of Churchill's address were shown in England, the

Windsors were cheered though Churchill was not.

In June, they were still around. Wallis, in a dress of Wallis blue and a sable scarf, presented fifteen hundred rosebuds to wounded veterans at the Valley Forge General Hospital. The Duke, reached for a fashion comment, said, "I think it's a silly rule that does away with trouser cuffs," and explained that the gray plaid suit he was wearing was ten years old.

In October, while the Oakes murder trial was getting under way, the Windsors were back again, visiting Wallis's ailing Aunt Bessie in a Boston hospital, and then going on by train to Newport for a series of parties. Reporters counted thirty-one pieces of luggage, and the Duchess commented, "I think this business of counting our bags is most extraordinary. It's also for a maid, a valet, and a secretary." As would be their perennial misfortune, the Windsors both continued to make comments to the press that tended to emphasize their extravagances and that would have been much better left unmade. Eight weeks later, they were still in the United States, busying themselves mostly with nightclubbing in New York. Peter Kriendler, of the "21" Club, said that though he appreciated their patronage their presence created problems. Patrons who had been about to leave would, when the Duke and Duchess entered, stay on and on just to gape at the pair, hopelessly tangling the restaurant's reservation system. But Kriendler defended the Windsors against current rumors that they were leaving large unpaid bills in their wake. *His* bills, he declared, were always promptly paid. During what turned out to be a two-month stay, the Windsors had few official engagements. They autographed copies of Queen Victoria's biography at a publisher's promotion party and reviewed a group of cadets at Yale.

In February 1944, back in the Bahamas, they entertained the vacationing Herbert Hoover for lunch, but by July they were back in New York for a month. It was the Duke's ninth trip to the United States since he had been appointed Governor four years earlier, and Wallis's seventh, and the purpose was another nightclubbing and shopping spree. When it was suggested to Wallis that her spending was drawing criticism in both England and America, she once more succumbed to her habit of overreacting and overexplaining, and replied, "You are out of your mind! Don't you think I know my people?" She bought, she said, "only about a hundred" new dresses a year, and most of them cost "only about two hundred and fifty dollars apiece," though she admitted that some gowns cost much more. From this comment, of course, simple arithmetic revealed that her annual budget for clothes came to at least twenty-five thousand dollars, which, in wartime 1944, seemed like a lot of money.

One wonders, too, what she meant by "my people." The British? The Americans? Perhaps she meant her public, which had been created for her by the media. The phrase calls to mind that of little Gloria Vanderbilt who, in the middle of a highly publicized battle for her custody between her mother and her aunt, went to her window one day and wanted to know, "Where are my photographers?"

In October, the Duke and Wallis visited the Duke's E. P. Ranch (for Edvardus Princeps) in Canada, sixty-five miles south of Calgary, Alberta. Here, on four thousand acres, with the help of a geologist named Dr. Barnum Brown, the Duke had been trying in vain to discover oil. A laboratory had been set up in the dining room of the main ranch house, and drillers marveled at the size of the Duke's refrigerator. "It's big enough to hold all the beer that all of us could buy with our liquor permits," one said. Wallis pronounced the ranch house uncomfortable and "too small," and added that she could never stand to live in Canada anyway, a remark that did not endear her to Canadians.

Whenever they returned to Nassau, Wallis complained about the heat, even though she had had Government House completely air-conditioned and managed to spend most of the hotter months in cooler climates. It was the terrible heat—not official displeasure over the Duke's handling of the Oakes case—that was given as one of the chief reasons for the Duke's premature resignation of the governorship early in 1945. Sir Oliver Stanley, the British Colonial Secretary, had called on the Windsors the previous December, and the Duke had expressed a wish to quit as soon as a replacement could be found. But the announcement that London had accepted his resignation, which came on March 15, appeared to catch everyone by surprise, including the Duke's official household and the Duke himself. An Associated Press correspondent who telephoned Government House that morning to ask for comment was told by an astonished aide that the Duke "doesn't know anything about it." However, after hurriedly canceling a golf date, the Duke announced that he was, indeed, resigning. The most surprising thing about the announcement was that it came only five months short of his completion of a full five-year term, the normal length of service for a colonial governor. In Nassau, the news was termed "His Second Abdication."

The Duke explained: "My resignation does not mean a permanent severance from public life. After the war, men with experience will be badly needed, and I'll fit in anywhere that I can be helpful. I shall go to England some day." Wallis said: "With the world as it is, one could not make a decision now. But we shall definitely visit France. Our possessions are scattered all over France. We must see what is left." The Duke added: "Both the Duchess and I love to travel. Nearly five years in Nassau is the longest I hope to spend in any place in the future. We have no immediate plan beyond going to New York, and probably to my ranch in Canada."

There were probably other reasons for his early resignation, in addition to the fact that five of Nassau's steamiest months lay ahead before the ending of his full term. After all, the war was nearly over, and the designers in New York and Paris were gearing up for their first postwar collections. There were chores, put off too long, that Wallis felt now needed to be done. In his farewell address to the people of the Bahamas, the Duke said, "You have not seen the last of us . . . *au revoir*." But it would be the last the Bahamas would see of them.

"I am *not* technologically unemployable," the Duke of Windsor told reporters emphatically. "I am not an obsolete man." But what could he do? Soon he would be fifty-one. He still talked wistfully about the governor-generalship of Canada, but under Mackenzie King that was an impossibility. His brother, the Duke of Gloucester, already had the governor-generalship of Australia, and the British were not likely to make the Duchess the Vicereine of India. The screen actor Chester Morris telephoned the Duke to offer him a contract as an actor, to star in his own life story, or to be a coproducer or technical adviser on such a film. The Duke actually considered this for a while, but in the end he and Wallis decided to go to New York for more nightclubbing and partying. That spring of 1945 they embarked upon a career that caused them to become known as the Wandering Windsors. Their wandering would consume the better part of three decades.

Wallis was just as efficient and well-organized a traveler as she was a housekeeper. Inside the top of each numbered trunk and suitcase was a list of the items each contained, and against these individual lists was a master list, itemizing each article for the voyage. Sublists itemized which articles were to be worn for which occasions, with alternative selections in case of unexpected changes in the weather, and inside each packing case each item was tagged with the date when it was to be worn, cross-referenced again against shoes, scarves, hats, sweaters, coats, and jewels which that item would accessorize. Nothing was left to chance or error. It was a job that kept a secretary busy.

From time to time, the Windsors made brief attempts to demonstrate civic-mindedness. During their New York visit in 1945, they visited the headquarters of the Salvation Army—she in sables, wearing pearls, a diamond clip, and aquamarine and sapphire earrings. When the Duke removed his topcoat, it turned out to be one from the early 1930's, with a label reading "H.R.H. The Prince of Wales" stitched on the inner lining. In April of that year President Roosevelt died, and later that summer the Duke paid a call on President Truman in Washington, "just to say hello," and told reporters afterward, "You know, I met him in France during the last war. I don't remember exactly the place." But the Duke's principal activity that summer involved renewed attempts to get the Royal Family to receive his wife, and he had written a number of imploring letters to Buckingham Palace. From Nassau, Wallis had also written to her mother-in-law, requesting that the Bishop of Nassau be given an audience by the Queen when he visited England. The letter had included an oblique suggestion of a reconciliation: "The horrors of war and the endless separations of family have in my mind stressed the importance of family ties." Though Queen Mary did receive the Bishop, there had been no direct reply to Wallis's letter. Some weeks later, however, Queen Mary had written to her son and added a sentence: "I sent a kind message to your wife." This had given the Duke reason to hope that his mother's resistance might at last be beginning to soften.

But by the time the Windsors sailed for France in September 1945, the Duke had still received no assurance that a meeting would take place between Wallis and his mother. At the sailing, he hinted to reporters that a new job possibility might be waiting for him in London. "Though I'm past the half-century mark," he said, "I still feel that I can be useful." Meanwhile, Walter

Winchell, the columnist, had begun attacking the Windsors in print, calling them "The Dook and Dookess." When they left New York, Winchell wrote, "Good riddance to them both—the snobs."

Arriving in Paris, the Windsors were shocked to discover that their house on the Boulevard Suchet had been sold. But the good news was that the new owner graciously invited them to stay at the house until they found a suitable new residence. Also, all their furnishings and possessions in the house had remained intact throughout the war; the Germans had guarded the house during the Occupation. The same situation had prevailed, they soon found out, at La Croë, where only a few small items were missing. The Germans had taken good care of them. When, in October, the Duke went to England to see his mother for the first time in nine years, the Duchess was not invited to accompany him and remained behind in Paris. In London, the Duke went immediately to Marlborough House to see his mother. What they discussed is not recorded, but later they were photographed strolling in the gardens, and his mother reportedly told him that she did not care for the green pork-pie hat he was wearing. A gray bowler would be more suitable, she said. That evening there was a family dinner at Buckingham Palace with his mother, his brother the King, and his sister, the Princess Royal. The subject of Wallis was studiously avoided. The next day the Duke played golf and then toured the bombed-out areas of the East End. Before flying home to Paris, he told reporters, "I shall certainly be coming back, and the next time the Duchess will be coming with me."

In Paris, in the meantime, the Duchess did what she seemed to love doing best. She shopped. She bought a number of Schiaparelli dresses, including a long green taffeta evening dress with a full skirt, and a tailored black moiré with—despite her sensitivity about her prominent collar bones—a revealingly low-cut neckline.

Still at loose ends, the Windsors wandered from party to party through the Paris winter season. Rumors continued to circulate that the Duke was drinking heavily—indeed they had throughout his adult life. Whether they were true it is difficult to say. At times, at parties, he would refuse drinks and ask for nothing but Vichy water. And no one actually saw him drinking too much. Yet there were times when he *appeared* to be drunk and disoriented, and at such times Wallis was observed flashing him sharp little looks of warning. Wallis herself also drank—in such a milieu, it was almost impossible not to—but her Scotches were carefully spaced so that she never, in public at least, lost her cool self-possession and extraordinary ability to remember names and faces.

In December, the Windsors left Paris for the south of France, and Wallis brought with her a new Riviera wardrobe by Hermes, including beach pajamas, color-coordinated scarves and coats, swimsuits, and a wide belt with "Wallis" embroidered across the front. By April, they were able to reoccupy La Croë and to begin entertaining there again. They were still at Cap d'Antibes in July, and still unemployed, when they gave a party for the United States press as part of an Air France publicity junket. Clementine Paddleford of the New York *Herald-Tribune* gushed, "Two ice-filled silver buckets—sandwiches one bite big—again and again came the silver trays with fresh glasses of the bubbling champagne!" At one point, someone commented that Gromyko had watched the Louis–Conn fight, and the Duke said, "That's one decision Gromyko couldn't veto." Everyone roared. Later the Duke staggered into a jardiniere and nearly fell, and the Duchess gripped his arm. He said something to her in a low voice, and she said, "Oh, shut up!" It was one of a number of promotional ventures into which the Windsors would find themselves drawn for the use of their names. For this one, the bill was picked up by Air France.

In September 1946, Wallis and the Duke crossed the Atlantic again, to revisit the Duke's Canadian ranch. Oil had still not been found. Their visit to Alberta created very little local stir, and it appeared that their neighbors could not have cared less about them. One neighbor asked columnist Cornelius Vanderbilt, Jr., "Who's he, mister?" Another said, "No one in Canada in their right mind has had anything decent to say about him as long as I can remember."

The following month the Duke went back to London, this time, as he had promised, bringing Wallis with him. The purpose of the visit was, again, twofold—to find a job for him, and to have Wallis received by the Royal Family. Once more, it was a fruitless mission on both fronts. Neither objective was reached, though the Duke visited and made a personal plea to Prime Minister Clement Attlee. Attlee's response was noncommittal. In England, the Windsors were guests at Ednam Lodge, the country home of the Earl of Dudley in Surrey. The Duke went to see his brother in London and, again, Wallis was excluded from the meeting by royal command. In Mayfair, the Windsors gave a small cocktail party for the press, at which they explained that they wanted only minimum publicity about their visit. But even this effort would prove to be in vain. Shortly afterward, there was a huge burst of publicity about the Windsors all over the world.

While Wallis and the Duke were dining out in London, a burglar climbed up a drainpipe and made his way into the Windsors' bedroom at Ednam Lodge. He—or perhaps they— took a gold watch belonging to the Duke, ignoring a number of other costly gold items, and then went into Wallis's jewel case. When Wallis discovered her loss, she immediately claimed that every piece of jewelry she owned had been stolen except what she had been wearing the night before. In banner headlines, the London *Daily Mail* announced that the stolen jewelry was worth in excess of $2 million. The Duke denied this as "hugely exaggerated," and said that the jewelry was actually worth no more than $80,000. The American press countered with the point that the jewelry had to be worth at least $1,000,000 since the Duke was known to have paid a bill in the amount of $600,000 to Cartier when he left England after the Abdication. The missing items were listed. They included a gold ring set with a 41.4-carat golden sapphire; a pair of diamond and sapphire earrings; a pair of shell-shaped earrings, one set with a blue sapphire, the other with a yellow sapphire; a double gold chain necklace with one large blue sapphire and one yellow sapphire; a ring set with a 7.81-carat square-cut diamond solitaire; an aquamarine and diamond brooch; an aquamarine ring with a huge 58.2-carat aquamarine solitaire; an aquamarine and diamond bracelet; a platinum and diamond bracelet; the Duchess's famous stork-shaped diamond clip; and the list ended with "etc."

Scotland Yard at the highest level was brought into the case, and R. M. Howe, Assistant Commissioner and one of England's foremost crime specialists, was placed in charge of the investigation. A reward of $8,000 was offered for information leading to the recovery of the jewels. Asked to comment on the robbery, the Duke said, "I don't think I will play very good golf this afternoon." Wallis said, "It was stupid. I've been kicking myself all over the place." Then, asked what she had been wearing for jewelry on the night the burglary took place, she said, not very cleverly, "A fool would know that with tweeds or other daytime clothes one wears gold, and that with evening clothes one wears platinum."

If they were not dead already, the publicity about the value and extent of the Duchess of Windsor's jewelry collection—along with the Duke's and Wallis's own unwise statements about it—killed, more or less permanently, the Duke's chances of ever being offered any sort of responsible government post. These two simply did not seem like responsible people. For all their talk of public service, they were a couple frivolously preoccupied with serving themselves. The news of such luxury, furthermore, did not sit at all well with the postwar, austerity-conscious British public, who were still being stringently rationed when it came to such day-to-day items as soap, eggs, and one of the foods they loved the most, chocolate. Wallis's haughty "A fool would know..." comment was mocked and parodied in every pub in England.

For all its much-vaunted sleuthing reputation, Scotland Yard was never able to come up with a clue as to who the thief might have been or what had become of the jewels, and the burglary was never solved.

There were a number of curious aspects to the case, in addition to the widely varying estimates of how much the Duchess's stolen jewelry was worth, and the bemusing "etc." Not long after the robbery, for instance, a number of the missing pieces were found scattered on the fairway of the Sunningdale golf course, next door to Ednam Lodge. Oddly, none of the earrings recovered matched. Many of these pieces had considerable value, but it was as though the burglar had discarded them as unwanted or not worth keeping.

Some months later, Mrs. Samuel Goldwyn, the motion picture producer's wife, was in a London jeweler's looking at photographs of jewels. Frances Goldwyn had a keen eye for stones, and she also knew the Duchess of Windsor slightly. Going through the photographs, she came to one that suddenly looked familiar; she was certain that she had seen Wallis wearing this piece, and she asked the jeweler about it. "Excuse me," he said quickly, "that photograph is in the wrong file. That piece is not for sale." Politely, he removed the photograph from Mrs. Goldwyn's hand and placed it in a drawer.

For years, friends who knew Queen Alexandra's jewelry

had claimed to have recognized stones from her collection in Wallis's, many of them reset in more modern settings. And so the rumor started, never confirmed or denied, that the actual burglar was Scotland Yard itself, assigned by Buckingham Palace with the cloak-and-dagger task of bringing back Queen Alexandra's stones to the coffers of the Royal Family. To do so, the Yard would have needed the expertise of London jewelers—an explanation, perhaps, of the misfiled photograph.

Wallis's jewels had of course been insured and were eventually replaced. But in November, jewelless, or practically so ("Well, really, there wouldn't be too many of them to bring, you know," the Duke told reporters), the Windsors headed back for New York, with none of their missions in England accomplished. Helpfully, Wallis described her outfit to newsmen. It was one of some fifty that she had brought along: "This is a blue wool suit with a red wool jersey, a striped silk hat— I guess that's what you'd call it—with a veil. And this is an alligator handbag, and this is a mink stole."

In December, the tenth anniversary of the Abdication, Wallis presided at a Little Sister beauty contest for the Boys' Club of New York, placed a star-studded coronet on the winner's head, and sat next to the new beauty queen on a gilded throne that had been painted for the occasion. Inez Robb of the International News Service asked the Duke if he'd do it again. "We'd do it!" he said. When they were at home, he explained, Wallis often whipped up Sunday night suppers herself, while his job was to get out a card table and set it up himself. "Now we're just a very happy middle-aged couple," he said. Later it was learned that the management of the Waldorf-Astoria had remonstrated with the Duke and Duchess for cooking on a hot plate in their room, which was against the hotel rules. It seemed that, in some ways, Wallis had never really left the East Biddle Street house and the stove where she had allegedly made fudge.

In February 1947, the Windsors were in Palm Beach for the season. In New York and Newport, they had not managed to gain acceptance by the highest echelons of society, but in the more heterogeneous, slightly more raffish atmosphere of Palm Beach, they were treated as true Royalty. Guests were required to assemble fifteen minutes before the arrival of the Duke and Duchess. When the royal pair made their appearance, the men bowed from the waist and the women performed deep curtsies. While the Duke and Duchess stood, everyone else stood, and when they sat, the others sat. At dinner, the Duke and Duchess went to the head of the table and were served first, simultaneously. No one could leave a party before the Duke and Duchess left, and since the Duke often enjoyed lingering late at parties, there were some protocol problems. Once, at a party that had gone on long after midnight, the hostess whispered to her guest of honor, "Sir, some of the others are beginning to look awfully tired. Why don't you pretend to say good night, drive around the block for a bit, and then come back after the others have gone?" The Duke thought this a splendid idea. Wallis, who was aware of the Duke's habit of staying on and on, had developed her own technique for dealing with it. When she felt it was time to go, she would turn to him and say sweetly, "Darling, have you no *home?*" He would immediately check his watch, down his last brandy, and say good night. Other social problems cropped up. Sometimes at parties, for no apparent reason, the Duke would insist on speaking only in German. Since German was a language with which most of the Palm Beach winter colony was not familiar, there were often evenings when, for long periods, no one had the slightest idea of what the Duke was talking about.

During the day, the male members of the Everglades Club would draw straws to see who would play golf with the Duke. The loser got him as a golfing partner; he was, it seemed, a painfully slow player, planning and discussing his shots for what seemed like hours.

And, in dealing with him, Wallis was not always sweet. When he occasionally became imperious, she would child him with, "Remember—you're not a King any longer!" Ever fashion-conscious, she decided that the white dinner jacket was becoming passé in warm climates. But the Duke insisted on wearing a white jacket at black-tie affairs until, at one of them, his wife suddenly snatched a tray of hors d'oeuvres from a passing waiter's hand and handed it to the Duke, saying, "Here! If you're going to dress like a waiter, you might as well act like one!" This outburst, like others, startled their friends, but the Duke took it with good grace. In fact, in his sheepish response—he never wore a white jacket again—he actually seemed to enjoy it. At the same time, she knew how to bolster his ego. During an after-dinner gin rummy game, one of her partners said to her, "I don't understand what you're doing. You've thrown away three kings!" With a wink, Wallis replied,

"But I kept the best one, didn't I?"

To those who observed the Duke and Wallis, it had become increasingly obvious that she completely dominated him. As for their friends, who now referred to him privately as "the poor Duke," their fondness for him was touched with pity. In Palm Beach that winter, he hinted that he might write his autobiography. "But it may take me a while," he said. "I use the hunt and peck system of typing." In his spare time, which was of course considerable, he pored through old letters and papers and photographs, which he liked to spread out on the floor around his chair. But whenever Wallis entered the room he would quickly gather the strewn papers up and assemble them in tidy piles on his desk. In March, when the Palm Beach season was waning, the Windsors returned to New York. They were briefly in the news again when the Duke helped put out a fire in the apartment of friends, the Baron and Baroness Egmont van Zuylen van Nuyvelt, two flights above the Windsors' own suite at the Waldorf Towers. The Duke had heard the alarm and, in black tie and dinner jacket, helped firemen haul out hoses to extinguish the blaze.

In May 1947, after six months in the United States, the Windsors headed back across the Atlantic again. Asked about a possible new job, the Duke's response was a pathetic echo of all the other answers given over the years to the same question. "Well," he said, "I might do something sometime, but I have nothing definite in mind. I never take life easy. I never have, and I never shall." En route to Paris, the Windsors stopped in London again for an "unofficial" visit, and when Wallis was asked about the three army trucks and two jeeps that had rather conspicuously deposited what appeared to be about two tons of luggage in front of Claridge's, where they were staying, she said, "We hardly brought anything!" And then, in the manner of Marie Antoinette, she added, "Things are fantastic in Paris now. No one will be able to buy clothes there any more if they keep putting the prices up." London was in the middle of a waiter-busboy strike, and the Duke commented, "If they had been better paid, they would not be striking. However, the spiral of pay and costs cannot continue indefinitely." Alas, the Duke had apparently not done his homework on the matter. The waiters and busboys were not striking for more pay, but for union recognition of their Union of General and Municipal Workers.

The Duke met with Prime Minister Attlee for forty minutes at 10 Downing Street, leaving by the back door to avoid reporters. Once more, there was a flurry of speculation about a possible job for him but, again, no offer was forthcoming. The Windsors crossed the Channel to France on their tenth wedding anniversary.

The previous winter it had been announced that *Life* had bought the rights to the Duke's memoirs for an undisclosed price, assumed to be in six figures. The sale led to speculation that, thanks to the Duchess's enthusiastic spending, the Windsors might be going broke. *Life's* editors were more concerned about whether the Duke could actually write a book, and a Time-Life editor, Charles J. V. Murphy, was selected to assist him with the chore. The summer of 1947 at La Croë had been set aside for this endeavor. In their own book, *The Windsor Story*, Mr. Murphy and his collaborator, J. Bryan III, tell of the three and a half years of travail involved in getting the Duke of Windsor to apply himself to the task of putting down on paper what would become *A King's Story* in 1951. The Duke's attention span, it seemed, was short. He was easily interrupted and distracted. As for the physical act of writing, the Duke had neither the taste for it nor the talent. In the end, Murphy would virtually write the Duke's "autobiography" for him.

In October of 1947, there was another snub from Buckingham Palace to deal with. The Duke and Duchess of Windsor were conspicuously missing from the list of people who had been invited to attend the November wedding of Princess Elizabeth and Philip Mountbatten. Back in New York in November, Wallis said of the noninvitation, to a gathering of fifty reporters, "It was purely a family matter." She also said, "People should wear skirts at the length most becoming."

In January 1948, Wallis headed the New York Dress Institute's ten best-dressed list for the third year in a row, but in her hometown of Baltimore which, the year before, had celebrated the 150th anniversary of its city charter, she did not fare so well. Baltimoreans had been polled to select their greatest citizen. Johns Hopkins came out the winner, and the Duchess of Windsor, way down on the list, received only twenty-one votes.

Though the Duke's memoirs, now his principal "job," were far from done, the Wandering Windsors were off again. In February 1948, they were guests at the wedding of Winthrop

Rockefeller and Mrs. Barbara "Bobo" Sears, the daughter of a Lithuanian coal miner. In March, a fire on the Duke's Alberta ranch destroyed twenty-four head of purebred Shorthorn cattle worth $20,000, but the Duke cheerfully announced that the animals were all insured, and appeared unconcerned as he pitched the first ball in the annual Society Softball Game at Palm Beach—his first time at the game. For the summer months that year the Windsors rented a huge French Provincial château-style house in Locust Valley, next to a golf course, and Locust Valley hostesses were somewhat put off when they were asked to submit their guest lists to the Duchess before she would agree to attend any parties, and were even more put off when these lists were returned with certain names crossed out.

No sooner had they settled in Locust Valley than they were off to a big party in Washington at the Robert R. Youngs'. They were also a part of the Youngs' large April gala for Mr. Young's newly refurbished Greenbrier Hotel in White Sulphur springs. This junket, to publicize the hotel, included three days in fourteen private railroad cars, and the Duchess required fourteen pieces of luggage for three days. At the hotel, the Duke got up on the stage and played the drums with Meyer Davis's band. His selection was "How Are Things in Glocca Morra?"

In May, Margaret Thompson Schulze Biddle, the former wife of Ambassador Anthony J. Drexel Biddle, entertained for the Windsors, and she wrote dinner-partner cards in verse that almost scanned. Her tribute to Wallis went:

> *The woman I most admire*
> *Is worth an entire Empire!*
> *She's witty, she's gay, she's sweet,*
> *And never gossip does she repeat.*

This latter observation was true. Though by 1948, Wallis appeared to have abandoned any pretense of caring what the general public thought of her, and to have settled into a life devoted entirely to her own and the Duke's pleasure, she was not a gossip. She still retained the "reserve" that her school-mates in Baltimore had noticed—the woman who entered a room ready to be kissed by her friends, but who did not return the kisses.

In June, the Duke and Wallis celebrated the Duke's fifty-fourth birthday with a party at the Stork Club in New York, and then it was off for France again, with 120 pieces of luggage. At Vallauris, they attended a show of Picasso's pottery, featuring strangely shaped vases, and jugs representing beasts and gods. "Beautiful," Wallis said, "but I wonder what use could be made of them?"

Early in 1949, the Windsors announced their intention to abandon the French Riviera and the house at La Croë. The Riviera, Wallis explained, was attracting all the wrong sort of tourists—the "riffraff" as she put it—and their new headquarters became a large mansion at 85 Rue de la Faisanderie in Paris, rented to them by the French industrialist Paul-Louis Weiller. The house in the Rue de la Faisanderie, of course, represented another redecorating project, and Wallis fell to this task with her customary enthusiasm and perfectionism. In April, however, it was back to New York again, and then—for the Duke—a trip to London to visit his ailing mother. In New York, where Wallis remained behind for a while before rejoining him, the fact that she had lately been showing up at parties and nightclubs with escorts other than her husband was suddenly more pronounced.

In November 1949, Wallis herself broke into print, and it began to seem as though the Wandering Windsors might be turning into the Writing Windsors. In an article for *Vogue* on entertaining, she wrote, "Any dinner of more than sixteen people I consider enormous. More than eight persons means no *soufflé*—always a melancholy omission.... Anybody who entertains a lot runs the risk of falling into a rut.... The hostess who relies on memory alone may find herself repeating... to friends precisely the same dinner, down to the *entremets*, that she provided six months before. It is a great pity that Mr. Thomas Watson's efficient International Business Machines Corporation has not already addressed itself to this challenging problem."

Was she writing with tongue in cheek? One rather hoped she was. But no, she insisted, she was absolutely serious.

"The Windsors are coming! The Windsors are coming!" These words would echo across the lawns of the Bath and Tennis Club in Palm Beach, the Clambake Club in Newport, the Piping Rock Club in Locust Valley, through hotel lobbies in Cannes, Venice, New York, St. Moritz, Acapulco ... wherever

the rich and idle gathered for drinks, for golf, for gossip, to discuss their divorces, their lawsuits, their murders, their love affairs . . . and hostesses would busily begin making little lists of who to ask and what to wear and what to serve and what to buy, and to see to it that guest bedrooms were in order. "What do you and the Windsors talk about?" Mrs. George F. Baker was asked. She seemed startled by the question. "Well, where they've just been and who they've just seen," she said at last.

22

Togetherness

WALLIS once complained that whenever she and the Duke appeared together in public they were required to talk animatedly to one another and smile at each other a great deal, and otherwise try to demonstrate affection. If they merely sat in silence, rumors immediately started that the Marriage of the Century was in difficulties. It was all a great bore, Wallis said, but she always did her best to act out the role of the loving wife.

In the autumn of 1950, however, when Wallis was alone in New York and the Duke remained behind in France, the talk of a marital rift grew serious. Wallis liked to go to parties, enjoyed being seen at fashionable gatherings, and when she went out she naturally preferred to have an escort—preferably one who was young, handsome, well-dressed and amusing. Most of these chic young men were homosexuals. The Duke, for his part, had always complained of feeling uncomfortable in the presence of homosexuals, and a psychologist might no doubt deduce a certain sexual confusion on his part from this aversion.

And yet, Wallis explained, it was almost impossible to put together a successful dinner party without drawing on the reserves of elegant young men from the international homosexual community. As she once said to her friend Cappy Badrut, "All the best-looking men in Paris are at the Club Sept," a fashionable homosexual restaurant and dance bar near the Place de l'Opéra.

Wallis had always had a certain affinity for homosexuals, and homosexuals had had an affinity for her, as well as for other women like her, who were famous, decorative, married, and no real threat to the gay way of life. To the women of Wallis's circle, homosexual men served a distinct purpose, and their relationships were symbiotic. If an escort was needed, or an extra man at dinner to pair off with a widow or a divorcée, one was always available. When it came to social climbing, the handsome homosexual probably had the easiest time of all. Furthermore, it was an international circle. All these men knew one another, kept up on all the latest stories, and were fun to have around.

Now, in New York, Wallis's favorite escort appeared to be a young man named Jimmy Donahue. In 1950, Jimmy Donahue was thirty-five and Wallis fifty-four. James P. Donahue, Jr., was not handsome exactly—he had a bland, rather slack-jawed face and a receding hairline—but he was slender and wore clothes well, and he was also very rich. His mother was the former Jessie Woolworth, and Jimmy Donahue had inherited some fifteen million dollars from his grandfather Woolworth, the five-and-ten-cent-store king. His first cousin was Barbara Hutton, and if she was "the richest girl in the world," he was among the richest boys. Wallis, like the Duke, was always magnetized by money, and Jimmy Donahue's wealth certainly added to his attractiveness.

And, though Jimmy Donahue had never worked a day in his life, devoting himself instead to harmless hedonism, he *was* attractive. He was saucy and impudent, a wonderful storyteller, and most important, he remembered everything. As such, he became a sort of message-bearer to the social gods he served. He fitted the then-current definition of a playboy perfectly, with one exception. He had no interest in playing with beautiful girls. His passion was for beautiful boys.

He made absolutely no bones about his sexual preferences, and in fact flaunted them outrageously. At parties, when a new man caught his fancy, he would drop his fork, rivet his attention on the newcomer, murmur appreciative comments, demand an introduction, and then flirt unconscionably. He also liked to point out that, since he was rich, he could afford to buy the best sex at the highest asking prices, which eliminated the chore of haunting bars and waiting for pickups. His methods were much more surefire. He talked so blatantly and flippantly about his life that it was—well, almost funny. Certainly it was titillating. His naughty talk was considered part of his wit, part of his charm. He had become the darling of fashionable parties on both sides of the Atlantic because, after all, who knew what shocking, campy thing Jimmy might say next?

He once told a rapt gathering at dinner that he had recently telephoned a young male hustler and asked him to come over to his house. The hustler had apparently been unavailable and had sent his roommate, an older and less attractive man, in his place. Jimmy was so furious about the substitution, he told his audience—who were all ears—that when the man had undressed, Jimmy had confiscated all his clothes and sent him out into the night naked. He also told of another male prostitute who had proved so disappointing that he had refused to pay the promised hundred-dollar fee until the man had eaten a sandwich spread with his own excrement. Such was international Café Society in Jimmy Donahue's day. Scatology and all—society found it amusing.

He was also an exhibitionist. Proud of his body, he thought nothing of receiving guests to his parties in the nude. He enjoyed putting on women's clothes, and he told the story—which no one knew whether to believe or not—that he had once entertained his mother's good friend Francis Cardinal Spellman in drag. He often asked his butler to take home movies of some of his more successful sexual encounters, and these he would cheerfully screen for interested friends.

To his credit, Jimmy Donahue was grandly generous, showering his friends with expensive gifts and flowers, seizing checks in nightclubs and restaurants and lavishly tipping waiters, chefs and hatcheck girls with hundred-dollar bills. Also, it should be mentioned that even the straightest of the "straight" men, who had been repelled by Jimmy Donahue's notoriety, found themselves, on meeting him, completely won over by him and came away from the experience muttering, begrudgingly, words like *charming...funny...good company*. This was the reaction of the Duke of Windsor when Jimmy Donahue came swimming gaily into their lives and anchored there for a while. He liked Jimmy too.

In New York, they often appeared as a threesome. In the summer of 1950, the three traveled to France together, a trip that was a long, extended party, and when the Duke retired early, Jimmy and Wallis were *à deux,* heads together deep in conversation until the wee hours, in a manner that recalled the days when Ernest Simpson had removed himself so that the Prince of Wales and Wallis could be alone together. Jimmy amused her, Wallis said. He also got her interested in collecting eighteenth-century snuffboxes, of which he had a large collection. In the afternoons, while the Duke struggled to continue to work on his memoirs, Jimmy and Wallis played cards, shopped, went to cafés, took drives in the country.

In November, the Windsors were scheduled to return to New York for another round of social engagements. The Duke, however, was now under pressure from his publisher to fulfill the contract for his book, which was still far from completion, and he suggested that they forgo the New York trip. But Wallis demurred. She wanted to go to New York, and she was willing to go alone. Left behind in Paris, without her as a distraction, he could work uninterruptedly. In New York, she would have Jimmy Donahue to escort her to the necessary parties. Surely the Duke would not object to that. He did not, and so Wallis set out for New York alone.

During the New York visit, rumors that the Duchess of Windsor and Jimmy Donahue were having an affair began in earnest. To be sure, it did not seem possible. Everyone knew what Jimmy Donahue was. And yet, when they appeared together, they seemed inseparable. They held hands. They whispered and giggled little secrets into one another's ears. They threw long looks at one another, and passed notes to one another across dinner tables. More and more of their doings were being reported in the press, and Cholly Knickerbocker wrote of how, at a nightclub, Jimmy Donahue had presented Wallis with a huge spray of red roses. She had been carrying a white-feather fan at the time, a gift from the Duke, and she discarded the fan in favor of the roses. Donahue himself was delighted with the furor the liaison was creating, and he fed the flames of the gossip with little tidbits of his own that quickly circulated through the homosexual community. He said of her, "She's marvelous! She's the best cock sucker I've ever known!" Such stories were lent credence by the report of at least one member of Parisian high society who claimed that after a party in Biarritz he mistakenly stepped into the wrong hotel suite to find Wallis and Jimmy Donahue in bed together.* As for Wallis, her disregard for public opinion seems to have become completely reckless—even perverse. That she was the storm center of another international scandal seemed not to worry her at all.

Reading the stories back home in Paris, the Duke became understandably alarmed. He immediately abandoned work on the book and made plans to join Wallis in New York. She was the first person up the gangplank of the *Queen Elizabeth* to meet him. The Duke, when asked about rumors of an estrangement, laughed and said, "That's the worst bunk ever written!" Before embarking at Cherbourg, he told reporters that the Duchess had "received several offers of jobs." But when she was asked about this at the reunion in New York harbor, she said, "I'm afraid that's a rumor," and then, glancing at the Duke, she added, "I have quite a full-time job now." Then, to dispel any doubts about their love, the Duke and Wallis embraced for photographers, and kissed, and held long kissing poses, a total of seven times. Finally, Wallis said, "Look, we're overdoing it!" The reporters had to admit that they had put on a good show. That evening, the Duke and Wallis were off to a New Year's Eve party to usher in 1951 at the Sherry–Netherland, with ex-King Peter and Queen Alexandra of Yugoslavia, just like old times.

All the same, the "affair" with Jimmy Donahue, if it was one, was by no means over. It would continue for fully three more years, appearing publicly as a kind of *menage à trois*. Donahue was with them wherever they went—to Palm Beach, and back to Paris again. He was the chief member of their retinue, and they were the chiefs of his. Throughout the early 1950's, they were the International Set's Merry Threesome, and hostesses who were unaware of the situation and who invited the Windsors without including Donahue were politely

---

*This story, though told to the author as gospel, has a ring of unlikelihood. Only a very careless guest would have wandered into the wrong hotel suite, and only very careless occupants would have left the door to the suite unlocked, unbolted and unchained.

reminded that an invitation for the third person would be appreciated—in fact, absolutely essential. The relationship seemed so consistent and mutually adoring that the inevitable rumor, which has never been laid to rest, began to circulate in the homosexual community that the Duke was also a homosexual, though there is absolutely no evidence of this.

What, then, did she—they—see in Jimmy Donahue, other than as a convenient drinking companion and bouncy court jester? Were they drawn to him by parental feelings? Did he represent the prankish, irrepressible son they would never have? This hardly seems likely. For one thing, Jimmy Donahue already had a mother, or Mother, though his relationship with Jessie Donahue was mercurial and up-and-down. In New York, Jimmy and his mother shared one of the biggest apartments in the city, a huge triplex at 834 Fifth Avenue. One minute, she would pamper and spoil him with lavish gifts of cash and luxuries, and the next, would berate him for extravagance and threaten to disinherit him.

As far as Wallis was concerned, the basis for her attraction to Donahue seems fairly clear. She had now spent more than fifteen years working hard to keep up the spirits of the abject Duke. It had been an uphill job. With each successive rebuff from Downing Street and Buckingham Palace, he had become gloomier and harder to divert, and trying to penetrate his sadnesses and dark moods had become increasingly difficult. With Jimmy Donahue it was just the opposite. Jimmy came with his own built-in diversions. Wallis didn't have to toil to keep him cheerful. He even helped her by sharing the burden of cheering up the Duke. Then there was the Duke's tightfistedness, which over the years must have become a considerable cross for his wife to bear. When *l'addition* arrived at a restaurant where the Duke and Duchess were entertaining guests for dinner, it was often downright embarrassing to watch the Duke gazing balefully at the presented check, fingering its corners suspiciously, then pushing it away from him just slightly, obviously in hopes that the bill would go away or that someone else would pick it up. With Jimmy Donahue in tow, there was no such problem. It was *always* his treat. Finally, and most important, Jimmy provided an active antidote to the thing Wallis feared the most—old age. He made her feel young.

The big house at 85 Rue de la Faisanderie, meanwhile, had provided a wonderful arena for Wallis's decorative talents, and

Jimmy's tastes, which matched her own, were no small help to her when it came to turning the mansion into yet another Windsor showcase. It was in the smart Sixteenth Arrondissement, near the Bois de Boulogne, an *hôtel particulier,* as the French call such privately owned town houses. Manicured shrubbery and flower borders flanked the house on the street side, and the entrance was through a pair of tall wrought-iron gates. In the large front entrance hall, portraits of His Royal Highness at various ages lined the walls—a huge one of him as the Prince of Wales in all his regalia, another as King of England. From the hall, leading to the floor above, stretched a wide staircase lined on either side from top to bottom with pots of densely thick white flowers—she insisted always on white flowers—and from the top of this regal climb the main entertaining rooms of the house presented themselves—the long drawing room, the dining room (too small, Wallis complained, since it would seat only twenty-four), the library, the small sitting room, the Duchess's study.

Wallis had become preoccupied with maintaining her thin figure, and her English-trained masseuse, Elizabeth Dupont, the manager of Elizabeth Arden's physiotherapy department, regularly treated her in a small room off the master bedroom. "Her figure was beautifully proportioned." Mme. Dupont, now Mrs. Elizabeth Gatehell, recalls, "slight, almost boyish, yet she was obsessed by two things—an imaginary roll of fat around her abdomen, and her hands, which were indeed curiously ugly—broad, short-fingered, with very small nails, incongruous with her impeccable body. Whenever possible she wore gloves. She'd say, 'Madame Dupont, put lots of Vitae cream on my hands, arms and wrists, and manipulate my hands and fingers. Hands are so important for a woman. And don't forget to go all out on that cellulite, that roll of fat around my tummy.' She was the sort of woman who'd never turn a hair or wince at these painful treatments. The more it hurt the better! She'd say, 'Don't spare the horses with that roll of fat!' She'd grit her teeth and say, 'Harder, harder! Go on!' I was terrified of bruising her flesh!"

Those who worked with her on her beauty treatments were surprised at how impatient, peevish, and even bullying she could be with the Duke. Once, during her massage, there was a terrible commotion from the bedroom next door, the sounds of dresser drawers and cupboard doors being opened and slammed shut. "That's the Duke," Wallis said. "He's lost something again. He always loses everything." Presently there was a tap on the door, and the Duke stepped in wearing a red silk dressing gown with white polka dots, and a white silk ascot with red polka dots. "Peaches," he said, "I can't find our travel itinerary, or our passports, or any of our documents." Needless to say, Wallis quickly found the necessary papers, scolding, "David, you always mislay everything!" Occasionally, Mme. Dupont would be forewarned by one of the servants, *"Attention,* Her Royal Highness is *not* in a good humor!" Earlier, it seemed, on one of these bad days, the Duke had knocked over a favorite vase containing a flower arrangement Wallis had just completed. The vase had shattered into tiny pieces. "She was furious," the maid whispered. "She told him to pick up all the pieces. And would you believe it? He got down on his hands and knees and did as he was told." The maid explained, "She's not easy. She has her little ways. But he—how nice he is with everyone. One would think *she* is the Royal Highness, and not he, she is so proud."

At Elizabeth Arden's Place Vendôme salon, where Wallis regularly went for hair and makeup appointments, her impending arrival always created a great stir. A bouquet of her favorite flowers was ordered from Harris, a florist on the Rue Cambon, and placed in a special cut-glass vase in her private treatment room. A special carpet was laid down on the floor. In the wings waited not one but three of her favorite *maître-coiffeurs,* Claude, Roger, and Manuel, ready to see which of them she might choose to minister to her hair that day and to apply the specially formulated secret dye, which she always carried with her whenever she traveled. Also awaiting her was Madeleine, Arden's facial and makeup expert, with another specially created foundation designed to enhance Wallis's purplish eyes and to draw attention away from her jutting jawline. All these little attentions, of course, had been dictated by the formidable Miss Arden herself. Once, when a British salesgirl in the salon did not immediately leave her French client when the Duchess made her entrance—to greet Wallis and escort her to the elevator, as all Arden employees had been instructed to do, whatever the circumstances—Wallis complained that she had not been "properly received and escorted." The luckless girl was sacked that night and sent packing back to England.

For all the special treatment she received at Arden's, Wallis was not known as a good tipper. Indeed she was a nontipper. To be sure, she would promise the favorites who served her—Mme. Dupont, Madeleine, the hairdressers—"I am going to tell Miss Arden that you are the *best*. And I know, I've tried them all." And, at Christmas, she presented each of her "technicians" with a little gift—for the women gold and diamond pins in the shape of the Prince of Wales's feathers and the motto *Honi soit qui mal y pense,* and for the men gold cufflinks stamped with the royal crest. The historical significance of these gifts was often lost on their recipients, who would have much preferred a check or cash.

After a day at Arden's, Wallis would customarily be picked up by Jimmy Donahue, and they would have a drink at the Cambon bar at the Ritz, and would then join the Duke for whatever festivities of the evening lay ahead. They continued to be careful to appear as a threesome, in order to put the lie to stories of a Duchess–Donahue romance, but there was at least one significant lapse. This occurred in the early spring of 1953, when the Duke returned—alone—to England to visit his dying mother. Queen Mary died on March 26, and on the day of her funeral Wallis, who had remained behind in New York, was seen at a nightclub with Jimmy Donahue. It was almost as though she were celebrating the death of the ever-unforgiving old Queen. Indeed, perhaps she was.

An evening with Jimmy Donahue, at any rate, was always unpredictable and, as a rule, reasonably alcoholic. In her autobiography, Lilli Palmer recalls one night on the French Riviera when the Duke and Duchess, in one of their borrowed yachts, had invited Miss Palmer and her husband, Rex Harrison, for dinner on the boat. The other guests had included Greta Garbo, her current escort George Schley, one or two others of lesser note, and of course Jimmy Donahue. The quality of the celebrities aboard the yacht anchored in the harbor had, understandably, drawn a large throng of the curious to the quayside, and during the dinner a particularly drunken American guest had launched into an unpleasant tirade against the English. This was intended to strike a sympathetic note with the Duke and Wallis, but in Miss Palmer's view it clearly failed, nor did she appreciate the line of conversation. Her husband, after all, was an Englishman. Several attempts were made to change the subject, all in vain, and even Wallis's celebrated talents as a hostess seemed not up to quieting her obnoxious guest. And so Jimmy Donahue, in black tie and emerald cufflinks, stood up, walked to the railing, and jumped into the sea. Amid cheering from the shore, Jimmy swam through the turbid harbor water to the dock. The drunken American seemed unaware of Jimmy's action and continued his nonstop jeremiad against the English. Presently Jimmy was back again, climbing aboard the yacht dripping wet, and excused himself briefly to change into fresh evening clothes and another set of jeweled cufflinks. Returning to the table as though nothing at all had happened, he could see that the American was still relentlessly on the same subject. Murmuring, "We'll just have to try again," he leaped into the sea once more. Needless to say, the evening ended in a shambles, with the Duke and Duchess retiring to their bedroom where they were audibly having "words."

As Lilli Palmer remembers in her book:

"Let's go," said Greta.

"Without saying goodbye?"

"Without."

There was no end to Jimmy Donahue's outrageousness. He used to boast that he had made a pact with his mother's butler, in which the butler agreed to telephone him in advance to warn him if his mother was planning an unannounced visit to his house on Long Island. He would then quickly deploy his retinue of young men to a motel suite nearby, which he maintained on a permanent basis just for that purpose. At the old El Morocco, then the most fashionable nightclub in New York, he enjoyed appearing with this or that well-known local madam, whom he would insist on dressing in a nightgown and bedroom slippers. Early one morning the peripatetic socialite-photographer Jerome Zerbe received a telephone call from a young woman friend of Donahue's named Toni Johnson. She and Jimmy, she explained, were at Jimmy's mother's apartment, and Jimmy was complaining that Zerbe didn't like him. Wouldn't Zerbe come over for some champagne and try to patch things up?

Zerbe arrived, and Jimmy Donahue repeated the question: "Why don't you like me?" Zerbe replied, "It's not that I dislike you. But I disapprove of you. I don't like the public spectacle you make of yourself—it's not fair to your nice mother. Nobody gives a fig what you do in your private life, but when you make a public display of it it's disgusting." Donahue listened to the lecture contritely, and promised to mend his ways. He escorted Zerbe soberly to the elevator. When the elevator arrived, and the door was opened by a handsome young elevator boy, Donahue cried out, "Oh, he's gorgeous!" and fell to his knees and kissed the elevator boy on the crotch.

Zerbe later ran into Donahue in Paris in a restaurant, and Donahue invited him to join his table. Once again he asked the question, "Jerry, why don't you like me?" Then he burst into tears.

Many years later, Zerbe was lunching with the Duchess at La Côte Basque in New York. He said to her, "The only thing you've ever done that I disapproved of was running around with Jimmy Donahue." Wallis replied, "Well, the Duke was getting tired of going to nightclubs, but I enjoyed it, and Jimmy made a pleasant escort." Zerbe said, "He was a man who destroyed everything he touched. He destroyed your reputation." Looking pensive, Wallis replied that she had never thought of it that way.

In the late spring of 1953, there was yet another snub from Buckingham Palace—at which point the Duke and Duchess must have lost count of how many there had been since 1936. Queen Elizabeth II was to be crowned on June 2. The Duke of Windsor had been invited to the Coronation. The Duchess had not. Of course they would not go. Instead, they watched it on French television in Paris.

The Jimmy Donahue affair lasted about another year and ended with more of a whimper than a bang. According to Bryan and Murphy, the three were having dinner in their hotel suite in Baden-Baden, and it is likely that the evening, as most had become, was again alcoholic. Something that Wallis said displeased Jimmy, and he kicked her sharply in the shin under the table. The kick tore her stocking and drew blood. In the confusion that followed, the Duke ordered Jimmy out of their lives forever. The Windsors and Jimmy Donahue never saw each other again.

The Windsors let it be known that they had simply had enough of his antics. But the fact that Jimmy—who, with a simple apology the next morning, or a gift of ten dozen roses, or a pair of diamond and ruby earrings, could easily have worked his way back into their good graces again—accepted his dismissal so casually, indicates that he also had had enough of them.

Without the stars of the Duke and Duchess of Windsor glittering in his social diadem, Jimmy Donahue's own star began to fade. Little was heard of him in the gossip columns, and from being a supernova he seemed to withdraw into a black hole. Drink and drugs were both taking their toll on his youth and figure. Surely he was never meant to be a man of forty, then forty-five, then fifty. On December 6, 1966, he was found dead by his mother in the apartment at 834 Fifth Avenue. For some reason, his death was not reported for more than a week. The New York Medical Examiner's office gave the cause of death as "acute alcoholic and barbiturate intoxication." Suicide was not entirely ruled out, but an associate medical examiner said, "I don't think this was a suicide, although the circumstances have not yet been determined. He had a moderate amount of alcohol in him and amounts of a quick-acting sedative, and the combination depressed the central nervous system. These barbiturates are dangerous, but unfortunately easily obtainable."

Jimmy Donahue was fifty-one years old. The following summer, Wallis would be seventy.

In December 1953, meanwhile—1953 was the year of the Coronation—Wallis and the Duke were in New York, and celebrated New Year's Eve at the old El Morocco—Wallis in a watermelon-pink silk coat by Dior and covered with jewels. At midnight, a tray filled with paper crowns appeared. The Duchess snatched a crown from the tray, and said, "Bring one for the Duke!" Then they put on the paper crowns, and wearing somewhat different smiles—hers mischievous, his sheepish—they posed side by side on a zebra-striped "throne" for photographers. When they left the club at around one in the morning, the Duchess tossed aside her paper crown, and said, "Coronation's over!"

23

Killing Time

THE year 1953, when Queen Elizabeth II ascended the throne, seemed to be the beginning of the final phase of the disintegration of both the Windsors. Deep in the toils of Jimmy Donahue, they seemed to have nowhere else to go. Perhaps both of them realized then, since the Duke had no heirs, that Elizabeth would have become Queen of England sooner or later no matter what happened. It must have given the Windsors a particular feeling of uselessness, of what-difference-did-it-make, of was-it-worth-the-candle. The long-ago drama of the Abdication began to seem an empty gesture. In the end it had counted for nothing, would have changed nothing.

There really were no real jobs to do, except to grow older and more out of touch with a reality they may not ever have understood. It was hard to keep up with the times when fewer and fewer of their friends could manage to live on the splendid scale—even if they had wanted to do so—which the Duke and Wallis had set as their standard. How many men were left who would openly admit that they could not live without a personal valet? Or, even if they could afford one, knew what a valet did? Still, there were days to be passed.

In 1952, the Duke and Wallis had acquired a 353-year-old mill near Gif-sur-Yvette, about forty-five minutes from Paris. The property consisted of a stone-floored millhouse, a large barn, and several smaller outbuildings. At first they leased the mill, but soon they were able to buy it. It was the first home they had actually owned.

Though the mill, which was called Le Moulin de la Tuilerie, had been made habitable by a previous owner, Wallis immediately began a renovation and redecoration project as ambitious and extensive as any of her others. The millhouse itself was to be the main residence. The old one-and-a-half-story barn was to be opened up to provide a summer dining room, outbuildings were to become guesthouses, and so on. When word got around that the Windsors were turning a seventeenth-century mill into a country castle, buying up and restoring old French mills became something of a craze.

The Duke decided to create an extensive garden out of what had once been a series of chicken runs. He threw himself wholeheartedly into the project, and it took him the better part of two years to achieve the effect he wanted—that of an informal English garden in central France. French gardens are typically geometrical and balanced; English gardens affect a more careless air: they spread and sprawl with grassy stretches, low walls and hedges, and apparently random dottings of shrubs and flower beds. The Duke's design for his garden succeeded brilliantly. In fact, gardening may have been his greatest single talent. To build a rock and water garden, he took a stream that flowed near the millhouse into the Mérantaise River, and re-channeled it through a series of cascades, with stepping-stones and rocks planted with alpine flowers and primulas. By pumping water from the river through underground pipes to the top of a rocky crag, he created a waterfall. Naturally, a garden of such scale and ambition required constant attention, and the Duke spent most of his days at Le Moulin tending his garden, moving rocks, and planting shrubs and fruit trees. At last, it seemed, the Duke of Windsor had a full-time job he was suited for.

Wallis applied the same meticulous attention to the design of the house. In the main living room she assembled mementos of her husband's youth—the steeplechasing trophies, regimental insignia of the Brigade of Guards, his midshipman's dirk and Field Marshal's baton, and various other objects and photographs collected during his travels as Prince of Wales. If the garden was to be a reminder of home in England, the house was to be a reminder of the Duke's past glories. Upstairs, Wallis's bedroom was all done in virginal white, her huge four-poster bed massed with lace-trimmed and embroidered pillows in all sizes. Down the hall, the Duke's bedroom was smaller, more masculine, almost barracks-like, his bed a narrow military cot, done in beige and gold, with chairs covered in felt and suede. The most impressive room, perhaps, was the main room of the old barn, which had been turned into a study–sitting room for the Duke, but was more nearly a royal museum. Royal standards stood against walls covered with portraits of the Prince of Wales and maps of the tours he had taken as a youth. The desk from which he had made his Abdication speech was here, along with other pieces that had come from Fort Belvedere. Everywhere were framed photographs of the Duke—as King, as Prince, as Governor, as Duke—and of his family and ancestors.

Some people claimed that Wallis's taste did not lend itself quite so well to a country cottage as it did to a city mansion and, after all, Wallis was admittedly a city woman. Harriet Culley, the wife of the head of the American Hospital in Paris, complained of "too much clutter. One had to pick one's way between tiny tables, each one covered with dozens of even tinier little *things*—bibelots, miniatures, little boxes." And the finicky Cecil Beaton, always difficult to please, found the Mill "overdone and *chichi*. Medallions on the walls, gimmicky poufs, bamboo chairs. Simply not good enough!"

But much of the fuss and clutter had to do with the fact that the Mill was designed as a place for entertaining weekend guests, and it was Wallis's conviction that, in order to make a guest's stay pleasant, no detail was to be overlooked. Certainly a weekend at the Windsors' was more luxurious than anything ever offered by the grandest hotel.

Invitations were usually issued by telephone from Wallis's secretary, Mlle. Hivet, followed by an engraved card emblazoned with the ducal crown in green and crimson that read: "This is to remind you that the Duke and Duchess of Windsor expect you on Saturday, June—, for the weekend at teatime."

Also enclosed was a carefully drawn *itinéraire* showing the principal motor routes to Le Moulin from Paris. The main guest cottage consisted of two bedrooms and baths, connected by a hall, which was lined with framed prints of the Coronation of George IV, and where the Duke's collection of some seventy walking sticks was on display. One bedroom had black and white quilted walls, and the bedspread and cushions were pink. In this room Wallis liked to place two vases of pink roses and one of pink gladioli. The sheets were by Porthault, appliquéd with the initials. W.W.W. in pink and white, with the ducal crown above. Pillows were lace-trimmed. (Wallis's own bed linen was changed twice daily—once in the morning, and again after her afternoon nap.) The bathroom was green-carpeted, with Chinese green and red wallpaper, and contained a tub surrounded by mirrors. A guest would find herself supplied with fresh cakes of pink Guerlain soap made especially for the Duchess (though servants were instructed to save the guest soaps after a guest's departure "for other uses") along with bath salts, bath oil, aspirin, Alka-Seltzer, and even an air freshener in a Porthault terry-cloth cover to match the towels, which were pink and white, appliquéd "E.R." In the bedroom was a telephone with an intercom connecting it to eighteen different posts, including the bedroom right across the hall.

This bedroom, if the guests were husband and wife, was the man's. It had walls of yellow felt with matching curtains, and contained a small bar supplied with whisky, gin, vodka, bitters, glasses, ice, and all conceivable cocktail garnishes. In this bedroom, a gentleman would find all the necessary shaving tools laid out—razor, soap, brushes, and bottles of shaving lotion and cologne arranged with their tops removed. Each bedroom was also supplied with a thermos of ice water, with the newest books on the bedside table, with writing paper and postcards (even stamps), pen, ink, cigarettes—filtered and unfiltered, plain and mentholated—matches (green folders with "Moulin de la Tuilerie" stamped in white), cigarette lighter, and a radio. One of Wallis's whimsies was her fondness for small needlepoint pillows with little sayings worked into them. One pillow in the guest cottage was inscribed, "Smile at the poorest tramp as you would at the Highest King." Another read, "You can't be too rich or too thin," one of the Duchess of Windsor's oft-quoted bons mots.

After tea, the newly arrived guest was expected to return to the guest cottage to rest and bathe and dress for dinner. There the guest would find that he had been completely unpacked, that everything had been freshly pressed, and that shoes had been polished. Dresser drawers and closet doors, furthermore, had been left open so that the guest could see at a glance where each unpacked item had been placed. The gentleman's dress shirt would be laid out, studs in place, white handkerchief folded in the breast pocket of his dinner jacket, socks turned inside out for proper toe-first donning. Saturday night dinner at the Mill was always black tie, though the Duke often wore one of his kilts. Upon retiring, the guest would find a menu card beside his bed, to be placed outside the door, on which he was asked to list what he wished for breakfast, and to say at what time he wished to be served. Breakfast was served in bed—in the pink-and-white bedroom on white china with a pink strawberry motif, along with a small vase of pink and white flowers—and, in the yellow bedroom, on yellow china with flowers. Later, weather permitting, there would be pre-luncheon cocktails on the terrace with the host and hostess, followed by lunch in the old barn. Quite often, the guest would be treated to one of Wallis's own culinary inventions, such as halves of avocado pear filled with daiquiris.

Despite Wallis's enormous organizational ability and eye for the tiniest detail, things occasionally went wrong. When they did, though, it was usually the fault of the guest, not the hostess. Thomas Kernan, the former editor of *Maison et Jardin*, recalls one luncheon for twelve where the main course was grouse. As the platter was being passed, it was clear to him that six grouse had been halved to provide one ample serving for each person. Kernan also watched as one thoughtless guest helped himself to two halves. It was clear to Kernan that, when the platter reached him, there would be no grouse left, only vegetables. Obviously he would have to make the best of the situation, but Wallis's ever-watchful eye had caught what had happened. She made a quick gesture to the butler, whispered something, and the butler vanished into the kitchen. Just as the meatless platter reached Kernan, Wallis spoke up. "Oh, Tommy—you and your damned diet! I hope at least you can eat a little steak." With that, a small tenderloin, perfectly grilled, arrived on another platter from the kitchen. It was all so cleverly done that no one but Wallis and Kernan knew what had happened. Later she whispered to him, "I guess you and I know who needs to diet at this party."

The host of Le Moulin was not always as clever as the hostess. On another occasion the dinner guests were the newly married Mr. and Mrs. William vanden Heuvel of New York. Mrs. vanden Heuvel was the former Jean Stein, the daughter of Jules Stein, the founding head of the Music Corporation of America and a man prominent in Jewish affairs in California. During dinner there was chatter about an American woman acquaintance who was suing her daughter over an inheritance. The Duchess was eager to hear all the details. Someone remarked that they hoped the woman had a good attorney, to which the Duke suddenly replied, "She's got some little kike lawyer from New York!" From such a situation there was almost no salvation, but Jean vanden Heuvel watched as Wallis gave her husband such a look that daggers were practically visible from one end of the table to the other. Though the conversation quickly turned to other matters, the Duke, on the receiving end of Wallis's glare, was so flustered that he had to get up and leave the table. He stepped outdoors, and William vanden Heuvel later swore to his wife that through a window he had seen the Duke of Windsor lift his kilt and urinate on the grass.

Meanwhile, in addition to decorating and entertaining, Wallis had embarked upon another, more commerical project. The Duke's book, *A King's Story,* when it was finally finished and published in 1951, had been a considerable success, and reportedly earned him, along with its movie sale, about a million dollars. Perhaps, with the Duke in the limelight again, Wallis felt herself beginning to be relegated to the shadows. Though she was still on best-dressed lists, she had begun to lose her first-place position to other, somewhat younger women, such as Mrs. Winston Guest and Mrs. William Paley. The trouble here, of course, was not just a difference in the women's ages. It was that the kind of fashion Wallis had personified was no longer fashionable. Her style in clothes continued to be classic—clean, simple, immaculate, with uncluttered lines—clothes designed for the display of precious stones, perfectly coordinated costumes. Fashion was now moving to a more baroque era. Self-confidence was becoming the key, and daring. The well-dressed woman now wore what she *chose* to wear; she was willing to experiment, to be different, to mix the expensive with the cheap. Precious stones were giving way to costume jewelry. In this new fashion mood, Wallis's standards were too rigid. She had become, in *Women's Wear Daily's* cruel phrase for women who looked *too* fashionable, a "victim of fashion," a prisoner of Mainbocher.

In any case, Wallis now decided to write her own memoirs, telling her side of the marriage-of-the-century story. They would, of course, turn out to be at variance with the Duke's on several points, including how, when, and where they met. Wallis assumed that her story would be even more of a money-maker. When the project was announced, there was the usual speculation about whether the Windsors were going broke. Certainly they weren't, but both of them operated on the principle, common among rich people, that no matter how much money one has, one can always use more. (Wallis, like the Duke, was not one to let a good financial prospect pass by; she had charged the *Woman's Home Companion* sixty thousand dollars for the rights to photograph Le Moulin.)

In the summer of 1955, Wallis appointed Cleveland Amory, then at the height of his fame as a chronicler of the rich and social, as her "editorial adviser," which was to say ghostwriter. Amory, a large, independent-spirited man, not known to be one who was bossed around easily, seemed, to those who knew them both, an ominous choice. Once again, two strong wills would be pitted against each other, and Wallis and the media appeared to be on a collision course again. Amory went to France and spent several months with Wallis, whom he found extraordinarily difficult to work with. Though she had promised to "tell all" in her book, her actual intention seemed to be something different—to gloss over unpleasantnesses like her Jimmy Donahue period, to alter facts, dates and even names, and to turn her tantalizingly indistinct China period into a romantic idyll dotted with jade-encrusted pagodas and tinkling temple bells. (Something more important *had* to have kept her in China for two years, Amory felt.) By October 1955 Amory and Wallis were at such odds over what the book should be and how it should be written—among other things, he wanted to call it *Untitled* and she did not—that Wallis fired him along with his unfinished manuscript.

When Amory returned to America, he explained that he and the Duchess of Windsor had disagreed on three basic points. She had wanted him to present her as one from the right side of the tracks, and wanted this fact stressed. She had wanted him to prove that she and the Duke were "happy and busy people." And she had wanted him to demonstrate that the British Royal Family had treated her "very meanly" by not allowing her to use the designation of Her Royal Highness. Amory said, "I told the Duchess that I didn't mind omitting facts. But I wouldn't distort them. She wanted a soap opera."

The Duke's secretary replied haughtily, "The Duchess of Windsor wishes it to be known that it was the unanimous recommendation of the three publishers of her memoirs—namely, David McKay, *McCall's* magazine and the London *Sunday Express*—that Mr. Amory's employment be terminated." Earlier, the announcement had been politer: 'Mr. C. Amory has now given all the assistance the Duchess felt was of value, and his employment has therefore been terminated." Now the Duchess stated that Amory had done "three hundred pages of unsatisfactory hack work"—fighting words to any author. Privately, too, she made a further accusation: Amory, she said, had been secretly feeding bits of "kitchen gossip" to Igor Cassini, the New York *Journal-America's* "Cholly Knickerbocker" columnist. In 1959, Amory was able to get back at the Duchess. In his *Celebrity Register*, published by Earl Blackwell and coedited by Sydney Cohn, Amory wrote of her, "She makes clear that her mother *never* took in boarders; she did, though, have an extraordinary number of people to dinner."*

---

*The next year, in *Who Killed Society?*, Amory seized another chance to even the score. He quoted Ernest Simpson's scathing appraisal of Wallis that Simpson had given him in an interview four years earlier: "Wallis never had dignity nor proportion. She never could take even minor criticism. She needed a strong man with judgment. If she was hurt she would fly into a tantrum. She was wild when she was angry and there was no end to her hate or temper. I think the Duke has always been mortally afraid of her." This indictment was a surprise, coming as it did from one who had always seemed the model of gentlemanly restraint and polite decorum when the subject of his former wife came up. For all anyone knew, he and Wallis had remained fond and supportive of one another. When Ernest had a heart attack in 1957, Wallis sent a dozen red roses to his hospital every day. When he died in 1958, she sent a large wreath to his funeral.

Later that fall, Kennett Rawson, an editor at David McKay, the firm that had contracted to publish the hard-cover book, announced that he himself would take on the task of ghost writing. "I have found the Duchess filled with desire to tell the truth!" he exclaimed. But in December the Duchess announced that she would write the book herself, without a ghost-writer. In the end, it fell to Charles Murphy, who had been the Duke's ghost, to be selected as her "collaborator." In *The Windsor Story*, he writes that he had grave misgivings about becoming involved in a second Windsor book. But on the whole working with the Duchess turned out to be somewhat easier than working with the Duke, thanks to Wallis's superior ability to organize her time, though the venture was not without its vicissitudes. At one point, the Duchess angrily fired Murphy, only to have the Duke come back to him, hat in hand, and beg him to carry on.

The first installment of the book, called "This Is My Side of the Story," appeared in the March 1956 issue of *McCall's*, and *The Heart Has Its Reasons* was published later that spring. In neither the magazine excerpts nor the book was anyone given ghostwriter or "as told to" credit.

In many ways, Wallis's was a better book than the Duke's. To be sure, she skirted around certain subjects. The hazy, lazy China years were left that way. Jimmy Donahue's name was not mentioned. Still, despite its title, the book reveals a woman with great strength of character. Reading between the lines it is possible to sense a deep and terrible bitterness over the way the Duke's family had treated them both for twenty years, but this is kept under control. Murphy has written that he found her much more candid than he had expected her to be, and Robert Sencourt has quoted Perry Brownlow as saying that Wallis's book was written with "an almost blinding veracity."

In September, to promote her book, Wallis and the Duke came to New York to appear on Edward R. Murrow's television show, *Person to Person*. It was an unusual interview, not only because it provided most Americans with their first view of the Windsors in the flesh, but also because of the banality of the conversation that took place in front of the television cameras. When Wallis was asked if she was familiar with the CBS show, she said yes, she and the Duke had once watched a televised interview with the Minsky burlesque people. "If only we could

come across the screen as nicely as the Minskys!" she said.
Murrow asked, "Do you think you would ever settle in New
York?" The Duke replied, "The Duchess prefers city life and
all that it has to offer women. I think better in country air."
The Duchess commented archly, "Well, he has 'aired' my
problems, I must say, in the fields." She then talked about her
superstitions—hats on beds, things hung on doorknobs, the
number thirteen, breaking mirrors. Murrow asked, "What about
the future?" The Duke said, "I think if one leads a decent life
and acts well, the future takes care of itself. There is so much
to do in life, and so little time to do it in."

Wallis proceeded to insert a strong plug for her book, holding it up for the camera to inspect front and back. Then she
picked at her dress and audiences were treated to the sight of
the Duchess of Windsor lurching across the screen to smooth
her husband's hair. When she was asked about the Abdication,
she said, "David, don't you remember we always said we
would never talk about what might have been? In fact, I think
we arranged that pact on our honeymoon." The Duke replied,
"It is a vow we have never broken." Then they talked about
the Duke's passion for gadgets, and her devotion to him. "I
want to make my husband happy. That's my only desire," she
said. On future travel plans, the Duke said, "I have been everywhere except in jail."

Despite Wallis's promotional efforts, the book did not do
nearly as well as *A King's Story*. It sold only 26,000 copies
in the American hard-cover edition, against the Duke's 120,-
000. There was no motion picture sale. David O. Selznick was
briefly interested, but when he was advised by British censors
that such a film could never be exhibited in England he abandoned the idea. The reviews ranged from the gently mocking
to the downright bad. One critic suggested that an appropriate
title for the Duchess of Windsor's memoirs might have been
Dear Me—a title later employed by Peter Ustinov. There was
of course a deep irony in the critical reaction. For twenty years,
in millions of words in print and over the airwaves, the media
had gotten mileage and a great deal of money out of Wallis's
spendthrift life. Now, when Wallis offered her own version of
it, they dismissed it as inconsequential.

Sales in England were even poorer, and so were the reviews.
In the stately *Times*, the lead review of the day—of a book

on alpine flowers—was long and detailed. Then came the following:

> *The Heart Has Its Reasons* (381 pp., Michael Joseph, 30s.) carries the memoirs of the Duchess of Windsor from her childhood in Baltimore to the present day.

Never would the British Establishment forgive her, never.

24

⚜

Withering Heights

In 1953, the Duke and Duchess of Windsor had been offered
the huge Paris mansion at 4 Route du Champ d'Entraînement, and moved there from the Rue de la Faisanderie
where, for some time, their neighbors had complained about
noise and the parking problems created in the street by their
parties. Their new house was much more secluded. Route du
Champ d'Entrainement is a short street tucked into the Neuilly
side of the Bois de Boulogne, so difficult to find that most
Parisians still do not know it exists, even though the house was
once the residence of President Charles de Gaulle. One wonders, in fact, why the house was ever given a street number.
There were no other houses on the street. Indeed, there were
no other houses in the Bois.

Windsor guests who had neglected to bring the *itinéraires*
sometimes wandered in the park for hours trying to find the
address, and discovered that even the park policemen did not
know where the street was; still, with Gallic crispness, they
always offered specific, if incorrect, directions. The house it-

self, hidden from the street behind high hedges, had an entrance gate unmarked except for a tiny notice that read *Attention aux petits chiens*. No one who did not know of the Windsors' fondness for little dogs would have had a clue that this was where they lived. Within, the grounds were a spacious two acres, but since the Windsors were the only people permitted to live within the Bois de Boulogne, they really had the entire park for their garden.

In her memoirs, Wallis wrote that they had obtained the house "on a long lease." This is not entirely correct. The house was one of a number of "grace and favor" houses owned by the city of Paris, and in yet another gesture of affection for the Windsors, the City Fathers had given the Windsors the lifetime use of the house for a token rent of less than a hundred dollars a year. There never was, in fact, a lease, and to the end Wallis remained convinced that at any moment the City Fathers might change their minds and take her house away. She did not understand Gallic gallantry and pride.

In the house in the Bois, the Windsors continued their entertaining—inviting, if not the true French aristocracy exactly, at least the celebrities and millionaires of the moment. They kept twenty-one servants in all, and their chef, Lucien, was acknowledged to be the finest in the city. From the moment one mounted the wide stone steps and passed through the canopied entrance, to be met by bowing footmen in royal livery and ushered into the great hall with its family portraits and array of standards and banners along the walls, one was quite aware of the carefully studied, formally royal atmosphere. Here Wallis could now entertain on a truly regal scale, though the Duke still enjoyed dressing up in a variety of evening suits, including his Highlander's kilts, and after dinner liked to take guests aside for games of gin rummy, poker or bridge.

Chips Channon visited the Windsors, whom he had not seen since the Abdication, in Paris. He found Wallis "elegant and gay and gracious," and reported to his diary that "The Duke, rather desséché, astonished me by his opening remark which was, 'Do you remember the night we dined together at the Saddle and Cycle Club in Chicago?' (This was in 1924 or 1925!) He watched me talking to Wallis; evidently he is still passionately in love. He came up three times and interrupted us by bringing her Scotch and water as he called it; each time she smilingly accepted the glass, and put it down undrunk.

There was certainly understanding and affection in her glance."

Wallis, at this time, had embarked upon what was to be a lengthy feud with another social arbitress, the late Elsa Maxwell. Like most social battles, the reasons behind this one were various and silly. Initially, Wallis was displeased with an article Miss Maxwell had published in March 1953 in the *American Weekly,* in which she stated that the Duchess of Windsor would have very much liked to have attended the Coronation of Elizabeth II, but had not been invited. Also, it had been reported to Wallis that Miss Maxwell had called her "stupid." Wallis had countered by referring to Miss Maxwell as "the old oaken bucket in the Well of Loneliness." The real reason for the feud was, if anything, sillier. At a New York party, Wallis had wanted to meet, and to be seated at the same table with, Marilyn Monroe. Miss Maxwell, however, had managed to get Miss Monroe seated at *her* table, and proceeded to monopolize the star the entire evening.

In 1955, Elsa Maxwell was organizing a cruise of the Greek Islands, sponsored by Stavros Niarchos, "for the two hundred top socialites and celebrities in the world." The Duke and Duchess of Windsor were not on the list. Actually, only 126 people showed up; both Grace Kelly and Jean-Pierre Aumont sent regrets. In the publicity surrounding the junket, Wallis was said to have called the group "Elsa's zoo." Wallis issued a statement with a correction. "I did not call it Elsa's zoo," she said. "I merely said that no boat has carried a queerer assortment of people since Noah's Ark." When Miss Maxwell was asked whether she had seen the Duchess lately, she said, "Which Duchess?" When told that Wallis was the Duchess in question, she said, "Oh her—only at a distance."

Miss Maxwell had also begun dropping hints that the Duchess of Windsor charged a fee for appearing at parties. This was not exactly true, though such a practice is not unknown among royalty. (Princess Margaret once asked a fee of $35,000 plus expenses to appear at a New York charity ball, and was furious when the event did not raise sufficient money to pay her.) The Duchess did not ask for sums of money outright, but planners of large benefits had learned that, if they wished their events to be graced by the Windsors' presence, a piece of jewelry from Van Cleef and Arpels or Cartier would usually ensure an appearance.

In the autumn of 1955, Mrs. George F. Baker gave a large

dinner party in honor of the Duke and Duchess at her estate in Locust Valley, Long Island. Among the guests were Mr. and Mrs. William Woodward, Jr.—he a wealthy sportsman and she a former model—who were also good friends of the Windsors'. Later that night, according to Mrs. Woodward's account, after the Woodwards had gone home and to bed in their separate rooms, Ann Woodward thought she heard a prowler outside her door. She got up, seized a shotgun that she kept beside her bed, opened her bedroom door and saw a shadowy figure in the hall. She fired pointblank at it, and when she turned on the light, the prowler turned out to be her husband. (The next morning, the Windsors' friend Mrs. Lyon Slater pulled together a hasty luncheon party to rehash the events on the night before and to discuss what sounded like an exciting new society murder.) When Wallis was interviewed by the police in her Waldorf suite, she said that she had always thought the Woodwards "an ideal couple." They had talked that evening, she said, mostly about Bill Woodward's racehorse Nashua. Elsa Maxwell, who also lived at the Waldorf under a reduced-rate arrangement similar to the Windsors', said that she thought the Duchess's observations were "very odd" since "everybody who is anybody knows that Bill and Ann Woodward have both had detectives spying on each other for months." In the end, a one-day grand jury found no evidence of crime in the shooting.

In May 1957, the Windsors found themselves on board the SS *United States* along with Elsa Maxwell. The Windsors had abandoned Cunard for the transatlantic trips in favor of the United States Lines, for a practical reason: The *United States* had graciously offered them, and Miss Maxwell, free passage whenever they wanted it, in return for the publicity. While everyone on board was speculating about what might happen should the two women meet, Miss Maxwell sent around a conciliatory note to the Windsors' cabin. Wallis, apparently in a forgiving mood, responded by inviting Elsa for cocktails, and the three-year period of bickering was ended. Elsa Maxwell said, "I once wrote of the Duchess that we were both strong personalities, and almost a law unto ourselves." She added, somewhat tartly, "She is charming. She can be *very* charming. The Duke is *always* charming." The following month, to prove that their respective hatchets were thoroughly buried, Wallis and Elsa walked hand in hand into lunch at the Paris Ritz.

Earlier that year, however, there had been another social setback for the Windsors in America. They had not been invited to a party given by the British Embassy in Washington for the visiting Queen Elizabeth and Prince Philip.

In 1956, the Duke and Wallis made another trip to Germany, and stayed at Schloss Fuschl, a hotel that had been Ribbentrop's country home during the Nazi era. As an honor, the Duke was given Ribbentrop's room and Ribbentrop's bed. In Munich, the Duke put on a false mustache and made a speech, in German, in a beer garden. He got rousing cheers. He said, "I am very glad to be back in Munich. It is a town I know very well. I have always loved Munich very much." There were more cheers, and waving of beer steins.

But the Duke's health was deteriorating. He looked not only dried out—he looked ill and old. He continued to complain of stomach troubles, and not long after his German visit he checked into a hospital to be treated for shingles. Wallis, in the meantime, had begun to worry about her own health. Always something of a hypochondriac, she had begun to fear that she had an ulcer, and went into hospitals for a series of tests and checkups. In 1959, a finger that had been pricked by a rose thorn became infected and she was hospitalized again—taking with her, as always, her own linens and personal maid. That same year she checked into the London Clinic, again as "Mrs. Robertson," for more facial work—though the official explanation was that she had cut her face when she tripped and fell over a suitcase during a transatlantic crossing. Two years later, another face lift was performed. The Duke had also begun having trouble with his eyes and, in 1965, the first of a series of eye operations was performed in the London Clinic. The Duke and Duchess had made many separate trips to England without Wallis's ever having been invited to meet a British Monarch. Now, while the Duke was recuperating in his fourth-floor hospital suite, the Queen paid her uncle a courtesy visit, and the Queen and Wallis exchanged a polite but cool greeting.

It was not that the young Queen bore any personal animus toward her uncle and his wife. She had been too young at the time of the Abdication to have had any feelings about it. But for nearly thirty years she had been living with her mother's and grandmother's feelings on the subject, and in 1965 Queen Mother Elizabeth remained just as stubborn and unyielding as old Queen Mary had been. The Queen Mother, furthermore, had kept no secret of the fact that she believed that the Abdication of Edward VIII, which had thrust the kingship so abruptly into his brother's untutored and unready hands, had helped shorten her husband's life. "My husband would be alive today if it hadn't been for that woman," she once told Lady Diana Cooper.

The hospital meeting was not regarded as an "official" meeting. This did not occur until 1967, and the circumstances struck many observers as ironic. The occasion was the unveiling at Marlborough House, on June 7, of a plaque marking the hundredth birthday of Queen Mary, who had died in 1953. The Queen, the Duke and Wallis all appeared at this ceremony. Thus Wallis was among those gathered to honor the woman who, throughout her life, had refused to honor her.

In January 1958, the Windsors' old friend Robert R. Young, the self-made railroad baron, troubled by increasing financial woes with his New York Central Railroad, had gone into the billiard room of his Palm Beach house and put a couple of shotgun cartridges through his head. Though his Central was in difficulties, Young's personal finances were in excellent shape and his widow found herself a splendidly rich woman. She started then to build a palatial new house in Palm Beach that would cost, before it was finished, over a million dollars and become perhaps the most expensive house ever built in the Florida resort colony. It was not only a labor of wealth but a labor of love, since Anita Young's stated intention was to build a house grand enough for entertaining the Windsors. Though the house seemed to take forever to finish—tiles had to be shipped back to Italy because they were the wrong color, windows had to be returned to Belgium to be remade—as soon as it was habitable, in the early sixties, Wallis and the Duke began spending at least part of every January-to-April "season" there as the guests of Anita Young. Palm Beach still treated the Windsors more royally than they were treated anywhere else, but it was noticed that the Duke seemed to be losing his famous memory, and possibly his hearing as well. When asked questions, he would often fail to answer. He would forget names and, for long periods, he would sit at parties silently staring into space, with an absent, melancholy look on his lined face. Once he was found wandering aimlessly in an upstairs hallway of Mrs. Young's house, looking lost. A butler took him by the arm and led him back to his room.

Wallis remained as animated as ever. In the south of France for a picnic, the sometime Best-Dressed Woman in the World put on sneakers, blue jeans, and a floppy felt hat and climbed up a high, rocky hill to the picnic site, though she made most of the ascent and descent from a sitting position because of her fear of heights. During that same southern visit, Françoise Wicart, whose aunt and uncle, M. and Mme. Jacques Ruiller, were close friends of Lord Louis Mountbatten, was on a beach chatting with the Earl of Burma when she suddenly saw the Duchess of Windsor, whom she had never met, approaching them across a terrace. Mlle. Wicart whispered to Earl Mountbatten, "Do I curtsy when I meet her?" Mountbatten replied, "It's not necessary. But she would appreciate it." The young woman did as was suggested, and is certain that this was the first time the Duchess had been curtsied to by someone wearing a minimal bikini.

In 1959, in Spain, Wallis visited Generalissimo Franco's daughter and went on to a gypsy nightclub. She refused to dance the flamenco, but she clapped her hands to the rhythm and shouted "Olé!" when the music ended. Still, there was time for more serious pursuits. Now that the Duke and Wallis were both published authors and had enjoyed the novel experience of making some money of their own, they looked earnestly for other commercial possibilities whereby their names could be exploited for profit. The Duke had begun to think of himself as just as much a fashion authority as his wife, and in July and August of 1960, *McCall's* published a two-part article by "H.R.H., The Duke of Windsor," called "Up to Date." This would become the basis of another, shortish book called *A Family Album*. Because of its misleading title, both readers and reviewers inferred that the book would contain intimate revelations about the British Royal Family, and were disappointed to discover that the book was almost entirely about clothes and the Duke's fashion philosophy.

That same year, not to be outdone, Wallis launched a Duchess of Windsor syndicated pattern service, which flourished for a while. The pattern service led, in February 1961, to a monthly column in *McCall's* called "All Things Considered," signed by "Wallis, Duchess of Windsor." The columns, which were ghostwritten by the writer Etta Wanger—though both Wallis and the Duke had final editorial approval—devoted themselves to predictable matters; only in the first one did Wallis let any of her feelings show. "The Duke and I pay our bills!" she emphasized. She also complained of being "picked on" by the press, and spoke of "the petty little digs, mostly inspired by the British." The second column talked about shopping at the Paris collections, and in April the topic was menus and entertaining. May described the Windsors' art collection, and June was devoted to vacations and travel. In September, Wallis became briefly "controversial," discussing the pros and cons of teenagers' "going steady," a question currently being aired from various American pulpits. In January 1962—the last of the twelve columns—Wallis offered a series of New Year's resolutions, including this one: "Release me from craving to try to straighten out everybody's affairs."

Etta Wanger recalls with the greatest pleasure the professional association with Wallis, which consisted of several meetings at the Neuilly house and at Le Moulin. Wallis liked Etta Wanger because, as she once told Mrs. Wanger's husband, "she doesn't know the difference between a Duke and a doorman." Etta Wanger was also impressed by Wallis's extraordinary considerateness. Once, at a seated gathering, Wallis had reached out unobtrusively to Mrs. Wanger to warn her that her stocking tops were showing. Whenever the Wangers arrived in Paris, Wallis sent flowers to their hotel room and, at Le Moulin, Mrs. Wanger's bedroom was always supplied with the makings of what Wallis had noticed was her favorite cocktail, a vodka martini. Before going down to the Mill, Harry Wanger had complained to his wife, "What am I going to do all day while you and she are working?" Wallis had already thought of this. Knowing that Harry Wanger was an artist, she telephoned Etta before departure, saying, "Tell Harry to bring his paints and brushes. There's a corner of the garden that the Duke's just finished, and he's sure Harry would love to do a painting of it." The two women developed an easy, informal relationship that was never based on ceremony. While waiting outside her hotel to be picked up by Wallis's car one morning, Etta Wanger found herself helping to guide a French motorist in a tiny French car out of a particularly tight parking space. Wallis appeared in her huge American limousine and watched as Etta directed the maneuver. "Well," Wallis said at last, "I never figured you for a traffic cop!" "Why not?" said Mrs. Wanger. "My father was a policeman." And once, learning that Mrs. Wanger had been stricken with a tourist's ailment the night before, Wallis wanted to know, "Why didn't you call me?" Etta explained that the attack had come upon her at three in the morning. "At least I could have called my doctor," Wallis said.

The collaboration was such a happy one that another Wanger–Windsor joint venture was planned to follow the series of articles—a Duchess of Windsor Etiquette Book. This project collapsed, however, when no publisher would come up with the $50,000 advance the Duchess's attorneys wanted.

Etta Wanger's dealings with Wallis were easy because, after all, it was a business arrangement. Social considerations were not involved. With the people whom Wallis considered of her social circle in Paris, Wallis was considerably more demanding. She was a difficult person to entertain. She still insisted on advance-screening the guest lists of parties to which she and the Duke were invited. All guests still had to be assembled fifteen minutes before the Windsors' arrival. She had to precede other women through doorways. No one could sit down until the Windsors sat. One could not speak to her until spoken to. Seating at dinner tables had to be according to strict diplomatic protocol, with Wallis and the Duke seated at the places of the highest honor. If a floral centerpiece interfered with the Duke's view of Wallis from where he sat, that would have to be removed. No one could leave until the Windsors left, and so on.

Because of this sort of thing, the Windsors' social position in the French capital had been declining steadily over the years, though the Windsors themselves may not have realized it. In the beginning, Windsor invitations had taken precedence over all others in Paris, but *le tout Paris* was now finding excuses to regret them, since acceptance meant reciprocation with an invitation for the Windsors. The French have a tendency to become impatient with protocol, and had begun to weary of the artifice of addressing her as "Your Royal Highness" when they knew she wasn't one. Though Wallis had often said that Paris was her favorite city in the world, she had also said that she didn't care all that much for France, or for the French, and these remarks had not been taken kindly. It began to seem to many Parisians that Wallis asked a great deal from Parisian society, but offered very little in return. The Windsors had never been accepted by the topmost level of the French aristocracy. Now they were gradually being dropped by the next layer down.

As for the Duke, though he was always pleasant and well-mannered, he was not really clever or amusing. "Sweet" was the adjective usually used to describe him as he approached old age. He liked, for example, to call the Avenue George V "Rue Papa," and the Hôtel George V, "Hotel Papa." He could talk well about gardening, about the history of English regiments, and he could tell family stories, but he was not really a lively conversationalist, a talent that the French admire. Wallis had learned to speak flawless French, but an inability to wisecrack in that language—her famous plays on words—made her more comfortable in English. The Duke's French, on the other hand, was terrible. When he tried to speak it, no one understood him, and the French have a famous tendency to resent anyone who misuses their beautiful language. They were also put off when he spoke German; the memory of the Occupation was still too close. Then, too, the Duke's increasing vagueness and absent-mindedness was irksome and, using his poor health as an excuse, the Windsors would often beg out of invitations at the last moment. Thus, by the late 1960's, most of the Windsors' guests at the big house in the Bois were second-rate French or visiting moneyed Americans—businessmen and their wives, department store executives, Texans, the new-rich Palm Beach crowd, entertainers and columnists: that amorphous potpourri that called itself the Jet Set.

In May 1972, Queen Elizabeth II, accompanied by her husband and their son Prince Charles, made a much-heralded state visit to France. In line with this visit, it was announced that the Queen would at last visit her ailing uncle, the Duke of Windsor, in Paris. In 1964, in America, the Duke had undergone an operation for an aneurism of the abdominal aorta, and the following year he had gone to London for operations on his left eye. In February 1972 he had a hernia operation at the American Hospital in Paris, and from this last operation he had never fully recovered. At the time of the Queen's state visit, the Duke was bedridden in the house in the Bois, and it was generally known that he was dying. In fact, there was distinct nervousness among members of the Queen's party that the Duke might indeed die during the royal visit, which would have been most awkward and embarrassing, to say the least. As the day of the Queen's "private call" on her uncle drew near, her aides were close to panic lest this might happen. At one of the many balls given for Her Majesty in Paris, a reporter asked one of her secretaries, Lord Charteris, if the Queen was aware of the seriousness of her uncle's condition. Charteris replied, "Look, *you* know he's dying, and *I* know he's dying. But *we* don't know he's dying."

The visit was scheduled to take place on the afternoon of May 18, and had been sandwiched into a tight royal schedule, between the running of an important race at Longchamp and a great ball that evening. The Duke's doctors had been begging him not to get out of bed to receive his niece. But he insisted that he did not want her to see him in bed; he wanted to be up and properly dressed, and seated in a chair, to receive the Queen of England. He also wanted to receive her in the main salon of the house, but the doctors refused to let him go down-stairs. He would have to see her in the upstairs sitting room.

Doctors and nurses worked on the Duke for more than seven hours to perpare him for the visit: dressing him, placing him in a chair, and hiding under his clothing the various tubes that ran in and out of his body so that the Queen might not see how very ill he really was. When the Queen, Prince Philip, and the new Prince of Wales arrived at 4 Route du Champ de l'Entraînement, Wallis, in a simple dark dress, was at the door to meet them, and curtsied low. The Queen was escorted up-stairs to the sitting room. The Duke did not rise to greet her with the bow that protocol demanded because he could not. She chatted with her uncle for about an hour before it was time to leave and dress for the ball.

In the press, her visit was termed a "reconciliation," but it was really no more than a necessary duty call. Wallis had wanted to go to Spain, to Marbella, in order to be out of the country while the Queen was in Paris. But the state of the Duke's health had prevented their going anywhere. Since the Queen's tour had been advertised as symbolic of improved Anglo-French relations, a resurgence of the spirit of *entente cordiale,* she was obliged to call on the Duke of Windsor, to whom the French had shown such kindness over the years. Because it seemed so obviously a political gesture, the Queen's visit to her uncle struck many as an ultimate example of the cynicism of the British Royal Family.

Some persons close to the present Queen of England have described her as a hardhearted, vindictive woman who never forgets a slight and never forgives a wrong when she believes one has been done to her. If Elizabeth did represent the third generation of women of the House of Windsor, who felt that the Duke's punishment should be relentless, and if she actually did believe that her uncle's Abdication had shortened her father's life, then she may have got her revenge that afternoon in Paris. The strain of the preparation for her visit undoubtedly helped shorten the Duke's life. The Queen left France on May 20. Eight days later, the Duke was dead.

25

Farewells

EVEN if the Queen of England were not a vindictive woman, her behavior after the Duke's death could hardly be character- ized as kindly. Everything she did in the days that followed was perfectly proper and polite, and yet there was a certain coldness and precision about her behavior which belied sym- pathy. She sent, for example, a formal message of condolence to Wallis, but did not, as she might have done, telephone her personally in Paris. On Wednesday, May 31, when the Duke's body was flown to England, and the next day, when it was removed to Windsor for burial in the royal burying ground at Frogmore, many people wondered why the Duke was not given the honor of lying in state at Westminster Hall. Buckingham Palace announced that "sometime in the 1960's"—the Palace did not say when—the Duke had requested that he be buried at Frogmore, where he had played as a child, and had made all the arrangements for his funeral, including the order of service and certain people he would like to ask as guests. He had also requested that Wallis lie beside him. All these requests the Queen had graciously granted.

Wallis did not accompany her husband's body on the plane, saying that she was too tired and unwell. She followed on Friday, June 2, and was met at Heathrow by Admiral of the Fleet Earl Mountbatten of Burma; she was then driven to Buckingham Palace, where she was to be the Queen's guest. She entered through the door the tourists use and signed the Guest Register. She was taken to her room, and then had lunch with the Queen and Princess Anne in the Queen's private apartments. The next day, Saturday, the Trooping of the Colour for the Queen's official birthday had been scheduled, and a special tribute to the Duke—two drum rolls surrounding a minute of silence—was added. It was announced that Wallis would not attend this ceremony, but would watch it on television from the palace. A memorable photograph was taken of her, looking sad and haggard, as she pulled aside a curtain at a palace window, to look down at the Queen's departure. Immediately after the ceremony, the Royal Family left for Windsor for the weekend as they usually did, leaving Wallis behind in the palace to occupy herself as best she could. On Saturday evening she was driven to Windsor to see her husband lying in state, and was escorted into the chapel by Prince Charles. It was, by coincidence, her thirty-fifth wedding anniversary, and she was heard to whisper, "Thirty-five years." Then she was driven back to London.

The funeral took place on Monday morning, June 5, at eleven-fifteen in St. George's Chapel, Windsor. Over the weekend, it was estimated that more than fifty-seven thousand people had trooped by the Duke's coffin, in tribute. At the service Wallis seemed disoriented, and it is likely that some tranquilizing drug was responsible for this. She did not weep, but she fidgeted, twisted her rings, and on at least two occasions her face broke into a sudden smile that was more like a grimace. At one point during the luncheon that followed she touched Princess Margaret's arm and whispered, "Are you having a good time, dear?" After the service, when Prime Minister Edward Heath stepped over to her to offer his condolences, she thanked him and then said, "You must come to Paris to see us. The Duke and I would so love to have you."

Immediately after the Duke's body was lowered into the ground, Wallis was driven back to Heathrow, escorted by the Lord Chamberlain. A member of the Queen's Household had been assigned to accompany her back to Paris. She had spent exactly three nights at Buckingham Palace, most of the time alone in the state suite on the first floor, overlooking the Mall, to which she had been assigned. The palace explained the lack of activities planned for her by saying that the Duchess was "tired and unwell and distressed." Was no member of the Royal Family available to meet her plane on Friday or to see her off on Monday? Could not even Prince Charles have been put to use? Apparently not, though many people thought that this would have been an appropriate gesture. The Queen was in charge of the proceedings, and Her Majesty did not wish to provide any of these extra touches. Wallis—a thin, tiny, veiled figure all in black—marched purposefully and quite rapidly up the steps, gripping the rail, and into the plane. She did not look back.

For several months, in Paris, Wallis remained in seclusion. With the Duke alive, there would have at least been someone with whom to share the bitterness. Now there was no one, except the dogs, and for comfort a glass of iced vodka in a silver cup. Vodka had replaced Scotch as her favorite drink. "The Duke would never touch a drop of drink before seven in the evening," the Duke's former private secretary John Utter told the British journalist David Pryce-Jones early in 1979. "But that is no guarantee of what can be drunk after seven, and sometimes the sound of their drunken bickering was unbearable." Now there was no one with whom to bicker, and Wallis drank alone. "Their life was essentially a life of entertainment," Mr. Utter said. "It was really empty as far as I could judge, but it was what they enjoyed. He had begun to tire of social life, but that was her great thing. She loved anything to do with a party. She had to make sure she never missed one. Was it enough? How could it be? They were wretched personalities." Now it was a solitary wretchedness, soothed and eventually put to sleep by vodka.

Little by little, Wallis began to go out again, with this or that young escort—what else was there to do? But she was sometimes a disconcerting date. Once her escort in Paris was the writer Patrick O'Higgins, and as they drove through the Place de la Concorde, past the lighted fountains, and turned into the Champs-Elysées, Wallis suddenly said, "Aren't the lights of Nice beautiful tonight?" Later she turned to him and wanted to know, "Who are you? Where are we going?" Perhaps it was the result of alcohol or perhaps it was the onset of arteriosclerosis, but the "twenty-four-hour memory," of which she had once boasted, was going. She faded in and out of focus. At times she would be perfectly lucid, her old self, able to introduce a roomful of fifty guests to one another without a single slip or stumble. At other times, she would turn to her dinner partner and ask, "What ever happened to——?" And the dinner partner would eerily realize that the person to whom she was referring was himself.

She began giving small dinners for eight, but the caliber of her guests was not what it had been when the Duke was alive. People who, out of fondness and respect for the Duke, had once broken previous engagements to come to his house, now sent excuses and regrets when they had other plans elsewhere. Also there were the times when the Duchess had to call off dinners because of ill health, or when, at the last minute, she felt too ill to appear at her own table, and remained upstairs while her guests dined without her.

Then there were the falls. In the autumn of 1973 she fell and broke her hip. The hip was repaired with a silver pin. Later, she fell again in Biarritz, tripping against a raised marble hearthstone, and sustained several broken ribs. When she entered the American Hospital in Paris again for more work on her hip, physicians feared that the anesthetic tube could not be inserted in her throat, which had become tightened by repeated cosmetic surgery.

Whenever she checked into a hospital, she arrived with her own personal maid and her own linens, which were changed twice daily. Her hospital rooms were filled with fresh flowers. And not long after her fall in Biarritz she was able to appear at a Versailles ball, using two sturdy male escorts, one at each elbow, for support. Several weeks after that, she began using a cane. In the spring of 1974 she was able to come to New York, where she put up, as usual, at the Waldorf Towers, though in a somewhat smaller suite. She and the Duke had always had 28-A. Now she took 40-F, which her friend Nathan Cummings, the art collector and food-processing magnate— for whom the Duke had once posed in a baker's bonnet as a publicity stunt—had helped her make pleasant with one of his Renoirs and one of his Sisleys. As usual, she added decorative touches of her own—small objets d'art, leopard throws on sofas—and filled the rooms with flowers. She lunched and dined with friends, and posed for photographers, supported on the arms of her friends Kay Chaqueneau and Cordelia Biddle Robertson. (For the photographers she asked Mrs. Chaqueneau to hold her cane.) Yes, she admitted during her visit, it was difficult to be alone, but she was not lonely, thanks to old friends. She spoke wistfully of "the old American friends," who were more loyal than the fair-weather French friends, and hinted that she might like to return to the United States one day. In Paris, it had begun to seem as though *le tout Paris* had deserted her—like "Rat Week" all over again.

She had become obsessive, almost hysterically so, about money, though it was hard to see quite why. Though royal wills are never made public, the Duke had died worth, by the most conservative estimates, well over £4,000,000 or $10,-000,000, and Wallis, as his "universal legatee," had got it all, with no death duties to pay. Shortly after the Duke's death, she sold three and a half acres of land in Marbella—on which they had at one point planned to build a house—for £82,000. In 1962, the Duke had sold his 4,000-acre ranch in Canada for £110,000. During the last years of his illness, they hardly ever visited Le Moulin, and after his death Wallis put it on the market—twenty-three acres of land with a ten-room main house and an additional fourteen rooms contained in guest cottages and outbuildings—through Previews, Inc., the international real estate firm, for one million dollars. When it didn't immediately sell, she lowered the price by half, suggesting a distress sale. But when the property finally sold, a year later, the price was £350,000, or very close to her original million-dollar asking price. The buyer, a Mr. Arthray, was identified as a "Swiss industrialist," and was reported to be acting as the agent for a Kuwaiti oil sheik. The furnishings of the Mill, many of them quite valuable, were sold at auction by Sotheby Parke Bernet, and more money entered the coffers of the money-maddened Duchess.

During his brother George VI's lifetime, the Duke had received a considerable rental income from the Duchy of Lancaster. At George VI's death, Queen Elizabeth had taken this income away from the Duke, and he had made several unsuccessful trips to London begging that it be restored. The matter had joined the long list of grievances the Duke had collected against his family. At his funeral, however, the Queen had assured Wallis that the income would be restored to her for her lifetime. The Duke's memoirs had earned roughly a million dollars, and her own had earned her $100,000. The city of Paris had assured her repeatedly that she could have the big house in the Bois for as long as she wishd for the same nominal rent. But Wallis, who never entirely trusted the French, remained suspicious that she might be evicted at any moment, and was furious when, after the Duke's death, the city removed the round-the-clock armed guards that had formerly been stationed outside her gates, arguing that these policemen were no longer necessary. To her, it was another example of French duplicity.

She also had her jewelry collection, amply replenished after the robbery, which was estimated to be worth over a million dollars. Perhaps from her years in the Orient she had developed a Chinese woman's feelings about jewels, which was that only under the most desperate and shameful circumstances should a woman ever sell her stones; they were her insurance.

There was also the persistent rumor, never confirmed but never denied, that when Jimmy Donahue died he had left her $300,000 in his will.

Why, then, with a palpably large fortune and a huge income, did Wallis have this fear of poverty? She had never been philanthropic. She had no direct heirs, no particular loved ones to pass her money on to, no relatives in the United States except a few obscure second cousins whom she barely knew. Perhaps it was because, throughout their marriage, the Duke had fretted about her spending, reminding her again and again that he was not as rich as he used to be. Or perhaps, in her old age, the echoes of the old days in Baltimore were coming back to her, when life had been pillar-to-post, dependent on the benefactions of relatives, with no security or way of telling how large rich Uncle Sol's check might be next month. In any case, following the Duke's death, Wallis's mindless fears of going to the poorhouse became her chief preoccupation.

Not long after the Duke's funeral, Lord Louis Mountbatten visited Wallis in Paris and tactfully suggested that some of the Duke's possessions—his uniforms, his medals, his decorations—ought properly to be returned to England. Wallis agreed. Mountbatten also recommended that the same thing be done with the ex-King's papers and documents. Wallis agreed again, and these were returned to England and placed in the Royal Archives at Windsor where, under the institution's rigid custodianship, they will probably never be seen again, nor will any interesting footnotes to history they may contain ever be known.

Mountbatten then brought up the delicate subject of her money. Since most of it had originally come from England, it seemed appropriate that it might eventually be returned, in some form or other, to that country. Mountbatten proposed that Wallis, in her will, establish a Duke of Windsor Foundation, which would aid worthy British causes. Initially, Wallis reacted favorably to this notion and promised to think about it.

While her obsessive worries about money were an affliction that she could at least try to cope with, the increasing hobbling of her famous memory was something that was much more difficult for her to bear. On this count, she was becoming a woman quite difficult to be around. As she drifted in and out of reality, it was impossible to predict where her mind might wander. On some days, she was as warm and bright and hospitable as ever, but on others she seemed lost in hallucination. At times, she not only lost track of names and faces and where she was, but also seemed to forget that the Duke was dead. "How very funny! I must tell the Duke," she would cry apropos of nothing in particular, while the faces of those around her struggled to compose themselves in appropriate expressions. Probably, too, it was her own anger and frustration over these lapses that brought on the sudden, violent bursts of temper and abuse that were also unpredictable. In the middle of a conversation that was trying to be pleasantly mundane, she would suddenly shout an insult across the table to the speaker. In her rages, too, she was often something that she had never been before—vulgar. After her 1974 visit to the Waldorf, which would be her last, the hotel staff talked for weeks about her abusive treatment of servants, waiters, busboys, and the drivers of her cars. The hotel chef was taken aback when he was called to the telephone and heard the Duchess of Windsor scream, "This is the Duchess of Windsor! Are you the son of a bitch that sent this fucking trout up here?" Of course her glasses of iced vodka did little to help her control these outbursts.

In 1973, *France-Dimanche,* never a particularly reliable source, had printed the news that the Duchess of Windsor would marry John Utter, who was one of her two private secretaries, and who had been the Duke's. There was no truth in this, and both denied the rumor. To those who knew them both the *France-Dimanche* report occasioned guffaws of laughter. John Utter had never cared for Wallis, and was caring for her even less in her new, often shrewish incarnation. Nor did Wallis care for Utter. He was a suave, elegant man who had been a Foreign Service officer with the U.S. State Department. But during the witch-hunting era of Senator Joseph McCarthy, who had made the State Department one of his chief targets, Utter had resigned in disgust. He had been recommended to the Duke by the U.S. Ambassador to Egypt. He and Wallis had locked horns often in the past. As the Duke's private secretary, Utter had the job of paying the household bills, and whenever an item of Wallis's spending required questioning, this responsibility fell to him. Wallis often accused him of keeping too tight a hold on her purse strings. But the Duke had been fond of Utter, and Utter had been fond of the Duke, and had offered to stay on to help Wallis make the transition into widowhood. He was an excellent secretary and, as Wallis was clever enough to realize, a shrewd financial manager.

After the Duke's death, to economize, she reduced the staff of the Paris household to fourteen. John Utter lasted until 1975, when, unable to cope with Wallis's increasing irascibility, he retired to private life in Paris. A second secretary, Johanna Schütz, lasted until 1978. Long gone by then, too, was Sidney Johnson, the magnificently proportioned handsome Bahamian, a great pet of the Duke's, who had come with him as the butler's "second man" from Nassau days. Black servants were a rarity in Paris, particularly one of Johnson's dimensions, and "Mr. Sidney," as he was always called, was, in his splendid uniform, almost a decorative item in the house. Wallis fired him summarily one day for asking for some time off. He departed, unpensioned, after nearly thirty years of service, and went to work for a Chilean family in Paris.

Wallis had begun to talk increasingly of going "home." But where was home? Baltimore, she insisted—but few friends remained there. The only thing that kept her in France, she said, was that from there she was able to take short, secret trips to Frogmore to visit the Duke's grave and to inspect the site of her own.

In 1974, another rumor circulated that Wallis would marry Prince Borromeo, the aging Italian ruler of the Borromean Islands and an old friend of the Windsors'. This rumor also proved to be without foundation. Still, even in old age, Wallis could be flirtatious. At a Paris party, the Duke's widow dabbed a few drops of cologne on her wrists, and said, "Perhaps if I use a little honey, a few bees will come."

By 1977, the famous blue eyes still sparkled, but they sometimes carried a wary, agitated look. More and more when she spoke, her mind, befuddled by age or vodka, wandered; she rambled, repeated herself, lost the thread. She became obsessed with the notion that certain of her possessions were being secretly spirited out of the house. To the visiting Lady Monckton, Wallis suddenly said, "I'm frightened! They've been here again! They've moved my things! It's the second time they've hijacked me." Lady Monckton could see that everything in the room was in its usual place.

Grown painfully thin, down to a mere eighty-five pounds, Wallis could not seem to eat, but one idea still burned brightly in her mind: her bitterness toward the British Royal Family, and in particular toward her sister-in-law, Queen Mother Elizabeth, the woman she continued to regard as the archvillainess in her life. Seizing a newspaper photograph of the Queen Mother and thrusting it in the face of a visitor, she cried angrily, "Would you call *that* regal?" She jabbed her finger at the plump little Queen Mum. "That plain, dumpy little Scotswoman in her beige shoes! *Anyone* could look more royal than that!" Of Queen Elizabeth II: "She's stupid—even stupider than her mother, if that's possible." As she spoke, her drink splashed across the front of her dress. The once-fastidious Duchess did nothing to mop it up. She had, however, liked Prince Charles. "Everything is going to Prince Charles—everything!" she once said. Gradually, though, even these strong images began to fade.

Soon it was no longer possible for her to come downstairs, and her activities were confined to the short trip between her bedroom and the upstairs sitting room, and it was not long before the perimeters of her life narrowed again, to the bedroom itself, and the little distance between her bed and a sofa. By 1978, she could no longer manage that, and the Duchess was bedridden.

Now the staff was further reduced—to Georges, the butler, whose main duty was to answer the telephone, which hardly ever rang; his wife, the housekeeper; the chauffeur, needed to collect groceries and medical supplies; and the laundress, needed because the meticulous Duchess had become incontinent. And of course the nurses, two at a time, in three shifts, around the clock. Visitors were limited to the doctor, Jean Thin, and the hairdresser, who continued to apply the secret dye to Wallis's glossy dark hair.

She lay there, a wasted ghostlike figure in the center of her big bed. She could not read, she could not watch television, and not even the sound of the radio playing—she had always kept up with the latest popular songs—seemed to divert her or to pull her out of the dark place where she had gone. Sometimes her eyes opened and darted about the room, but mostly she slept. Occasionally she spoke, but seldom coherently. Under medication, of course, her drinking days were over. Her favorite treat was candy. As her hairdresser lifted the fragile body to the wash basin to shampoo her hair, Wallis suddenly said, "I wish someone would put a sweet in my mouth." The hairdresser complied, but the nurse was cross. "I wish you wouldn't do that," she snapped. "You don't have to clean her up."

The year 1979 passed in this fashion. In June 1980, Wallis would be eighty-four. There was longevity in her genes. Her Aunt Bessie Merryman had lived to celebrate her hundredth birthday.

26

Enter Maître Blum

IT is a final irony that the woman who had so successfully organized and managed the life of one of the world's most famous men should in the end need to be managed by strangers: Nurses, doctors, hairdresser—professional despots, well trained in the care of the senile, but able to return to their homes and more pleasant chores when the day's work was done. One of her lifelong fears—fears of the dark, of flying, of high places— had been a fear of being alone. Now, with the exception of hired help, she was alone.

To the few old friends who remained, it was as though, since Wallis was not dead, she had simply gone away and become a memory. Both she and the Duke were now spoken of in the past tense. Those who remembered spoke of Wallis's toughness and determination, and also of her self-mocking good humor and her occasional wicked little barbs. Once, arriving a little late at a friend's house in Paris, Wallis apologized and explained that she had been kept waiting by her hairdresser, Alexandre. "I don't mind being kept waiting for a *person*," she said, "but I do object to being kept waiting by a *thing*." The "thing," she explained, was an elaborate hairpiece that Alex-andre was creating for Elizabeth Taylor. It had to be finished and rushed to Orly airport so that it could reach Miss Taylor in time for her wedding—another Wedding of the Century— to Richard Burton in 1964. The hairpiece Wallis described was a mass of dark curls and braids intertwined with yellow ribbons. "Of course everyone knows," Wallis said with a wink, "that yellow is *la couleur du cocu"*—the cuckold's color. There were also memories of the Duke's gentle ways, of how once, when a dancing partner accidentally stepped on his foot and apologized, the Duke murmured, "Don't mention it—the other foot is jealous."

In June 1974, Wallis had turned seventy-eight, but that same summer she startled a friend by suddenly saying, "Do you know that I'm really eighty-one?" This, naturally, rekindled old rumors that Wallis had long lied about her age, and it seemed peculiar that she should at this point decide to tell the truth. But the remark must have been the result of Wallis's increasing mental disorientation. Though the birth records have disappeared from Blue Ridge Summit, it is known that her debutante season was 1914–1915, and that the coming-out ritual is traditionally for eighteen-year-olds. Surely if Wallis was actually twenty-one when she came out, her friends and contemporaries would have remembered this uncommon de-parture from custom, and would have told the world about it.*

Early in 1973, when the Duke had not yet been dead a year, the plans for a Duke of Windsor Foundation were abruptly abandoned, and the London law firm of Allen & Overy, which had long handled the Duke of Windsor's affairs, was advised by the Duchess that its services were no longer required. All matters, legal and financial, would now be handled by her French lawyer, Maître Suzanne Blum of Paris.†

Maître Blum is a tall, slender, elegant woman the same age as the Duchess, who manages to appear at least twenty years younger than she is, with a high-cheekboned, *haute-juive* face

---

*Iles Brody, in *Gone with the Windsors*, claims possession of two letters from contemporaries which assert that Wallis was actually born in 1890, six years earlier than the date ordinarily given, but admits that jealousy on the part of these correspondents cannot be ruled out.

†"Maître" is the standard designation for all members of the French legal profession, regardless of sex; in the United States, women lawyers are increasingly using "Esquire."

and a slim, aristocratic nose. She has for many years lived and worked in a beautifully appointed apartment in the Rue de Varenne, on the Left Bank, and her reputation as a trial lawyer is for toughness, astuteness and cool-headedness. Over the years she has represented many distinguished clients, a number of them Hollywood personalities, including Darryl Zanuck, Jack Warner, Walt Disney, and Charlie Chaplin. In 1958, she represented Rita Hayworth in the famous divorce from Aly Khan. Maître Blum has also enjoyed another career, as an author. She has published books on classic French legal cases and a number of mystery and detective novels. When, in the late 1970's, Wallis began to disappear from view, Maître Blum became the storm center of a many-faceted mystery of her own.

She first met the Windsors in 1937, and began her professional relationship with them ten years later. As the sole executor of the Duke's will, she acquired complete authority over the affairs of the disintegrating widow. It was she who handled the final paring-down of the Duchess's staff—dismissing the last three footmen, the chef, the sous-chef, the parlormaids, and the gardeners under condtions which, Maître Blum insists, were very generous. But by late 1978, her role had become much more important than that. She was the vociferous protector and defender of the memory and reputation of the Duke, and of Wallis as well. She was their outspoken champion, the keeper of the flame.

It all began with the publication of Lady Frances Donaldson's biography, *Edward VIII*, which many historians greeted as the most thorough and exhaustive volume on the subject ever written. Not so Suzanne Blum. The Donaldson work is, she insists, mostly "lies and inaccuracies," and she has said that it would take a volume at least four hundred pages long—nearly as long as the Donaldson book, which clocked in at 477 pages—to set the record straight and to correct all the Donaldson errors and misinterpretations. Furthermore, says Maître Blum, the book is both a libel and an invasion of her clients' privacy, though of course the Duke never read the book, nor has Wallis, nor will she ever.

In 1978, Thames Television, which had acquired the film rights to *Edward VIII*, announced its plans to produce a seven-segment dramatization of the book, with Lady Donaldson serving in the capacity of historical adviser. The dramatization would cover the period between the meeting of the Prince of

Wales and Mrs. Simpson through their wedding in 1937.* No sooner was the first episode on the air than Maître Blum fired off an angry broadside. The series, she stated in a release to the Associated Press on November 20, 1978, was "largely and essentially a fable based on incorrect or distorted interpretation of the facts." It contained, she said, a "wave of calumnies" and then dropped a tantalizing bit of news. A historian—she did not give his name—who was holding the private papers of the Duke of Windsor might decide to publish them soon. These papers, including "the complete correspondence in 1936" between the Duke and the Duchess, "will make known everything that was said" between them. Some newspapers reported that there were perhaps twenty "love letters" in this heretofore-unknown correspondence. Others said that there were as many as a thousand.

One of Maître Blum's most outraged objections to the television series—and, of course, to the Donaldson book—was the implication (only ever-so-subtly hinted at in the television drama) that prior to her marriage to him Wallis Simpson had been the King's mistress. That the question of whether the King and Wallis had slept together out of wedlock should assume such importance at the end of Wallis's long life and marriage seemed odd, and yet to Maître Blum, the "mistress" allusions constituted defamation of the highest order. The 1936–1937 "correspondence" between the two would put the lie to these allegations, she said, and the letters would prove that until the wedding band was placed on Wallis's finger she and the Duke "were linked only by friendship."

"She did *not* sleep with him," Maître Blum has said firmly. "His fascination with her was based on her reserve, her hard-to-get quality. She made him laugh, made him have fun. She wouldn't take him too seriously. Her pose was that of a well-bred southern girl who, if in love with a man, wouldn't sleep with him without marriage."

Maître Blum had already proved herself a formidable defender of the Windsors' honor. In 1974, two photographers with telephoto lenses concealed themselves outside the Neuilly house and managed to photograph the wizened Duchess being lifted onto a garden chaise by a uniformed nurse. The photo-

*The series, called *Edward and Mrs. Simpson*, was broadcast in Britain in November and December 1978. American viewers were offered it early in 1980.

graphs were published in *France-Soir*, and were shown on French television. On Wallis's behalf, Maître Blum promptly sued for invasion of privacy, and Wallis was awarded damages of about thirty thousand dollars. Earlier, on the Duke's behalf, Maître Blum had sued about a story that Edward VIII had often returned, in the red boxes from Fort Belvedere, official documents blotted with whisky stains and ringed where glasses had been set down on them. In this libel action, damages were also awarded and collected, and turned over to charity. She would, she announced, have sued Thames Television over the premarital sex allegation, except for the technicality in British law which required that the complainant in such an action appear in court in person. This, obviously, the Duchess was no longer able to do.

On November 27, 1978, Maître Blum was further quoted in *The Times*. When the long-suppressed letters were published, she said, "People will be amazed to discover how seriously they have been fooled. Mrs. Simpson, the Duchess of Windsor, has been portrayed [in the television series] as a cheap adventuress, determined to get hold of the Duke of Windsor [sic], determined to marry the King and destroy the King. The reverse is true. She was the reluctant partner. What has particularly distressed her—and myself—has been the allegation that she was Edward's mistress. This was quite untrue. The King did not want a mistress, and if he had, no doubt he would not have abdicated. He wanted a wife and the support of this one woman for the rest of his life."

But how, those close to the situation wanted to know, could Wallis be "distressed" by anything that was going on beyond the confines of her bed in Neuilly? Suzanne Blum conceded to the press that the Duchess was unaware of the television series, and that there was no way she could ever be. She also admitted that the course of history would not have been changed if Wallis and the Duke *had* slept together before marrying, but she still insisted vehemently that they had not—even though the sexuality of both partners would be called into question upon evidence of such prim restraint. The letters, she repeated, would reveal everything. If that was the case, she was asked, and the letters would make a mockery of everything the television series—and the Donaldson book—had to say, why not produce them now? What better timing? Her client's reputation as an easy woman would be cleared in a single stroke—and

cleared, furthermore, while she was still living. Or, if not all
the letters, just a judicious sampling of the collection would
prove the point. Even a pertinent sentence or two might do the
trick. "No, the time is not yet right." Are the letters being
saved, perhaps at the Duchess's request, for posthumous publication? "I cannot tell you that." Where are the letters? "I
cannot tell you that, either." Who will publish the letters? "An
historian, someone whom the Duchess trusts." But isn't the
Duchess now beyond caring, much less trusting? "That is not
important." Has the historian already been selected? "I cannot
answer that." To the suggestion that she herself—since she
has written books—may be the historian, her reply, accompanied by a mocking look, is an elliptical one: "Please do not
take me to be a fool."

Meanwhile, some of those close to the controversy began
to get the eerie feeling that a phenomenon of intense identifi-
cation was taking place. In her ardor to defend her client's
reputation, Suzanne Blum seemed to be *becoming* the Duchess
of Windsor.

At the time of Maître Blum's November 27 jeremiad in *The
Times*, the reaction at Thames Television was one of bemuse-
ment. By then, only two of the segments of the series had been
broadcast, and the rest had not even been given final editing.
Wallis Simpson had barely been introduced as a character, and
it was assumed that Suzanne Blum's anger stemmed from
Thames Television's refusal to let her see the scripts before
production. At the same time, her attempted intervention and
the ensuing newspaper stories had helped build a record audience for the show—an estimated thirteen million viewers.
"We could never have bought such publicity," Verity Lambert
at Thames told David Pryce-Jones for the New York *Times*.

Others who had known the Windsors had different objections. Lady Alexandra Metcalfe, the widow of the Duke's old
friend Fruity Metcalfe, complained that the series was not faithful *enough* to Lady Donaldson's book. In a letter to *The Sunday
Times* of London, which was published on November 26, 1978,
she wrote:

The first installments [sic], when not factual, are an imaginary version of his [the Prince of Wales's] private life,
focusing on episodes and intimate conversations with the
three ladies with whom he was closely involved. What peo-

ple see on "the box" tends to be remembered—the early episodes will be thought by millions to be a correct picture of the Prince of Wales, of his character, life and behaviour. For the sake of history, I think it is only fair that certain important aspects of his life not mentioned should be remembered.

In Lady Donaldson's excellent biography, the role played by the Prince in those early years, the endless exhausting tours all over the world, the ceaseless round of work at home, the unique charm and personality which captivated the world is vividly described. She quotes letters of praise and admiration from Queen Mary and King George, as well as many extracts from the press, especially *The Times*. This proves he was not, as portrayed in the film, just a pleasure-seeking lightweight, lacking in most essential qualities, evading his duties whenever possible, seemingly never doing more than escaping to ride, play golf, dance, yacht, ski and fall in love.

He enjoyed all those things, but for years he had done his job superbly well—un-royal, un-grand, mixing with all naturally, preferring a game of darts in a working men's club to a state function. This is what gained him the place in the hearts of the people all over the world. Because it did not fit into the type of film, no mention is made of these outstanding gifts; consequently, in my humble opinion, the portrait is unjust and unfair.

At the conclusion of the series, Lady Metcalfe remained disappointed in the depiction of the man at whose wedding her husband had served as best man. "They made him into a frivolous playboy," she said. "They emphasized how he had disappointed his parents and everybody around him. They didn't point out how terribly proud his parents had been of him as Prince of Wales." As for Maître Blum's attempted intervention in the series, she said, "I suppose it is awfully hard for her not to try to defend someone who is—pitiful."

Lady Diana Cooper, meanwhile, who also appeared as a "character" in the television series ("They paid me a thousand pounds—not bad, I thought!"), objected more to the portrayal of Wallis than of the King. Well in her eighties, but still blond and creamy-skinned and extraordinarily beautiful, she receives guests for cocktails in the bedroom of her house in Maida Vale wearing a fluffy bed jacket, propped up by dozens of lacy pillows and in a bed that has been turned into a work space of sorts—scattered with note pads, pencils, books, telephone and directory, appointment calendar, cosmetics case and manicuring tools, spectacles for various uses, a small dog that is shy of strangers, and, seemingly, a great deal else. "I am *not* bed-ridden," she says firmly. "It is just that I have reached the stage of life when, if I do not have to get out of bed, I find it more pleasant to stay in bed." Of the television series, she has this to say:

The actress [Cynthia Harris] who played Wallis was all wrong. I suppose she was cast because of a certain physical resemblance. But she played Wallis as an ingenue—all soft and innocent and helpless. She tried to do it in a southern accent, which was a mistake. Wallis had a sort of drawl, but it was a drawl that came out fast, if you see what I mean. And Wallis wasn't soft. Wallis was *hard*. There were other niggling inaccuracies, which I told them about. For instance, Wallis *couldn't* have heard the Abdication broadcast in France. British radio didn't travel that far in those days. And when Royalty takes a drink, it doesn't say "Cheers." They asked me, "Well, then what does it say?" I said, "It doesn't say *any*thing. It just takes a drink and everybody else goes glug-glug-glug."

As for the implication that the two had slept together before their wedding night, Lady Diana says "Who knows, and who gives tuppence?" Earlier, however, she had told a reporter, "I have been asked constantly if I thought they went to bed together on the *Nahlin* and so on. I tell them all, 'I haven't the least idea. How should I know?' Though I'm perfectly sure they did. But I don't think she was scheming from the start. She was enjoying it, and then it got beyond her."

In Paris, Maître Blum found more to object to in the script. "There was a scene of a trip to Deauville, for example, with Mrs. Merryman, who hints—almost *leeringly*—that the two young people ought to be left alone. Mrs. Merryman would never have done that. She was the most dignified, most proper woman. Then there's a scene where Mrs. Simpson and the chef at Fort Belvedere sit around a kitchen table while she tells him how to make club sandwiches. Wallis was too dignified ever to do a thing like that." To be sure, the club-sandwich episode was not part of Lady Donaldson's historical account, and there are other points where the script is at variance with what Donaldson presented as the facts (the manner in which Wallis learned of the death of George V, for example). These changes were obviously made to enhance the film's dramatic impact, and as the historical adviser, Lady Donaldson apparently went along with them as incidents that *might* have happened.

Maître Blum's contentions with Frances Donaldson go far beyond the confines of the television drama. One, which Lady Donaldson goes into considerable detail about, is the Windsors' rendezvous with the Germans in Portugal at the outset of World War II, and she quotes extensively from recovered Nazi documents to support her view. This, Maître Blum now says, is "lies—all of it—lies. I was with them in Portugal at the time. They were terrified, they were so eager to get out—that was all they cared about. They were so eager that they left before I did, and I had to take a later boat." Then how does one explain the German documents? "Forgeries—all of them." But who would commit these forgeries and for what purpose? "Malice. Deception." And yet these documents were officially published by the British Foreign Office. "There is no limit to how far they will go to try to discredit the Duke and Duchess. The letters and documents will disclose all the lies." Again, is not this the ideal moment to produce the exonerating letters and documents, and to set the record straight once and for all? Maître Blum shakes her head. "From what I know of the lawsuits in which the Duke of Windsor himself obtained complete satisfaction, but no practical results, it is not very encouraging to try 'setting the record straight.'"

Maître Blum classifies the Donaldson "lies" about the Portuguese connection along with "all the other lies that have been told about them—such as the one that the Royal Court paid for her hairdresser, or the one that she was leaving all her money to Lord Snowdon, or to her dogs." (Maître Blum certainly knows to whom the Duchess is leaving her money, but professional ethics naturally prevent her revealing who or what the beneficiary will be.) Then there is another lie: "Every two months, for instance, there is an article about the jewels of Queen Alexandra, which the Duke never received." This is an astonishing revelation. In practically everything published about the Duke and Wallis since the mid-1930's, Queen Alexandra's vast jewelry collection has been mentioned. Over the years, a number of people have claimed to have recognized various of Queen Alexandra's jewels on Wallis, and it was assumed, first, that the Prince had given them to her and, second, that the Royal Family wanted them back, which would have been understandable. Furthermore, following the jewel theft at Ednam Lodge, the rumors have persisted that the Royal Family had engineered the robbery in order to retrieve its property. Only the Duchess's room had been entered. Only her jewel case had been opened. Only certain pieces had been taken. The rumors made sense. But now, in 1979, Maître Blum was claiming that the Duke had never had any of his grandmother's jewels—"Not one, not a single stone." Instead, Maître Blum explained, the Duchess's jewels—all bought for her by the Duke—were a movable feast over the years. Stones were sold, privately or at auction, and were replaced by more desirable pieces. As for the Ednam Lodge robbery, Maître Blum points out with logic, "If the Royal Family were behind that, it would have put them in the position of conspiring with Scotland Yard to defraud the insurance company." One accepts this view, of course, only if one also believes that the British Royal Family, by virtue of being royal, would never stoop to the skulduggery of common folk who attempt to defraud insurance companies.

Early in the spring of 1979, the Paris-based British journalist Sam White, a longtime card-playing crony of the Duke's and an official Windsor-watcher for many years, learned in the course of news gathering that a plane of the Queen's Flight had landed in Paris and had been met by an official from the British Embassy. The party had driven immediately to the house in the Bois de Boulogne and had left shortly afterward with certain boxed items to return to London. White placed the date of this incident in mid-February of 1979, but when he questioned Embassy officials in Paris about it he found the entire affair shrouded in secrecy.

Asked about it in early April, Maître Blum denied that anything of the sort had taken place that recently. "It was not six weeks ago," she said. "It was perhaps six *years* ago—and it was all very complicated. Too complicated to go into." In London, however, Buckingham Palace had a different version of what had happened. "Yes," said Michael O'Shea, the palace press attaché, "there was a recent flight—one of a series over the past few years. Their purpose has been to return certain personal effects and papers of the Duke's to the Royal Archives at Windsor. This has been in accordance with the Duke's wishes, and at the express inspiration of the Duchess." Of the whereabouts of Queen Alexandra's jewels, however, Mr. O'Shea was more vague. "I doubt that anyone, even anyone in the Royal Family, could tell you where Queen Alexandra's jewels are today," he said. Thus it must be inferred that the fabled collection, once conservatively estimated to be worth three million dollars—and at today's prices undoubtedly worth a great deal more—has vanished, or at least that no one knows where it is.

In Paris, other ghoulish stories had by 1979 begun to circulate—to the effect that certain valuable possessions were disappearing from the Neuilly house: Wallis's jewels, bibelots, art objects, antiques, furs. Alas, this sort of thing has been known to happen to the ill and wealthy. When Barbara Hutton died after a long illness and months of being surrounded by a large and changing coterie of paid and unpaid attendants and protectors, a number of things that she was once known to have owned could not be found. It is one of the penalties the rich must one day expect to pay—the cormorants descending to pick over the remains of the dying. Maître Blum offers another explanation: "These stories are being spread by a few disgruntled former servants. They are all lies." (Disgruntled—despite the fact that the terms of the dismissals were, she insists, generous.)She also adds that, not long after the Duke's death, a number of his friends came to call on Wallis and, in the course of these visits, pointed out certain valuable objects which, they claimed, the Duke had promised in his lifetime to give them. Shocked at such callousness and greed, Wallis immediately ordered the objects in question placed in storage. This accounts for certain "holes" that may have been noticed among the furnishings of the Neuilly house. Everything, Maître Blum says, is accounted for. The furs and jewels are stored in vaults; everything is inventoried and catalogued in triplicate. The finances are in perfect order—"though the Duchess is not that rich. There are a great many women richer than she."

In Miss Hutton's case, there was at least that hovering coterie of sycophants about her until the end. By 1979, Wallis's situation had become much more stark and ghastly. No one—with the exception of the attending nurses, the doctor, the hairdresser, and of course Maître Blum—was permitted to see her. This of course could be interpreted as a kindness to someone who could no longer care for herself, who no longer even had fragmented moments of lucidity. But would not the sight of a few old friends' faces divert her and brighten her days? No, says Maître Blum. At one point this was tried, but it did not work. "It is very difficult to talk to someone who is in bed," says Maître Blum. "People came to see her, they talked about the latest gossip, the latest parties, what the women wore. It frustrated her. Her blood pressure shot up immediately. The doctor ordered it—no more visitors." (The reaction of the blood pressure, of course, would indicate some degree of comprehension.)

In an interview with David Pryce-Jones, "A golfing companion of the Duke's" complained, "I promised the Duke I'd look after Wallis, and I'd like nothing better. But I can't get near her. Meanwhile, explain to me why her possessions are apparently disappearing into the blue!" Others complain of the prisonlike isolation in which she is kept, the gates to the house locked and bolted, burglar alarms everywhere. "They say visitors make her blood pressure go up," says one friend. "But doesn't blood pressure also rise when one is happy or excited?"

Meanwhile, no one could question Maître Blum's singleminded devotion to her cause, to the woman who has become almost her alter ego. Her main quarrel with the Thames Television series—aside from the interpretations of the characters, about which she remains incredulous—was that it should have been done at all. She argues that the ailing Duchess should be allowed some privacy at the end of her life, away from the glare of further publicity. This would constitute a telling and indisputably humane point if it were not for one fact. For half her life Wallis's doings had been intensely publicized, and like many famous people who complain of too much publicity, she missed the publicity when it went away. After the Duke's death when, after all, the romance and marriage of the century were over and the attention of the public was inevitably straying elsewhere, Wallis seemed to encourage publicity for herself. Though her body and mind were already failing her, she switched from a "no-interview" policy to one whereby she was surprisingly accessible to the press. She was interviewed by *Time* in November 1973, by *Women's Wear Daily* in May 1974, by *People* in August 1974, and by the London *Times* in April 1975. Perhaps, by 1978, even though she was unaware of it, Wallis would have enjoyed being at the center of another controversy.

On March 18, 1979, David Pryce-Jones's article on the Windsors appeared in the *New York Times Magazine*—the "abominable article" Maître Blum called it. In it, Mr. Pryce-Jones questioned some of Maître Blum's principal assertions: that the Duke and Wallis never went to bed with each other before their marriage, that there had been no wartime encounter with the Germans in Portugal. He spoke of Wallis's "dreadful" isolation in the Neuilly house, of former servants who appeared to have been silenced by Maître Blum, and he quoted Sidney Johnson, the Bahamian butler, as saying, "You must ask Maître Blum for permission to speak to me. I've signed a paper about it." Pryce-Jones cited the "panic" of the Duchess's hairdresser lest Maître Blum find out that he had been successfully tracked down and interviewed.

As several other people had begun to do—among them Sam White in Paris—David Pryce-Jones questioned the existence of the "letters" and of the "historian" who will one day publish them. After all, he pointed out, if the letters exist they would have to have been written between early December 1936 and late April 1937, the only period when the Duke and Wallis were apart for any length of time. It was during this period, furthermore—while they languished in Austria and Cannes respectively—that Fruity Metcalfe, who was with the Duke throughout these months, tells in letters to his wife of how much of each ducal day was spent in marathon telephone calls to Wallis, the bills for which so alarmed the Baron de Rothschild. In her memoirs Wallis also speaks of the long daily hours on the telephone. After so much telephoning, what can have remained to be said in letters? Wallis was not known as a letter writer; she preferred the telephone or telegrams, and her thank-you notes usually took the form of engraved cards. Charles Murphy has reported the Duke's extreme difficulty with the chore of getting words on paper. But of why Maître Blum should boast of letters that do not exist, Pryce-Jones is at a loss for an explanation. To discredit the television series and Lady Donaldson? Perhaps.

When the Duke was Prince of Wales, however, he apparently did write letters to Freda Dudley Ward. Discreet to the end, she rather recently burned them all. Were they love letters?

Discretion rules. Had she loved him? "Oh, no, he was much too abject," she told Mr. Pryce-Jones.

No sooner had Maître Blum read the Pryce-Jones article than she—having decided that an international lawsuit against the *Times* was impractical—dashed off a long and angry letter to the editor in which she said:

> Mr. Pryce-Jones's article merely repeated constant rumors, ignoring corrections and denials—even lawsuits won by the Duke and Duchess of Windsor. The article is filled with malice and it is difficult to separate the derisory from the defamatory . . .
>
> Mr. Pryce-Jones reopens accusations, legally closed by the British Government, that the Duke entertained supposed relations with German agents in 1940, when his patriotism was never in doubt.
>
> When Mr. Pryce-Jones gives details, they are false; for example: the amount of money the Duke received after abdication, the parliamentary act forbidding the King to marry a divorcée, the statement that the Duchess had never read a certain book nor made a certain remark, the dismissal without reason of faithful servants, the isolation which is supposedly aggravating her health, etc.
>
> The remarks attributed to myself are incorrect.
>
> To demonstrate his hostility to the Duke and Duchess, Mr. Pryce-Jones has turned to witnesses likely to share his animosity, and accounts based on proof or indisputable fact are treated as fables.

Later, Maître Blum would claim that she had been "tricked" into an interview by Mr. Pryce-Jones and that the ruse had been the suggestion of Pryce-Jones's aunt, the Baroness Elie de Rothschild, for a three-way meeting between the baroness, Maître Blum, and the British journalist.

"That is not true," countered Pryce-Jones. "I wanted to meet Maître Blum, and mentioned this to my aunt, the Baroness Rothschild. My aunt said, 'Look, I know her, we'll ask her to lunch'—that was it. She may have accepted the invitation for snobbish reasons, because my aunt was the Baroness Rothschild. But I explained at the outset that I was writing a story on the Windsors for the *Times,* and that my questions to her were for my story. I took careful notes during the interview, and made it clear to her that everything she said would be for possible quotation."

Mr. Pryce-Jones went on to say, "Actually, I thought my story was sympathetic to the Duchess, since I found her situation so tragic. The great love story—for it to end up like this. There were other horror stories I could have told, grueling stories. There were more devastating things I could have said about the Duke, too. Martin Gilbert, who is doing a biography of Churchill, has come up with evidence that when the Duke was in Portugal he wanted to make a speech asking England to make peace with Hitler. In order to stop him, Churchill had to threaten him with a court-martial, to keep him quiet." Of the silenced former servants of the Windsors', Pryce-Jones says, "I got the distinct impression that they'd been told they'd get something in her will if they didn't talk. If they broke the contract, they'd get nothing." This would be in line with earlier Windsor practice: when servants complained of longer-than-average hours at lower-than-average salaries, they were reminded that service on the Windsor staff would sit well with future employers, and also that for loyal service they would be rewarded "in the will."

"I can only conclude that Madame Blum's talk about secret unpublished letters is a fantasy." Pryce-Jones says. "Meanwhile, there are two general theories about what is going on—the English and the French. The English, who love conspiracies, think that there's a lot of dirty work at the crossroads, that there's a conspiracy to get things away from the Duchess. The French, who tend to be more philosophical, shrug and say it's inexplicable."

Maître Blum continues to be nothing if not consistent: Wallis was never drunk. She never slept with the Duke until they were man and wife. She never wanted to be Queen of England. She never even wanted to marry the King. "It was he. She was terrified of being Queen. She just wanted to get out. But he insisted. He would have followed her anywhere. She once said to me, 'If I had gone to China, he would have followed me there. There was nothing I could do to stop him—nothing.' He forced her to marry him." The letters will reveal all this apparently.

What was the secret of Wallis's fatal allure? Maître Blum produces a portrait by the photographer Man Ray which she keeps in her office. There Wallis stands, full length, in a long dress of the utmost simplicity. Her chin is tucked in slightly, to relieve the sharp line of her jaw and to throw a softer light on her large nose. Her eyes are cast slightly upward in a glance that is innocent, demure, almost winsome. Her hands are concealed behind her. She looks slim, cool, elegant and—Maître Blum's favorite word for her—dignified. Never pretty, in the Man Ray photograph she looks almost beautiful. "Look at that," says Maître Blum. "Can you imagine a woman of such—dignity—ever agreeing to be the mistress of any man?"

That, then, was Wallis Warfield Simpson: the Man Ray photograph.

As she sat in her bed in Maida Vale—London's "Little Venice"—Lady Diana Cooper said, "She made him look good, that was her great talent. She made him appear brighter than he was. I got into it because of Wallis—he invited people to Fort Belvedere and on the *Nahlin* to keep her company. I liked her, but we were never intimate, we never talked about any love affair. In the long run, it's been a blessing. He would not have been a good King. He liked gardening. Like all the English, we end up gardening, with our bulbs and cuttings. We were lucky to get George VI and Elizabeth—they were by far the better loved in the end. Of course all the Royal Family were pro-German in the beginning. After all, they *were* German. Old Queen Mary could barely speak English, which most people don't realize—she was always working with tutors. But the Duke was the worst. He'd make terrible anti-Semitic remarks. Sir Ernest Cassel was one of his grandfather's best friends, but whenever his name came up the Duke would say, 'What can you expect from these Jews?' And Sir Ernest's granddaughter was married to Dickie Mountbatten, the Duke's own cousin! Whenever he talked like that, I'd shut my trap. Wallis never talked that way, to give her credit. Yes, in the end it was a blessing that Wallis came along and took him away. But what a pity—in the beginning it was all such a lark for her—that it has to end in such a sordid way, with everybody motivated by what's in her will, grubbing, grubbing for her money. I hope not one of them inherits anything."

One institution—or institution-to-be—that expects to inherit from Wallis surfaced on the same letters-to-the-editor page of the *New York Times Magazine* as Maître Blum's scathing letter. Mr. Joseph A. Moore of New York wrote that he had the pleasure and honor of being chairman of the Advisory Committee to The Wallis, Duchess of Windsor, Museum and Fine Arts Center, to be built on the campus of her alma mater, the Oldfields School, outside Baltimore, after her death. "One of the objectives of the museum," Mr. Moore wrote, "will be to 'set the record straight' in the future by making available to writers research materials previously unpublished." Up to that point, few people were aware of this proposed project, and some saw ironies—again—in the thought that whatever treasures Wallis leaves behind will find their way back to a not-quite-fashionable school in Baltimore, where the not-quite-fashionable Wallis began her extraordinary career.

And so what, in the end, did her life add up to? Hers was certainly not a particularly productive journey on this earth—the years of shopping, dancing, traveling, party-going, with clothes, jewels, photographers with popping flashbulbs, gossip, publicity, and a husband, like one of her obedient puppies, following her in the life she chose to lead. Did she ever, one wonders, see the fickleness and hollowness—and also the terrible dangers—that lurked in that world, a world of money and possessions, but also a world of jealousy and fear, of locks, burglar systems, attack dogs, of loaded guns by Chippendale bedside tables, of adultery and violence brought on by boredom and alcohol and sleeping pills? Harry Oakes, William Woodward, Charles Bedaux, Jimmy Donahue, Robert Young—their names and deaths rang like baleful gongs throughout her life. "What a pity it has to end in such a sordid way..."

She had married a man who, though stubborn, obviously adored her and filled her with a great sense of being needed. As his old friend Sam White has said of him, "He was an extremely *nice* man. He was like a good little Boy Scout. If you overlooked his politics, he was good company. He never seemed bored, but then he had spent his life doing boring things in an agreeable way. His heart was essentially in the right place. It's been said that the Duke's tragic flaw was the Duchess, but that's not true. Without her, he would have been nothing at all."

But *was* he anything at all?

For years he had blamed the vindictiveness and meanspiritedness of the Royal Family and the British government for depriving him of the opportunity to do worthwhile and productive work. True, they had failed consistently to offer him a post he considered worthy of his exalted birth. But if he had really wanted work, there was plenty that he could have done in areas where his family had no influence.

Any one of a hundred international corporations would have been delighted to have created a distinguished position for the Duke of Windsor if he had ever asked for one. Any number of philanthropies or charitable foundations would have been happy to have had him on their boards, if he had indicated the slightest interest. He had often said that his serious interests—fashion and gardening were just hobbies—were "housing" and "working conditions." But he had never approached any organization—the Ford, the Carnegie, the Rockefeller foundations, for example—devoted to such causes and asked what he might do to help. And so it is impossible not to conclude that his protestations about wanting to be useful were self-serving, face-saving lies or fancies. And yet it would be wrong to conclude that he was simply lazy, that he preferred a life of idleness to work. The fact seems to be that he did not understand the concept of work. To him, work was rank and status. It did not involve contributing something. Instead, it involved the opposite: receiving titles, honors, prestige, perquisites. Though servile by nature, he had no idea of what though her mother, who had gone to work, had understood it. But then Wallis had always been a little ashamed of her mother—for actually working.

And yet, despite all this, she was, by many American standards, a success. She had achieved what every American shopgirl of the 1920's and 1930's dreamed about and prayed for. As a little girl who had started out without much money and without much in the way of looks, she had married the handsome scion of the Most Ancient Splendid Royal House in the World. Wouldn't any American girl be happy with this? With it had come money, power, position, fame, huge houses, footmen who bowed from the waist, maids who curtsied as they entered and left—and a place in British history which, she said, she didn't mind at all.

Several years ago, the New York mansion of the Windsors' friend Mrs. George F. Baker, at 67 East Ninety-third Street just off Park Avenue, briefly went on the market for sale or lease (it eventually was kept by the family). At the time the house was being shown, most of its furnishings had been re-moved, except for those in one room, the bedroom occupied by the Duke and Duchess of Windsor when they had been Edith Baker's frequent house guests. It had been kept intact—perhaps as some sort of memorial to the famous sometime occupants. On each of the two beds was a large pillow, worked in need-lepoint—the kind of pillow Wallis liked to scatter about—and on each was embroidered a motto. They were the mottoes, perhaps, that the Duke and Wallis had at least tried to live by. On the Duke's pillow were the words NEVER EXPLAIN. On Wallis's, NEVER COMPLAIN.

Source References

Two unusual sources were made available to the author in the preparation of this book. First was the London *Evening Standard*, through the kindness of its editor, Mr. Jeremy Deeds, which permitted me access to certain of the *Evening Standard*'s uncatalogued files for the period leading up to the Abdication of Edward VIII. In the references that follow, these *Evening Standard* uncatalogued files will be referred to as ESUF.

Second was the massive collection of Windsoriana gathered by the late Dowager Lady Christabel Aberconway of London, a contemporary and friend of both the Prince of Wales and Wallis Simpson. Lady Aberconway, in typical English fashion, had consuming hobbies. Hers were collecting stories about unusual murders and stories about the Windsors. The scrapbooks she compiled with her private secretary and companion, Mrs. Maeve Bowman-Vaughan, were annotated with her own personal comments, in ink. Though many of the clippings the scrapbooks contained were unidentified and undated, and came from all over the world, it was often possible to approximate their dates. At the same time, when Lady Aberconway, Mrs. Bowman-Vaughan and the author went through the scrapbooks, their contents often inspired further verbal recollections and impressions. The difficulty of separating the press clippings from the handwritten comments and the accompanying oral commentary they elicited has necessitated citing this source as "Aberconway scrapbooks and conversations."

1. A Girl of Slender Means

2. Husband Number One

3. Husband Number Two

4. "Strangers When We Meet"

35–36	The first version of the meeting: ESUF (1936).
36	The second version: Ibid.
36	"scarcely knew": Duchess of Windsor, *The Heart Has Its Reasons*, p. 155.
36–37	"I seem to be having": Aberconway scrapbooks and conversations.
37	The third version of the meeting: E. H. Wilson, *Her Name Was Wallis Warfield*, pp. 85, 20.
37	Variant of the third version: I. Brody, *Gone with the Windsors*, p. 104.
37	The fourth version: Duke of Windsor, *A King's Story*, p. 256.
37	"extremely fond of horses": Brody, p. 106.
38	The first conversation: Duke of Windsor, p. 257.
39	Thelma Furness on the first meeting: G. Vanderbilt and T. Furness, *Double Exposure*, p. 288.
39	"Wallis and I became": Ibid., pp. 288–289.
39	The book caption: Duke of Windsor, illus. following p. 244.
40	The expensive new dresses: Duchess of Windsor, p. 154.
40	The acceptance of the invitation: Ibid., p. 155.
41	"How nice": Ibid. p. 162.
41	"Uncle Arthur": Ibid., p. 163.
41	"But, Sir": Ibid., p. 164.
42	"When her turn": Duke of Windsor, p. 163.
43	Wallis's presentation clothes: Duchess of Windsor, p. 163.

5. At the Summit

45–46	Wallis's jaw and hands: Aberconway scrapbooks and conversations.
46	Thelma Furness's description: G. Vanderbilt and T. Furness, *Double Exposure*, pp. 287–288.
46	Beaton's description: Quoted in J. Bryan and C. J. V. Murphy, *The Windsor Story*, p. 79.
46	Channon's description: H. Channon, *Chips*, p. 23.
46	Opinions of the Simpsons' flat: Channon, p. 51; Beaton, quoted in Bryan and Murphy, p. 50.
46–47	"No good will come": ESUF (1936).
47	"out of the blue": Duchess of Windsor, *The Heart Has Its Reasons*, p. 169.
48	"I'm afraid the Prince": Ibid., p. 182.
49	"She . . . said suddenly": Vanderbilt and Furness, p. 306.

49   "But I am boring you": Duchess of Windsor, p. 183.
49   "Sir, would you care": Ibid.
50   "tactfully": Ibid.
51   "Darling, you know": Vanderbilt and Furness, p. 312.
51   "I think he likes me": Ibid., p. 184.
51   "Wallis looked": Vanderbilt and Furness, p. 313.
52   "She is a jolly": Channon, pp. 29–30.
52   "Mrs. Simpson has": Ibid., p. 33.
52   "we were joined": Ibid., pp. 34–35.
53   "Now, David": Interview with Harriet Culley.
53   "Let me be candid": Duchess of Windsor, p. 179.
54   "She has already": Channon, p. 30.
54   "immaculate, soignée"; Quoted in Bryan and Murphy, p. 219.
54–55   "You don't have to worry": Duchess of Windsor, p. 191.
55   "I can't describe it": Ibid., p. 192.

6. "What Could It Be He Sees in Her?"

58   "he was the open sesame": Duchess of Windsor, *The Heart Has Its Reasons*, p. 192.
58   "None of her features": Quoted in J. Bryan and C. J. V. Murphy, *The Windsor Story*, p. 20.
58   "she did not have the chic": G. Vanderbilt and T. Furness, *Double Exposure*, p. 287.
59   "have small-penis complexes": Interview with A. R. St. Johns.
59   "heir-conditioned": Bryan and Murphy, p. 483.
59   "a seedless Raisin": Ibid., p. 21.
59–60   "Right then I made": Ibid., p. 93.
60   "He had the charm": Cole Lesley, *Remembered Laughter: The Life of Noël Coward*, p. 188.
61   "[The Prince] is Mrs. Simpson's": Channon, *Chips*, p. 60.
62   "who first modernised": Ibid., p. 50.
62   "For the 26 years": Ibid.
62   "he has the easy gift": Ibid.
62   "he drank next to nothing": Ibid., pp. 50–51.
62–63   "She has always": Ibid., p. 51.
63   "No man has ever": Ibid., p. 54.
63   "good, dull, dutiful": Ibid., pp. 51–52.
64   "while amusing and witty": Ibid., p. 40.
65   "The Prince of Wales": New York *Journal*, Sept. 12, 1934.
65   "I had taken": Duchess of Windsor, p. 198.
65   The skiing trip: Ibid., p. 199.

7. Prince to King

68–69   "It was once said": Duke of Windsor, *A King's Story*, p. 28.

69   "My father was frightened": R. Churchill, *Lord Derby*, p. 159.

69–70   The alligator pear incident: Aberconway scrapbooks and conversations.

70   "My father doesn't": Ibid.

70   "I have always": J. Pope-Hennessy, *Queen Mary*, p. 391.

70   "His Royal Highness wishes": Duke of Windsor, p. 28.

71   "The Navy will teach David": Ibid., p. 59.

71   The hazing at Osborne: Ibid., p. 62.

72   "I would never recommend": Aberconway scrapbooks and conversations.

72   "Bookish": I. Brody, *Gone with the Windsors*, p. 79.

72   The Prince's morning apple: Ibid.

73   "to show that": C. Hibbert, *Edward the Uncrowned King*, p. 10.

73   "What does it matter": Duke of Windsor, p. 111.

73   "Thank Heavens he's going": Hibbert, p. 31.

74   "The King was afraid": Ibid.

77   "At the same time": Ibid., p. 8.

78   "I was troubled": Duchess of Windsor, *The Heart Has Its Reasons*, p. 202.

78   "I think you ought to know": Duke of Windsor, p. 263.

79   "It's all over": Duchess of Windsor, p. 210.

79   "The King is dead": F. Donaldson, *Edward VIII*, p. 186.

79   "Why shouldn't I": Brody, p. 73.

8. Rumblings

82   The clocks episode: F. Donaldson, *Edward VIII*, p. 190.

82   "the glittering tip": Duchess of Windsor, *The Heart Has Its Reasons*, p. 207.

83   "The thought came to me": Ibid., p. 212.

84   "almost at once": J. Bryan and C. J. V. Murphy, *The Windsor Story*, pp. 157–158.

85   "Are you quite sure": Duchess of Windsor, p. 214.

86   "That was a very": Bryan and Murphy, p. 190.

86   The footnote: Aberconway scrapbooks and conversations.

89   "That may be difficult": Duchess of Windsor, p. 217.

89   "It's got to be done": Ibid., p. 216.

91   "Mrs. Simpson has stolen": Bryan and Murphy, p. 187.

91   "In the notes": Donaldson, p. 173.
92   "I don't want": Bryan and Murphy, p. 132.
92   "I think I make": Interview with Lady Diana Cooper.
93   "frantic and unreasonable": H. Hardinge, *Loyal to Three Kings*, p. 61.
94   "After I'm dead": K. Middlemas and J. Barnes, *Baldwin*, p. 976.
94   "I pray to God": Countess of Airlie, *Thatched with Gold*, p. 61.

9. Cruising

98   "No marriage": Lord Beaverbrook, *The Abdication of Edward VIII*, p. 70.
98   "with a lie": Duke of Windsor, *A King's Story*, p. 340.
100 Mrs. Simpson's jewels: H. Channon, *Chips*, pp. 73, 77, 85.
101 "We can't have": Duke of Windsor, p. 284.
101 "Couldn't have been me": ESUF (1936).
101 "Nowadays princes": Ibid.
101 The Archbishop's visit: Duke of Windsor, p. 275.
102 The golf balls: ESUF (1936).
102 "You are no longer": I. Brody, *Gone with the Windsors*, p. 165.
103 "We were all left": D. Cooper, *Autobiography*, p. 414.
104 "I've told them": Ibid., p. 423.
105 "Please send" and "Your family papers": Interview with Martin Shallenberger.

10. Divorce Number Two

109–112 The court proceedings: I. Brody, *Gone with the Windsors*, pp. 178–183.
113 Earl Winfield Spencer's comments: ESUF (1936).
114 "If what the newspapers": *Time*, Oct. 5, 1936.
114 "And would your life": ESUF (1936).
114 The tabloid headline: F. Donaldson, *Edward VIII*, p. 247.

11. Villains

119 "If only Queen Mary": ESUF (1936).
120 "Let us see": A. R. St. Johns, *The Honeycomb*, p. 434.
120 "patently impossible": Interview with A. R. St. Johns.

121   Woollcott on Wallis's wit: St. Johns, *Honeycomb*, p. 441.
121–122   Hellman on the King's marriage: Ibid., pp. 446–447.
123   "A lot of this": Ibid., p. 458.
123   "W.R. wants me": Ibid., p. 461.
124   St. Johns's first installment: Ibid., p. 476.
126   "looked surprised": H. Nicolson, *Diaries and Letters*, p. 279.
128   "The reasons he gave": Lord Beaverbrook, *The Abdication of King Edward VIII*, p. 30.
129   "She appeared to me": Ibid., pp. 34–35.
130   "To bugger Baldwin!": Interview with Sam White.
131   "The King's Private Secretary": F. Donaldson, *Edward VIII*, p. 255.
132   "there is but one course": K. Middlemas and J. Barnes, *Baldwin*, p. 988.
132   "your association": Ibid.
132–133   Hardinge's letter: *The Times* (London), Nov. 29, 1955.
133   "They had struck": Duke of Windsor, *A King's Story*, p. 328.
134   "If there was any question": Middlemas and Barnes, p. 988.

12. Needs and Wants, Ways and Means

140   "I want you to be": K. Middlemas and J. Barnes, *Baldwin*, p. 995.
141   "Sir, this is": Ibid.
141   Beaverbrook's opinion of Baldwin: Beaverbrook, *The Abdication of King Edward VIII*, p. 40.
141   "It can be simply stated": J. Pope-Hennessy, *Queen Mary*, p. 573.
143   "pleasant but distant": Duchess of Windsor, *The Heart Has Its Reasons*, p. 217.
145   "astonishing": Ibid., p. 239.
145   "strange and almost inhuman": Duke of Windsor, *A King's Story*, p. 341.
146   "on the executioner's block": Ibid., p. 346.
147   The King and Wallis as possible security risks: F. Donaldson, *Edward VIII*, pp. 197, 203–204.
148   "it would become publicly": Beaverbrook, pp. 61–62.

13. Storm...and Flight

150   "was under no compulsion": Lord Beaverbrook, *The Abdication of King Edward VIII*, p. 61.

150   "of sending": Ibid.

151   "a policy of": Ibid., p. 62.

152   "The King's matter": J. Bryan and C. J. V. Murphy, *The Windsor Story*, p. 260; also Beaverbrook, p. 65.

156   "You must wait": Duchess of Windsor, *The Heart Has Its Reasons*, p. 247.

158   "always had": Ibid., p. vii.

159   "kept telling the detective": *Time*, Mar. 29, 1937.

161   The Ann Bridge episode: ESUF (1936).

14. The End of Edward VIII

166   "uncertain": Duke of Windsor, *A King's Story*, p. 364.

167   "The Conspiracy": Ibid., p. 393.

167   Views of the *Catholic Times:* Lord Beaverbrook, *The Abdication of King Edward VIII*, p. 71.

167   "I plead for time": New York *Times*, Dec. 6, 1936.

168–169   "I want you to go": Beaverbrook, p. 79.

169   "Our cock": Ibid., p. 80.

170   "Mrs. Simpson throughout": Duchess of Windsor, *The Heart Has Its Reasons*, p. 264.

170   "Go ahead": Ibid.

173   "When the King": New York *Times*, Jan. 22, 1939.

15. "Rat Week"

179   "We had her": H. Channon, *Chips*, p. 97.

179   could not "stick": Ibid.

181   Channon on Baldwin and the Cabinet: Ibid., p. 99.

182   The Stanleys' dinner party: Ibid., p. 100.

16. Other People's Houses

184   "He had a craving": I. Brody, *Gone with the Windsors*, p. 233.

184–185   Beaverbrook in the dentist's office: Lord Beaverbrook, *The Abdication of King Edward VIII*, p. 107.

185   "Halt!": Brody, p. 233.

187   The hate letters: J. Bryan and C. J. V. Murphy, *The Windsor Story*, p. 350.

187   The loaded pistol: Duchess of Windsor, *The Heart Has Its Reasons*, p. 271.

189–193   The Duke at Enzesfeld: Brody, pp. 237–238.

190   The Duke at cards: Aberconway scrapbooks and conversations.

191   "As far as I'm concerned": Brody, p. 237.

191   The thank-you note: F. Donaldson, *Edward VIII*, quoting Metcalfe's letter, pp. 333–334.

193   The pension arrangements: Brody, p. 241.

194   Wallis blue: Brody, p. 242.

194   The dispute over money: ESUF (1937).

195–196   The Duke's income and assets: Donaldson, pp. 310–311.

201   "She twisted and twirled": C. Beaton, *The Wandering Years*, p. 306.

201   "Wallis hovered": Ibid., p. 309.

17. Unemployed

203   The railroad car: I. Brody, *Gone with the Windsors*, p. 245; ESUF (1937).

204   "I have had": J. Bryan and C. J. V. Murphy, *The Windsor Story*, p. 361.

206–207   The Duchess's shopping: ESUF (1938).

207   "I've lost a friend": Brody, p. 247.

208   The visit to Berchtesgaden: New York *Times*, Oct. 23, 1937.

208   "In one respect": Duchess of Windsor, *The Heart Has Its Reasons*, pp. 300–301.

209   "The tour of the Fatherland": ESUF (1937).

210   "Bedaux made his money": Ibid.

212   "We want him back!": Ibid.

212   "Harassed, unreasonable": Hector Bolitho, *King Edward VIII*, p. 278 ff.

18. Limbo

218   "Keep the change": ESUF (1937).

218   "slight lapses": F. Donaldson, *Edward VIII*, p. 379.

220–221   "No one will ever": Aberconway scrapbooks and conversations.

221   "If Wallis were ever": Quoted by Lady Diana Cooper to the author.

222   "I'm sure that I": Duchess of Windsor, *The Heart Has Its Reasons*, p. 311.

222   "I want to offer": Ibid., p. 312.

223   Playing for Mussolini's troops: ESUF (1939).

19. On the Road

226–227   "They arrived": F. Donaldson, *Edward VIII*, p. 372.
231   "Well, darling": Duchess of Windsor, *The Heart Has Its Reasons*, p. 334.
232–233   "had two long": Donaldson, p. 391.
233   "When he gave": Ibid.
233–234   "The message which": Ibid., p. 399.
235   "The confidant": Ibid., p. 400.
235   ". . . it is . . . likely": Ibid., p. 401.

20. Decorating

240   "While she had a look": A. R. St. Johns, *The Honeycomb*, p. 524.
241–242   "I did everything": Ibid., p. 524.
242   "Her deep concern": Ibid., p. 525.
242   "You know, when": Interview with A. R. St. Johns.
242–243   St. Johns's twin conclusions: Ibid.
244   "In my country, sir": St. Johns, pp. 531–532.
245   "David, darling": Interview with St. Johns.
245   "I felt a cloud": St. Johns, p. 537.

21. Wandering

250   The first face lift: ESUF (1942).
251   "I think this business": Aberconway scrapbooks and conversations.
251   "You are out of your mind!": ESUF (1944).
254   The letter to Queen Mary: Duchess of Windsor, *The Heart Has Its Reasons*, pp. 347–348.
254   "I send a kind message": Ibid., p. 348.
255   The Duke's meeting with Queen Mary: ESUF (1945).
258   "A fool would know": Ibid.
261   The Duke and the waiter-busboy strike: Ibid.

22. Togetherness

269   Donahue and the male prostitute: Interview with Michael Greer.
271   "She's marvelous!": Ibid.

273   "Her figure": Interview with Mme. Elizabeth Wakefield Dupont (later Mrs. Edward Gatchell).

274   The shattered-vase episode: Ibid.

274   The firing of the Arden salesgirl: Ibid.

276   Donahue's two swims: L. Palmer, *Change Lobsters—and Dance*, pp. 219–222.

276   Donahue's didoes: Interview with Jerome Zerbe.

277   "The only thing": Ibid.

277   The end of the Donahue affair: J. Bryan and C. J. V. Murphy, *The Windsor Story*, p. 516.

278   "I don't think": New York *Times*, Dec. 14, 1966.

23. Killing Time

281   "too much clutter": Interview with Harriet Culley.

281   "overdone and *chichi*": J. Bryan and C. J. V. Murphy, *The Windsor Story*, p. 522.

283–284   The grouse luncheon: Interview with Thomas Kernan.

284   The Duke's gaffe: Interview with Jean vanden Heuvel.

286   Amory and Igor Cassini: Interview with Etta Wanger.

286   "Wallis never had": C. Amory, *Who Killed Society?*, p. 238.

287   Murphy as the Duchess's ghostwriter: Bryan and Murphy, p. 553.

287   "an almost blinding veracity": R. Sencourt, *The Reign of Edward the Eighth*, p. 38.

287–288   The Murrow interview: ESUF (Sept. 1956).

289   *The Times* "review": *The Times* (London), Sept. 27, 1956.

24. Withering Heights

292   "elegant and gay": H. Channon, *Chips*, p. 445.

293   "Which Duchess?": ESUF (1955).

294   "everybody who": Ibid.

295   "I am very glad": Ibid. (1956).

296   "My husband would be": Interview with Lady Diana Cooper.

297   The bikini curtsy: Interview with Mme. Pablo Lozada de Echinique (Françoise Wicart).

298   "The Duke and I": Duchess of Windsor, "All Things Considered," *McCall's*, Feb., 1961.

301   "Look, *you* know": Interview with Sam White.

25. Farewells

304 "You must come": Interview with Patrick O'Higgins.

305 "The Duke would never": D. Pryce-Jones, "TV Tale of Two Windsors," *New York Times Magazine*, Mar. 18, 1979, p. 110.

309 "This is the Duchess of Windsor!": Interview with Michael Greer.

311 "I'm frightened!": J. Bryan and C. J. V. Murphy, *The Windsor Story*, p. 604.

311 "Would you call *that*": Interview with the Duchess of Windsor.

311 "Everything is going": Bryan and Murphy, p. 606.

312 "I wish someone": Interview with David Pryce-Jones.

26. Enter Maître Blum

314 "Of course everyone knows": Interview with Harriet Culley.

314 "Don't mention it": Ibid.

314 "Do you know": Ibid.

315 "She did *not*": Interview with Suzanne Blum.

317–318 The Windsors' love letters: Ibid.

318 "We could never": D. Pryce-Jones, "TV Tale of Two Windsors," *New York Times Magazine*, Mar. 18, 1979, p. 38.

319 "They made him": Interview with Lady Alexandra Metcalfe.

319–320 Lady Diana's comments: Interview with Lady Diana Cooper.

320 "I have been asked": D. Pryce-Jones, "TV Tale of Two Windsors," p. 108.

321 "From what I know": Interview with S. Blum.

322 "If the Royal Family": Ibid.

322 "It was not": Ibid.

323 "I doubt that anyone": Interview with Michael O'Shea.

323 The disappearance of Barbara Hutton's possessions: Interview with Gustavus Ober.

323 "though the Duchess": Interview with S. Blum.

324 "It is very difficult": Ibid.

324 "I promised the Duke": D. Pryce-Jones, "TV Tale of Two Windsors," p. 111.

326 "Mr. Pryce-Jones's article": *New York Times Magazine*, May 13, 1979.

326 Maître Blum "tricked": Interview with S. Blum.

326–327 "That is not true": Interview with D. Pryce-Jones.

327–328 "It was he": Interview with S. Blum.

328   "She made him look good": Interview with Lady Diana
            Cooper.
329   "One of the objectives": *New York Times Magazine*, May
            13, 1979, p. 94.
329   "He was an extremely": Interview with Sam White.

Bibliography

Aberconway, Christabel, Lady. Scrapbooks. *See* the introduction to the Source References.

Airlie, Mabell, Countess of. *Thatched with Gold*. Edited by Jennifer Ellis. London: Hutchinson, 1962.

Amory, Cleveland. *Who Killed Society?* New York: Harper, 1960.

Beaton, Cecil. *The Wandering Years*. Boston: Little, Brown, 1962.

Beaverbrook, Lord. *The Abdication of King Edward VIII*. New York: Atheneum, 1966.

Bolitho, Hector. *King Edward VIII*. London: Lippincott, 1937.

Brody, Iles. *Gone with the Windsors*. Philadelphia: Winston, 1953.

Brookman, Laura Lou. *See* Wilson, Edwina H.

Bryan, J., III, and Charles J. V. Murphy. *The Windsor Story*. New York: Morrow, 1979.

Channon, Sir Henry. *Chips: The Diaries of Sir Henry Channon*. Edited by Robert Rhodes James. London: Weidenfeld and Nicolson, 1967.

Churchill, Randolph. *Lord Derby, King of Lancashire*. London: Heinemann, 1959.

Cooper, Diana. *Autobiography*. Salisbury: Russell, 1979.

Donaldson, Frances. *Edward VIII*. Philadelphia: Lippincott, 1975.

Evening Standard, London. Uncatalogued files, 1930–1939. Referred to in the Source References as ESUF.

Furness, Thelma, Lady. *See* Vanderbilt, Gloria.

Hardinge, Helen. *Loyal to Three Kings*. London: Kimber, 1967.

Hibbert, Christopher. *Edward the Uncrowned King*. New York: St. Martin's, 1972.

Lesley, Cole. *Remembered Laughter: The Life of Noël Coward*. New York: Knopf, 1976.

Middlemas, Keith, and John Barnes. *Baldwin*. London: Weidenfeld and Nicolson, 1969.

Nicolson, Harold. *Diaries and Letters, 1930–1963*. Edited by Nigel Nicolson. London: Collins, 1966.

Palmer, Lilli. *Change Lobsters—and Dance*. New York: Macmillan, 1975.

Pope-Hennessy, James. *Queen Mary*. London: Allen and Unwin, 1957.

Pryce-Jones, David. "TV Tale of Two Windsors," *New York Times Magazine*, March 18, 1979.

St. Johns, Adela Rogers. *The Honeycomb*. New York: Doubleday, 1969.

Sencourt, Robert. *The Reign of Edward the Eighth*. London: Anthony Gibbs and Phillips, 1962.

Tree, Ronald. *When the Moon Was High: Memoirs of Peace and War, 1897–1942*. London: Macmillan, 1975.

Vanderbilt, Gloria, and Thelma, Lady Furness. *Double Exposure: A Twin Autobiography*. New York: McKay, 1958.

Wilson, Edwina H. (pseud. of Laura Lou Brookman). *Her Name Was Wallis Warfield*. New York: Dutton, 1936.

Windsor, Duchess of. *The Heart Has Its Reasons*. New York: McKay, 1956.

——. "All Things Considered." Series of twelve articles in *McCall's*, February 1961–January 1962.

Windsor, Duke of. *A King's Story*. New York: Putnam's, 1951.

INDEX